Mastering

ENGLISH

from day one

Mastering English from day one aims at enabling learners without any prior knowledge of English language to learn it by themselves. Starting with the alphabet and very basic speech patterns, it helps the learners to gradually attain a level of proficiency where they may take part in conversation, take competitive exams and face interviews for jobs. I am well aware of the availability of excellent English language learning books. However, learning an alien language in one's native country where most of the time one uses one's native tongue for day-to-day business, is baffling indeed. Having been involved with bilingual writing and teaching, I am aware of the challenges faced by Hindi-speaking people in learning English and vice versa. There is a real need for a book that focuses on the requirements of this category of learners. *Mastering English from day one* is specially designed to cater to the specific needs of the Hindi-speaking people. Nevertheless, it could be profitably used by everybody—beginners, advanced learners doing just some remedial work, and teachers looking for more comprehension examples and extended practice material.

Where needed, reference has been made to comparable Hindi language structures for unambiguous and enhanced comprehension.

Everything has been explained in simple spoken Hindi. A few chapters at the beginning of the book have been fully transcribed in Hindi to enable the beginners to learn correct pronunciation. Tabular illustration of the language structures makes the book specially valuable and user-friendly for new learners.

By the same author

Hindi-English

- Hindi For Non Hindi Speaking People Grammar
- Hindi For Non Hindi Speaking People (WORK BOOK)
- Speak Hindi from Day One
- English Hindi Phrasebook

Hindi-German

- Namaste - Einfeuhrung in die Grammatik und den praktischen Gebrauch de Hindi (Main Book)
- Namaste - Einfeuhrung in die Grammatik und den praktischen Gebrauch de Hindi (Work Book)
- Hindi - German Phrasebook

Hindi-Spanish

- Manual de hindi para hispanohablantes
- Gramática de hindi

Hindi

- Vyakaran - Ek navin Dristikon

English

- Mira - The Emancipated Soul

Mastering

ENगLISH

from day one

GRAMMAR AND PRACTICE BOOK

With focus on special needs of Hindi speaking people

Kavita Kumar

BLUEJAY

Bluejay Books Pvt. Ltd.
A-8/76, Ist Floor,
Sector 16, Rohini,
Delhi 110 085
info@bluejaybooksindia.com

First published in 2013 by
Bluejay Books Pvt. Ltd.

Printed and bound in India

CONTENTS

EVERY DAY EXPRESSIONS

VOCABULARY

PROVERBS

I wish to thank :

- all my students over the years for their questions and curiosity which prompted me to think and dwell upon the genuine problems of Hindi speaking learners of English language.
- friends for their sustained encouragement and support.
- Solveigh Mcintosh who, with her knowlede of Sanskrit and Hindi language, promptly and gladly read through some of my bilingual presentations of usages, answered several queries to my satisfaction and helped me to comprehend the comparative nuances before including in the book..
- ***Bluejay Books Pvt Ltd*** for agreeing to publish this much needed study material with focus on the difficulties of Hindi speaking people.

For learners

A detailed table of contents and an index at the end should help the learner to easily find what he/ she is looking for. However, for absolute beginners, I have an advice. Read, reread, comprehend and work all the exercises of chapters 1-17 pg. 1-84, based on the basic tenses.

1 ALPHABET वर्णमाला

A	**B**	**C**	**D**	**E**	**F**	**G**	**capital letters**	बड़े अक्षर
a	**b**	**c**	**d**	**e**	**f**	**g**	**small letters**	छोटे अक्षर
ए	बी	सी	डी	ई	एफ़	जी		देवनागरी लिपि में
H	**I**	**J**	**K**	**L**	**M**	**N**	**capital letters**	बड़े अक्षर
h	**i**	**j**	**k**	**l**	**m**	**n**	**small letters**	छोटे अक्षर
एच	आइ	जे	के	एल	एम	एन		देवनागरी लिपि में
O	**P**	**Q**	**R**	**S**	**T**	**U**	**capital letters**	बड़े अक्षर
o	**p**	**q**	**r**	**s**	**t**	**u**	**small letters**	छोटे अक्षर
ओ	पी	क़्यू	आर	एस	टी	यू		देवनागरी लिपि में
V	**W**	**X**	**Y**	**Z**			**capital letters**	बड़े अक्षर
v	**w**	**x**	**y**	**z**			**small letters**	छोटे अक्षर
वी	डबल्यू	एक्स	वाइ	ज़ैड				देवनागरी लिपि में

Consonants कॉन्सोनेन्ट्स (व्यंजन)

b c d f g h j k l m n p
q r s t v w x y z

Vowels वावल्स (स्वर)

a e i o u

☞ *प्रत्येक अंग्रेज़ी सीखने के इच्छुक व्यक्ति का, जिसकी मात भाषा अंग्रेज़ी नहीं है, अध्ययन के प्रारम्भ में कुछ कठिनाइयों से सामना होता है । एक स्वर की एक ही ध्वनि न होने के कारण उच्चारण की समस्या बनी रहती है। जैसे :—*

cat	कैट	a	=	ऐ
car	कार	a	=	आ
care	केअर	a	=	ऐअ
hair	हेअर	ai	=	ऐअ
hut	हट	u	=	अ
put	पुट	u	=	उ
read	रीड	ea	=	ई
reed	रीड	ee	=	ई
receive	रिसीव	ei	=	ई
relieve	रिलीव	ie	=	ई
red	रैड	e	=	ऐ
read	रैड	ea	=	ऐ
role /roll	रोल	o	=	ओ
coal	कोल	oa	=	ओ
soul	सोल	ou	=	ओ
hot	हॉट	o	=	औ
caught	कॉट	au	=	औ
thought	थॉट	ou	=	औ

☞ *इसी प्रकार कुछ शब्द ऐसे हैं जिनका उच्चारण एक सा होता है परन्तु वर्तनी एवम् अर्थ भिन्न होता है। जैसे :—*

soar	सोर	ऊँचा उड़ना
sore	सोर	दु:खद, घाव

assent	*असैन्ट*	सहमति
ascent	*असैन्ट*	चढ़ाव

☞ अंग्रेज़ी में कुछ अक्षर **silent** होते हैं, अर्थात बोले नहीं जाते। जैसे **walk** (वॉक) चलना, **talk** (टॉक) बोलना। इन में "**l**" बोला नहीं जाता। प्रत्येक नए शब्द को उच्चारण एवम् वर्तनी के साथ सीखें। (**pg. 431- 432**)

☞ अंग्रेज़ी में प्रत्येक वाक्य के आरम्भ में आनेवाला शब्द बड़े अक्षर (**capital letter**) से शुरू होता है। अन्य शब्द छोटे अक्षरों (**lower capital**) में लिखे जाते हे़।

☞ अंग्रेज़ी में वाक्य के आरम्भ में कर्ता, दूसरे स्थान पर क्रिया और उसके बाद शेष वाक्यांश आता है। यह हिन्दी से भिन्न है। उदाहरण :

Hindi word order	**English word order**	
1. यह कमरा है।	यह है कमरा।	**This is a* room.** दिस इज़ अ /ए रूम।
2. वह भारतीय है।	वह है भारतीय।	**He is an Indian.** ही इज़ एन इंडियन ।
3. यह किताब है।	यह है किताब।	**This is the book.** दिस इज़ द बुक।

☞ आपने देखा कि उपरोक्त वाक्यों में:
room से पहले **a, Indian** से पहले **an, book** से पहले **the** का प्रयोग किया गया है। इन तीनों को अंग्रेज़ी में **article** (आर्टिकल) कहते हैं। ये दो प्रकार के होते हैं, **definite article** (डेफ़िनेट आर्टिकल) **'the'** (द, दी) और **indefinite article** (इनडेफ़िनेट आर्टिकल) **a, an**(अ/ ए, ऐन ।)

■ **Indefinite article** ***(इनडेफ़िनेट आर्टिकल)*** —जैसा कि इनके नाम से स्पष्ट है, इनका प्रयोग किसी अनिश्चित वस्तु या व्यक्ति के लिए होता

है। जब कोई शब्द vowel (स्वर) से शुरू होता है तो उसके पूर्व an (एन) लगता है, अन्यथा a (अ/ए).

a man	अ/ए मैन	एक आदमी
a room	अ/ए रूम	एक कमरा
a boy	अ/ए बॉय	एक लड़का
a country	अ/ए कण्ट्री	एक देश
an old man	एन ओल्ड मैन	एक बूढ़ा आदमी
an Indian	एन इण्डियन	एक भारतीय

* 'a' के दो उच्चारण है, 'अ' और 'ए'। 'अ' उच्चारण ज़्यादा प्रचलित है। बलाघात हेतु 'ए' का प्रयोग होता है।

■ **Definite article 'the'** *(डेफ़िनेट आर्टिकल 'द')* —जैसा कि इसके नाम से स्पष्ट है, इसका प्रयोग किसी वस्तु या व्यक्ति विशेष के लिए होता है। जैसे कि:

the man	द मैन	एक आदमी
the room	द रूम	एक कमरा
the boy	द बॉय	एक लड़का
the country	द कण्ट्री	एक देश
the old man	दी ओल्ड मैन	एक बूढ़ा आदमी
the Indian	दी इण्डियन	एक भारतीय

☛ 'the' के दो उच्चारण हैं, 'द' और 'दी'। Consonant से पूर्व आने पर 'द' और vowel से पूर्व आने पर 'दी' का प्रयोग होता है।

2 Pronoun (प्रोनाउन)

living प्राणीवाचक *सर्वनाम*

	1st person		2nd person	3rd person	
subject	**I**	**we**	**you**	**he /she**	**they**
	आइ	वी	यू	ही/ शी	दे
	मैं	हम	तू, तुम, आप	वह, यह	वे/ये
object	**me**	**us**	**you**	**him /her**	**them**
	मी	अस्	यू	हिम, हर	दैम
	मुझ	हम	तुझ, तुम, आप	उस, इस	उन, इन

- **I** like **her/ him.** — मैं *उसको* पसन्द करता हूँ।
  आइ लाइक हर/हिम।
- **We** like **them.** — हम *उनको* पसन्द करते हैं।
  वी लाइक दैम।
- **They** like **us.** — *वे हमें* पसन्द करते हैं।
  दे लाइक अस।
- **Do you** like **them**? — क्या तुम *उनको* पसन्द करते हो?
  डू यू लाइक दैम?

non living अप्राणीवाचक *सर्वनाम*

subject			object		
it	इट	यह	it	इट	यह
they, those	दे, दोज़	वे	them	दैम	उन,इन

☞ अप्राणीवाचक third person (अन्यपुरुष) में singular (एकवचन) में subject और object दोनों 'it' हैं, जबकि plural (बहुवचन) में प्राणीवाचक की तरह 'them' का प्रयोग होता है।

☞ किस और किन, दोनों के लिए whom का प्रयोग होता है। उदाहरण के लिए : किसको/ किनको = to whom; किसके लिए/ किनके लिए for whom etc.

1. I like **it**. — मैं इसे पसन्द करता हूँ।
   आइ लाइक इट।
2. Give **it** to me. — इसे मुझको दे दीजिए।
   गिव इट टु मी।
3. I like **these** . — मैं ये पसन्द करता हूँ।
   आइ लाइक दीज़।
4. Give **them** to me. — इन्हें मुझको दे दीजिए।
   गिव दैम टु मी।

Ex. 1: Translate into English.

1. इसमें 2. उसमें 3. उनसे 4. उनपर 5. उनको 6. मुझसे 7. हमसे 8. आप लोगों से 9. किसको/किनको 10. किससे/ किनसे 11. हमको; 12.इससे 13. उससे 14. उनमें 15. किसमें / किनमें।

Ex.2: Complete the sentences with object pronouns:

1. They want to meet her but she doesn't want to meet ....
2. I want to meet him but he doesn't want to meet ....
3. Savita is a nice lady. I lke......very much.
4. This is our new house. Do you like ....?
5. All these are our houses. Do you like ....?
6. You may have this book. I don't require ....anymore.
7. Take these DVDs. I don't need ....
8. She is calling you. Please go to ....
9. He wants this CD. Can you give...........to............
10. I need those pictures. Could you bring............for ....
11. "Is this job interesting?" "yes, ... is."
12. "Are these your keys?" "Yes, ... are."
13. "Is this hotel very expensive?" " No, ...is not at all expensive."
14. "Are the banks closed today." "yes .... are."
15. " Where did you buy these picture frames?"
    " I bought .... at Saturday bazaar."

Key 1

1. in it / him / her	2. in that / him/her	3. from them
4. on them	5. to them	6. from me
7. from us	8. from you people	9. to whom
10. from whom	11. to us	12. from it/him/her
13. from that/him her	14. in them	15. in whom

Key 2

1. them	2. me	3. her	4. it
5. them	6. it	7. them	8. her.
9. it, him	10. them , me.	11. it	12. they
13. it	14. they	15. them	

3 Verb "to be" *(होना)*

Present tense: is इज़**, are** आर**, am** ऐम

I am.	आइ ऐम।	मैं हूँ।
We are.	वी आर।	हम हैं।
you are.	यू आर।	तू है।/तुम हो।/ आप हैं।
He/She is.	ही/ शी इज़।	वह / यह है।
They are.	दे आर।	वे / ये हैं।
What is?	व्हाट इज़?	क्या है?
Who is?	हू इज़?	कौन है?
Who are?	हू आर?	कौन हैं?

Examples:

I am happy.	आइ ऐम हैपी।	मैं खुश हूँ।
The party is good.	द पार्टी इज़ गुड।	दावत अच्छी है।

Past tense: was वॉज़**, were** वर

I was.	आइ वॉज।	मैं था / मैं थी।
We were.	वी वर।	हम थे / हम थीं।
You were.	यू वर।	तू था /तू थी।
		तुम थे / तुम थीं।
		आप थे / आप थीं।
He / She was.	ही/शी वॉज़।	वह था। / वह थी।
They were.	दे वर।	वे थे / वे थीं।

What was?	व्हाट वॉज़?	क्या था?
Who was?	हू वॉज।	कौन था/ कौन थी?
Who were?	हू वर।	कौन थे/ कौन थीं?

Examples:

I was happy.	आइ वॉज़ हैपी।	मैं खुश था/थी।
The party was good.	द पार्टी वॉज़ गुड।	दावत अच्छी थी।

Future tense: will be / shall be विल बी/ शैल बी।

I will be / shall be.	आइ विल बी/ शैल बी।	मैं हूँगा/ मैं हूँगी।
We will be / shall be.	वी विल बी/ शैल बी।	हम होंगे/हम होंगी।
You will be.	यू विल बी।	तू होगा / तू होगी। तुम होगे/तुम होगी। आप होंगे/आप होंगी।
He / She / It will be.	ही / शी / इट विल बी।	वह होगा/वह होगी।
They will be.	दे विल बी।	वे होंगे/वे होंगी।
What will be?	व्हॉट विल बी?	क्या होगा?
Who (sg.) will be?	हू (sg.) विल बी?	कौन होगा / कौन होगी?
Who (pl.) will be?	हू (pl.) विल बी?	कौन होंगे / कौन होंगी?

Examples:

I will be happy.	आइ विल बी हैपी।	मैं खुश हूँगा/हूँगी।
The party will be good.	द पार्टी विल बी गुड।	दावत अच्छी होगी।

☞ ***प्रश्नवाचक बनाने के लिए क्रिया को वाक्य के शुरू में रखें।***

Examples:

Is she happy?	इज़ शी हैपी?	क्या वह खुश है?

Was she happy?	वॉज़ शी हैपी?	क्या वह खुश थी?
Will she be happy?	विल शी बी हैपी?	क्या वह खुश होगी?

Ex.1: Fill in the blanks with 'am, are, is':

1. She..... busy.
2. They.... hungry.
3. He...... sick
4. We.... happy.
5. This box.... heavy.
6. Varanasi.... a city of temples.
7. .... you ill?
8. I.... a student.
9. .....he the teacher?
10. Delhi.... the capital of India.
11. I...... diligent; you...... lazy!
12. This camera..... expensive; that one..... cheap.
13. This bread..... not fresh; it..... stale.
14. Rani..... tall; her sister..... short.
15. I...... optimistic; my friend..... pessimistic.

Ex. 2: Fill in the blanks with 'was', 'were'.

1. Weather .... pleasant last week.
2. We .... disappointed.
3. They .... very tired.
4. This time last week I .... in the US
5. ....the exam easy?
6. Where .... you last night?
7. ....they late?
8. Who all .... at the party.
9. The hotel .... expensive but not comfortable..
10. They .... here last month.

Ex.3: Fill in the blanks with ' will be'.

1. Next week I .... in Delhi.
2. I ....be a little late.
3. I am sure they .... very tired.

4. This time next week we .... in the US
5. They .... proably eat out this evening.
6. Where .... you.......... after 6 O' clock in the evening.?
7. ....they arrive on time?
8. I think there .... many people at the party.
9. He ....sixty tomorrow..
10. They .... here the day after tomorrow.

Ex. 4: Translate into English:

1. आज सोमवार है। 2. वे मितभाषी हैं। 3. तुम महत्त्वाकांक्षी हो। 4. हिन्दी भारत की राष्ट्रभाषा है। 5. औरत मिलनसार है। 6. मैं चिंतित हूँ। 7. बच्चा भूखा-प्यासा है। 8. यात्री थके हैं।

9. किताब महँगी थी। 10. दही खट्टा था। 11. आम मीठा था। 12. लड़का बीमार था। 13. यात्री दयालु था। 14. वह कैसे था? 15. वहाँ कौन था? 16. हम परेशान थे।

17. वह खुश होगा। 18. कल धूप होगी। 19. माता जी परेशान होंगी। 20. अध्यापक नाराज़ होंगे। 21. बहन उदास होगी। 22. अगले हफ़्ते आसमान साफ़ होगा। 23. पुस्तक मेला कब होगा? 24. कल तापमान ज़्यादा होगा।

Key 1

1. is	2. are	3. is	4. are
5. is	6. is	7. Are	8. am
9. Is	10. is	11. am, are	12. is, is
13. is, is	14. is, is	15, am, is	

Key 2

1. was	2. were	3. were	4. was
5. was	6. were	7. were	8. were
9. was	10 . were		

Key 3

1. will be	2. shall be	3. will be	4. shall be
5. will	6. will, be	7. will	8. will be
9. will be	10. will be		

Key 4

1. It is Monday today. 2. They are reticent. 3. You are ambitious. 4. Hindi is the national language of India. 5. The woman is friendly. 6. I am worried. 7. The child is hungry and thirsty. 8. The travelers are tired.

9. The book was expensive. 10. Yogurt was sour. 11. Mango was sweet. 12. The boy was sick. 13. The traveler was kind. 14. How was he? 15. Who was there? 16. We were upset.

17. He will be happy. 18. It will be sunny tomorrow. 19. Mother will be upset. 20. Teacher will be displeased. 21. Sister will be sad. 22. Sky will be clear next week. 23. When will the book fare be.? 24. Temperature will be higher tomorrow

It's Nice To See You!

Rani :	Hello, Kamla!
Kamla :	Hi, Rani!
Rani :	It's nice to see you.
Kamla :	Nice to see you too. I would like you to meet my friend Manju.
Rani :	Hello, I am pleased to meet you.
Manju :	Pleased to meet you too. I hear you are a student?
Rani :	Yes, I am studying law at B.H.U.
Kamla :	How is your brother, Rani?
Rani :	He is fine, thank you.
Kamla :	Tell him I said, "hello'.

4 Imperative

■ हिन्दी में मध्यम पुरुष (second person) के 'तू', तुम', 'आप' तीन औपचारिक (formal) एवम् अनौपचारिक (informal) रूपों के लिए, अंग्रेज़ी में एक ही 'you' का प्रयोग होता है और imperative वाक्य रचना भी एक ही है। औपचारिकता हेतु वाक्य के आरम्भ में Please का प्रयोग करते हैं। एक और बात हिन्दी भाषियों को ध्यान में रखनी चाहिए कि अंग्रेज़ी में प्रत्यक्ष एवम् परोक्ष विधिलिंग का कोई भेद नहीं। *उदाहरण के लिए :* **Verb come (*कम*) *आना*!**

अनौपचारिक (informal) *प्रयोग में:* तू आ/ तुम आओ (प्रत्यक्ष) तू/ तुम आना। (परोक्ष)	Come! (कम)
औपचारिक (formal) *प्रयोग में* आप आइए (प्रत्यक्ष) आप आइएगा। (परोक्ष)	Please come! (प्लीज़ कम)

Comprehension:

1. Put the book here. पुट द बुक हिअर। किताब यहाँ रखो।
2. Make the bed. मेक द बैड। बिस्तर बनाओ।
3. Come to the kitchen. कम टु द किचन। रसोई-घर में आओ।
4. Go to the living room. गो टु द लिविंग रूम। बैठक में जाओ।
5. Give me the money. गिव मी द मनी। मुझे पैसे दो।
6. Tell him the secret. टैल हिम द सीक्रेट। उसे रहस्य बताओ।

7. Wash your hands.	वाश योअर हैंड्स	अपने हाथ धोओ
8. Brush your teeth.	ब्रश योअर टीथ।	अपने दाँत साफ़ करो।
9. Put them here.	पुट दैम हिअर।	उन्हें यहाँ रखो।
10. Play the piano.	प्ले द पिआनो।	पिआनो बजाओ।
11. Tell him the truth.	टैल हिम द ट्रूथ।	उसे सच्चाई बताओ।
12. Turn the light off.	टर्न द लाइट ऑफ़।	बत्ती बुझा दो।
13. Turn the television off.	टर्न द टैलीवियन ऑफ़।	दूरदर्शन बन्द कर दो।
14. Please put the garbage out.	प्लीज़ पुट द गारबेज आउट।	कृपया कचरा बाहर रख दीजिए।

■ 'us' imperative (Let's + infinitive)

☞ This is used while asking others to join you in an activity.
जब व्यक्ति दूसरों को अपने साथ मिलकर कुछ करने को कहता है तो निम्नलिखित रचना का प्रयोग होता है।

Let's go. लैट्स गो।	आइए, चलें।/ चला जाय।
Let's watch TV. लैट्स वॉच टी.वी.।	आइए, दूरदर्शन देखें।/ दूरदर्शन देखा जाय।
Let's sing and dance. लैट्स सिंग ऐण्ड डान्स।	आइए, नाचें, गाएँ।/ आइए, नाचा, गाया जाय।
Let's meet in front of the cinema at 8 p.m. लैट्स मीट इन फ्रण्ट ऑफ़ द सिनेमा ऐट एट पी.ऐम. ।	रात को आठ बजे सिनेमा के सामने मिलें।/ मिला जाय।

Let's not eat out. = Don't let's eat out.
Let's not watch TV = Don't let's watch TV.

Ex.1: Translate into English:

1. आप यहाँ बैठिए।
2. आप बाज़ार जाइए।
3. अंधविश्वासी न बनिए।
4. आप चाय पीजिए।
5. तुम कॉफी बनाओ।
6. तुम नीचे बैठो।
7. तुम बाहर जाओ।
8. नल बन्द करो।
9. नल खोलो।
10. पौष्टिक भोजन खाइए।
11. घर साफ़ कीजिए।
12. सूई में तागा डालो।

Ex.2: Translate into English:

1. सड़क सावधानी से पार करना।
2. सहपाठियों से सद्व्यवहार करना।
3. रात को देर तक बाहर मत रहना।
4. अपने स्वास्थ्य का ध्यान रखना।
5. विदेश जाकर अपनी संस्कृति मत भूलना।
6. अपनेसे कमज़ोर लोगों को मत सताना।
7. ग़रीबों की मदद करना।
8. समय व्यर्थ न गँवाना।
9. फ़िज़ूल ख़र्च मत करना।
10. तुम मुझे सोमवार को सुबह नौ बजे मिलना।
11. मुझे धर्म संकट में न डालिएगा।
12. कभी मेरे घर आइएगा।

Ex. 3: Translate into English:

1. चलिए, सैर करने चलें।
2. आज शाम को बाहर खाया जाय।
3. तैरने चला जाय।
4. इस हफ़्ते शाकाहारी भोजन खाया जाय।
5. इस हफ़्ते मांसाहारी भोजन न खाया जाय।
6. आज घर पर रहकर दूरदर्शन देखा जाय।
7. आज रात जल्दी सोया जाय।
8. कल नौका-विहार किया जाय।
9. आइए, कुछ व्यायाम किया जाय।
10. चलिए, बस का इन्तज़ार न करके टैक्सी ली जाय।

Key 1

1.Please sit here. 2. Please go to the market. 3. Please don't be superstisicious. 4. Please have tea. 5. Prepare coffee. 6. Sit down. 7. Go out. 8. Turn the tap off. 9. Turn the tap on. 10. Please eat nutritious food. 11. Please clean the house. 12. Thread the needle.

Key2.

1.Cross the road carefully. 2. Behave nicely with your class mates. 3. Don't stay out late at night. 4. Take care of your health. 5. Don't forget your culture after going abraod. 6. Don't trouble those who are weaker than you. 7. Help the poor. 8. Don't waste time. 9. Don't waste money. 10. Meet me on Monday at 9 O'clock in the morning. 11. Please don't put me in a dilemma. 12. Please come to my house sometime.

Key 3

1.Let's go for a walk. 2. Let's eat out today. 3. Let's go to swim. 4. Let's eat vegetarian food this week. 5. Let's not eat non-vegetarian food this week. 6. Let's stay at home today and watch TV. 7. Let's sleep early tonight. 8. Let's do a boat ride tomorrow. 9. Let's do some physical exercise. 10. Come, let's not wait for the bus and take a taxi.

I Guess So / I Hope So

Cherry	:	Hello, Rani!
Rani	:	Hi, Cherry, It has been a long time.
Cherry	:	Yes, the last time we met was in September, 2011.
Rani	:	I guess so.
Cherry	:	How is everything with you?
Rani	:	About the same.
Cherry	:	Going somewhere during the summer vacation?
Rani	:	I hope so.

5 Present Indefinite Tense

(प्रेज़ेन्ट इन्डेफ़िनेट टेन्स)

■ **Affirmative:** | **subject +** | **verb** | **+** | **object** |

- I eat rice. — मैं चावल खाता/खाती हूँ ।
  आइ ईट राइस।
- We eat rice. — हम चावल खाते/खाती हैं ।
  वी ईट राइस।
- You eat rice. — तू चावल खाता/खाती है।
  यू ईट राइस। — तुम चावल खाते/खाती हो।
  आप चावल खाते/खाती हैं।
- He / She / It eats rice. — वह चावल खाता/खाती है।
  ही/शी/इट ईट्स राइस।
- They eat rice. — वे चावल खाते/खाती हैं।
  दे ईट राइस।

■ इन वाक्यों को नकारात्मक बनाते समय **I, we, you, they** के साथ **do not/ don't** और **he, she, it** के साथ **does not/doesn't** लगाएँ।

- I do not/ don't eat rice. — मैं चावल नहीं खाता/खाती ।
  आइ डू नॉट/डोंट ईट राइस।
- We do not/ don't eat rice. — हम चावल नहीं खाते/खातीं।
  वी डू नॉट/डोंट ईट राइस।

- You do not/ don't eat rice. — तू चावल नहीं खाता/खाती ।
  यू डू नॉट/डोंट ईट राइस। — तुम/आप चावल नहीं खाते/खातीं।
- He /She/ It does not/ doesn't eat rice — वह चावल नहीं खाता/खाती।
  ही/शी/ इट डज़ नॉट/डज़न्ट ईट राइस।
- They do not/ don't eat rice. — वे चावल नहीं खाते/खातीं ।
  दे डू नॉट/डोंट ईट राइस।

■ **Interrogative** (प्रश्नवाचक) बनाते समय वाक्य के शुरू में **I, we, you, they** के पहले **do** और **he, she, it** के पहले **does** लगाएँ।

- Do you eat rice? — क्या तू चावल खाता/खाती है?
  डू यू ईट राइस? — क्या तुम चावल खाते/खाती हो?
  क्या आप चावल खाते/खाती हैं?
- Does he /she/ it eat rice? — क्या वह चावल खाता/खाती है?
  डज़ ही/शी/ इट ईट राइस?
- Do they eat rice? — क्या वे / ये चावल खाते/खातीं हैं?
  डू दे ईट राइस?

■ **Interrogative negativce** (नकारात्मक प्रश्नवाचक) बनाते समय वाक्य के शुरू में **I, we, you, they** के पहले **do not /don't** और **he, she, it** के पहले **does not** या **doesn't** लगाएँ।

- Don't you eat rice? — क्या तू चावल नहीं खाता/खाती?
  डोंट यू ईट राइस? — क्या तुम/ आप चावल नहीं खाते/खातीं?
- Doesn't he/she/ it eat rice? — क्या वह चावल नहीं खाता/खाती?
  डज़न्ट़ ही / शी/ इट ईट राइस?
- Don't they eat rice? — क्या वे चावल नहीं खाते/खातीं ?
  डोंट दे ईट राइस?

Present simple tense के प्रयोग :

1 **Activities that one does and events that take place usually, always*, never, sometimes, once a week, once in five years etc i.e activities and events that follow a regular frequency patern in one's routine:**

सामान्य जीवन में नियमित रूप से(प्रायः, सदैव, कभी-कभी आदि) होने वाली क्रियाए एवम् घटनाएँ **present simple tense** में कही जाती हैं।

☞ ***always** का प्रयोग **present simple continuous** में भी सम्भव है। देखें **pg.** 29

1. She lives in Delhi. शी लिव्स इन डेल्ही।	वह दिल्ली में रहती है।
2. I eat a lot of salad and fruit. आइ ईट अ लॉट ऑफ़ सैलेड ऐण्ड फ्रूट।	मैं बहुत सलाद और फल खाती हूँ /खाता हूँ।
3. He always carries a stick. ही ऑलवेज़ कैरीज़ अ स्टिक।	वह हमेशा छड़ी साथ रखता है।
4. I usually have bread and jam for breakfast. आइ यूश्वली हैव ब्रैड ऐण्ड जैम फ़ॉर ब्रेकफ़ास्ट।	मैं प्रायः नाश्ते में डबल रोटी और 'जैम' लेता हूँ।
5. Mother goes to temple every day. मदर गोज़ टु टैम्पल ऐवरी डे।	माँ प्रतिदिन मंदिर जाती हैं।
6. She sometimes reads the Filmfare. शी सम-टाईम्ज़ रीड्स द फ़िल्म फ़ेअर।	वह कभी-कभी फ़िल्म फ़ेयर पढ़ती है।
7. We never eat out. वी नेवर ईट आउट।	हम कभी बाहर नहीं खाते।

2 **Seminars, concerts, meetings, trains, buses, flights** *आदि के* **time tables** *संबंधी भविष्य के लिए* **:**

1. What time does the concert finish.
   व्हाट टाईम डज़ द कॉन्सर्ट फ़िनिश?
   गोष्ठी कितने बजे ख़त्म होगी।
2. What time does the next train to New Delhi leave?
   व्हाट टाईम डज़ द नेक्स्ट ट्रेन टु न्यू डेल्ही लीव?
   नई दिल्ली के लिए अगली गाड़ी कितने बजे छूटेगी?
3. The aeroplane lands at 9 a.m.
   दी एरोप्लेन लैण्ड्स ऐट नाइन ए•एम•।
   हवाई जहाज़ सुबह नौ बजे उतरेगा।

3 **Eternal truth:** (शाश्वत सत्य)

1. The sun rises in the east.
   सन राइज़िज़ इन दी ईस्ट।
   सूर्य पूर्व में निकलता है।
2. The earth revolves round the sun.
   अर्थ रिवॉल्व्स राउण्ड द सन।
   धरती सूर्य के गिर्द घूमती है।
3. Water boils at 100° celsius.
   वॉटर बौएल्स एट हण्ड्रड डिग्रीज़ सैलसियस।
   पानी १०० अंश सेल्सियस पर उबलता है।
4. The moon goes round the earth in about 27 days.
   द मून गोज़ राऊँड दी अर्थ इन अबाउट ट्वेण्टी-सैवन डेज़।
   चाँद लगभग २७ दिन में पृथ्वी के गिर्द चक्कर लगाता है।

4 **Running commentaries:** (आँखों देखे हाल का वर्णन)

1. The guests take their respective
   मेहमान अपना-अपना स्थान ग्रहण

seats. द गैस्ट्स टेक देअर रिस्पैक्टिव सीट्स।	कर रहे हैं।
2. The chief guest arrives. द चीफ़ गैस्ट अर्राइव्ज़।	मुख्य अतिथि आ रहे हैं।
3. The crowd cheers. द काउड चीर्अज़।	भीड़ हर्षध्वनि से प्रोत्साहित कर रही है।

Ex. 1: Which is correct?

1. Where do / does Piush work?
2. How do / does aeroplanes fly?
3. What do / does mother say?
4. What time do / does the film begin?
5. What do / does they want from me?
6. He speak / speaks several languages.
7. We read / reads Hindi magazines.
8. They always eats / eat vegetarian food.
9. She work / works hard.
10. We buy / buys and read / reads newspaper every day.

Ex.2: Change the sentences given below from the present simple affirmative to the present simple interrogative form as shown.

1. I study English.	Do you study English?
2. She teaches three languages.	How many.........................?
3. Mother prepares breakfast in the morning.	what ....?
4. We have cereal and fruit for breakfast.	what ....?
5. He looks very sick.	How...................................?
6. They like music.	Who ....?

7. I have a hot bath in the morning. What................................?
8. Anil works hard. Who................................?
9. Water boils at 100° celsius. What................................?
10. Shops close at 7 p.m. When................................?

Ex. 3: Write complete sentences:

1. He / always / buy / child proof toys. ....
2. This vehicle /not/use / much fuel. ....
3. I / not / speak Spanish. ....
4. You / know how/ use / computer?...
5. Where / you / come from? ....
6. What / this / word mean?..
7. What time / post office / open? ....
8. Which newpaper / you/ subscribe? ....
9. They / eat / non-vegetarian food?...
10. Get up / what time / usually / your mother?...............................
11. How much / to /phone / New Delhi / it / cost?...............................
12. Where / live / your fiance?..
13. She / want / what / for breakfast?...
14. Often / rain / it / in your city? ....
15. Your/ family / like music? ....

Ex. 4: Translate into English:

1. कमला और मैं एक दूसरे को पत्र लिखते हैं। 2. मैं गर्म और कड़क चाय पीता हूँ। 3. खिलाड़ी तेज़ दौड़ता है। 4. बच्चा बाग़ीचे में खेलता है। 5. मैं प्रतिदिन अख़बार पढ़ता हूँ। 6. हम अध्यापक/अध्यापिका से प्रश्न पूछते हैं। 7. वे सप्ताहान्त पर तैरते हैं। 8. हम रोज़ ताज़ा फलों का रस पीते हैं। 9. मैं सुबह सात बजे स्कूल ज़ाता हूँ । 10. शाम को मैं दूरदर्शन पर धारावाहिक देखता हूँ । 11.मैं रात को कहीं नहीं ज़ाता। 12. क्या आप रेडियो सुनते हैं? जी, मैं रेडियो सुऩता हूँ । 13. 'क्या आप दूरदर्शन देखते हैं?' 'जी, मैं

child proof = जिससे बच्चों को हानि न हो।

दूरदर्शन देख़ता हूँ ।' 14. 'क्या आप उपन्यास पढ़ते हैं?' 'जी, मैं उपन्यास पढता हूँ।' 15. 'क्या आप सैर करते हैं?' 'जी, मैं रोज़ सैर कर्ता हूँ ।' 16. 'क्या आप क्रिकेट खेलते हैं?' 'जी नहीं, मैं क्रिकेट नहीं खेल्ता; मैं हाकी खेलता हूँ ।' 17.वह वाहन बहुत तेज़ चलाता है। 18.वह अक्सर अपने ही घर का रास्ता भूल जाती है। 19. मैं साँपों से घ णा करता हूँ। 20. गाड़ी दो बजे छूटती है। 21. हम लहसुन और प्याज़ कभी नहीं खाते। 22. बच्चे तैरना पसन्द करते हैं। 23. वह सदैव अपने माता-पिता की बात सुनता है। 24. मैं प्रतिदिन प्रात:काल योगाभ्यास करता हूँ। 25. वह अपना भोजन स्वयं बनाती है।

Key 1

1. does	2. do	3. does	4. does	5. do
6. speaks	7. read	8. eat	9. works	10. buy, read

Key 2

2. ... languages does she teach?
3. ...does mother prepare in the morning?
4. ... do you have for breakfast?
5. .... does he look?
6. ... ..like music?
7. .....do you have in the morning?
8. ... works hard?
9. ... boils at 100° Celsius?
10. .. do the shops close?

Key 3

1. He always buys child proof toys.
2. This vehicle does not use much fuel.
3. I do not speak Spanish.
4. Do you know how to use computer?
5. Where do you come from?
6. What does this word mean?
7. What time does the post office open?
8. Which newpaper do you subscribe?
9. Do they eat non-vegetarian food?
10. What time does your mother usually get up?
11. How much does it cost to phone New Delhi?
12. Where does your fiance live?

13. What does she want for breakfast?

14. Does it rain often in your city?

15. Does your family like music?

Key4

1. Kamla and I write letters to each other. 2. I drink hot and strong tea. 3. The athlete runs fast. 4. The child plays in the park. 5. I read the newpaper every day. 6. We ask the teacher questions. 7. They swim on weekends. 8. We drink fresh fruit juice every day. 9. I go to school at seven a.m. 10. In the evening, I watch serials on TV. 11. At night, I don't go anywhere. 12. 'Do you listen to the radio?' 'Yes, I listen to the radio.' 13.'Do you watch television?' 'Yes, I watch television. ' 14. 'Do you read novels?' ' Yes I read novels.' 15. 'Do you go for a walk?' 'Yes I go for a walk every day.' 16. 'Do you play cricket?' 'No, I don't play cricket. I play hockey.' 17. He drives very fast. 18. She usually loses the way to her own house. 19. I hate snakes. 20. The train leaves at 2 O'clock. 21. We never eat garlic and onion. 22.Children enjoy swimming. 23. He always listens to his parents. 24. I practise yoga every morning. 25. She cooks her meals by herself.

Could You Tell Me....?

A: Can you tell me the way to Parliament House?
B: It's straight down the street, but it is not very near. You will need to take a bus or a taxi.
A: Could you tell me which bus goes there?
B: Numbers 407 and 502, both will take you there.
A: Thank you. By the way, how often do these buses run?
B: Every 15 minutes.
A: But I have been standing here for 30 minutes!
B: Yes, sometimes it takes longer in heavy traffic.
A: I'd rather take a taxi.
B: Look, there comes the bus!

6 Present Progressive Tense

■ **Aff.:** **subj. + am, is, are + (v..ing) + obj. (if any)**

- I am eating rice. — मैं चावल खा रहा/रही हूँ ।
  आइ एम ईटिंग राइस।
- **You** are running. — *तुम* दौड़ रहे/रही हो।
  यू आर रनिंग। — *आप* दौड़ रहे/रही हैं।
- **He / she / It** is eating rice — *वह / यह* चावल खा रहा/रही है।
  ही/ शी/ इट इज़ ईटिंग राइस।
- **They / we** are running. — *वे/ ये / हम* दौड़ रहे/रही हैं।
  दे / वी आर रनिंग।

■ **Neg.:** **subj. + am, is, are + not + (v.. ing) + obj. (if any)**

- I am not eating rice. — मैं चावल नहीं खा रहा/रही ।
  आइ एम नॉट ईटिंग राइस।
- **He / she / It** is not eating rice — *वह* चावल नहीं खा रहा/रही ।
  ही / शी / इट इज़ नॉट ईटिंग राइस।
- **They / You / we** are not laughing. — *वे/ ये/तुम/ आप/ हम* हँस नहीं रहे/रहीं।
  दे / यू / वी आर नॉट लाफ़िंग।

■ **Int. :** **Am / Is / Are + subj. + (v..ing) + obj. (if any)**

- **Is he / she / it** eating rice? — *क्या वह* चावल खा रहा/रही है ?
  इज़ ही / शी/ इट ईटिंग राइस?

- **Are you** running? आर यू रनिंग? — ***क्या तुम*** दौड रहे/रही हो? ***क्या आप*** दौड रहे/रही हैं?
- **Are they / we** laughing?. आर दे / वी लाफ़िंग? — ***क्या वे / ये/ हम*** हँस रहे/रही हैं?

■ **Neg. int. :** **Am / Is / Are + subj. + not + v..ing + obj. (if any)**

- **Is he / she / it** not eating rice? इज़ ही/ शी/ इट नॉट ईटिंग राइस? — ***क्या वह*** चावल नहीं खा रहा/रही?
- **Are they / you / we** not laughing?. आर दे / यू / वी नॉट लाफ़िंग? — ***क्या वे/ ये/ आप/ तुम / हम*** हँस नहीं रहे/रहीं?

Present simple progressive tense *के प्रयोग* :

1 Activities or events taking place at the time of talking:
बात करते समय किसी कार्य या घटना के हो रहे होने पर :

• It is snowing.	इट इज़ स्नोइंग।	बर्फ़ पड़ रही है।
• We are climbing up the tree. .	वी आर क्लाइमिंग अप द ट्री ।	हम पेड़ पर चढ़ रहे / रही हैं।

2 Activities or events taking place for shot extended period at present:

कभी-कभी वर्तमान में अल्प कालावधि में की जानेवाली क्रियाओं के लिए भी इस ढाँचे का प्रयोग करते हैं। जैसे:

- These days we are swimming every day. — आजकल हम रोज़ तैर रहे हैं।

दीज़ डेज़ वी आर स्विमिंग ऐव्री डे।

- These days we are playing all day. — आजकल हम दिन भर खेल रहे हैं।
  दीज़ डेज़ वी आर प्लेइङ्ग ऑल डे।

3 **Activities or events taking place in the near future:**
निकट भविष्य में की जानेवाली क्रियाओं के लिए भी इस ढाँचे का प्रयोग करते हैं।

subj. + am, is, are + (v.ing) + obj. (if any)+ fut. time clause

- We **are playing** cricket **tomorrow.** — हम कल क्रिकेट खेल रहे हैं।
  वी आर प्लेइंग क्रिकेट टुमौरो।
- **I am not working next month.** — मैं अगले महीने काम नहीं कर रहा/रही।
  आइ एम नॉट वर्किन्ग नेक्स्ट मन्थ।

■ **Present simple progressive tense** *का प्रयोग नहीं होता :*

1 **Seminars, concerts, meetings, trains, buses, flights** *आदि के* **time tables** *के लिए* **present simple progressive** *का प्रयोग* नहीं *होता;* **present simple tense** *का प्रयोग होता है।* देखें **pg.** 21

2. **"hear", "smell'. 'taste'** *के साथ* **present simple progressive tense** *का प्रयोग* नहीं करते। देखें **pg.** 130

3 *निम्नलिखित* **verbs** *के साथ* **present simple progressive** *का प्रयोग सामान्यता नहीं होता; यदि होता है तो किसी बिशेष अर्थ में:*
like, prefer, love, hate, need, want, know, mean, understand, believe, remember, forget, depend, realise, suppose, belong, seem.

- मैं आज कुछ ख़रीदारी करना — I want to do some

चाह रही हूँ। | shopping today. (√)

I am wanting to do some shopping today. (x)

- आप समझ रही हैं ? — Do you understand? (√)

  Are you understanding?(x)
- आप कहना क्या चाह रही हैं? — What do you mean? (√)

  What are you meaning? (x)

Present simple *और* **present progressive tense**
दोनों का प्रयोग संभव :

[1] **'look', 'feel'** *के साथ :* **see pg. 130**

[2] **think** *के साथ :*

☞ *जब* **"think"** *किसी धारणा, अथवा राय की अभिव्यक्ति होता है, तो* **present simple** *का प्रयोग करते है, निम्नलिखित वाक्य* **1,2:**

☞ *जब* **think** *से अर्थ किसी विषय वस्तु पर सोचने की प्रक्रिया हो तो* **present simple progressive** *का प्रयोग करते है। नीचे दिए वाक्य* **3, 4 :**

1. I think this is a good bargain. — मुझे लगता है यह अच्छा सौदा है।/ आइ थिंक इट इज़ ए गुड बारगेन।
2. What do you think of this project. — आपको यह योजना कैसी लगती है।/ लग रही है ? व्हाट डु यू थिंक ऑफ़ दिस प्रॉजेक्ट।
3. I am thinking of settling in the US. — मैं अमरीका में बसने की सोच रहा हूँ। आइ ऐम थिंकिंग ऑफ़ सैटलिंग इन दी यू . ऐस .
4. I am thinking of going regularly to some gym. — मैं नियमित रूप से किसी 'जिम' में जाने की सोच रहा हूँ। आइ ऐम थिंकिंग ऑफ़ गोइंग रैग्युलरली टु सम जिम।

3 **always *के साथ* present simple progressive *का प्रयोग* :**

***सामान्यता* always *के साथ* present simple tense *का प्रयोग होता है* / (see pg. 19) *परन्तु जब तात्पर्य किसी काम के ज़रूरत से ज़्यादा या बार बार होने के अर्थ में हो तो* always *के साथ*present simple progressive *का प्रयोग करते हैं* /**

1. They are always complaining. वे हमेशा शिकायत करते रहते हैं।
   दे आर ऑलवेज़ कम्प्लेनिंग।
2. She is always listening to the . radio. वह हमेशा रेडियो सुनती रहती है।
   शी इज़ ऑलवेज़ लिसेनिंग टु द रेडियो।

Compare and comprehend 1	
present simple tense	**present simple progressive tense**
1. He plays the sitar. वह सितार बजाता है।	He is playing the sitar. वह सितार बजा रहा है।
2. Ravina usually works at this time. रवीना सामान्यता इस समय काम करती है।	She is not working today. रवीना आज काम नहीं कर रही।
3. I have a shower twice a day. मैं दिन में दो बार नहाता हूँ।	I am having a shower. मैं नहा रहा हूँ।
4. Water boils at 100 celsius. पानी १०० अंश सेल्सियस पर उबलता है।	Water is boiling. पानी उबल रहा है।

Compare and comprehend 2:

Use of present simple progressive for future:

(1) is / are / am + v.....ing ☞ जब व्यक्ति भविष्य में कुछ करने का निर्णय लेता है और साथ ही उसे कार्यान्वित करने की व्यवस्था भी कर लेता है। **Examples 1, 2:**

(2) is / are / am + going to + infinitive ☞ *जब व्यक्ति भविष्य में कुछ करने का निर्णय तो लेता है परन्तु उसके कार्यान्वयन से संबंधित कोई सुनिश्चित व्यवस्था नहीं की गई।* **Examples 3, 4 :**

1. I am changing jobs next Monday . मैं अगले सोमवार को 'जॉब' (नौकरी) बदलूँगा।
   आइ एम चेंजिंग जॉब्स नेक्स्ट मन्डे।
   (भविष्य में धंधा बदलने का निर्णय और उसके कार्यान्वयन से संबंधित सब व्यवस्था हो चुकी है।)
2. We are having a party on Sunday. हम रविवार को दावत करेंगे।
   वी आर हैविंग ए पार्टी ऑन सण्डे।
   (रविवार को दावत देने का निर्णय और उसके कार्यान्वयन से संबंधित सब व्यवस्था भी हो चुकी है।)
3. I am going to change jobs soon. मैं जल्दी जॉब (नौकरी) बदलने वाला हूँ।
   आइ एम गोइंग टु चेंज जॉब्स सून।
   (भविष्य में काम बदलने का निर्णय हो चुका है, परन्तु उसके कार्यान्वयन से संबंधित कोई व्यवस्था नहीं की गई।)
4. We are going to have a party on Sunday. *हम रविवार को दावत करेंगे।*
   वी आर गोइंग टु हैव ए पार्टी ऑन सण्डे।
   (रविवार को दावत देने का निर्णय लिया जा चुका है, परन्तु उसके कार्यान्वयन से संबंधित कोई व्यवस्था नहीं की गई।)

Ex. 1: Complete the sentences given below in the present simple progressive tense using the verbs in brackets:

1. She................... (work).
2. I.......(read).....a newpaper.
3. They ....(have)......lunch.
4. The students...............(play)
5. We .... (do) ...... our home work.
6. The sun .... (shine)
7. The athletes .... (run)
8. Mother ....(cook).
9. We ....(stay)....... at Hotel Taj.
10. Some boys ......(swim).

Ex. 2: Write sentences using the cues given below as shown:

> **she/wash/ her hair?**
> => **Is she washing her hair?**

1. Who/ have/ shower/ at this time?
2. What/students/do?
3. She/learn/classical music?
4. What/ you guys/ do?
5. She/ wash/ her hair?
6. Who/ sit/ on the chair?
7. Whose/ children/ cry?
8. Rain/now?
9. Why/ dog/ bark?
10. Why/ she/ tell/ a lie?

Ex. 3: Complete the sentences in the present simple progressive tense using the words given below.

chirp	deliver	cross	repair
tell	mew	clean	teach
read	think	mend	

1. The cobbler..................my shoes.
2. The birds ....
3. The postman .... mail.
4. The old woman............................ the road.

5. The electrician .... electricity.
6. She ....not...............the truth.
7. My cat ....
8. Rani .... her desk.
9. She ....me to swim.
10. I ....not.......; I ....

Ex. 4: Write sentences using the cues given below as shown:

> **I / not/ come to the wedding party tomorrow.**
> **=>I am not coming to the wedding party tomorrow.**

1. She / go to/ the physician this evening.
2. They / come / tomorrow?
3. He / play / one day cricket match / tomorrow.
4. What / they / do / during summer vacation?
5. She / go to/ music concert tonight?
6. We / go away / next week.
7. I / meet / my boss tomorrow.
8. He / get / married next year.

Ex. 5: Write sentences using the cues given below as shown:

> **I / buy / some clothes next week**
> **=>I am going to buy some clothes next week.**

1. Bhoomi / have / a garage sale next Sunday.
2. What / you / wear to the party tonight.?
3. I / have / a shower before dinner.
4. Mother / buy / me an apartment for my 21st birthday.
5. Are you / watch / a movie tomorrow?
6. What / you / do / after your graduation?

Ex. 6: Change as shown:

I am returning this gadget next week => I am going to return this gadget next week.

1. We are watching a film tonight. It begins at 6 p.m.
2. I am traveling by air on Sunday. The airplane takes off at 8 O' clock in the morning.
3. Some guests are coming to our house on Tuesday. Their train arrives at 10 a.m.
4. Tomorrow I am going to the book fare. It ends next week.
5. I am staying at home all day tomorrow.
6. I am buying a new washing machine this week.

Ex. 7: Translate into English.

1. वह लंगड़ा रहा हैं। 2. बूढ़ा आदमी खाँस और छींक रहा है। 3. छात्र नारे लगा रहे हैं। 4. जमादार 'हॉल' में झाड़ू लगा रहा है। 5. वे कहाँ जा रहे हैं? 6. डाकिया द्वार पर खटखटा रहा है। 7. लड़के आम के पेड़ पर चढ रहे हैं। 8. मैं कैंची खोज रहा/ रही हूँ । 9. कुत्ता कराह रहा है। 10. राम समाचारपत्र पढ रहा है। 11. क्या आपकी घड़ी ठीक चल रही है?12. पक्षी आकाश में ऊँचे उड़ रहे हैं। 13. क्या आप लोग आज रात को गोष्ठी में आ रहे हैं? 14. मैं आज शाम को सहेलियों के साथ भोजन कर रहा/रही हूँ । 15. मेरे भाई शाम को जा रहे हैं । 16. मेरे दोस्त रात को आठ बजे भोजन करने लौट रहे हैं। 17. तुम कल शाम को क्या कर रहे हो? 18. खाने का पैसा कौन दे रहा है? 19. वे सोमवार को कितने बजे पहुँच रहे /रही हैं? 20. वे यहाँ सोमवार को सुबह आठ बजे पहुँच रहे /रही हैं।

Ex.8: Compare, comprehend and translate into English:

1a. मैं सप्ताहान्त पर घर में रहती हूँ।	1b. इस सप्ताहान्त पर मैं बाहर जा रही हूँ।
2a. क्या वह घर साफ़ करती है?	2b. क्या वह घर साफ़ कर रही है?
3a. वह हमेशा बहुत परिश्रम करता है।	3b. वह आजकल बहुत परिश्रम कर रहा है।
4a. मेरे चाचा इस शहर में रहते हैं।	4b. मैं आजकल अपने चाचा के साथ रह रहा हूँ।

Key 1

1. is working	2. am reading	3. are having
4. are playing	5. are doing	6. is .shining
7. are running	8. is cooking	9. are staying
10. are swimming		

Key 2

1. Who is having a shower at this time? 2. What are the students doing? 3. Is she learning classical music? 4. What are you guys doing? 5. Is she washing her hair? 6. Who is sitting on the chair? 7. Whose children are crying? 8. Is it raining now? 9. Why is the dog barking? 10. Why is she telling a lie?

Key 3

1. is mending	2. are chirping	3. is delivering
4. is crossing	5. is repairing	6. is....... telling
7. is mewing	8. is cleaning	9. is teaching
10. am not reading; am thinking.		

Key 4

1. She is going to the physician this evening. 2. Are they coming tomorrow? 3. He is playing one day cricket match tomorrow. 4. What are they doing during summer vacation? 5. Is she going to the music concert tonight? 6. We are going away next week. 7. I am meeting my boss tomorrow. 8. He is getting married next year.

Key 5

1. Bhoomi is going to have a garage sale next Sunday. 2. What are you going to wear to the party tonight? 3. I am going to have a shower before dinner. 4. Mother is going to buy me an apartment for my 21st birthday. 5. Are you going to watch a movie tomorrow? 6. What are you going to do after your graduation?

Key 6

1. We are going to watch a film tonight. It begins at 6 p.m. 2. I am going

to travel by air on Sunday. The airplane takes off at 8 O'clock in the morning. 3. Some guests are going to come to our house on Tuesday. Their train arrives at 10 a.m. 4. Tomorrow I am going to go to the book fare. It ends next week. 5. I am going to stay at home all day tomorrow. 6. I am going to buy a new washing machine this week.

Key 7

1. He is limping. 2. The old man is coughing and sneezing. 3. The students are shouting slogans. 4. The sweeper is sweeping the hall. 5. Where are they going? 6. The postman is knocking at the door. 7. Boys are climbing up the mango tree. 8. I am looking for a pair of scissors. 9. The dog is whimpering. 10.Ram is reading the newspaper. 11. Is your watch running on time? 12. The birds are flying high in the sky. 13. Are you coming to the concert tonight? 14. I am eating with friends this evening. 15. My brother is leaving in the evening. 16. My friends are returning at 8 p.m. for dinner. 17. What are you doing tomorrow evening? 1 8. Who is paying for the meal? 19. What time on Monday are they arriving? 20. They are arriving here on Monday at 8 O' clock in the morning.

Key 8

1a.	Usually I stay at home at the weekend.	1b.	This weekend I am going out.
2a.	Does she clean the house?	2b.	Is she cleaning the house.?
3a.	He always works hard.	3b.	He is working hard these days.
4a.	My uncle lives in this city.	4b.	I am staying with my uncle these days.

Wisdom From Grandma 

- Live and let live.
- Ignorance is bliss
- Reap as you sow.
- Distant fields look greener.
- Slow and steady wins the race.

Ask For Directions

(1)

A: Execuse me!

B: Yes?

A: I wonder if you could help me? I am looking for a telephone booth around here.

B: Ah yes. There is one over there round the corner.

A: Thank you. Can you make international calls from there?

B: Oh yes, you can call anywhere in the world. You can also make collect calls, or use your credit card.

A: Ah, that's very convenient indeed. Thanks again. Goodbye.

(2)

A: May I help you, Sir?

B: I want to meet the Principal. Which way is his office, please?

A: Have you got an appointment, Sir?

B: Yes, I have an appointment with him at half past ten.

A: Okay... go down this corridor till you come to a staircase. Go up the stairs to the 2nd floor. There you take the corridor on the right. The Principal's room is the last but one. Anything else, Sir?

B: No, thanks.

(3)

A: Excuse me?

B: Yes?

A: I think I am lost! I want to go to the railway station. Is this the road to the station?

B: I am afraid you are going the wrong way; this is the road to the airport.

A: Oh dear! I might miss the train. Could you put me right for the station?

B: Walk straight ahead, turn right at the first crossing; then take the next turn left; walk down two blocks. You can't miss the station.

A: Thanks very much indeed. Goodbye.

7 Past Habitual Tense
(पास्ट हेबिचुअल टेन्स)

- **Past habitual tense is used to talk about things that one used to do in the past but doesn't do them anymore.**
  जो काम व्यक्ति पहले करता था, परन्तु अब नहीं करता, उस के लिए **Past habitual tense** का प्रयोग करते हैं।

Language structure

aff. :	**subj.**	**+**	**used to**	**+**	**v. inf.**	**+**	**obj.**
neg.:	**subj.**	**+**	**didn't use to**	**+**	**v. inf.**	**+**	**obj.**
int. :	**Did**	**+**	**subj. + use to**	**+**	**v. inf.**	**+**	**obj. ?**
int. neg.:	**Didn't**	**+**	**subj. + use to**	**+**	**v. inf.**	**+**	**obj.?**

aff. : I used to smoke. — मैं धूम्रपान करता था/करती थी।

Neg.: I didn't use to smoke. — मैं धूम्रपान नहीं करता था/नहीं करती थी।

Int. : Did you use to smoke? — क्या तुम धूम्रपान करते थे/करती थी?

Int. neg.: Didn't you use to smoke? — क्या तुम धूम्रपान नहीं करते थे/नहीं करती थीं?

Comprehension:

1. I used to collect stamps. — मैं डाक टिकट इकट्ठे करता था/किया करता था।
2. She used to go for a morning walk every day. — वह रोज़ सुबह सैर करने जाती थी/जाया करती थी।

3.	This hotel didn't use to be here.	यह 'होटल' यहाँ नहीं हुआ करता था।
4.	She didn't use to have short hair.	उसके बाल छोटे नहीं हुआ करते थे।
5.	Did you use to study a lot?	क्या तुम बहुत पढ़ा करते थे?
6.	Did they use to go out for morning walks?	क्या वे सुबह घूमने जाया करते थे?
7.	Didn't you use to learn classical music?	क्या तुम शस्त्रीय संगीत नहीं सीखा करते थे/सीखा करती थीं?
8.	Didn't you use to go to the movies every week?	क्या तुम हर हफ़्ते सिनेमा देखने नहीं जाया करते थे/जाया करती थीं?

■ **'Would' is used to talk about repeatedly done actions in the past that are not done any more.**

1.	We **would** often **bunk** classs,, **go** to the movies and **have** fun.	हम अकसर कक्षा से ग़ायब होकर फ़िल्म देखने जाते और मौज मस्ती करते।
2.	Father **would buy** us balloons and kites and we **would play** for hours together.	पिता जी हमें गुब्बारे और पतंगें ख़रीदकर देते और हम घण्टों मिलकर खेला करते!

Ex. 1: Fill in the blanks with 'used to'/'use to'.

1. I .... play the guitar. Now I play the sitar.
2. We .... have a big house. We sold it some time ago.
3. I .... go to work by car. These days I go on foot.
4. We ....live in Delhi. We moved to Amritsar two years ago.
5. Didn't they ....live in your neighborhood.?
6. Didn't you ....wear glasses when you were a student?
7. What languages did you ....speak when you were

abroad.

8. Did you ....have long hair when you were a little girl?
9. I never .... like coffee, but I drink it a lot these days.
10. I .... sleep very late. Now I go to bed very early.

Ex.2: Change as shown using 'I remember + v.. ing' :

> **I used to go to the movies every Sunday.**
> **=> I remember going to the movies every Sunday.**

1. Father always brought presents for us.

   ....

2. Mother always prepared delicious food for us.

   ....

3. My older sister always shouted at me.

   ....

4. We used to play cricket in the field every evening.

   ....

5. I used to climb up the tamarind tree and eat tamarind.

   ....

Ex. 3: Translate into English:

1. मेरा भाई एक 'बैंक' में काम करता था / किया करता था। 2. मैं 'कनाडा' में रहता था/ रहा करता था। 3. मैं अध्यापक हुआ करता था। 4. इस सड़क पर एक जूतों की दुकान होती थी / हुआ करती थी। 5. दादी बहुत फ़िल्में देखती थी / देखा करती थीं। 6. जब हम छोटे थे, हम बहुत खाते थे / खाया करते थे। 7. हम प्रतिदिन गंगा में नहाते थे / नहाया करते थे। 8. मैं हर शाम को अपनी प्रेमिका से मिलता था / मिला करता था। 9. मेरे पिता जी हर सप्ताहान्त पर दूरदर्शन देखते थे / देखा करते थे। 10. हम हर गर्मी में समुद्रतट पर जाते थे /जाया करते थे। 11. जब मैं विद्यार्थी था, मैं कम से कम आठ घण्टे रोज पढ़ता था / पढ़ा करता था। 12 . यह होटल एक फ़र्नीचर की दुकान हुआ करता था। 13. क्या आपके शहर में संगीत गोष्ठियाँ होती थीं / हुआ करती थीं? 14. क्या आप 'कार' से स्कूल जाती थीं/जाया करती थीं? 15. क्या वह स्कूल में कक्षा से ग़ायब नहीं होता था / हुआ करता था?

Key 1

1, 2, 3, 4 9, 10 used to 5,6, 7, 8 use to

Key 2

1. I remember father bringing presents for us.
2. I remember mother preparing delicious food for us.
3. I remember my older sister always shouting at me.
4. I remember playing cricket in the field every evening.
5. I remember climbing up the tamarind tree and eating tamarind.

Key 3

1. My brother used to work in a bank. 2. I used to live in Canada. 3. I used to be a teacher. 4. There used to be a shoe shop in this street. 5. Grandmother used to watch a lot of films. 6. We used to eat a lot when we were younger . 7. We used to bathe in the Ganges every day. 8. I used to meet my girl friend every evening. 9. My father used to watch television every weekend.10. We used to go to the beach every summer. 11. I used to study at least eight hours every day when I was a student. 12. This hotel used to be a furniture shop. 13. Did there use to be music concerts in your town? 14. Did you use to go to school by car? 15. Didn't he use to bunk classes at school?

Vocabulary : Adjectives

1.	hungry	हंग्री	2.	thirsty	थर्सटी
3.	independent	इण्डिपेन्डैन्ट	4.	lazy	लेज़ी
5.	cruel	क्रुएल	6.	miserly	माइज़र्ली
7.	slim/thin	स्लिम/थिन	8.	illiterate	इल्लिटरेट
9.	impatient	इम्पेशन्ट	10.	incorrigible	इन् कॉरिजॅबल
11.	incompetent	इनकम्पीटेण्ट	12.	selfish	सेलफ़िश

1. भूखा 2. प्यासा 3. स्वतन्त्र 4. आलसी 5. क्रूर 6. कंजूस
7. दुबला-पतला 8. अनपढ़ 9. अधीर 10. असुधार्य 11. असमर्थ 12. स्वार्थी

8 Past Simple Tense

■ **We use past simple tense for elapsed time.**
English has (1) Regular verbs (2) Irregular verbs.
The past and past-participle forms of regular verbs are made by adding '-ed' to it, for example work. worked, worked.
Irregular verbs do not follow any set pattern and a student needs to learn these forms:

go	**went**	**gone**
eat	**ate**	**eaten**
buy	**bought**	**bought**

☞ **Some verbs remain the same in all three positions:**

cost	**cost**	**cost**
hurt	**hurt**	**hurt**
shut	**shut**	**shut**
hit	**hit**	**hit**

Affirmative: **subj. + verb in the past tense + obj. (if any)**

I, We			मैंनें, हमने	
You	worked	hard.	तुमने, आपने,	परिश्रम किया।
He, She	ate	rice.	उसने, इसने,	चावल खाया।
They	watched	television.	उन्होंने, इन्होंने,	दूरदर्शन देखा।
	listened	to the radio		'रेडियो' सुना।
Who			किसने	

☞ **To make negative and interrogative sentences in the past simple tense, use the auxiliary verb 'did' with the main verb in the present tense. We don't use two past tense verbs in one sentence.**

Negative: नकारात्मक भाषा ढाँचा

I, We		मैंनें, हमने,	
You	did not work hard.	तुमने, आपने,	परिश्रम नहीं किया।
He	did not eat rice.	उसने, इसने,	चावल नहीं खाया।
She	did not watch television.	,, ,,	दूरदर्शन नहीं देखा।
They	did not listen to the radio.	उन्होंने, इन्होंने,	'रेडियो' नहीं सुना।

Interrogative: प्रश्नवाचक भाषा ढाँचा

Did	you	work	hard?	क्या	तुमने, आपने,	परिश्रम किया?
	he,she	eat	rice?		उसने, इसने,	चावल खाया?
	they	watch	television?		उन्होंने,इन्होंने	दूरदर्शन देखा?
Who		listened to the radio?		किसने,	क्न्होंने,	'रेडियो' सुना?

Comprehension

1. Nitu fell from the 5th floor window and died. — नीतू पाँचवीं मंज़िल की खिड़की से गिर कर मर गई।

   नीतू फ़ैल्ल फ़्रॉम द फ़िफ़्थ फ़्लोर विण्डो ऐण्ड डाइड।

2. The boy tore all of his new books. — लड़के ने अपनी सब नई किताबें फाड़

द ब्वाय टोर ऑल ऑफ़ हिज़ न्यू बुक्स। ई।

3. The taxi drivers went on strike for a week.
द टैक्सी ड्राइवर्ज़ वैण्ट ऑन स्ट्राइक फ़ॉर ए वीक।
टेक्सी चालक एक हफ्ते के लिए हड़ताल पर चले गए।

4. Did you water the plants?
डिड यू वॉटर द प्लाण्ट्स?
क्या तुमने पौधों को पानी दिया?

5. They visited India in 1992.
दे विज़िटिड इण्डिया इन नाइनटीन-नाइन्टी टू।
वे सन् उन्नीस सौ बानवे में भारत आए।

6. Some robbers robbed the bank.
सम रॉबर्ज़ रौब्ड द बैंक।
कुछ डाकुओं ने बैंक लूटा।

7. The electrician mended the fuse.
दी इलैक्ट्रिशियन मैण्डेड द फ़्यूज़।
बिजली मिस्त्री ने फ़्यूज़ ठीक किया ।

8. The police arrested the killers.
द पोलीस अर्रैस्टिड द किल्लर्स।
पुलीस ने हत्यारों को पकड़ लिया।

Ex.1: Write sentences in the the past simple tense using the cues given below.

I / sell / my house. => I sold my house.

1. The child /break / the window.
2. He / drink / two glasses / orange juice.
3. She / open / her box.
4. I / write / a letter.
5. We / eat / 'nan' and 'sag-panir'.
6. He / watch / a movie.
7. I / speak / with Maria.
8. She / count / the money.

9. You / study/ this morning?
10. He / give / us / a foolproof proposal..
11. I / wash / dishes.
12. Her servant / open / the door.
13. Where / you / go / last week?
14. Y:ou / take / a bath / or / shower?
15. She / gift / her TV to a colleague.

Ex.2: Change the sentences given below from the past simple affirmative to the past simple interrogative and negative as shown:

1. I fed the dog at noon.	Did you feed the dog at noon? I didn't feed the dog at noon.
2. His mother encouraged him .	....
3. We found their house easily.	....
4. She apologised to me.	....
5. My uncle lived in a haunted house.	....
6. His dog once bit me.	....
7. I found this book very interesting.	....
8. Mother let me go to the movies.	....
9. She left the office at 5 p.m.	....
10. I visited many countries when I was young.	....
11. Grandfather narrated stories to us.	....
12. The teacher allowed the students to go for a picnic.	....

Ex.3: Translate into English.

1. बाढ़ में कई लोग बेघर हो गए । 2. उसकी टाँग टूट गई । 3. हमने कल एक अच्छी फ़िल्म देखी । 4. उसने झांसी की महारानी लक्ष्मीबाई पर किताब पढ़ी । 5. हमने एक गुप्त सुरंग खोज ली । 6. मैंने उसे सब सच्चाई बता दी। 7. मैंने 'पैकिट' नहीं खोला । 8. क्या तुमने पत्र डाल दिया? 9. क्या उसने अपने माता/ पिता को लिखा ? 10. मैंने पूरियाँ

foolproof = कभी ग़लत न होनेवाला।

तलीं। 11 मैंने फूल घर में रख दिए ? 12 मैंने अपनी माता जी को सारा प्रसंग लिख दिया । 13. मुझे चोट लग गई । 14. उसकी बाँह टूट गई । 15. आतंकवादियों ने इस शहर पर पिछले महीने दो बार हमला बोला। 16. आज मैं डाकघर नहीं गई । 17. परसों हमारे पड़ोसी छुट्टी मनाने मनाली गए । 18. अनिल की गाड़ी छूट गई। 19. मैं छह बजे की उड़ान से लौटा / लौटी। 20. दर्ज़ी ने मेरा माप लिया। 21. हमें उनका घर आसानी से मिल गया। 22. तुम्हें भारत पहुँचने में कितना समय लगा? 23. मुझे भारत पहुँचने में सोलह घण्टे लगे। 24. आप भारत कब आए? 25. मैं भारत सन् २००२ में / नौ वर्ष पूर्व आया।

Key 1

1. The child broke the window. 2. He drank two glasses of orange juice. 3. She opened her box. 4. I wrote a letter. 5. We ate 'nan' and 'sag-panir'. 6. He watched a movie. 7. I spoke with Maria. 8. She counted the money. 9. Did you study this morning? 10. He gave a foolproof proposal. 11. I washed the dishes. 12. Her servant opened the door. 13. Where did you go last week? 14. Did you take a bath or a shower? 15. She gifted her TV to a colleague.

Key 2

2. Did his mother encourge him?
   His mother didn't encourage him .
3. Did you find their house easily?
   We didn't find their house easily.
4. Did she apologise to you?
   She didn't apologise to me.
5. Did your uncle live in a haunted house?
   My uncle didn't live in a haunted house.
6. Did his dog bite you?
   His dog did not bite me.
7. Did you find this book very interesting?
   I didn't find this book very interesting.
8. Did mother let you go to the movies?
   Mother didn't let me go to the movies.
9. Did she leave the office at 5 p.m.?
   She didn't leave the office at 5 p.m.
10. Did you visit many countries when you were young?

I didn't visit many countries when I was young.

11. Did grandfather narrate stories to you?
    Grandfather didn't narrate stories to us.
12. Did the teacher allow the students to go for a picnic?
    The teacher didn't allow the students to go for a picnic.

Key 3

1. Many people became homeless in the floods. 2. He broke his leg. 3. We watched a good movie yesterday. 4. He/ She read the book on Lakshmi Bai, the Queen of Jhansi.. 5. We discovered a secret tunnel. 6. I told him the entire truth. 7. I did not open the packet. 8. Did you mail the letter. 9. Did he/she write to his/her parents. 10. I fried the 'poories'? 11 I put the flowers in the house.? 12. I wrote the entire incident to my mother. 13. I hurt myself. 14. She broke her arm. 15. Terrorists attacked this city twice last month. 16. I did not go to the post office today. 17. The day before yesterday our neighbours went to Manali on vacation. 18. Anil missed the train. 19. I returned by 6 O' clock flight. 20. The tailor took my measurements. 21. We found their house easily. 22. How long did it take you to arrive in India? 23. It took me 16 hours to arrive in India. 24. When did you come to India? 25. I came to India in 2002 / nine years ago.

★★★★★

Letter From A Pen Friend

A: Today I received a letter from my Indian pen friend.

B: Did you? How long have you been writing to each other?

A: This is his first letter. He told me he got my name through his Spanish language teacher. His Spanish teacher has been to several countries and has many pen pals himself.

B: That sounds interesting. Have you had pen pals before?

A: No, I am just starting! In fact I am quite excited. At the same time I am nervous too. I know Hindi but I have never written a letter in this language.

B: Don't worry. If you make a couple of mistakes. Its okay. It's not your mother tongue. Your friend will understand. By the way, where does he live in India?

A: He lives in Udaipur, a city in Rajasthan. He said it is called the 'Venice of the East'. It is a very quiet and lovely place with several lakes and low hills.

9 Past Simple Progressive Tense

■ भूतकाल में किसी एक समय पर किसी काम को कर रहा होना या किसी काम का हो रहा होना बताने के लिए इस का प्रयोग होता है। वाक्य रचना ठीक pres. simp prog. tense (see pg. 25) की तरह होती है; मात्र 'is, are, am + v..ing' की जगह 'was, were + v..ing' लगाते हैं।

Comprehension:

1. Robert was learning Hindi. — राबर्ट हिन्दी सीख रहा था।
   राबर्ट वॉज़ लर्निंग हिन्दी।
2. The Principal was giving prizes to the students. — प्रधानाचार्य छात्रों को पुरस्कार दे रहा था।
   द प्रिन्सिपल वॉज़ गिविंग प्राइज़िज़ टु द स्टुडेण्ट्स।
3. The passengers at the platform were bargaining with the porters. — प्लेटफ़ॉर्म पर यात्री कुलियों से मोलभाव कर रहे थे।
   द पैसिंजर्स ऐट द प्लैटफ़ॉर्म वर बारगेनिंग विद द पोर्टर्स।
4. Father was working at the computer. — पिता जी कम्प्यूटर पर काम कर रहे थे।
   फ़ादर वॉज़ वर्किंग ऐट द कम्प्यूटर।

past simple tense vs past simple progressive tense

☞ past simple tense = one time completed activity or situation in the past. (समाप्त क्रिया अथवा परिस्थिति)

☞ past simple progressive tense = incomplete activity or situation in the past. (ऐसा काम जो शुरू हो चुका था परन्तु अभी समाप्त नहीं हुआ था।)

1.	I saw her in the post office. She was buying stamps.	मैंने उसे डाकघर में देखा। वह टिकट ख़रीद रही थी।
2.	The doorbell rang when I was going to bed.	जब मैं सोने जा रही थी, दरवाज़े की घण्टी बजी।
3.	When they came in, we were watching television	जब वे अन्दर आए, हम दूरदर्शन देख रहे थे।
4.	When he arrived , I was having lunch.	जब वह पहुँचा, मैं दिन का भोजन कर रहा था / रही थी।
5.	She phoned while I was having a shower.	उसका 'फ़ोन' आया जब मैं स्नान कर रहा था / रही थी।

Ex. 1: Write sentences in the past continuous tense using the cues given below as shown:

> **He / wear / red pullover.**
> **=> He was wearing a red pullover.**

1. She / carry / books.
2. Mother / go / the optician.
3. Children / eat / chocolates.
4. The old man / carry / a stick.
5. She / drive / her father's car.
6. Rain / when / you / go out?
7. They wait / you / in front of / cinema hall?
8. Who / wash / your car this morning?

Ex. 2: Complete the sentences in the past progressive tense using the words given in the brackets.

1. Everybody ....in the party. (dance and sing)
2. Those days I ....Premchand's novels. (read)
3. My sister .... her hair. (wash)
4. The washerman........................... clothes. (dry)
5. The fruitseller .... fruit. (sell)
6. What .... the customer ....? (buy)
7. Why .... you guys ....so much noise? (make)
8. The teacher .... math to the students. (teach)
9. The students .... the teachers questions. (ask)
10. The painters................our house. (paint)
11. The birds .... (chirp)
12. The postman .... mail. (deliver)
13. The old woman........................... the road. (cross)
14. The electrician .... electricity. (repair)
15. She .... a lie. (tell)
16. My cat .... (mew)
17. Rani .... her desk. (clean)
18. She ....me archery (teach)
19. I ....not.......; I .... (sleep, rest)
20. She ....giving up her job. (think of)

Ex. 3: Translte into English:

1. मैं अपने मित्र को ढूँढ रहा था।
2. वे दूरदर्शन देख रहे थे।
3. तुम लोग चाय पी रहे थे।
4. हम धूप सेक रहे थे।
5. वे संग्रहालय की तस्वीरें खींच रहे थे/रही थीं।
6. मैं गाड़ी का इन्तज़ार कर रहा था।

7. आप क्या कर रहे थे? / रही थीं?
8. मैं आराम कर रहा था/रही थी।
9. मैं अपनी माता जी से बात कर रहा था / रही थी।
10. बच्चे सो रहे थे।
11. छात्र पढ़ रहे थे।
12. मैं अपनी गाड़ी ठीक कर रहा था।
13. हम दिन का खाना पका रहे थे।
14. वह सितार बजा रही थी।

Ex. 4: Translte into English:

1. जब मैं रानी के कमरे में गया, वह पढ़ रही थी।
2. जब मैं नाश्ता कर रहा था, वे हमारे घर आए।
3. जब वह पेड़ से टकराई, वह वाहन बहुत तेज़ चला रही थी।
4. जब तुम उससे मिलीं, उसने क्या पहना हुआ था?
5. जब 'फ़ोन की घण्टी बजी, मैं संगीत सुन रही थी।
6. जब माँ ने हमें अन्दर बुलाया, हम फुटबॉल खेल रहे थे।

Key 1

1. She was carrying books.
2. Mother was going to the optician.
3. Children were eating chocolates.
4. The old man was carrying a stick.
5. She was driving her father's car.
6. Was it raining when you went out?
7. Were they waiting for you in front of the cinema hall?
8. Who was washing your car this morning?

Key 2

1. was dancing and singing
2. was reading
3. was washing
4. was drying
5. was selling
6. was ....buying
7. were.............making
8. was teaching
9. were asking
10. were painting

11. were chirping	12. was delivering
13. was crossing	14. was repairing
15. was telling	16. was mewing
17. was cleaning	18. was teaching
19. was .... sleeping; was resting.	20. was thinking of

Key 3

1. I was looking for my friend. 2. They were watching TV. 3. You guys were drinking tea. 4. We were sitting in the sun. 5. They were taking pictures of the museum. 6. I was waiting for the train. 7. What were you doing? 8. I was resting. 9. I was talking to my mother. 10. The children were sleeping. 11. The students were studying. 12. I was repairing my car. 13. We were cooking lunch. 14. She was playing the sitar.

Key 4.

1. When I went into Rani's room, she was studying. 2.They came to our house while I was having breakfast. 3. She was driving very fast when she hit against the tree. 4. What was she wearing when you met her? 5. When the phone rang, I was listening to music. 6. When mother called us in, we were playing football.

A Tourist In India

A: What places do you want to visit in India?
B: Primarily I want to visit Varanasi. I have heard it is the oldest city in the world. It sounds like an interesting place to me. I want to see all the temples there.
A: How long are you planning to stay there?
B: For two weeks. How far is it from Varanasi to Nepal?
A: It is quite far.
B: Well, after Varanasi I want to go trekking in Nepal.
A: It is a very good idea. But you had better tell your travel agent and make advance bookings for everything.
B: Thank you for your advice. Goodbye!

10 Present Perfect Simple

has/have + past participle

Language Structure	
aff.:	subject + has/have + pp + object (if any)
Neg.:	subject + has/have + not + pp + object (if any)
Int.:	Has/Have + subject + pp + object (if any)?
Int. neg.:	Hasn't/Haven't + subject + pp + object (if any)? or Has/Have + subject + not + pp + object (if any)?

aff.:	I, We, You, They	+ have	+	cleaned	+	the house.
	He, She it	+ has	+	cleaned	+	the house.
Neg.:	I, We, You, They	+ have not	+	cleaned	+	the house.
	He, She, It	+ has not	+	cleaned	+	the house.
Int.	Have	+ you, they	+	cleaned	+	the house?
	Has	+ he, she, it	+	cleaned	+	the house?
Int. neg.:	Haven't	+ you, they	+	cleaned	+	the house?
	Hasn't	+ he, she, it	+	cleaned	+	the house?

Comprehension:

1. I have read this book. — मैंने यह किताब पढ़ ली है।
2. The servant has opened the window. — नौकर ने खिड़की खोल दी है।
3. My watch has stopped. — मेरी घड़ी रुक गई है।
4. Have the children gone to sleep? — क्या बच्चे सो गए हैं?

pp = past participle

Use of the present perfect tense

1 **New information about completed activities connected with present :**

वर्तमान से जुड़े किसी समाप्त हो चुके कार्य के बारे में सूचित करते हुए :

• It has stopped raining.	बारिश बन्द हो गई है।
• The Principal has expelled two students from school.	प्रधानाचार्य ने दो विद्यार्थियों को स्कूल से निकाल दिया है।

2 **'already', 'yet', 'just'** के साथ :

• We have not eaten **yet.**	हमने अभी नहीं खाया।
• I have **already** been to the bank.	मैं बैंक हो आया हूँ।
• The train has **just** departed.	गाड़ी अभी-अभी छूटी है।

3 **'today', 'this month', 'this year', 'this week', 'this term'**

☞ के साथ भी **present perfect tense** प्रयोग होता है बशर्ते बात करने के समय तक कथित काल अवधि समाप्त न हुई हो।

1. I have eaten six bananas today.	मैंने आज छह: केले खाए हैं।
2. Have you watched any movie this week?	क्या तुमने इस सप्ताह कोई फ़िल्म देखी है?
3. Our teacher hasn't finished the course this term.	हमारे अध्यापक ने इस सत्र में पाठ्यक्रम पूरा नहीं किया।

4 **With time period until now such as 'for a long time', 'since the morning', 'for several days' etc :**

☞ अब तक की काल अवधि के साथ जैसे **recently, for a long time, since the morning, for several days etc.**

1. Have you heard from Amulya **recently?**	क्या तुम्हें हाल में अमूल्य से कोई ख़बर मिली है?
2. Several people have visited me **during the last few days.**	पिछले कुछ दिनों में मेरे यहाँ कई लोग आए हैं।
3. I haven't had a drop of water **since yesterday morning.**	मैंने कल सुबह से एक बूँद पानी नही पिया।
3. I haven't met my daughters **for a long time.**	मैं बहुत समय से अपनी बेटियों को नही मिली हूँ।

Ex. 1: Write sentences in the present perfect simple tense using the given cues.

> **She / just / have / breakfast.**
> **=> She has just had breakfast.**

1. I / just / meet / her / once. => ....
2. Father / not / read / newspaper => ....
   yet ....
3. They / not / arrive / yet. => ....
4. I / not / tell / her / about my wedding plans / yet. => ....
5. She / ride / horse / ever? => ....
6. You / ever / be / in India? => ....
7. You / ever / meet / a famous film star? => ....
   ....
8. She / no eat / anything since last night. => ....
   ....
9. I / never / drive / a car in my life. => ....
   ....

10. How many cups of coffe / you / have / since the morning? =>..

11. I / misplace / my glasses. =>..

12. Anil / give up /smoking. =>..

13. Your sister / already be /bank. =>..

14. We / decorate / our house / for Diwali. =>..
....

Ex. 2: Read the situation and complete the sentences using the verb given in the brackets:

Sushma is looking for her book. She can't find it.
=>Sushma has lost her book. (to lose)

1. Jigyasa cannot write. Her hand is in plaster.
   Jigyasa..(to break)
2. Last month the price of sugar was 25 rupees per kilo. Now it is Rs. 40.
   The price of sugar ....(to go up)
3. Amy's Hindi was not very good. Now it is better.
   Amy's Hindi..(to improve)
4. Last month the temperature was 37 degrees. Now it is 25.
   The temperature...(to fall)

Ex. 3: Translate into English: Use just, yet, already where required.

1. गाड़ी अभी-अभी आई है। 2. बच्चे अभी-अभी लौटे हैं। 3. फ़िल्म अभी-अभी शुरू हुई है। 4. मैंने अभी-अभी पत्र डाला है। 5. उन्होंने अभी-अभी किराया दिया है। 6. हमने अभी-अभी खाना खाया है। 7. उसने अभी-अभी मेरी 'कार' की मरम्मत की है। 8.

उन्हें अभी-अभी नया घर मिला है। 9. अध्यापक अभी-अभी कक्षा में आया है। 10. मैं अभी-अभी इस शहर में आया हूँ। 11. गाड़ी अभी नहीं छूटी। 12. दर्ज़ी ने अभी तक कपड़े नहीं सिए। 13. वह अभी तक बैंक नहीं गई। 14. मैंने अभी भोजन नहीं बनाया। 15. उसने अभी अपना भाषण तैयार नहीं किया। 16 क्या आपने यह किताब पढ़ ली है? 17. क्या उसने पाठ तैयार कर लिया है? 18. क्या खेल समाप्त हो गया है? 19. क्या बर्फ़ पड़नी बन्द हो गई है? 20 क्या उन्होने दरवाज़े और खिड़कियाँ बन्द कर दिए है?

Ex. 4: Translate into English:

1. तुम लोगों ने ठीक सुना है। 2. उसने सब काम ठीक से किया है। 3. क्या आपने उनको सच बताया है?। 4. आज आपने हमारे लिए क्या पकाया है? 5. मैंने ये पुस्तकें पुस्तकालय से ली हैं। 6. फूलदान किसने तोड़ा है? 7. उन्होंने भारतीय संगीत के लिए अपना प्रेम प्रकट किया है। 8. मैं पिछले सोमवार से उसे नहीं मिला/मिली। 9. तुमने अपने आभूषण कहाँ रखे हैं? 10. तुम लोगों ने अपने कपड़े धोए हैं? 11. तुमने अपने दाँत साफ़ किए हैं ? 12. देश में हर जगह भ्रष्टाचार फैला हुआ है। 13. तुमने पहले कभी 'कार' चलाई है? 14. मैंने पहली बार 'कार' चलाई है। 15. क्या तुम पहले कभी इस आदमी से मिले हो? 16. मैने इस आदमी को पहली बार देखा है।

Key 1

1. I have just met her once.
2. Father has not read the newspaper yet.
3. They have not arrived yet.
4. I have not told her about my wedding plans yet.
5. Has she ever ridden a horse?
6. Have you ever been in India?
7. Have you ever met a famous film star?
8. She hasn't eaten anything since last night.
9. I have never driven a car in my life.
10. How many cups of coffe have you had since the morning?
11. I have misplaced my glasses.
12. Anil has given up smoking.
13. Your sister has already been to the bank.
14. We have decorated our house for Divali.

Key 2

1. ....has broken her hand. 2. ....has gone up.

3. ....has improved. 4. ....has fallen.

Key 3

1. The train has just arrived. 2. The children have just returned. 3. The film has just started. 4. I have just mailed the letter. 5. They have just paid the rent. 6. We have just had dinner. 7. He has just repaired my car. 8. They have just found a new house. 9. The teacher has just come into the classroom. 10. I have just arrived in this city. 11. The train has not departed yet. 12. The tailor has not stitched the dresses yet. 13. She has not gone to the bank yet. 14. I have not cooked food yet. 15. She / He has not prepared her / his speech yet. 16. Have you already read this book? 17. Has she already prepared the lesson?18. Has the game finished ? 19. Has it stopped snowing? 20. Have they closed the doors and windows?

Key 4

1. You have heard correct. 2. He / She has done everything properly. 3. Have you told them the truth? 4. What have you cooked for us today? 5. I have taken these books from the library. 6. Who has broken the flower vase? 7. They have evinced their love for Indian music. 8. I haven't met her since last Monday. 9. Where have you kept your ornaments?10. Have you guys washed your clothes? 11. Have you brushed your teeth?12. Corruption has spread everywhere in the country. 13. Have you ever driven a car before?. 14.This is the first time I have driven a car. 15. Have you met this man before? 16. I have seen this man for the first time

Wisdom From Grandma 

- Blood is thicker than water.
- Honesty is the best policy.
- Silence is golden.
- Love is blind.
- Still waters run deep.

11 Present Perfect Progressive

has/have + been + v.. ing

	Language Structure										
aff. :	**subj.**	**+**	**has or have**	**+**	**been**	**+**	**v.. ing**	**+**	**obj.**	**+**	**time clause *since/for.....**
neg.:	**subj.**	**+**	**has or have**	**+**	**not been**	**+**	**v..ing**	**+**	**obj.**	**+**	**time clause since/for.....**
int.:	**Has or Have**	**+**	**subj.**	**+**	**been**	**+**	**v..ing**	**+**	**obj.**	**+**	**time clause since/for.....**
int. neg.:	**Hasn't. or Haven't**	**+**	**subj.**	**+**	**been**	**+**	**v..ing**	**+**	**obj.**	**+**	**time clause since/for.....**

aff.:	The servant has been cleaning the house for four hours / since the morning.	नौकर चार घण्टे से/सुबह से घर साफ़ कर रहा है।
neg.:	The servant has not been cleaning the house for four hours / since the morning.	नौकर चार घण्टे से/सुबह से घर साफ़ नहीं कर रहा।
Int.:	Has the servant been cleaning the house for four hours / since the morning?	क्या नौकर चार घण्टे से/सुबह से घर साफ़ कर रहा है?
Int. neg.:	Hasn't the servant been cleaning the house for four hours / since the morning?	क्या नौकर चार घण्टे से/सुबह से घर साफ़ नहीं कर रहा?

Use of present perfect progressive:

1 किसी दीर्घ कालावधि में कोई काम निरन्तर बार-बार किए जाने पर :

- He has been playing chess since he was six.
  वह जब से छह साल का था, शतरंज खेल रहा है।
- We have been eating at this restaurant for years.
  हम सालों से इस रेस्टरो में खा रहे हैं।

2 कोई काम कभी पहले शुरू हो कर अब तक हो रहा होने या फिर तुरन्त अभी-अभी समाप्त हुए होने पर :

- It has been snowing since yesterday (and it is still snowing.)
  कल से बर्फ़ पड़ रही है (और अभी भी पड़ रही है।)
- She has been studying since early morning (and is still studying.)
  वह सुबह से पढ़ रही है (और अभी भी पढ़ रही है।)

3 यदि कोई कार्य किसी अनिश्चित काल से अब तक होता आ रहा हो, संभवता अभी और आगे तक होता रहे, या फिर यहीं समाप्त हो जाय, तो **'How long ....** से शुरू होने वाले प्रश्न और उनके उत्तर में वाक्य रचना **present perfect progressive** में और काल अवधि के साथ **since** या **for** का प्रयोग करें।

A.	How long have you been learning Hindi?	आप कब से हिन्दी सीख रहे हैं?
B.	I have been learning Hindi for four years / since 2006.	मैं चार साल से/ सन् २००६ से हिन्दी सीख रहा हूँ।
A.	How long have you been mowing the lawn?	आप कब से 'लॉन' की घास छील रहे हैं?
B.	We have been mowing the lawn for 2 hours / since 10 O' clock.	हम दो घण्टों से/दस बजे से 'लॉन' की घास छील रहे हैं।

Compare and comprehend: Past simple, present perfect simple and present perfect continous tense:

1a.	I cleaned the house yesterday.	मैंने कल घर साफ़ किया।
1b.	I have cleaned the house.	मैंने घर साफ़ कर लिया है।
1c.	I have been cleaning the house since the morning.	मैं सुबह से घर साफ़ कर रहा हूँ।
2a.	When did you learn French?	आपने फ़्रांसीसी कब सीखी?
2b.	How long have you learnt French?	आपने फ़्रांसीसी कितना समय सीखी है?
2c.	How long have you been learning French?	आप कबसे फ़्रांसीसी सीख रहे हैं?

1a., 2a. past simple tense: . इन वाक्यों से ***कार्य के अमुक समय पर समाप्त होने का बोध होता है।***

1b., 2b. present perfect simple:. इन वाक्यों से यह बोध तो होता है कि काम समाप्त हो गया है, परन्तु यह बोध नहीं होता कि काम कब खत्म हुआ।

1c., 2c. present perfect continuous: इन वाक्यों से बोध होता है कि कार्य किसी अनिश्चित काल से अब तक होता आ रहा है, संभवता अभी और आगे तक होता रहे, या फिर यहीं समसप्त हो जाय।

Ex. 1: Write sentences using the cues given below as shown:

He / wait / long?
=> Has he been waiting long?

1. What / he / do / since he arrive/ here?
2. How long / you / write / books?
3. How long / save / for the trip?
4. How long / children / watch TV?

5. The children / watch TV since 5 p.m.
6. How long / audience / wait / for the minister?
7. The audience / wait /for the minister for a long time.
9. How long / she / fish / in this pond.

Ex. 2: Combine the sentences given below using the present perfect continuous tense as shown:

> **My mother was cooking two hours ago.**
> **She is still cooking.**
> **=> My mother has been cooking for two hours.**

1. Grandfather was watching TV in the morning.
   He is still watching it.
   ....

2. The children were playing in the park in the afternoon.
   They are still playing.
   ....

3. I began to learn Hindi when I was 10 years old.
   I am still learning it.
   ....

4. The reporter was interviewing her at 4 p.m.
   He is still interviewing her.
   ....

5. He was doing maths in the morning.
   He is still doing maths.
   ....

Ex.3: Translate into English: How long has X been doing something:

1. आप कब से एक ही दुकान में काम कर रहे हैं? 2. मैं दो साल से एक ही दुकान में काम कर रहा हूँ । 3. आप कितने समय से हिन्दी सीख रहे हैं? 4. मैं चार महीने

से हिन्दी सीख रहा हूँ। 5. आप कब से इन्तज़ार कर रहे हैं? 6. मैं आधे घण्टे से इन्तज़ार कर रहा हूँ। 7. वह कब से आपकी घड़ी ठीक कर रहा है? 8. वह तीन घण्टों से मेरी घड़ी ठीक कर रहा है।

Key 1

1. What has he been doing since he arrived here?
2. How long have you been writing books?
3. How long have you been saving for the trip?
4. How long have the children been watching TV?
5. The children have been watching TV since 5 p.m.
6. How long has the audience been waiting for the minister?
7. The audience has been waiting for the minister for a long time.
8. How long has she been fishing in this pond.

Key . 2

1. Grandfather has been watching TV since the morning.
2. The children have been playing in the park since the afternoon.
3. I have been learning Hindi since I was 10 years old.
4. The reporter has been interviewing her since 4 p.m.
5. He has been doing maths since the morning.

Key 3

1. How long have you been working at the same store? 2. I have been working at the same store for two years. 3. How long have you been learning Hindi? 4. I have been learning Hindi for four months. 5. How long have you been waiting? 6. I have been waiting for half an hour. 7. How long has he been repairing your watch? 8. He has been repairing my watch for three hours.

A.D. ईसा मसीह के जन्म से बाद का समय
(लैटिन भाषा में anno domini)
e.g. 560 A.D., 1280 A.D.

B.C. ईसा मसीह के जन्म से पहले का समय
e.g. 200 B.C., 3000 B.C.

12 Past Perfect Simple Tense

had + past participle

Language Structure							
aff.:	**subj.**	**+**	**had**	**+**	**pp**	**+**	**obj. (if any)**
neg.:	**subj.**	**+**	**had not**	**+**	**pp**	**+**	**obj. (if any)**
Int.:	**Had**	**+**	**subj.**	**+**	**pp**	**+**	**obj. (if any)?**
Int. neg.:	**Hadn't**	**+**	**subj.**	**+**	**pp**	**+**	**obj. (if any)?**

aff.:	Ram had finished the work.	राम ने काम समाप्त कर लिया था।
neg.:	Ram hadn't finished the work.	राम ने काम समाप्त नहीं किया था।
int.:	Had Ram finished the work?	क्या राम ने काम समाप्त कर लिया था?
int. neg.:	Hadn't Ram finished the work?	क्या राम ने काम समाप्त नहीं किया था?

Uses of past perfect simple tense

1 **In narration of events that happened long time ago.**
(काफ़ी समय पहले हुई घटना का विवरण करते हुए :)

2 **In the reported speech as past of the present perfect:**
☞ **Direct speech** मे **present perfect simple** में कही हुई बात को

reported speech में past perfect simple में कहते हैं।

Direct: "The student is ill. He has not come to school".
विद्यार्थी बिमार है। वह स्कूल नहीं आया।

Reported: The student was ill. He hadn't come to school.
विद्यार्थी बिमार था। वह स्कूल नहीं आया था।

Direct: "I am not thirsty. I have just had a large glass of beer".
मुझे प्यास नहीं है। मैंने अभी-अभी एक बड़ा गिलास 'बीअर' पीया है।

Reported: He was not thirsty. He had just had a large glass of beer.
उसे प्यास नहीं थी। उसने उसी समय एक बड़ा गिलास 'बीअर' पीया था।

3 **When we talk about two events that happened in the past in sequence, the first event is in past perfect simple tense and the following event is in past simple tense.**

1. When I reached his house, he had already left.	जब मैं उसके घर पहुँचा , वह जा चुका था।
2. All the arrangements for the wedding had been made before we arrived.	हमारे पहुँचने से पहले, शादी की सब तैयारियाँ हो चुकी थीं।
3. They were obliged to me for the help I had given to them in their time of need.	जो मदद मैंने उन्हें उनकी ज़रूरत के समय दी थी, उसके लिए वे मेरे आभारी थे।
4. When they arrived at the theatre, the play had already begun.	जब वे 'थिएटर' में पहुँचे, नाटक शुरू हो चुका था।

Ex. 1: **Write sentences in the past perfect simple tense using the cues given below as shown:**

> **She / come / into my office.**
> **=> She had come into my office.**

1. The city / change / a lot in my absence.
2. The concert / already / begin.
3. Someone / break / into their house.
4. Mother / never / travel by air / before.
5. I / /not / meet / him for 10 years.
6. She / work hard / all week
7. The boys / quarrel / all day.
8. The concert / already / begin.
9. They / wait / at the bus stop for more than an hour.
10. We / look forward to / our vacation for months when I suddenly broke my arm.

Ex. 2: Translate into English: Past perfect simple.

1. खाना किसने बनाया था ? 2. छात्रों ने बहुत परिश्रम किया था। 3. क्या तुमने खरीदने से पहले 'कार' चलाई थी? 4. उसने सारी रात किताब पढ़ी थी। 5. मैंने उसे कुछ नहीं बताया था। 6. मैंने पैसे अलमारी में रखे थे। 7. वे अमरीका आने से पहले दस साल भारत में रहे थे। 8. खिड़कियाँ किसने खोली थीं? 9. मेरी माता जी ने दावत के लिए पर्याप्त पकौड़े नहीं बनाए थे। 10. क्या तुमने देवदास' फ़िल्म देखी थी? 11. दावत से पहले नौकर ने घर का कोना-कोना साफ़ किया था। 12. उन्होंने हमें बहुत ज़रूरी सूचना दी थी। 13. उसने दो महीने अपने बाल नहीं धोए थे। 14. उन्होंने तुम्हारी मदद के लिए क्या किया था? 15. उन्हों ने अपनी समस्याओं का समाधान अपने से कर लिया था। 16. मैंने पूजा से पहले दो बार स्नान किया था। 17. क्या तुमने खाने से पहले अपने हाथ धो लिए थे? 18. उसने मुझसे झूठ कहा था। 19. हमने जाने से पहले सब खिड़कियाँ और दरवाज़े बन्द किए थे। 20. मैं पिछले सप्ताह से पहले अनिल से कभी नहीं मिला था।

Ex. 3: Translate into English : Past simple and past perfect simple.

1.वह सब पत्र टंकित करने के बाद दफ़्तर से गया। 2. प्रधानाचार्य ने विद्यार्थियों से पूछा कि वे देर से क्यों आए थे। 3. उसने मुझसे पूछा कि मैंने भारत में कौन-कौन से स्थान देखे थे। 4. अग्निशमन वाहन के पहुँचने से पहले उन्होंने आग पर काबू पा लिया था। 5. हिन्दी सीखना इतना आसान नहीं था जितना मैंने सोचा था। 6. पुलीस के पहुँचने से पहले चोर भाग गया था। 7. जब हमारी बेटी का जन्म हुआ, हमारी शादी को छः साल हो चुके थे। 8. उन्हें जल्दी एहसास हो गया कि उन्हों ने बहुत बड़ी ग़लती की थी।

9. वह हमारे साथ नहीं आई क्योंकि उसकी एक मित्र ने उसे पहले से खाने पर बुलाया हुआ था। 10. वह घबराया हुआ था क्योंकि वह पहले कभी इतने श्रोतागण के समक्ष नहीं बोला था। 11. जब हम पहुँचे, सब खा चुके थे।

Key 1

1. The city had changed a lot in my absence.
2. The concert had already begun.
3. Someone had broken into their house.
4. Mother had never traveled by air before.
5. I had not met him for ten years.
6. She had worked hard all week.
7. The boys had quarrelled all day.
8. The concert had already begun.
9. They had waited at the bus stop for more than an hour.
10. We had looked forward to our vacation for months when I suddenly broke my arm

Key 2

1. Who had prepared the food? 2.The students had worked very hard. 3. Had you driven the car before buying. 4. He/ She had read the book all night. 5. I had not told him/her anything. 6. I had kept the money in the cupboard. 7.They had lived in India for ten years before coming to America. 8. Who had opened the windows? 9. My mother had not prepared sufficient 'pakoras' for the party. 10. Had you seen the film "Devdas"? 11. Before the party, the servant had cleaned every nook and corner in the house. 12. They had given us very important information. 13. She / He had not washed her / his hair for two months. 14. What had they done to help you? 15. They had solved their problems themselves. 16. I had had bath twice before the 'puja'. 17. Had you washed your hands before eating? 18. She had told me a lie. 19. We had shut all the doors and windows before leaving. 20. I had never met Anil before last week.

Key 3

1. He left the office after he had typed all the letters.
2. The Principal asked the students why they had come late.
3. She asked me what places I had visited in India.
4. They had controlled the fire before the fire brigade arrived.

5. It was not as easy to learn Hindi as I had imagined.
6. The thief had fled before the police arrived.
7. We had been married for six years when our daughter was born.
8. They soon realised that they had made a big mistake.
9. She didn't come with us since a friend of hers had already invited her to dinner.
10. He was nervous because he had never spoken in the presence of such large audience before.
11. When we arrived there, everybody had already eaten

★★★★★

Vocabulary: Professions

1. baker	बेकर	2. pilot	पायलट
3. butcher	बूचर	4. teacher	टीचर
5. greengrocer	ग्रीनग्रोसर	6. grocer	ग्रोसर
7. postman	पोस्टमैन	8. gardener	गार्डनर
9. architect	आर्कि टैक्ट	10. doctor	डॉक्टर
11. lawyer	लॉ'यर	12. judge	जज
13. engineer	इन्जीनियर	14. travel agent	ट्रैवल एजैन्ट
15. patient	पेशैन्ट	16. plumber	प्लम्बर
17. goldsmith	गोल्ड स्मिथ	18. ironsmith	आयरन स्मिथ
19. painter	पेन्टर	20. sweeper	स्वीपर
21. carpenter	कार् पैन्टर	22. cook; chef	कुक/शैफ़
23. officer	ऑफ़िसर	24. director	डायरैक्टर

1. नानबाई 2.वायुयान चालक 3. कसाई 4. शिक्षक/शिक्षिका 5. सब्ज़ीवाला 6. पंसारी 7. डाकिया 8. माली 9. वास्तुकार 10. चिकित्सक 11. वकील 12. न्यायधीश 13. अभियन्ता 14. अभिकरण 15. मरीज़ 16. नलकार 17. सुनार 18. लोहार 19. चित्रकार 20. जमादार 21. बढ़ई 22. महाराज/महाराजिन 23. अधिकारी 24. निदेशक ।

13 Past Perfect Progressive

had been + (v.ing)

1 किसी ऐसी घटना का ज़िक्र करते हुए जो दूरस्थ भूतकाल में किसी एक समय पर शुरू हो कर भूतकाल में ही बात करते समय तक अभी हो रही थी तो 'had been + v..ing का प्रयोग होता है।

■ **Affi:** **subj. + had been + (v.ing) + obj. (if any)**

- She **had been watching** TV since afternoon. — *वह अपराह्न से* दूरदर्शन *देख* रही थी।

■ **Neg:** **subj. + had + not been + (v.. ing) + obj. (if any)**

- She **had not been watching** TV since afternoon. — *वह अपराह्न से* दूरदर्शन नहीं *देख* रही थी।

■ **Int:** **Had + subj. + not been + (v.. ing) + obj. (if any)**

- **Had** she **been watching** TV since afternoon**?** — *क्या वह अपराह्न से* दूरदर्शन *देख* रही थी?

Comprehension:

1.	How long had they been mowing the lawn when you arrived there?	जब आप वहाँ पहुँचे वे कब से 'लॉन' की घास छील रहे थे?
2.	When we arrived there, they had already been mowing the lawn for 2 hours / since 10 O' clock.	जब हम वहाँ पहुँचे वे दो घण्टों से/दस बजे से 'लॉन' की घास छील रहे थे।
3.	How long had the audience been waiting for the minister?	श्रोतागण कबसे मंत्री जी की प्रतीक्षा कर रहे थे?
4.	The audience had been waiting for the minister for a long time / since the morning.	श्रोतागण लम्बे समय से/सुबह से मंत्री जी की प्रतीक्षा कर रहे थे।
5.	When the terrorists entered the concert hall, the musician had already been playing for two hours.	जब आतंकवादी गोष्ठी-कक्ष में पहुँचे, संगीतकार दो घण्टे पहले से वाद्य बजा रहे थे।

2 किसी एक घटना से पूर्व यदि कार्य होता रहा हो, तो उसे past perfect progressive.में, और कार्य समापत हो चुका हो तो past perfect में कहते हैं। जैसे:—

- Mother looked tired. She had been cooking since the morning.
  माँ थकी हुई लग रही थीं। वे सुबह से खाना बना रही थीं।
- Mother lookd tired. She had cooked all day.
  माँ थकी हुई लग रही थीं। उन्होंने दिन भर खाना बनाया था।

14 Simple Future Tense

will / shall

■ **'will / shall '** का प्रयोग:

1 सामान्य भविष्य में होने वाली घटनाओं एवम् बिना पूर्व नियोजन के तत्काल लिए गए निर्णयों/वक्तव्यों के लिए **'will'** का प्रयोग होता है।

☞ **'I, We '** के साथ **'will'/ 'shall'** दोनों में से कोई भी प्रयोग करें।
'you, he, she, it, they' आदि के साथ **'will'** का प्रयोग करें।
वैसे समकालीन अंग्रेज़ी में **'will'** का प्रयोग व्यापक रूप से तीनों पुरुषों में होता है।

	Spontaneous decisions			
aff.:	**subj.**	**+ will**	**+ v.inf.**	**+ obj. (if any)**
neg.:	**subj.**	**+ will not /won't**	**+ v.inf.**	**+ obj. (if any)**
int.:	**Will**	**+ subj.**	**+ v.inf.**	**+ obj. (if any)?**
Int. neg.:	**Won't**	**+ subj.**	**+ v.inf.**	**+ obj. (if any)?**

aff.:	I will / shall buy this book.	मैं यह किताब खरीदूँगी।
neg.:	I will not /won't buy this book.	मैं यह किताब नहीं खरीदूँगी।
int.:	Will you buy this book?	क्या आप यह किताब खरीदेंगी?
int. neg.:	Won't you buy this book?	क्या आप यह किताब नहीं खरीदेंगी?

Comprehension:

1. I shall / will be seventy-five tomorrow. — मैं कल पचहत्तर वर्ष का होऊँगा/की होऊँगी।

2. How will you use the money that you have won?	आप उस पैसे का क्या करेंगे जो आपने जीता है?
A. I will go round the world.	मैं विश्व भ्रमण करूँगा।
B. I will buy myself a house with a big garden and a swimming pool.	मैं अपने लिए घर ख़रीदूँगा जिस जिसमें बड़ा-सा बागीचा एवम् तरणताल हो
C. I will establish a school for orphans.	मैं अनाथों के लिए स्कूल की स्थापना करूँगा।
D. I will invest the money and become multimillionaire one day	मैं पूंजी निवेश करूँगा और एक दिन करोड़पति बन जाऊँगा।

2 **Planned future activities:** (भविष्य में होने वाली पूर्व नियोजित क्रियाओं और घटनाओं की वाक्य रचना में निम्नलिखित ढाँचे का प्रयोग होता है।)

subj.	**+**	**is, are, am**	**+**	**planning to intending to going to**	**+**	**v. inf.**	**+**	**obj. (if any)**
subj.	**+**	**is, are, am**	**+**	**thinking of**	**+**	**v..ing**	**+**	**obj. (if any)**

☞ **negative** वाक्यों में **is, are, am** के बाद **not** लगाएँ।

☞ **Interrogative** वाक्यों में **is, are, am** से शुरू करें।

affirmative:

1. I am planning to buy this book.	मैं यह किताब खरीदने की सोच रही हूँ।
2. She is intending to go abroad.	वह विदेश जाने की सोच रही है।

3. We are thinking of buying a house next year.	हम अगले साल नया घर ख़रीदने की सोच रहे हैं।

negative

1. I am not planning to buy this book.	यह किताब ख़रीदने की मेरी कोई योजना नहीं है।
2. She is not intending to go abroad.	विदेश जाने का उसका कोई इरादा नहीं है।
3. We are not thinking of buying a new house.	हम नया घर ख़रीदने की नहीं सोच रहे।

interrogative:

1. Are you planning to buy this book?	क्या आप यह किताब खरीदने की सोच रही हैं?
2. Is she intending to go abroad?	क्या वह विदेश जाने की सोच रही है ?
3. Are you thinking of buying a new house next year?	क्या आप अगले साल नया घर ख़रीदने सोच रहे हैं?

Comprehension:

1. We are planning to go to Delhi by car.	हम 'कार' से दिल्ली जाने की सोच रहे हैं।
2. She is thinking of studying the Ayurvedic system of medicine.	वह आयुर्वेदिक चिकित्सा पद्धति सीखने की सोच रही हैं।
3. What are you planning to wear to the party this evening?	तुम आज शाम को दावत में क्या पहनने की सोच रही हो?
4. How are you planning to spend your summer vacation?	तुम अपनी गर्मी की छुट्टियाँ कैसे बिताने की सोच रहे हो?

■ **Other language structures for planned future:**

सामान्य भविष्य से जुड़ी हुई पूर्व निर्णीत और पूर्व नियोजित क्रियाओं और

घटनाओं की वाक्य रचना के लिए उपरोक्त के अतिरिक्त अन्य भाषा ढाँचे:

1 **is, are, am + going to + v. inf. + obj. (if any) see pg. 30**

2 **is, are, am + v .... ing + obj. (if any) see pg. 30**

3 ***subj + will/shall + be + v - ing........ see pg. 77**

☞ बोलचाल की भाषा में **(1) is, are, am + v..ing', (2) is/are/am + going to + verb infinitive** और **(3) 'will + be + (v..ing)',** ये तीनों वाक्य रचनाएँ लगभग समानार्थी हैं और एक दूसरे के स्थान पर प्रयोग की जा सकती हैं।

- **is, are, am + v..ing'** और **is/are/am + going to + verb infinitive** के तुलनात्मक प्रयोग के लिए देखें **pg. 30**
  प्रयोग की शुद्धता की दृष्टि से ***इन के अन्तर इस प्रकार हैं। :—***
- **is, are, am + v..ing'** का प्रयोग (1) ***पूर्व निर्णीत और पूर्वनियोजित क्रियाओं*** के लिए, (2) सिर्फ़ निकट भविष्य के लिए ही किया जा सकता है; और इसके साथ समय सूचक अभिव्यक्ति **(time clause)** का होना अनिवार्य है।
- **'will + be + (v..ing)'** का प्रयोग (1) ***किसी सन्दर्भ विशेष में*** (2) दोनों, निकट एवम् दूरस्थ ***भविष्य*** से जुड़े तत्काल कथन के लिए (3) समय-सूचक अभि-व्यक्ति के साथ या उसके बिना भी किया जा सकता है।

Compare and comprehend:

1a. She is going to leave India next week. — वह अगले हफ़्ते भारत छोड़ेगी।
(भारत छोड़ने का निर्णय हो चुका है, परन्तु उसके लिए कोई व्यवस्था नहीं हुई।)

1b. She is leaving India next week. — वह अगले हफ़्ते भारत छोड़ रही है।
(भारत छोड़ने का निर्णय और उससे संबंधित व्यवस्था हो चुकी है।)

1c. She will be leaving India next **week.** — वह ***अगले हफ़्ते*** भारत छोड़ेगी।

(यह किसी सन्दर्भ विशेष में भविष्य से जुड़ा तत्काल कथन है।)

2a. We are buying a new house . next month. — हम अगले महीने नया घर ख़रीद रहे हैं।

(निकट ***भविष्य*** में नया घर ख़रीदने का निर्णय और उसके लिए व्यवस्था हो चुकी है।)

2b. We are going to buy a new house next month. — हम अगले महीने नया घर ख़रीदेंगे।

(निकट ***भविष्य*** में नया घर ख़रीदने का निर्णय हो चुका है, उसके लिए किसी प्रकार की व्यवस्था नहीं की जा चुकी।)

2c. We will be buying a new house. — हम नया घर ख़रीदेंगे।

(यहाँ घर ख़रीदना पूर्वनियोजित नहीं है। घर ख़रीदना निकट ***या दूरस्थ भविष्य*** में कभी भी हो सकता है। यह मात्र ***किसी सन्दर्भ विशेष में भविष्य*** से जुड़ा तत्काल कथन है।)

Ex. 1: Complete the sentences using (is/are/ am + going to) and one of the verbs given below.

snow	wash	gift	walk
stay	travel	rest	buy

1. I......................my hair.
2. We........................to school.
3. He .... with us.
4. How ....you.................to Mumbai, by train or by plane?
5. Mother is exhausted. She ....for a while.
6. It ....during the night.
7. They ....a new house.
8. My husband and I ....a car to our daughter.

Ex.2: Translate into English.

1. मैं अगले महीने साठ वर्ष का हूँगा/होऊँगा। 2. मैं रॉबर्ट को शाम को मिलूँगा। 3. आज से दुकानें आठ बजे बन्द होंगी। 4. इस साल दीवाली किस महीने में होगी? 5. मैं बड़ा होकर विदेश भ्रमण करूँगा। 6. हम जल्दी ही अनाथों के लिए एक स्कूल शुरू करेंगे। 7. आज हम सब किसी रेस्टोरेंट में खाएँगे। 8. कल सुबह मैं जल्दी उठूँगा। 9. हम अपने सारे कर्ज़ अगले साल लौटाएँगे। 10. तुम धूम्रपान करना कब छोड़ोगे? 11. शायद वह अगले साल शादी करेगा।

Ex.3: Translate into English

1. मैं अगले हफ़्ते मुम्बई जाने की सोच रही हूँ। 2. पिता जी जल्दी ही नया व्यापार शुरू करने की योजना बना रहे हैं। 3. हम आज शाम को सिनेमा जाने की सोच रहे हैं। 4. आप कौन सी 'कार' ख़रीदने की सोच रहे हैं। 5. मेरा भाई विदेश में पढ़ने की सोच रहा है। 6. हम अपने घर का बीमा कराने की सोच रहे हैं।

Key 1

1. am going to wash	2. are going to walk
3. is going to stay	4. are ....going to travel
5. is going to rest	6. is going to snow
7. are going to buy	8. are going to gift

Key 2

1. I will be 60 next month. 2. I will meet Robert in the evening. 3. From today shops will close at 8 O' clock. 4. In which month will Diwali be this year? 5. When I grow up, I will travel abroad. 6. We will soon start a school for the orphans. 7. Today we will all eat in some restaurant. 8. I will get up early tomorrow morning. 9. We will return all our debts next year. 10. When will you stop smoking.?11 Perhaps he will marry next year.

Key 3

1. I am thinking of going to Bombay next week. 2. Father is planning to start a new business soon. 3. We are intending to go to the movies this evening. 4. Which car are you planning to buy? 5. My brother is thinking of studying abroad. 6. We are planning to have our house insured.

15 Future Progressive Tense

will be v..ing

Language structure						
aff.:	subj.	+	will be		+ (v..ing)	+ obj. (if any)
neg.:	subj.	+	will not be or won't be		+ (v..ing)	+ obj. (if any)
int.:	Will	+	subj.	+ be	+ (v..ing)	+ obj. (if any)?
int. neg.:	Won't	+	subj.	+ be	+ (v..ing)	+ obj. (if any)?

aff. : Mother will be cooking at this time tomorrow. — माँ कल इस समय खाना पका रही होंगी।

neg.: Mother will not be cooking at this time tomorrow. — माँ कल इस समय खाना नहीं पका रही होंगी।

int.: Will mother be cooking at this time tomorrow? — क्या माँ कल इस समय खाना पका रही होंगी?

int. neg.: Won't mother be cooking at this time tomorrow? — क्या माँ कल इस समय खाना नहीं पका रही होंगी?

■ **will be v..ing** *के प्रयोग:*

1 ***भविष्य में अमुक समय पर कोई काम कर रहे / हो रहे होने पर :***

1. This time tomorrow I will be traveling. — कल इस समय मैं यात्रा कर रहा हूँगा/कर रही हूँगी।
2. The Prime Minister will be having a meeting after 6 p.m. today. — आज शाम छः बजे के बाद प्रधानमंत्री एक बैठक कर रहे होंगे।

2 **will be v..ng** ***का प्रयोग सामान्य भविष्य के अर्थ में :***

1.	We will be going to Srinagar this year.	हम इस साल श्रीनगर जाएँगे।
2.	The Presidents of both the countries will be signing a trade treaty soon.	दोनो देशों के राष्ट्रपति जल्दी ही एक व्यापार सन्धि पर हस्ताक्षर करेंगे।
3.	Who will be playing the flute at the concert tonight?	आज रात को गोष्ठी में बांसुरी कौन बजाएगा?
4.	This time I will be staying at my brother's place.	इस बार मैं अपने भाई के यहाँ ठहरूँगी।

☞ **'will be v..ing', 'is, are, am + v..ing'** और **is, are, am + going to + infitive'** के सामान्य ***भविष्य के लिए*** तुलनात्मक प्रयोग के लिए देखें पष्ठ 73

3 **'will + be + v..ing' is used to indicate activities extended over a period in future.**

'will + be + v..ing' का प्रयोग उन क्रियाओं के लिए भी होता है जो भविष्य में किसी अवधि विशेष में फैली हों।

1.	I wonder where they will be spending their vacation this summer.	मैं सोच रहा हूँ /रही हूँ वे यह ग्रीष्म अवकाश कहाँ बिताएँगे।
2.	In a week's time we shall be enjoying the warmth of the Indian plains.	हफ्ते भर में हम भारतीय मैदानों की गर्मी का आनन्द लेंगे / ले रहे होंगे।
3.	We shall be watching cricket matches on TV all next week.	हम सारा अगला हफ़्ता दूरदर्शन पर क्रिकेट मैच देखेंगें।
4.	My husband will be working overtime for the next three months.	अगले तीन महीने मेरे पति अतिरिक्त काम करेंगे।

Ex.1: Translate into English: Use fut. prog. simple where possible.

1. आपकी जानकारी के लिए बता दूँ कि मैं अगले हफ़्ते अपने दोस्त के यहाँ रहूँगा।
2. क्या रविवार को तुम्हारा भाई अपना 'कैमरा' प्रयोग करेगा? मैं उससे कुछ घण्टों के लिए उधार लेने की सोच रहा हूँ ।
3. अगले मंगलवार को इस समय मैं हवाईजहाज़ में बैठा होऊँगा।
4. मौसम बदल रहा है। जल्दी ही पत्तियाँ रंग बदलेंगी।
5. वह हमें अगले वर्ष नहीं पढ़ाएगा। वह लम्बी छुट्‌टी पर जा रहा है।
6. राष्ट्रपति ओबामा आज शाम को भारत के संसद को सम्बोधित करेंगे।
7. उसके बाद वे विभिन्न संस्थानों के विद्यार्थियों से बातचीत करेंगे।
8. क्या कल सचिन तेन्दुलकर क्रिकेट खेलेंगे?
9. मैं सकूल के वार्षिक खेलों में भाग नहीं लूँगा क्योंकि मेरे पैर में मोच आ गई है।
10. आज रात को आप कहाँ खाएँगे, घर पर या रेस्टोरेण्ट में?
11. कल प्रार्थना के समय में प्रधानाचार्य विद्यार्थियों को भाषण दे रहे होंगे।
12. मैं यह पत्र उन तक पहुँचा पाऊँगा। मैं दफ़्तर जाते हुए उसके घर के सामने से गुज़रूँगा।
13. क्या आप भारत में ताजमहल देखने जाएँगे/जाएँगी?
14. मैं जल्दी ही नया काम स्वीकार करूँगा।

Key 1

1. For your information I will be staying at my friend's house next week.
2. Will your brother be using his camera on Sunday? I am thinking of borrowing it from him for a few hours.
3. At this time next Tuesday I will be sitting in the aeroplane.
4. The season is changing. Soon the leaves will be changing color.
5. He will not be teaching us next year. He is going on a long leave.
6. President Obama will be addressing the Indian Parliament this evening.
7 Later he will be talking to the students from various Institutions.
8. Will Sachin Tendulkar be playing the cricket match tomorrow?
9. I will not be taking part in the annual school sports as I have sprained

my ankle.

10. Where will you be having dinner tonight, at home or in a restaurant?
11. The Principal will be giving a talk to the students during the prayer hour tomorrow.
12. I could deliver this letter to him; I will be going past his house on my way to the office.
13. Will you be visiting the Taj Mahal in India?
14. I will be accepting the new job soon.

Future Plans

A. What do you plan to do in the future?

B. I am thinking of becoming an astrologer.

A. That's interesting. Why an astrologer?

B. Everyone seems to be interested in knowing their future. I guess I will always be in demand and make plenty of money!

A. Sounds great! Tell me one thing, do you really believe in the science of astrology?

B. Of course, I have no doubt that forces beyond this planet condition the happenings in the lives of individuals. Planetary vibrations, in varying degrees and qualities, influence our minds and bodies. Believe me, the scope of astrology is really vast. It doesn't limit itself to individual existence but encompasses the whole idea of human existence itself.

A. I really don't understand all this. Anyway, I do wish you good luck with your future plans.

B. Thank you.

16 Future Perfect Simple

will have + past participle

Language Structure					
aff. :	**subj.**	**+ will have**		**+**	**pp + obj. (if any) + time clause**
neg.:	**subj.**	**+ will not have**		**+**	**pp + obj. (if any) + time clause**
int. :	**Will**	**+ subj.**	**+ have**	**+**	**pp + obj. (if any) + time clause?**
int. neg.:	**Won't**	**+ subj.**	**+ have**	**+**	**pp + obj. (if any) + time clause?**

aff.: I will have finished this work by tomorrow.
मैं कल तक यह काम समाप्त कर चुका हूँगा/ चुकी हूँगी।

neg.: I won't have finished this work by tomorrow.
मैं कल तक यह काम समाप्त नहीं कर चुका हूँगा/चुकी हूँगी।

int.: Will you have finished this work by tomorrow?
क्या आप कल तक यह काम समाप्त कर चुके होंगे/चुकी होंगी?

int. neg.: Won't you have finished this work by tomorrow?
क्या आप कल तक यह काम समाप्त नहीं कर चुके होंगे/ चुकी होंगी?

Comprehension

1. I will have written the letter by 12 O' clock. — मैं 12 बजे तक पत्र लिख चुका हूँगा/ लिख चुकी हूँगी।
2. She will have cooked dinner by 8 p.m. — वह शाम को आठ बजे तक रात का खाना पका चुकी होगी।
3. By next year they will have saved enough money to visit America. — वे अगले साल तक अमरीका जाने के लिए पर्याप्त पैसा बचा चुके होंगे।

4. You will have learnt English by next year.	तुम अगले साल तक अंग्रेज़ी सीख चुके होगे।
5. I will have arrived in Delhi by 7 a.m. tomorrow.	मैं कल सुबह 7 बजे तक दिल्ली पहुँच चुका हूँगा/पहुँच चुकी हूँगी।

Ex.1: Write sentences in the future perfect tense using the cues given below as shown.

> **The film / finish/ by 6 p.m.**
> **=> The film will have finished by 6 p.m.**

1. By the end of May / the teacher / complete / the course.
2. By the end of this month / he / play/ thirty cricket matches.
3. The tickets for the cinema / sold out / by this evening
4. By the end of this year you / learn/ enough English to speak the language fluently
5. By the end of this month, 15 million more children / be born in this country.
6. The concert / begin / before you arrive.
7. She / finish / dinner by 8 p.m.

Ex.2: Translate into English.

1. गोष्ठी रात दस बजे तक ख़त्म हो चुकी होगी।
2. आधे घण्टे में सब घर जा चुके होंगे।
3. अगर आप हमारे यहाँ सुबह दस बजे के बाद आएँगे, तो मेरे पति अपने कार्यालय जा चुके होंगे।
4. मुझे डर है कि जब तक तुम सिनेमाघर पहुँचोगे, फ़िल्म शुरू हो चुकी होगी।
5. यात्रा ख़त्म होने तक हमने लगभग 50,000 मील तय कर लिए होंगे।
6. इस साल के अन्त तक वे 25 देशों की यात्रा कर चुके होंगे।
7. बैठक शाम को चार बजे तक ख़त्म हो चुकी होगी।

8. हम रात को आठ बजे खाना खा चुके होंगे।

9. सन् 2014 में हमारी शादी को 50 साल हो चुके होंगे।

10. मैं नौ बजे तक नाश्ता कर चुका होऊँगा।

Key 1

1. By the end of May, the teacher will have completed the course.
2. By the end of this month, he will have played thirty cricket matches.
3. The tickets for the cinema will have been sold out by this evening.
4. By the end of this year, you will have learnt enough English to speak the language fluently.
5. By the end of this month, 15 million more children will have been born in this country.
6. The concert will have begun before you arrive.
7. She will have finished dinner by 8 p.m.

Key 2

1. The concert will have finished by 10 p.m.
2. Everybody will have gone home in half an hour.
3. If you come to our place after 10 a.m, my husband will have gone to work by then.
4. I am afraid, the film will have begun by the time you get to the cinema hall.
5. We will have travelled about 50,000 miles by the end of the journey.
6. They will have visited 25 countries by the end of this year.
7. The meeting will have ended by 4 p.m.
8. We will have had dinner by 8 O ' clock .
9. In 2014 we will have been married for fifty years.
10. I will have finished breakfast by 9 O' clock.

17 Future Perfect Progressive

will have been + (v..ing)

Language Structure	
aff. :	**subj. + will have been + (v..ing) + obj. (if any) + *TC**
neg.:	**subj. + won't have been + (v..ing) + obj. (if any) + *TC**
int. :	**Will + subj. + have been + (v..ing) + obj. (if any) + *TC ?**
int. neg.:	**Won't + subj. + have + (v..ing) + obj. (if any) + *TC. ?**

☞ ***TC =Time clause; This may be placed at the end of the sentence or at the beginning of the sentence.**

aff. I will have been working here for twenty years by the end of this year.
इस वर्ष के अन्त तक मुझे यहाँ काम करते हुए बीस वर्ष हो जाएँगे।

neg.: I won't have been working here for twenty years by the end of this year.
इस वर्ष के अन्त तक मुझे यहाँ काम करते हुए बीस वर्ष नहीं हुए होंगे।

int.: Will you have been working here for twenty years by the end of this year?
क्या इस वर्ष के अन्त तक आपको यहाँ काम करते हुए बीस वर्ष हो जाएँगे?

int. neg.: Won't you have been working here for twenty years by the end of this year?
क्या इस वर्ष के अन्त तक आपको यहाँ काम करते हुए बीस वर्ष नहीं हो जाएँगे?

Comprehension

1. She will have been learning Hindi for four years by next year.
   अगले साल उसे हिन्दी सीखते हुए चार वर्ष हो जाएँगे।
2. This theatre will have been under construction for five years by the end of May.
   मई के अन्त तक इस 'थिएटर' को बनते हुए पाँच वर्ष हो जाएँगे।
3. By the end of 2015 he will have been driving trains for thirty years.
   सन् दो हज़ार पंद्रह तक उसको गाड़ियाँ चलाते हुए पैंतीस वर्ष हो जाएँगे।
4.. By next Diwali I will have been teaching Hindi for thirty two years.
   आगामी दीवाली तक मुझे हिन्दी पढ़ाते हुए बत्तीस साल हो जाएँगे।

Let's Do Yoga!

1. Stand straight. Fold your hands and keep them at the centre of your chest.
2. While inhaling, stretch your hands up; take them as far back as you can. Keep your arms straight. Bend your body from the waist upwards as far as you can.
3. Bring your arms forward and bend your body down; put the palms of your hands on the ground and place them beside your feet.
4. Take the left leg backward, bend your right knee, with the hands remaining on the ground. Inhale.
5. Exhale. Take your right leg to the position of your left leg. Make sure your heels are completely on the ground. Raise your hips upwards.
6. Touch your chest with your chin. Place all your limbs on the ground. Lie down on your stomach. Breathe normally.
7. Raise the front portion of your body up to the chest. Inhale. Bend your neck as far back as possible.
8. Repeat exercises from 2 to 5 in reverse order. Return to the position 1. Bring your hands down.

18 'will' – अन्य प्रयोग

■ **'will' is used with following expressions given in bold.**

1. He will **probably** be a little early today.	संभवता वह आज कुछ जल्दी आएगा।
2. You must meet my daughter; **I am sure** you will like her.	आप मेरी पुत्री से अवश्य मिलें। मेरा विश्वास है कि आप उसे अवश्य पसन्द करेंगे।
3. **I bet** you will pass the test.	मैं शर्तिया कह सकती हूँ कि तुम परीक्षा में उत्तीर्ण होओगे / होओगी।
4. **Do you think** I will get this job?	आपको लगता है कि मुझे यह नौकरी मिलेगी?
5. **I suppose** we shall / will meet at Ann's party on Sunday.	मेरे विचार में हम रविवार को ऐन की दावत में मिलेंगे/मिलेंगी।
7. **I think** she will leave for the United States by Monday.	मुझे लगता है कि वह सोमवार तक अमरीका चली जाएगी।

■ **will + activities that will always happen:**
'will' is stressed here.

☞ ***कुछ ऐसी घटनाएँ , नियति सिद्ध परिस्थितियाँ जिनका नियमित रूप से होना निश्चित होता है , उनमें* 'will' *का प्रयोग होता है।***

ध्यान दें कि बोलते समय **'will'** पर बलाघात होता है।

1. Summer will come.	ग्रीष्म ऋतु आती रहेगी।
2. Nations will fight.	राष्ट्र लड़ते रहेंगे।

3. Human nature will never change. मानव प्रकृति कभी नहीं बदलेगी।
4. Children will be children. बच्चे बच्चे ही रहेंगे।
5. There will always be wars. युद्ध हमेशा होंगे/होते रहेंगे।
6. Accidents will take place. दुर्घटनाएँ हमेशा होती रहेंगी।

■ **'Will' is used to express future with following verbs:**

(1) some auxiliary verbs such as 'to be, to have',
(2) sense verbs such as' look, seem, feel, taste' etc,
(3) verbs of emotion such as 'happiness, disappointment, thought, possession':

☞ *अंग्रेज़ी में* **(1)** *कुछ सहायक क्रियाओं* **'to be, to have', (2)** *ज्ञानेद्रियों से जुड़ी हुई क्रियाओं* **' look, seem, feel, taste etc'**, **(3)** *भावना, विचार, आधिपत्य बताने सम्बन्धी क्रियाओं* **'happiness, disappointment, thought, possession** *आदि के साथ* **will'** *का प्रयोग होता है।*

1. She **will be** here next Monday. वह अगले सोमवार को यहाँ होगी।
2. They **will have** time to visit the museum. उनके पास संग्रहालय जाने का समय होगा।
3. Mother **will worry** where I am. माँ चिन्ता करेंगी कि मैं कहाँ हूँ।
4. You **will know** my decision by tomorrow. आपको कल तक मेरा निर्णय पता लग जाएगा।
5. When **will** you **discover** the truth? आपको सच्चाई कब पता लगेगी?
6. Take this medicine; you **will feel** better. आप यह दवाई ले लीजिए। आपको अच्छा लगेगा।
7. Add a pinch of salt and a little sugar. It **will taste** better. चुटकी-भर नमक और थोड़ी-सी चीनी मिला लीजिए। इसका स्वाद और अच्छा लगेगा।
8. Buy this one. It **will look** good on you. यह वाला ख़रीद लीजिए। आप पर अच्छा लगेगा।

■ **Announcement of future plans, weather forecasts, news broadcasts:**

☞ भविष्य में कार्यान्वित होने या की जाने वाली योजनाओं के बारे में, मौसम का ब्योरा देने में, समाचार पत्रों में, एवम् रेडियो, टेलिवियन पर प्रसारित होने वाली भविष्य से जुड़ी सूचनाएँ देते समय **'will'** का प्रयोग करते हैं।

1. The Prime minister will inaugurate the TV center in Varanasi tomorrow. — प्रधानमंत्री कल बनारस में दूरदर्शन केंद्र का उद्‌घाटन करेंगे।
2. There will be rain in the eastern region next week. — अगले सप्ताह पूर्वी क्षेत्र में वर्षा होगी।
3. Mist will continue all over northern India. — उत्तरी भारत में सर्वत्र धुंध रहेगी।

■ **Invitations:** निमन्त्रण में अंग्रेज़ी में प्रायः **'will'** का प्रयोग करते हैं, जबकि हिन्दी में ऐसा नहीं है।

1. Will you have dinner with us next Sunday? — कृपया आप आगामी रविवार को हमारे साथ भोजन कीजिए।
   (= Would you like to have dinner with us next Sunday?)
2. Will you have a cup of tea? — चाय पीजिएगा?/कृपया चाय पीजिए।
   (= Would you like to have a cup of tea?)

■ **Requests:** अनुरोध, निवेदन में **'will'** का प्रयोग करते हैं।

1. Will you help me to move the table? — कृपया यह मेज़ हटाने में मेरी मदद कीजिए।
   (= Could you help me to move the table please?)
2. Will you pass me the salt please? — कृपया नमक मेरी ओर खिसकाइए।
   (= Could you pass me the salt please?)
3. Will you bring the chair out into the garden? — कृपया कुर्सी बाहर बागीचे में लाइए।
   (= Could you bring the chair out in the garden?)

- **Commands:** (आदेश देने में:)

1. You will sit here all evening and study! — तुम सारी शाम यहाँ बैठकर पढ़ोगे/पढ़ोगी।
2. Will you stop making noise? — तुमलोग शोर मचाना बन्द करो।
3. Will you shut the door before you sit down? — तुम बैठने से पहले दरवाज़ा बन्द कर देना।
4. You will go to school today. No excuses. — तुम आज स्कूल जाओगे/जाओगी। कोई बहाना नहीं चलेगा।

- **Negative commands: (** नकारात्मक आदेश देने में:**)**

1. You will not go to the movies. — तुम सिनेमा देखने नहीं जाओगे/जाओगी।
2. You will not move from here till I return. — जब तक मैं न लौटूँ, तुम यहाँ से नहीं हिलोगे/हिलोगी।।
3. You will not watch television for one week. — तुम एक सप्ताह तक दूरदर्शन नहीं देखोगे।

- **Offering to do something for somebody:**

  (किसी के लिए कुछ करने की पेशकश में।)

1. Don't worry! I will help you. — चिन्ता मत करो। मैं तुम्हारी मदद करूँगा/करूँगी।
2. If you are short of money, let me know. I will lend you some. — अगर तुम्हारे पास पैसे कम हों, तो मुझे बता देना। मैं तुम्हें कुछ दे दूँगा/दे दूँगी।

- **Promise** किसी को आशा दिलाने, विश्वास दिलाने, वचन देने में **'will'** और **'shall'** का प्रयोग।

1. She will be here to help you. — वह तुम्हारी मदद के लिए यहाँ होगी।
2. You shall have your books by tomorrow morning. — कल शाम तक तुम्हें तुम्हारी किताबें मिल जाएँगी।
3. I won't tell anyone what you told me. — जो आपने मुझे बताया, मैं किसीको नहीं बताऊँगा/बताऊँगी।

4. I shall return this book to you on Saturday.	मैं शनिवार को तुम्हें यह पुस्तक लौटा दूँगा।

■ **Threats:** धमकी देने की भाषा में **'will'** का प्रयोग:

1. Mother will punish you if you tell lies.	अगर तुम झूठ बोलोगे/बोलोगी, तो माँ तुम्हें दण्ड देंगी।
2. I will hit you if you utter another word.	अगर तुम एक शब्द और बोलोगे/बोलोगी, तो मैं तुम्हें मारूँगा/ मारूँगी।

■ **Refusals: (Use of 'won't */ wouldn't' :)**

1. My moped won't start.	मेरी गाड़ी (मोपेड) चल ही नहीं रही।
2. She won't listen to anyone (refuses to listen to anyone).	वह किसी की बात सुनने को तैयार ही नहीं।
3. I have asked Anil to help me with math but he won't.	मैने अनिल से गणित में मदद माँगी परन्तु उसने मना कर दिया।
4. The fever wouldn't go . (= refused to go)	बुख़ार उतर के ही नहीं दिया।/बुख़ार उतरा ही नहीं ।
5. The prisoner wouldn't speak. (= refused to speak)	बन्दी बोला ही नहीं।/बन्दी बोल के ही नहीं दिया।

■ **I, We + will/would, shall/should to express determination:**

☞ द ढ़ संकल्पसूचक वाक्यों में **will / would, shall / should** के साथ I, We का प्रयोग :

1. I will help him when he needs me.	जब उसे मेरी ज़रूरत होगी, मैं उसकी मदद करूँगा/ करूँगी।
2. I will never see him again.	मैं उसे फिर कभी नहीं मिलूँगा/ मिलूँगी।
3. We shall counter attack and we shall be victorious.	हम पलटवार करेंगे और हम अवश्य जीतेंगे।
4. Don't worry. I shall be there on time.	चिन्ता न करें, मैं वहाँ समय पर होऊँगा/ होऊँगी।

* X 'will not = X won't

■ **'you / he / she / they' + 'will/would' to express obstinate determination:**

☞ *दुराग्रही इरादोंवाले सकारात्मक और नकारात्मक वाक्यों में* **'you, he, she, it , they'** *के साथ* **'will/would'** *का प्रयोग* **:**

1. If you will go out (= insist on going out) in the rain without an umbrella, you will fall ill.	अगर तुम बिना छाते के बारिश में जाओगे तो बीमार हो जाओगे।
2. If he will eat (insists on eating) restaurant food every day, he will ruin his health.	अगर वह रोज़ रेस्टोरेण्ट में खाना खाएगा, तो अपना स्वास्थ्य बर्बाद कर लेगा।
3. She would do it (= insisted on doing it) in spite of my advising her against it.	मेरे समझाने के बावजूद उसने यह किया।

■ **'will / would' + 'you / he / she / it / they' in the interrogative to ask someone about his/her agreement/approval to do something.**

☞ *किसी कार्य को करने या किसी कार्य में भाग लेने के लिए सहमति प्राप्त करने हेतु भी* **'you, he, she, they'** *के साथ* **'will, would'** *का प्रयोग होता है।*

1. Will / Would you dance at the Institute's annual function?	आप संस्थान के वार्षिक समारोह में नृत्य करेंगे?
2. Will / Would you take part in the debate tomorrow?	आप कल की बहस में हिस्सा लेंगे न?/ले रहे हैं न?

■ **Normally we don't use 'will'/ would in the 'if ' clause. How ever ☞ 'Would, is used in ' if 'sentences :**

(1) to be very polite. **see sentences 1-3**

(2) to express willingness of 2nd person or 3rd person to do something. **see sentences 4-5**

1 **'If you would'** *का विनम्रता-सूचक निवेदन करने के अर्थ में प्रयोग :*

1. If you would help me in this matter, I would be extremely grateful to you.	यदि आप इस मामले में मेरी मदद करेंगे तो मैं आपका अत्याधिक आभारी हूँगा।
2. If you would sign here. (= please sign here).	कृपया यहाँ हस्ताक्षर कीजिए।
3. If you would write your name and address at the bottom of this page.	कृपया इस पृष्ठ पर नीचे के भाग में अपना नाम और पता लिखिए।

2 **If + he/they/ you + will/would = If he is/ If you are willing to do so:**

मध्यम और *अन्य* पुरुष के द्वारा कुछ करने की सहमति सूचक *प्रयोग* :

4. **If he will / would** confide in me, I will try to solve his problem.	यदि वह मुझ पर भरोसा करके अपना रहस्य बता दे, तो मैं उसकी समस्या सुलझाने का प्रयास करूँगा/करूँगी ।
5. **If you will / would** tell me (if you are willing to tell me) what you want for breakfast, I will have it prepared for you.	यदि आप मुझे बता दें कि आपको नाश्ते में क्या चाहिए, तो मैं आपके लिए बनवा दूँगा/दूँगी ।

■ **Use of 'will / won't', 'would / wouldn't' to talk about assumptions.**

पूर्वानुमान सूचक वाक्यों में निम्नलिखित भाषा ढाँचों का प्रयोग होता है।

will/won't + be	**will/won't + have + pp**
would /wouldn't + be	**would / wouldn't + have + pp**

1. That will be the machine — यही वह मशीन होगी जो आप माँग

	you are asking for.	रहे हैं।
2.	That will be the milkman, I hope.	मैं आशा करती हूँ वह दूधवाला ही होगा।
3.	He will have heard the news by now.	अब तक उसने समाचार सुन लिया होगा।
4.	He won't have heard it yet.	उसने अभी तक नहीं सुना होगा।

At The Market

A: How much do a dozen bananas cost?

B: Well these big ones are 8 rupees for a dozen and these smaller ones are 6 rupees.

A: Wow.... That's quite expensive. Do you have any cheaper ones?

B: Madam.... these are are really tasty bananas. The prices are very reasonable.

A: I'll give you six rupees for a dozen of large bananas.

B: Six rupees!... No. Seven rupees is my last price.

A: Okay.... give me six large ones. How much are these apples?

B: Twenty five rupees for a kilo.

A: Give me one kilo of apples too.

B: Here you are!

A: Thanks!

19 Uses of 'would'

■ **'Would'= past tense of 'will' in reported speech.**
असाक्षात कथन में **'would'** का प्रयोग **'will'** के **past tense** रूप में होता है। **pg. 324.**

1. "I will help you".	मैं तुम्हारी मदद करूँगी।
• She said she would help me.	उसने कहा वह मेरी मदद करेगी।
2. "I will be on time".	मैं समय पर आऊँगी।
• She promised she would be on time.	उसने वचन दिया कि वह समय पर आएगी।
3. "I shall visit you tomorrow".	मैं कल तुम्हारे यहाँ आऊँगी।
• She promised she would visit me the following day.	उसने वचन दिया कि वह अगले दिन मेरे यहाँ आएगी।
4. "I will not go out so frequently".	मैं इतना अक्सर बाहर नहीं जाऊँगी।
• She promised she would not go out so frequently.	उसने वचन दिया कि वह इतना अक्सर बाहर नहीं जाएगी।
5. "I shall be home before it gets dark".	मैं अंधेरा होने से पहले घर पर होऊँगी।
• She promised she would be home before it got dark.	उसने वचन दिया कि वह अंधेरा होने से पहले घर पर होगी।

■ **'Would' is used while talking about repeated actions in the past that are not done any more. See pg. 38**

■ **'would rather / would sooner' - to talk about preferences in general see page 170**

subj. + would rather + infinitive + obj. X + than + obj. Y

= **subj. + prefer + (v..ing) + obj. X + to + (v..ing) + obj. Y (see pg. 170)**

■ **Would rather / would sooner + have + past participle is used to talk about preference in the past. (see pg. 172)**

☞ would rather/would sooner + have + past participle का प्रयोग भूतकाल में किसी वस्तु या कार्य की वरीयता दिखाने के लिए होता है। देखें **Past preferences (see pg. 172)**

■ विनम्रतासूचक प्रयोग: **'If you would like / care' is almost the same as 'if + you want / wish', but more polite form.**

☞ **'If you would like / care'** और **'if you want / wish'** दोनों समानार्थी हैं परन्तु **'If you would like / care'** का प्रयोग ज़्यादा विनम्र है।

1. If you would like / care to come with us, I will take you along.	यदि आप मेरे साथ चलना चाहें, तो मैं आपको अपने साथ ले चलूँगा।
2. If you would like / care to go to the movies, I shall buy advance tickets.	यदि आप सिनेमा देखनाा चाहें, तो मैं पहले से टिकट ख़रीद लूँगा।
3. If she would like to buy this property, I shall talk to the property dealer.	यदि वह ये जायदाद ख़रीदना चाहे, तो मैं 'प्रौपर्टी डीलर' से बात करूँगा।

20 shall should

■ Interrogative use of 'shall' :

☞ कुछ प्रश्नवाचक वाक्य जो वास्तव में सलाह लेने, विनम्रता पूर्वक किसी कार्य हेतु अनुरोध करने, अनुमति माँगने के लिए होते हैं, उनमें **'shall'** का प्रयोग होता है।

1. Let's go to bed, shall we? **(suggestion)** — चलिए सोएँ, सो जाएँ न?
2. Shall we go by bus? **(ask for approval of a suggestion)** — बस से चलें?
3. What shall I do with your plants in your absence? **(request for instructions)** — तुम्हारी ग़ैरमौजूदगी में तुम्हारे पौधों का क्या करूँ?
4. Where shall we be at this time tomorrow? **(speculation)** — हम कल इस समय कहाँ होंगे?
5. Shall I shut the window? **(politely letting the other person know one's preference and ask for permission)** — मैं खिड़की बंद कर दूँ?
6. Where shall we go this weekend? **(ask for suggestion)** — इस सप्ताहान्त पर हम कहाँ जाएँ?
7. What time shall I call you tomorrow? **(ask for permission)** — मैं तुम्हें कल कितने बजे 'फ़ोन' करूँ?
8. What shall we have for breakfast? **(ask for suggestion or other person's preference)** — हम नाश्ते में क्या लें?
9. Who all shall I invite to the party? **(ask for advice)** — मैं किन-किन को दावत में बुलाऊँ?

■ **'Shall / should' are used with 'he, she, it, they, you' (where shall / should is stressed) to indicate the determination of the speaker about the activities of the persons other than him=self, i.e. where the other person has no choice; but will have to comply with the determined decision of the speaker:**

☞ जहाँ किसी दूसरे आदमी की क्रिया को लेकर वक्ता की पूर्व निर्धारित दृढ़ धारणा का संकेत हो, जहाँ किसी काम को करनेवाले के लिए वक्ता द्वारा कही गई बात को मानना अनिवार्यता हो, वहाँ **'he, she, it, they, you'** के साथ **'shall, should'** का प्रयोग होता है। जैसे:

1. He shall come with you. — वह तुम्हारे साथ आएगा।
   (I insist on his coming with you)
3. She shall marry him. — वह उसीसे शादी करेगी।
   (I insist on her marrying him).

■ **Use of 'shall' with 'I', 'we' in simple future tense (see pg. 70)**

■ **Use of 'should' = 'ought to' (see pg. 179)**

Writing the date: British, American

British use:	**date**	**.**	**month**	**.**	**year**
	27th	**.**	**October**	**.**	**2011**
	27	**.**	**10**	**.**	**2011**
American use:	**month**	**.**	**date**	**.**	**year**
	October		**27**	**.**	**2011**
	10	**.**	**27**	**.**	**2011**

21 can, could, be able to

ability or inability language structures

■ *कुछ काम कर सकने या न कर सकने के अर्थ में :*

☞ **present tense** में **can** और **'is / are / am + able to'** का प्रयोग होता है।

☞ **Past tense** में **'could'** और **'was / were + able to'** का प्रयोग होता है।

☞ **can** का **present perfect / past perfect** और **future tense** के लिए कोई रूप नहीं। इन के लिए क्रमशः **'has/ have been able to'**, **'had been able to'** ,**'will be able to'** का प्रयोग होता है।

☞ **subj.** एक वचन के साथ **'can'** के साथ **'s'** नहीं लगता।

■ **Present simple tense: Affirmative**

subj.	**+**	**can**	**+**	**v. inf.**	**+**	**obj. (if any)**
subj.	**+**	**is / are / am able to**	**+**	**v. inf**	**+**	**obj. (if any)**

- You can cook. तुम पका सकते हो।

= You are able to cook. ' ' ' '

Interrogative

can	**+ subj.**		**+**	**v. inf.**	**+**	**obj. (if any)?**
is / are / am	**+ subj.**	**+ able to**	**+**	**v. inf.**	**+**	**obj. (if any)?**

See use of 'can't" for negative presumption page 107-108

- Can you cook? क्या तुम पका सकते हो?

= Are you able to cook? " " " " "?

Negative

subj.	+	**cannot**	+	**v. inf.**	+	**obj. (if any)**
subj.	+	**is / are / am not able to**	+	**v. inf.**	+	**obj. (if any)**

- You cannot cook. तुम नहीं पका सकते।

= You are not able to cook. " " " " "

- Can't yout cook? क्या तुम पका नहीं सकते?

= Are you not able to cook? " " " " "

■ **Past tense:**

ठीक उपरोक्त ढाँचे की तरह है। मात्र **can** *के स्थान पर* **could** *और* **is / are/ am able to** *के स्थान पर* **was / were able to** *लगाएँ।*

aff.: They could understand Hindi. वे हिन्दी समझ सकते थे।

= They were able to understand Hindi.

int.: Could they understand Hindi? क्या वे हिन्दी समझ सकते थे?

= Were able to understand Hindi?

neg.: They could not understand Hindi. वे हिन्दी नहीं समझ सकते थे।

= They were not able to understand Hindi.

■ **Ability structure: Present or past perfect tense**

subject + has / have or had + been able to + v. inf.

- I have been able to learn English. मैं अंग्रेज़ी सीख पाया हूँ /पाई हूँ।
- I had been able to find his house. मैं उसका घर ढूँढ़ पाया था /पाई थी।

☞ *ध्यान दें– किसी स्थिति विशेष में कर्ता के एक बार कुछ कर पाने या न कर पाने की हालत में* **could** *न लगाकर* **was / were not able to** *का प्रयोग ज़्यादा ठीक है।*

• I was able to talk her into doing it.	मैं उसे ऐसा करने को राज़ी कर पाया।
• They were able to bring the people out of the house before it collapsed.	वे घर ढहने से पहले उस में से लोगों को निकाल पाए।
• Although everybody had lost hope, the pilot was able to land the plane safely.	यद्यपि सभी उम्मीद छोड़ बैठे थे, चालक हवाई जहाज़ को सुरक्षित नीचे उतार पाया था।

☞ परन्तु जब बात कर्ता के सामान्य सामर्थ्य की हो, तो **could** का प्रयोग सही है। जैसे **'She can usually talk people into doing what she wants.'** ठीक है क्यों कि यहाँ बात कर्ता के एक बार कुछ कर पाने या न कर पाने की नहीं है। यहाँ बात उस के सामान्य सामर्थ्य की है।

■ **Future tense:**

aff.	**subj.**	**+**	**will be able to**	**+**	**v. inf.**	**+.....**	
int. :	**will**	**+**	**subj. + be able to**	**+**	**v. inf.**	**+..... ?**	
neg.:	**subj.**	**+**	**will not be able to**	**+**	**v. inf.**	**+.......**	

aff. :	You will be able to speak English.	आप अंग्रेज़ी बोल सकेंगे।
int.:	Will I be able to speak English?	क्या मैं अंग्रेज़ी बोल सकूँगा?
neg.:	You will not be able to speak English.	आप अंग्रेज़ी नहीं बोल सकेंगे।

Comprehension:

1. He can play the sitar well.	वह सितार बहुत अच्छा बजा सकता है।
2. She can swim.	वह तैर सकती है।
3. My daughter can speak several foreign languages.	मेरी बेटी कई विदेशी भाषाएँ बोल सकती है।
4. She could not remember his address.	उसे उसका पता याद नहीं रहा।
5. Earlier I could high jump but I cannot do it anymore.	पहले मैं ऊँची छलाँग लगा सकती थी, लेकिन अब नहीं।
6. I can't find my glasses; I don't know where I put them.	मुझे अपनी ऐनक नहीं मिल रही। पता नही मैंने कहाँ रख दी !

■ Uses of can, could

1 **for asking permission** (इजाज़त माँगने के अर्थ में।)

इजाज़त माँगने के अर्थ में **can** और **could** के स्थान पर **may** का प्रयोग संभव है। ।(देखें **UNIT 23- page 115)**

1. Can I (or Could I) speak to Mr. Sharma please?	क्या मैं श्री शर्मा से बात कर सकता हूँ?
2. Can I leave now?	क्या मैं अब जा सकता हूँ?
3. Could I use your car for a few hours?	क्या मैं कुछ घण्टे आप की 'कार' प्रयोग सकता हूँ?
4. Students can use the hostel phone.	विद्यार्थी छात्रावास के दूरभाष का प्रयोग कर सकते हैं। = (विद्यार्थियों को छात्रावास का दूरभाष प्रयोग करने की इजाज़त है।)

2 **Giving permission**

☞ *ध्यान दें- इजाज़त देने के अर्थ में* **'can'** *का प्रयोग होता है, परन्तु* **could** *का प्रयोग नहीं होता।*

1. You can drink / smoke / play here. — आप यहाँ शराब पी सकते हैं। /धूम्रपान कर सकते हैं। /खेल सकते हैं।

☞ *यहाँ* **'can'** *के स्थान पर* **'could'** *नहीं लग सकता।* **'may'** *का प्रयोग हो सकता है।*

1. You may (=can) leave now. — अब आप जा सकते हैं।
2. You may smoke if you want to. — आप चाहें तो धूम्रपान कर सकते हैं।

3 **Offering to do something for somebody.**

☞ **'can'** *का प्रयोग – किसीके लिए कुछ करने की पेशकश करते हुए।*

1. Can I give you a hand in carrying it? — मैं इसे ले जाने में आपकी मदद करूँ
2. Can I get you a glass of water? — मैं आपके लिए एक गिलास पानी लाऊँ?

☞ *ध्यान दें- इस अर्थ में* **'can'** *के स्थान पर* **'may'** *का प्रयोग भी संभव है। विशेषकर औपचारिक बातचीत में जैसे जब दुकानदार गाहक से बात करता है तो* **'May I help you?'** *का प्रयोग ज़्यादा विनम्रताबोधक होता है।*

■ **Uses of could** (**could** के प्रयोग)

1 **For realistic statements:** ☞**Realistic statements** में **could** का प्रयोग **can** के **simple past tense** के रूप में होता है।

1. I could not go to the bank. — मैं बैंक नहीं जा सका/सकी।
2. I could not read my email this morning. — मैं आज सुबह अपनी 'ई-मेल' नहीं पढ़ सका/सकी।
3. She could take liquids, but could — वह तरल पदार्थ ले सकती थी परन्तु

not swallow anything solid. कुछ ठोस नहीं निगल सकती थी।

4. How could I have gone to the party leaving my ailing mother alone? मैं अपनी बीमार माँ को अकेली छोड कर दावत में कैसे जा सकता था ! (अर्थात नहीं जा सकता था)

2 **For possible and probable actions or events in the present or future tense.** **(see page 115)**

संभावित क्रियाओं के लिए :

1. They could be here any moment. वे किसी भी क्षण यहाँ हो सकते हैं।
2. What he told you could be true. However, I don't believe him. उसने जो तुम्हें बताया, वह सच हो सकता है। फिर भी मुझे उसपर विश्वास नहीं।
3. The weather is bad. It could be worse. मौसम ख़राब है। लेकिन इससे भी ख़राब हो सकता है।
4. Your book could be on your bed under your pillow. तुम्हारी किताब तुम्हारे पलंग पर तुम्हारे सिरहाने के नीचे हो सकती है।

3 **For requests:**

किसीसे कुछ निवेदन के अर्थ में। ☞ यद्यपि **'could' 'can'** का **past tense** रूप है, इसका निवेदनार्थक प्रयोग **present** या **future** के लिए होता है।

1. Could you come to my house tomorrow evening? आप कल शाम को मेरे यहाँ आइए।
2. Could you look after my dog in my absence next week? क्या आप मेरी अनुपस्थिति में मेरे कुत्ते की देखभाल कर पाएँगे?
3. Could you turn off the light please? कृपया बत्ती बुझा दीजिए।
4. Could you pass me the butter please? कृपया मक्खन मेरी ओर खिसका दीजिए।

4 **Use of could for things that could have taken place in the past but did not :** ***कुछ होते होते रह जाने के अर्थ में।***

1. You could have hurt yourself.	तुम्हें चोट लग सकती थी।
2. He could have fallen sick.	वह बीमार पढ़ सकता था।
3. Why did you drive so fast? You could have had an accident.	तुमने वाहन इतना तेज़ क्यों चलाया? तुम दुर्घटनाग्रस्त हो सकते थे।
4. The exam was not easy. But it could have been more difficult.	परीक्षा सरल नहीं थी। परन्तु और कठिन हो सकती थी।
5. You could have applied for this job.	तुम इस नौकरी के लिए आवेदन कर सकते थे।

5 **for apprehensions:** ***आशंका, भय आदि के लिए***

1. You could hurt yourself.	तुम्हें चोट लग सकती है।
2. They could have killed you!	वे तुम्हें मार भी सकते थे।

6 **for unrealistic statements :** ***असम्भव बात कहने में :***

1. I am so thirsty. I could drink buckets full of water.	मुझे इतनी प्यास लगी है। मैं बाल्टियाँ भर पानी पी सकता हूँ।
2. I like your house immensely. I could spend my whole life here.	मुझे तुम्हारा घर बहुत पसन्द है। मैं यहाँ आजीवन रह सकता हूँ।

7 **for expressing superabundance / excess of a situation :** *इन्तहाई बयान करते वक्त :*

1. We had a really good time in India. It could not have been better.	भारत में हमारा समय बहुत बढ़िया बीता। इससे अच्छा कुछ हो ही नहीं सकता था।

See comparative use of 'could not" , may/might pg. 117

Ex. 1: Write sentences using the cues and the verb 'can' as shown:

I / not / play / guitar. => I can not play the guitar.

1. My sister / speak / French.
2. You / change / 50 dollars?
3. We / not come / your birthday party tomorrow.
4. You / hear / me?
5. She / not find / her wallet.

Ex. 2: Write sentences using the cues and the verbs 'could' / 'could not.' as shown:

She / not / work. => She could not work.

1. I was sick. I / not eat / anything
2. She / not go / meeting / yesterday. She was not in town.
3. I / not study / today. Some guests came.
4. Electricity went out. We / not / watch TV all day.
5. My daughter / pass the exam /with very good marks.
6. The exam / be / worse.

Ex .3: Translate into English:

1. क्या आप तैर सकते हैं? 2. जी, मैं तैर सकता हूँ। 3. क्या वह कोई वाहन चला सकती है? 4. नहीं, वह कोई वाहन चला सकती। 5. क्या वे क्रिकेट खेल सकते हैं? 6. जी, वे क्रिकेट खेल सकते है। 7. क्या आप मुझे देख सकते थे? 8. मैं अपनी किताब नहीं ढूँढ पाया। 9. क्या आप आज शाम को हमारे घर आ सकेंगे? 10. मुझे खेद है मैं आज शाम को आपके घर नहीं आ सकूँगा। 11. आज मैं डाकघर नहीं जा सका/सकी। 12. मेरे पैर में चोट लग गई थी। मैं सैर करने नहीं जा सकी। 13. क्या मैं आपका छाता उधार ले सकता हूँ? 14. क्या हम कुछ समय बात कर सकते हैं? 1 5. किसी भी क्षण बारिश आ सकती हैं। 16. महँगाई अभी और बढ़ सकती हैं। 17. भयंकर दुर्घटना थी। कोई मर भी सकता था। 18. वे तम्हें मार भी सकते थे। 19. मुझे यह कमरा पसन्द

है। व्यक्ति यहाँ से समुद्र देख सकता है। 20. उसे यह नौकरी इसलिए मिली क्योंकि वह तीन भाषाएँ बोल सकती है। 21. क्या आप मुझे सिर्फ़ आज भर के लिए कुछ पैसा उधार दे सकेंगे? 22. अभियुक्त सर्वोच्च न्यायालय में पुनर्रावेदन कर सकते है। 23. हम छुट्टियों में सिनेमा देखने जा सकते थे। 24. विद्यार्थी छात्रावास में अपने पालतू जानवर नहीं ला सकते थे।

Key 1

1. My sister can speak French. 2. Can you change 50 dollars? 3. We can not come to your birthday party tomorrow. 4. Can you hear me? 5. She cannot find her wallet.

Key 2

1. I was sick. I could not eat anything. 2. She could not go to the meeting yesterday. She was not in town. 3. I could not study today. Some guests came. 4. Electricity went out. We could not watch TV all day. 5. My daughter could pass the exam with very good marks. 6. The exam could be worse

Key 3

1. Can you swim? 2. Yes, I can.swim. 3. Can she drive? 4. No, she cannot drive. 5. Can they play cricket? 6. Yes, they can play cricket. 7. Could you see me? 8. I was unable to find my book. 9. Will you be able to come to our house today in the evening? 10. I am sorry, I will not be able to come to your house this the evening. 11. I could not go to the post offfice today. 12. I hurt my foot . I could not go for a walk. 13. Could I borrow your umbrella, please? 14. Could we talk for a while? 15. It could rain any moment. 16. Inflation could go higher still. 17. It was a horrible accident. Someone could have died. 18. They could have even killed you. 19. I like this room. One can see the ocean from here. 20. She got this job because she can speak three languages. 21. Do you think you could lend me some money just for today. 22.The accused can appeal to the Supreme Court. 23. We could go to the movies during the holidays. 24.The students could not bring their pets into the hostel.

22 must can't

to express presumption

■ Present Presumption

subject	+	must be	+	attribute or noun

- She must be intelligent. वह अवश्य बुद्धिमान होगी।
- She must be Chinese. वह अवश्य चीन की रहनेवाली होगी।
- That must be the postman at the door. वह दरवाज़े पर अवश्य डाकिया होगा।
- You must be very tired. तुम अवश्य बहुत थके होगे।

■ Present Progressive Presumption

subject	+	must be	+	v..ing.

- He must be studying a lot these days. वह आजकल बहुत पढ़ रहा होगा।
- She must be coming. वह आ रही होगी।
- Mother must be cooking at this time. माँ इस समय खाना पका रही होगी।
- Father must be reading the newspaper now. पिता जी अब अख़बार पढ़ रहे होंगे।

■ Present Perfect Presumption

subject	+	must	+	have	+	pp

- They must have gone by now. वे अब तक चले गए होंगे।
- She must have worked hard. उसने बहुत परिश्रम किया होगा।

pp= past participle

• It must have been very difficult.	यह अवश्य कठिन रहा होगा।
• They must have been asleep.	वे अवश्य सोए हुए होंगे।

■ **Presumption and the verbs 'know', 'like', 'have'**

subject + must + know / like / have + object

• Solveigh has been in India for a long time. She must know many Indians.	सॉलवे़ बहुत समय से भारत में है। वह ज़रूर कई भारतीयों को जानती होगी।
• Rani always travels by air. She must have a lot of money.	रानी हमेशा हवाई जहाज़ से यात्रा करती है। उसके पास बहुत पैसा होगा।

■ **Negative Presumption : Use of 'can't'**

☞ ***ध्यान दें – नकारात्मक सम्भावना में (अर्थात जब व्यक्ति की धारणा अमुक बात के सम्भव न होने की ओर संकेत करती है) तो* must *नहीं ,* can't *का प्रयोग होता है। जैसे:***

■ **Negative Present Presumption**

subject + can't be + attribute or noun

• He can't be an Indian.	वह भारतीय नहीं हो सकता।
• She can't be sick.	वह बीमार नहीं हो सकती।
• They can't be his friends.	वे उसके मित्र नहीं हो सकते।

■ **Negative Present Progressive Presumption**

subject + can't be + v..ing + ...

• She can't be studying at this time.	वह इस समय पढ़ नहीं रही होगी।
• They can't be watching a movie every day.	वे हर रोज़ फ़िल्म नहीं देखते होंगे।

can't be = negative presumption.

must not = advice against doing something.

• Mother can't be cooking on Sundays.	माँ रविवार को खाना नहीं बनाती होंगी।

■ **Negative Present Perfect Presumption**

subject	+ can't	+ have	+ pp

• She can't have driven fast.	उसने वाहन तेज़ नहीं चलाया होगा।
• He can't have worked hard.	उसने परिश्रम नहीं किया होगा।
• They can't have drunk unboiled water.	उन्होंने बिना उबला पानी नहीं पीया होगा।

■ **Negative Present Presumption with 'know', 'like', 'have'**

subject	+ can't	+ know / have / like	+ obj.

• She can't know the truth.	वह सच्चाई नहीं जानती होगी।
• She can't have much money.	उसके पास बहुत पैसा नहीं होगा।
• She can't like him.	वह उसे पसन्द नहीं करती होगी।

Ex. 1: Write presumptive sentences using the cues given below as shown:

> • Mother has been working all day. She / must / tired.
> => Mother has been working all day. **She must be tired.**
>
> • They haven't contacted us. They can't / receive / our message.
> => They haven't contacted us. **They can't have received our message.**

1. Sapna passed the exam with really good grades. Her family / be /proud of her.

2. She always wears very expensive clothes. She / be / very rich.
3. "I can't find my bag." "You / left / it on the metro."
4. "I can't find one of my ear rings." " You / dropped / it somewhere."
5. They arrived in no time. They / came / by taxi.
6. Our neighbors have a party every other day. They /not be / short of money.
7. My friend did exactly the opposite of what her boss told her to do. She / not / understood / the instructions.
8. Their house is very near the airport. It / not be/ peaceful place to live.
9. They came to live here recently. They not / know many people.
10. You just had a big meal. You / not be / hungry again so soon.

Ex. 2 : Change the sentences given below using 'can't / could not + have + pp' as shown:

> **She certainly did not steal.**
> **=> She could not have stolen.**

1. He certainly did not cheat during the exam.

   ....

2. He certainly did not abuse his power.

   ....

3. Her husband certainly was not cruel to her.

   ....

4. There was heavy rain this morning. The children certainly did not go for a picnic.

   ....

5. Kamla knew nothing about our plans. She certainly did not overhear our conversation.

   ....

Ex.3: Change the sentences given below using 'must + have + past participle" as shown:

> **She certainly learnt spoken English while she lived in England.**
> **=> She must have learnt spoken English while she lived in England.**

1. He was certainly happy.

   ....

2. The baby certainly cried for a long time.

   ....

3. They certainly visited the temples of Varanasi.

   ....

4. Someone certainly followed you when you came here.

   ....

5. She was certainly very pretty when she was young.

   ....

6. Her mother was certainly very religious.

   ....

Ex.4: Change the sentences given below using 'must + have + been + v..ing' as shown:

> **He was certainly dreaming.**
> **=> He must have been dreaming.**

1. He was certainly driving fast.

   ....

2. She was certainly working hard.

   ....

3. The children were certainly playing in the field.

....

4. Rani was certainly swimming in the river when she got caught in the whirlpool.

....

5. There was a woman standing under the tree in front of your house. She was certainly waiting for somebody.

....

6. Rahul hit his car against a tree. He was certainly not looking ahead.

....

Ex. 5 Translate into English:

1. परीक्षा अगले महीने है। कमल ज़रूर दिनभर पढ़ता होगा।
2. रानी बहुत समय पंजाब में रही है; वह अवश्य पंजाबी खाना बनाना जानती होगी।
3. आजकल बहुत गर्मी है। आप अवश्य अक्सर तरणताल जाते होंगे।
4. आजकल घरेलू नौकर आसानी से नहीं मिलते। वह अवश्य घर का सारा काम स्वयं करती होगी।
5. विद्यार्थी इस समय मैदान में खेल रहे होंगे।
6. आजकल वे भारत में मौज मस्ती कर रहे होंगे।
7. मैंने बहुत देर तक द्वार खटखटाया, परन्तु कोई बाहर नहीं आया। अवश्य सब सोए होंगे।
8. आज दोपहर 'हाई–वे' पर एक कार–दुर्घटना हो गई। अवश्य चालक तेज़ चला रहा होगा।
9. इस इत्र की सुगन्ध बहुत अच्छी है। अवश्य महँगा होगा।
10. आप कई साल भारत में थे। आपने ताजमहल अवश्य देखा होगा।
11. इस वर्ष हाईस्कूल की परीक्षा में हमारे स्कूल के सभी छात्र प्रथम श्रेणी

उत्तीर्ण हुए। अवश्य परीक्षा पत्र बहुत सरल रहे होंगे।

12. माता जी अब तक दिल्ली पहुँच गई होंगी।
13. दर्ज़ी अब तक अवश्य कपड़े सी चुका होगा।
14. चौकीदार मुख्य द्वार बन्द करना भूल गया होगा।
15. रातभर बिजली जल रही थी। तुम अवश्य बन्द करना भूल गई होगी।
16. उसका राष्ट्र छात्रवृत्ति के लिए चयन हो गया है। उसने अवश्य परिश्रम किया होगा।
17. दो बज गए हैं। अब तक डाक आ गई होगी।
18. आप तो पहले भी भारत आ चुके हैं। आप अवश्य ही यहाँ के रीति–रिवाजों को जानते होंगे।

Key 1

1. Sapna passed the exam with really good grades. Her family must be proud of her.
2. She always wears very expensive clothes. She must be very rich.
3. "I can't find my bag." "You must have left it on the metro."
4. "I can't find one of my ear rings." " You must have dropped it somewhere."
5. They arrived in no time. They must have come by taxi.
6. Our neighbors have a party every other day. They can't be short of money.
7. My friend did exactly the opposite of what her boss told her to do. She can't have understood the instructions.
8. Their house is very near the airport. It can't be a peaceful place to live.
9. They came to live here recently. They can't know many people.
10. You just had a big meal. You can't be hungry again so soon.

Key 2

1. He could not have cheated during the exam.
2. He could not have abused his power.
3. Her husband could not have been cruel to her.
4. There was heavy rain this morning. The children could not

have gone for a picnic.

5. Kamla knew nothing about our plans. She could not have overheard our conversation.

Key.3

1. He must have been happy.
2. The baby must have cried for a long time.
3. They must have visited the temples of Varanasi.
4. Someone must have followed you when you came here.
5. She must have been very pretty when she was young.
6. Her mother must have been very religious.

Key 4

1. He must have been driving fast.
2. She must have been working hard.
3. The children must have been playing in the field.
4. Rani must have been swimming in the river when she got caught in the whirlpool.
5. There was a woman standing under the tree in front of your house. She must have been waiting for somebody.
6. Rahul hit his car against a tree. He can't have been looking ahead.

Key. 5

1. The exams are next month. Kamal must be studying all day.
2. Rani has lived in Punjab for a long time. She must know how to cook Punjabi food.
3. It is very hot these days. You must be going to the swimming pool often.
4. These days domestic servants are not easily available; she must be doing all the housework herself.
5. The students must be playing in the field at this time.
6. They must be enjoying themselves in India these days.
7. I knocked at the door for a long time but no one came out. Everyone must have been asleep.
8. A car accident took place on the highway this afternoon. The driver must have been driving fast.
9. This perfume smells very good. It must be expensive.

10. You were in India for several years. You must have seen the Taj Mahal.
11. This year all the students of our school passed the high school examination in first division. The exam papers must have been very easy.
12. Mother must have reached Delhi by now.
13. The tailor must have sewn the clothes by now.
14. The watchman must have forgotten to shut the main gate.
15. The light was on all night; you must have forgotten to turn it off.
16. He has been selected for national scholarship. He must have worked very hard.
17. It is 2 O' clock. The mail must have come by now.
18. You have visited India before. You must know the customs and traditions here.

At The Railway Station

A: Good afternoon. May I help you, sir?

B: Could you give me some information about the trains from Varanasi to Delhi? I prefer trains departing during the day.

A: Just a moment please. Yes, there is the Kashi Vishwanath Express. Its departure time is 1.50 p.m. and it arrives in Delhi the next day at 6.40 a.m.

B: Thanks very much. Where can I buy the ticket?

A: At the booking office window, No. 1. Go straight ahead and then turn right. It's just there.

B: Thanks again. Goodbye.

23 may might perhaps

Uses of may, might, perhaps:

1 **May / might are used to express probability of some action or event happening in the present tense.** (*किसी कार्य अथवा घटना की सम्भावना के अर्थ में* प्रयोग)

☞ **For real situations, both 'may' or 'might' can be used.**
(*वास्तविक स्थिति में* **'may' or 'might'** *दोनों का प्रयोग होता है।*)

☞ **For unreal situations, only 'might' can be used, not 'may'.**
काल्पनिक स्थिति में सिर्फ़ **'might'** *का प्रयोग करें,* **'may'** *का नहीं।*

☞ ***Alternatively, could can be used for 'may' or 'might'.**
(*वैकल्पिक रूप से* **could** *का प्रयोगं* **'may' or 'might'** *के स्थान पर होता है।*) **e.g.**

- **It could be true.** *यह सच हो सकता है। =*

= **It may/might be true.** *सम्भवता/शायद यह सच है।*

Comprehension

1. You must stay at home today. Mother might / could need you. — तुम्हें आज घर पर रहना चाहिए। हो सकता है माता जी को तुम्हारी आवश्यकता हो।
2. Let me know when you sell your car. I might buy it. — जब तुम अपनी कार बेचो, तो मुझे बताना। हो सकता है /शायद मैं ही

*(see page 102)

	ख़रीद लूँ।
3. My daughter might visit us in July.	हो सकता है मेरी बेटी जुलाई में हमारे यहाँ आए।
4. I might not be able to come to the wedding as some guests are expected in the house.	हो सकता है मैं शादी में न आ पाऊँ क्योंकि घर में कुछ मेहमान आनेवाले हैं।

■ **Could not be≠ (is not the same as) may / might not be.**
could not be = ***हर हाल में नहीं*** **(probability 0 %)**
may not be / might not be = probability 50 %
= ***हो भी सकता है, नहीं भी हो सकता***
For example:

• It could not be true.	यह (किसी भी हाल में) सच नहीं हो सकता।
• It may/might not be true	शायद यह सच नहीं (परन्तु सच हो भी सकता है।) **(see pg.117)**

■ **'May' to mean permission (*इजाज़त के अर्थ में*):**

☞ **Also 'might' is used as past tense of 'may' to imply permission.**

1. Mother said to the child, 'you may go out and play with your friends now". (permission).	माँ ने बच्चे से कहा,' अब तुम बाहर जाकर अपने मित्रों के साथ खेल सकते हो।
• Mother told the child that he might go out and play with his friends.	माँ ने बच्चे को बताया कि वह बाहर जाकर अपने मित्रों के साथ खेल सकता था।
3. "You may spend this money as you like", said the father	पिता ने पुत्र से कहा,' तुम यह पैसा जैसे चाहो ख़र्च कर सकते हो।'

to his son.	हो।'
• Father told the son he might spend that money as he liked.	पिता ने पुत्र को बताया कि वह उस पैसे को जैसे चाहे ख़र्च कर सकता था।

■ **Might - to make a suggestion** (*सुझाव के अर्थ में*)

1. It is very cold. You might turn the radiator on.	बहुत ठण्ड है। रेडियेटर लगा लो।
2. You might give some thought to what you are doing.	तुम जो कर रहे हो उस पर ज़रा विचार कर लो।
3. You might visit your parents more frequently (suggestion).	तुम अपने माता पिता को मिलने कुछ अधिक जाया करो।
4. You might talk to your boss regarding study leave.	तुम अपने अधिकारी से पढ़ाई हेतू अवकाश की बात कर लो।

Compare and comprehend:

could not	**may/might not**
1a. He could not have worked hard enough to pass the Entrance Test. उसने प्रवेश परीक्षा मे उत्तीर्ण होने हेतु पर्याप्त परिश्रम नहीं किया होगा।	1b. He might not have worked hard enough to pass the Entrance Test. हो सकता है उसने प्रवेश परीक्षा मे उत्तीर्ण होने हेतु पर्याप्त परिश्रम न किया हो।
2a. He could not have been of Indian origin. वह भारतीय मूल का नहीं हो सकता।	2b. He might not have been of Indian origin. हो सकता है वह भारतीय मूल का न रहा हो।

Ex.1: Rewrite the sentences given below using 'may/might' with reference to the present:

> **Perhaps she is at home.**
> **=> She may / might be at home.**

1. Perhaps she likes cold coffee. ....
2. Perhaps they are engaged to ....
   be married. ....
3. Perhaps she is telling a lie. ....
4. Perhaps he is a school teacher. ....
5. Perhaps they are watching TV. ....
6. Perhaps mother knows about it. ....

Ex. 2: Rewrite the sentences given below using 'may/might/ with reference to the past:

> **Perhaps he was not in town.**
> **=> He may / might not have been in town.**

1. Perhaps she was having a bath.
   ....
2. Perhaps the children were in the playground.
   ....
3. Perhaps they went to the movies.
   ....
4. Perhaps you dropped your key somewhere.
   ....
5. Perhaps Ram was not invited to the party.
   ....
6. Perhaps she was daydreaming.
   ....

Ex.3: Rewrite the sentences given below using 'may / might' with reference to the future as shown:

> **Perhaps I will go to Sarnath next Sunday.**
> **=> I might go to Sarnath next Sunday.**

1. Anil will perhaps go to Los Angeles to study gemology.

   ....

2. Perhaps they will win the game.

   ....

3. Perhaps we will meet at the concert tonight.

   ....

4. Perhaps she will marry one of her colleagues.

   ....

5. Perhaps the river will be flooded by tomorrow.

   ....

Ex. 4 Write sentences with the help of cues given below. Use 'might' indicating present tense.

> **She / be / her study room.(present)**
> **=> She might be in her study room.**

1. Mother / go / bed / early. ....
2. He /not be/ his office. ....
3. She / come / see the painting exhibition. ....
4. They / visit / us next Sunday. ....
5. Mother / be / kitchen. ....
6. The doctor / be / busy ....

Ex. 5: Make sentences from the words given below. Use might indicating past tense.

> **She / went / doctor. (past)**
> **=> She might have gone to the doctor.**

1. Mother / went / bed / late.

   ....

2. He / left / his watch / restroom.

   ....

3. She / not / knew / about the meeting.

   ....

4. She / went / visit her family.

   ....

5. She / spent / the day with her old friends.

   ....

Ex. 6: Translate into English: Possibility...present / future tense.

1. हो सकता है हम ग्रीष्म अवकाश में हांगकांग जाएँ।
2. हो सकता है वह उसे आपका संदेश देना भूल जाए।
3. हो सकता है कल बारिश हो।
4. हो सकता है आज मेरे पति देर घर से आएँ।
5. हो सकता है जल्दी ही बर्फ़ानी आँधी आए।
6. हो सकता है जब वह अगले सप्ताह दिल्ली आए, वह हमें मिलने न आ सके।
7. हो सकता है आज रात को हम बाहर खाएँ।
8. हो सकता है वे सही हों।
9. हो सकता है वे जानते हों।
10. हो सकता मैं घर पर ही रहूँ और कुछ न करूँ।
11. हो सकता मैं दिनभर समुद्रतट पर पड़ा रहूँ।

Ex. 7: Translate into Englishi: Possibility...past tense.

1. हो सकता है वे बाहर गए हों।
2. हो सकता है वह बीमार रही हो।
3. हो सकता है उन्हें सच्चाई न पता रही हो।
4. हो सकता है वह अपना बटुआ टेक्सी में छोड़ आया हो।
5. हो सकता है उन्हें आपका पत्र न मिला हो।

Key 1

1. She might like cold coffee.
2. They might be engaged to be married.
3. She might be telling a lie.
4. He might be a school teacher.
5. They might be watching TV.
6. Mother might know about it.

Key 2

1. She might have been having a bath.
2. Children might have been in the play ground.
3. They might have gone to the movies.
4. You might have dropped your key somewhere.
5. Ram might not have been invited to the party.
6. She might have been day-dreaming.

Key 3

1. Anil might go to Los Angeles to study gemology.
2. They might win the game.
3. We might meet at the concert tonight.
4. She might marry one of her colleagues.
5. The river might be flooded by tomorrow.

Key 4

1. Mother might go to bed early.
2 He might not be in his office
3. She might come to see the painting exhibition.
4. They might visit us next Sunday.
5. Mother might be in the kitchen.
6. The doctor might be busy.

Key 5

1. Mother might have gone to bed late.
2. He might have left his watch in the restroom.
3. He might not have known about the meeting.
4. She might have gone to visit her family.
5. She might have spent the day with her old friends.

Key 6

1. We might go to Hongkong during the summer holidays.
2. She might forget to give your message to him.
3. It might rain tomorrow.
4. My husband might come home late today.
5. There might be a snowstorm soon.
6. She might not be able to visit us when she comes to Delhi next week.
7. We might eat out tonight.
8. They may be right.
9. They may / might know.
10. I might just stay indoors and do nothing.
11. I might lie down on the beach all day.

Key 7

1. They may / might have gone out.
2. She may / might have been ill.
3. They may / might not have known the truth.
4. He may / might have left his wallet in the taxi.
5. He may / might not have received your letter.

Wisdom from Grandma

- Every cloud has a silver lining.
- Actions speak louder than words.
- Even walls have ears.
- Look before you leap.
- Absence makes hearts grow fonder.

24 Predictions

Given below is a table of expressions used in prediction structures to correspond to the degree of probability.

Degree of probability	Expressions	
100%	certainly, bound to, definitely	निश्चित ही
75%	probably, I should think so, I expect so, , likely to	संभवता, मेरा अनुमान है,
50%	may, might be, perhaps, could	शायद, हो सकता है
25%	probably not, I shouldn't think that, I don't expect that	संभवता ऐसा नहीं, मेरा अनुमान है ऐसा नहीं,
0%	Certainly not, definitely not	ऐसा बिलकुल नहीं,

1. The Indian economic situation will **certainly** improve in the next ten years.
   आगामी दशक में ***निश्चित ही*** भारत की आर्थिक स्थिति सुधरेगी।
2. Consequently more employment opportunities are **bound to** arise.
   परिणामस्वरूप ***निश्चित ही*** अधिक रोज़गार होंगे।
3. The new government will **probably** be able to control inflation.
   नई सरकार ***संभवता*** मँहगाई रोक पाएगी।
4. **I should think** computers will be used all over the country in every sphere in the immediate future.
   मेरा अनुमान है कि निकट भविष्य में देश भर में हर क्षेत्र में कम्प्यूटर प्रयोग

किए जाएँगे।

5. The railway employees **may** go on strike next week.
   शायद अगले हफ़्ते रेल कर्मचारी हड़ताल करेंगे।
6. There will **perhaps** be mid-term elections soon.
   शायद जल्दी ही मध्यावधि चुनाव होंगे।
7. I **don't expect** any war between India and her neighbours
   मुझे उम्मीद नहीं कि भारत और उसके पड़ोसी देशों में कोई युद्ध हो।
8. **I doubt** if he will attend the meeting.
   मुझे नहीं लगता कि वह सभा में आएगा।
9. I **certainly won't** sell the house at that price.
   निश्चित ही मैं इस दाम पर मकान नहीं बेचूँगा।/बेचूँगी।

Ex.1: Complete the sentences using one of the expressions given below:

bound to	**likely to, probably**	**certainly not**
certainly never	**perhaps**	**should expect**
shouldn't think that	**don't expect**	**may / might**

1. He is .... pass the entrance test. (100%)
2. After months of hard work, she is .... be tired. (100%)
3. Since she is going away from her family for the first time, she is .... miss home. (100%)
4. There is.................. be much traffic on the roads on Deepavli.(75%)
5. We are .... go to Agra next Monday. (75%)
6. It is .... not safe in India to drink unboiled water.(100%)
7. They know I am not friends with Rajat. I .... they have invited him to the party.(25%)
8. They will .... be at home at this time. (0%)
9. I .... them to be at home at this time. (25%)
10. She has .... gone to visit her friend. (75%)
11. Mother is...................... leave for Mumbai tomorrow. (75%)

12. I have............................seen her before. (0%)
13. .... we will go to the mountains on vacation this summer. (50%)
14. I .... not be able to visit you when I come to Delhi. (50%)
15. From what I know of Pranav, **I** .... him to donate generously for this purpose. (75%)

Key1

1, 2, 3, bound to	4, 5, 11 likely to
6. certainly	7. shouldn't think that
8 certainly not	9. don't expect
10 probably	12. definitely not
13 perhaps	14 . may / might
15 expect	

Conditional Predictions

■ **'Unless', 'except if', 'as long as' and 'provided that' are used in conditional predictions.**

☞ **As long as' and 'provided that' are used in optimistic predictions.**

☞ **As long as, provided that = but only if.**

☞ **Unless' and 'except if ' are used in pessimistic predictions and warnings.**

☞ **Unless = except if = if not.**

☞ **Even though referring to the future, the present tense will follow them.**

Examples:

1. They may allow you to have the party in their house **provided that / as long as** you don't play loud music.

शायद वे तुम्हें अपने यहाँ दावत करने दें बशर्ते कि तुम ऊँचा संगीत न बजाओ।

2. She will probably lend you her camera **as long as / provided that** you handle it carefully.
   वह तुम्हें सम्भवता अपना कैमरा उधार देगी बशर्ते कि तुम उसे ध्यान से इस्तेमाल करो।
3. You will certainly pass the exam **provided that** you work hard.
   तुम निश्चित ही परीक्षा में उत्तीर्ण होगे बशर्ते कि तुम परिश्रम करो।
4. You will definitely miss the train unless/ except if you hurry.
   जब तक आप जल्दी नहीं करोगे, आपकी गाड़ी निश्चित ही छूट जाएगी।
5. You will certainly miss the train if you don't hurry.
   यदि आप जल्दी नहीं करेंगे, तो आपकी गाड़ी निश्चित ही छूट जाएगी।
6. This gadget could be dangerous if you don't follow the instructions.
   यदि आप अनुदेशों का अनुसरण नहीं करेंगे, तो यह उपकरण ख़तरनाक को सकता है।।
7. There will probably not be any more wars **provided that** nations respect each other's sovereignty.
   संभवता कोई और युद्ध न हो बशर्ते कि राष्ट्र एक दूसरे के अधिराज्य का आदर करें। ।
8. Rani is bound to go abroad **provided that** she gets a scholarship.
   रानी निश्चित ही विदेश जाएगी बशर्ते कि उसे छात्रवृत्ति मिल जाए।

Ex. 1: Rewrite the sentences as shown in the model:

> **She won't pass the entrance test unless she completely dedicates herself to studies.**
> **=> She will pass the entrance test provided that she completely dedicates herself to studies.**

1. You won't be able to complete this task successfully unless you follow the instructions carefully.

2. I will not support him unless he himself asks for my help.
3. I will not accompany you to the party unless I get an invitation.
4. You are not allowed in this gym unless you are a member.
5. You will not reach the station in time unless you go by taxi.
6. You will not be able to speak Hindi fluently unless you make many Indian friends.

Ex. 2: Translate into English:

1. तुम यह काम सफलतापूर्वक पूरा नहीं कर पाओगे जब तक तुम सब हिदायतों का ध्यान से अनुसरण नहीं करोगे।
2. बहुत-सी कम्पनियों के जल्दी ही बन्द हो जाने की सम्भावना है जब तक कि अर्थव्यवस्था में कोई चमत्कार ही न हो।
3. अगले चुनाव में कांग्रेस जीत सकती है बशर्ते कि वे अतिविस्त त भ्रष्टाचार पर क़ाबू पा लें।
4. आगामी पूर्णिमा की रात को हम नौका विहार के लिए *जाएँगे* बशर्ते बारिश या बर्फ़ न पड़े।
5. जब तक आपका जन्म इस राज्य में न हुआ हो, आप यहाँ ज़मीन-जायदाद नहीं ख़रीद सकते।
6. आप जल्दी ही धाराप्रवाह अंग्रेज़ी बोल पाएँगे बशर्ते आप बहुत से विदेशी मित्र बनाएँ।

Key 1

1. You will be able to complete this task successfully provided that you follow the instructions carefully.
2. I will support him provided that he himself asks for my help.
3. I will accompany you to the party provided that I get an invitation.
4. You are allowed in this gym provided thaf you are a member.
5. You will reach the station in time provided that you go by taxi.
6. You will be able to speak Hindi fluently provided that you make many Indian friends.

Key 2

1. You won't be able to complete this task successfully unless you

follow the instructions carefully.

2. Many companies are likely to close down soon unless there is some miracle in the economy.
3. Congress could win the coming elections provided that they control rampant corruption.
4. We shall go for a boat ride on coming fullmoon night provided that there is no rain or snowfall.
5. You cannot buy property here unless you were born in this State .
6. You will be able to speak English fluently very soon provided that you make many foreign friends.

At The Doctor's - 1

Patient : Good evening.
Doctor : Good evening. What's the matter?
Patient : I have got a terrible pain in my right knee.
Doctor : How long have you had it?
Patient : Oh, about two weeks.
Doctor : Is there any swelling?
Patient : Yes, doctor. There is some swelling around the knee. There is a shooting pain while walking or bending.
Doctor : Well, try these tablets. Take one twice daily and drink plenty of water. Come back again after one week and if here is no improvement, I shall change the medicine. I may have to give you injections. Meanwhile go to Ward number ten. Meet the physiotherapist. She will show you some exercises. Do them regularly and don't worry. You will get well soon.
Patient : Thanks, doctor. Goodbye.

Related Vocabulary: 447-449

25 Sense verbs

look, seem, feel, taste, sound, smell

1. It looks new.	यह नया लगता है / दिखता है।
2. He looks happy	वह खुश लगता है / दिखता है।
3. Your dress looks expensive.	तुम्हारी पोशाक महँगी लगती है।
4. She seems to be rich.	वह धनी प्रतीत होती है।
5. He seems to be fond of dogs.	वह कुत्तों का शौकीन लगता है।
6. They seem to have lived abroad.	वे विदेश में रहे लगते हैं।
7. It feels cold in here.	यहाँ अन्दर ठण्ड लग रही है।
8. This table feels sticky.	यह मेज़ चिपचिपा लग रहा है।
9. The floor feels slippery.	फ़र्श फिसलना लग रहा है।
10. This fabric feels rough.	यह कपड़ा खुरदुरा लगता है।
11. This perfume smells terrific.	यह इत्र बहुत बढ़िया महकता है। /महक रहा है।
12. This place smells of cigarettes.	इस जगह सिगरेट की महक आ रही है।
13. He did not sound honest.	यह ईमानदार नहीं लगा।
14. This plan does not sound good.	यह योजना बहुत अच्छी नहीं लग रही।
15. My new guitar sounds horrible.	मेरे नए गिटार की ध्वनि बहुत ख़राब लगती है।
16. These mangoes taste very good.	ये आम बहुत स्वादिष्ट लग रहे हैं।

17. The bread tastes stale. — यह डबलरोटी बासी लग रही है।
18. This food tastes tinned. — यह खाना डिब्बे का लगता है।
19. This curry tastes Indian. — यह 'करी' भारतीय लग रही है।

ध्यान दें :—

1 **'see', 'hear', 'smell'. 'taste'** ***के साथ*** **present continuous tense** ***का प्रयोग नहीं करते।***

- Do you see that red car over there? (√)
- Are you seeing that red car over there? (x)
- This place smells of rotten eggs.(√)
- This place is smelling of rotten eggs. (x)
- This curry tastes delicious. (√)
- This curry is tasting delicious. (x)
- I hear some funny sound. (√)
- I am hearing some funny sound.. (x)

2 **'look', 'feel'** ***के साथ यदि वाक्य में*** **'now', 'these days'** ***हो, तो*** **present simple** ***और*** **present continuous tense** ***दोनों का प्रयोग संभव है।***

- She looks well these days. (√)
- She is looking well these days. (√)
- I feel strong now. (√)
- I am feeling strong now. (√)

Ex. 1 Translate into English.

1. वह उदास और खिन्न लगी। (दिखने में)
2. वह उदास और खिन्न लगी।(आवाज़ से)
3. तुम्हारा 'केक' बहुत बढ़िया महक रहा है।

4. इस कॉफ़ी का स्वाद कुछ अजीब-सा लग रहा है।
5. तुम ठीक तो हो? तुम्हारा चेहरा बहुत उतरा हुआ लग रहा है।
6. भोजन बहुत स्वादिष्ट लगा।
7. सुबह से माँ कुछ नाराज़ लग रही हैं।
8. कभी-कभी पके हुए कटहल का स्वाद बहुत ख़राब होता है।
9. राहुल अपने नए काम को लेकर बहुत उत्तेजित लगा।
10. इस पेड़ की पत्तियाँ मख़मली लगती हैं।

Key 1

1. She looked depressed.
2. She sounded depressed.
3. Your cake smells terrific.
4. This coffee tastes somewhat strange.
5. Are you okay? You look so pale.
6. The meal tasted delicious.
7. Since the morning mother seems somewhat annoyed.
8. Sometimes ripe jackfruit tastes horrible.
9. Rahul sounded very excited about his new job.
10. The leaves of this tree feel velvety.

So Do I / Let's + infinitive

A. I don't feel like cooking today.
B. Neither do I.
A. Let's eat out.
B. Okay.
A. I feel like going to the movies today.
B. So do I. Let's first go to a restaurant and eat. Then we can watch a film.
A. Good! Let's go.

26 Talking about time

1. What time is it? कितने बजे है?
2. It is.... ....बजे है।
3. It is 1.00 / one 0'clock. एक बजा है।
4. It is 1.30 / one-thirty / half past one. डेड़ बजा है।
5. It is 2.30 / two thirty / half past two. ढाई बजे हैं।
6. 1.15 / one fifteen / a quarter past one. सवा एक
7. 2.15 / two fifteen / a quarter past two. सवा दो
8. 12.45 / twelve fortyfive / a quarter to one. पौना एक
9. 1.45 / one fortyfive / a quarter to two. पौने दो
10. 1.10 / one ten / ten past one एक बजकर दस मिनट
11. 12.50 / twelve fifty / ten to one. एक बजने में दस मिनट
12. 2.20 / two twenty twenty past two. दो बजकर बीस मिनट
13. 1.40 / one forty / twenty to two. दो बजने में बीस मिनट

> Q. How long does it take (subject) (to do something)?
> A. It takes (subject)(time) (to do something) .

Q How long does it take you to get ready?
आपको तैयार होने में कितना समय लगता है?

A. It takes me ten minutes to get ready.
मुझे तैयार होने में दस मिनट लगते हैं।

Q How long did it take you to write this book?
आपको यह पुस्तक लिखने में कितना समय लगा?

A It took me seven years to write this book.
मुझको यह पुस्तक लिखने में सात साल लगे।

Q. How long has it taken him to achieve his goal?
उसको अपना लक्ष्य प्राप्त करने में कितना समय लगा है?

A. It has taken him twenty years to achieve his goal.
उसको अपना लक्ष्य प्राप्त करने में बीस वर्ष लगे हैं।

Q. How long will it take them to do this work?
उन्हें यह काम करने में कितना समय लगेगा?

A. It will take them at least one week to do it.
उन्हें यह काम करने में कम-अज़-कम एक हफ़्ता लगेगा?

(For more examples see the pages 59, 62, 69)

Ex.1: Write sentences using 'has / have been v-ing' and the cues given below.

1. How long / you / cook?..
2. How long / you / write / books?..
3. How long / you / save / for the trip?...
4. How l ong / your sister / learn / Spanish?.......................................
....

Ex.2: Write sentences using 'has / have + past participiple' and the cues given below.

1. How long / you had this dress? ....
2. How long / you know Jigyasa. ....
3. How long / your daughter / be in the U.S.? ....
....
4. How long / you lived / in Indiai?..

Ex.3: Translate into English:

1. आप भारत में कब से हैं?
2. मैं भारत में तीन महीने से/जनवरी से हूँ।
3. आप भारत कब आए?

4. मैं सन् २०२० में भारत आया।

5. आपने अंग्रेज़ी कितना समय सीखी हैं?

6. मैंने अंग्रेज़ी दस वर्ष सीखी हैं।

7. आप अंग्रेज़ी कितने समय से सीख रहे हैं?

8. मैं अंग्रेज़ी दस वर्ष से सीख रहा/रही हूँ।

9. आपने अंग्रेज़ी कब सीखी?

10. मैंने अंग्रेज़ी दस वर्ष पहले सीखी।

11. उसके पास यह घर कबसे है?

12. उसके पास यह घर छह साल से/ 2006 से है।

13. वे कितने समय से एक-दूसरे को जानते हैं?

14. वे लम्बे समय से/बचपन से एक-दूसरे को जानते हैं।

Key 1

1. How long have you been cooking? 2. How long have you been writing books? 3. How long have you been saving for the trip? 4. How long has your sister been learning Spanish?

Key 2

1. How long have you had this dress? 2. How long have you known Jigyasa.3. How long has your daughter been in the U.S.? 4. How long have you lived in India?

Key 3

1. How long have you been in India? 2. I have been in India for three months / since January. 3. When did you come to India? 4. I came to India in 2010. 5. How long have you learnt English? 6. I have learnt English for ten years. 7. How long have you been learning English? 8. I have been learning English for ten years. 9. When did you learn English ? 10. I learnt English ten years ago. 11. How long has he had this house? 12. He has had this house for six years / since 2006. 13. How long have they known each other? 14. They have known each other for a long time/since childhood.

27 Causative Verb

प्रेरणार्थक क्रिया

Have passive structure (i.e. to have something done by somebody).

जब कोई कार्य स्वयं न करके किसी और से करवाया जाता है तो विभिन्न काल-ढाँचे कुछ इस प्रकार है।

■ **Present Indefinite Tense**

subj. + have / get + obj. + pp + by agent

aff.:	I have / get my clothes sewn by tailor.	मैं अपने कपड़े दर्ज़ी से सिलवाती हूँ।
neg.:	I don't have my clothes sewn by tailor.	मैं अपने कपड़े दर्ज़ी से नहीं सिलवाती।
int.:	Do you have your clothes sewn by tailor?	क्या आप अपने कपड़े दर्ज़ी से सिलवाती हैं?

■ Use of the causative verb in other tenses: Follow the above given examples to make negative and interrogative sentences.

- **Past Habitual Tense**
  I used to have my clothes sewn by tailor. — मैं अपने कपड़े दर्ज़ी से सिलवाती थी।
- **Past Simple Tense**
  I had my clothes sewn by tailor. — मैंने अपने कपड़े दर्ज़ी से सिलवाए।

- **Present Perfect Tense**

I have had my clothes sewn by tailor — मैंने अपने कपड़े दर्ज़ी से सिलवाए हैं।

- **Past Perfect Tense**

I had had my clothes sewn by the tailor. — मैंने अपने कपड़े दर्ज़ी से सिलवाए थे।

- **Future simple**

She will have a drama staged by her college students in January. — वह जनवरी में अपने कॉलिज के विद्यार्थियों से एक नाटक करवाएगी।

- **Planned Future Activity**

She is planning to have a drama staged by her college students in January. — वह जनवरी में अपने कॉलिज के विद्यार्थियों से एक नाटक करवाने की योजना बना रही है।

- **Present Compulsion Structure**

I have to have my clothes sewn by tailor. — मुझको अपने कपड़े दर्ज़ी से सिलवाने पड़ते हैं।

- **Past Compulsion Structur**

I had to have my clothes sewn by tailor. — मुझको अपने कपड़े दर्ज़ी से सिलवाने पड़े।

- **Future Compulsion Structure**

I will have to have my clothes sewn by tailor. — मुझको अपने कपड़े दर्ज़ी से सिलवाने पड़ेंगे।

- **probability and have passive**

I may have to have my clothes sewn by tailor. — मुझको अपने कपड़े दर्ज़ी से सिलवाने पड़ सकते हैं।

- **Continuative Action**

He keeps getting his work done by others. — वह अपना काम दूसरों से करवाता रहता है।

☞ ध्यान दें- वाक्य लिखने या बोलने में **agent** का प्रयोग आवश्क नहीं।

Ex. 1: Rewrite the sentences given below using 'have passive' as shown:

> **I washed my hair myself.**
> **=> I had my hair washed at the beauty parlor.**

1. She teaches her children herself. ....
2. I clean my house myself. ....
3. She is repairing her watch herself..
4. He is washing his car himself. ....
5. We used to decorate our house at Diwali ourselves. ....
....
6. We used to wash our dirty clothes ourselves. ....
....
7. She baked this cake herself. ....
8. I trained my dog myself. ....
9. I have watered these plants myself.
....
10. Mother has cooked the food herself. ....
11. I shall embroider this tablecover myself. ....
....
12. Anil will make this piece of furniture himself. ....
....
13. I haven't developed the film yet. ....
14. Are you thinking of piercing your ears?..
....
15. They are going to paint their house themselves next month.
....

Ex. 2: Translate into English:

1. रानी अपने बाल श्रृंगार गृह में कटवाती है।
2. क्या आप भी अपने बाल श्रृंगार गृह में कटवाती हैं?
3. नहीं, मैं अपने बाल श्रृंगार गृह में नहीं कटवाती।
4. मैं अपना घर नौकर से साफ़ करवाती हूँ।
5. क्या आप भी अपना घर नौकर से साफ़ करवाती हैं?
6. नहीं, मैं नौकर से घर साफ़ नहीं करवाती।
7. मैंने नौकरानी से बरतन साफ़ करवाए।
8. क्या आपने भी नौकरानी से बरतन साफ करवाए?
9. नहीं, हमने नौकरानी से बरतन साफ़ नहीं करवाए।
10. हमने 'स्टूडियो' में अपनी तस्वीरें खिंचवाई हैं।
11. उन्होंने अपनी तस्वीरें' स्टूडियो' में नहीं खिंचवाई हैं।
12. क्या आपने अपनी तस्वीर 'स्टूडियो' में खिंचवाई है?
13. मैंने यह चित्र एक महान कलाकार से बनवाया था।
14. क्या आपने कभी किसी महान कलाकार से अपना चित्र बनवाया है?
15. नहीं मैंने कभी किसी महान कलाकार से अपना चित्र नहीं बनवाया।
16. मैं अगले हफ़्ते अपनी आँखों की जाँच करवाने की सोच रही हूँ।
17. वे अगले महीने अपना घर दोबारा रंगवाऐंगे।
18. हो सकता है हम रात का खाना 'रेस्टोरन्ट' से मँगवाऐं।
19. मैं अगले हफ़्ते अपने शयनकक्ष के पर्दे बदलवा रही हूँ।
20. मुझे लगता है आपको अपनी रसोई की मरम्मत करवाने की ज़रूरत है।
21. मुझे अपने वातानुकूलन यंत्र की मरम्मत कितनी अकसर करवानी पड़ेगी?
22. व्यक्ति को अपने वातानुकूलन यंत्र की मरम्मत साल में एक बार नियमित रूप से करवानी चाहिए?

Key 1

1. She has her children tutored (by a school teacher).
2. I have my house cleaned. (by the servant)
3. She is having her watch repaired. (by watchmender)

4. He is having his car washed. (at the garage)
5. We used to have our house decorated at Diwali.
6. We used to have our dirty clothes washed (by a washerman)
7. She had this cake baked (at the bakery).
8. I had my dog trained (by a dog trainer).
9. I have had these plants watered (by the gardener).
10. Mother has had the food cooked (by the servant). .
11. I shall have this tablecover embroidered.
12. Anil will have this piece of furniture made (by a carpenter).
13. I haven't had the film developed yet.
14. Are you thinking of having your ears pierced ?
15. They are going to have their house painted next month.

Key 2

1. Rani has her hair cut at the beauty parlour. 2. Do you also have your hair cut at the beauty parlour? 3. No, I do not get my hair cut at the beauty parlour. 4. I get my house cleaned by the servant. 5. Do you also get your house cleaned by the servant? 6. No, I do not get the house cleaned by the servant. 7. I had the utensils cleaned by the maid . 8. Did you also have your utensils cleaned by the maid? 9. No, we did not have our utensils cleaned by the maid . 10. We have had our photographs taken at the studio. 11.They have not had their photographs taken at the studio. 12. Have you had your photograph taken at the studio? 13. I had had this portrait painted by a great painter. 14.Have you ever had your portrait painted by any great painter? 15. No I have never had my portrait painted by any great painter? 16. I am thinking of having my eyes tested next week. 17. They are going to have their house repainted next month. 18. We might have the evening meal brought from the restaurant. 19. I am having the curtains in my bed room changed next week. 20. I think you need to have your kitchen repaired. 21. How often will I have to have the air conditioner serviced? 22. One ought to have the air conditioner serviced regularly once a year.

28 Habit structure

'to be used to'something or activity'

• • • • • • • का आदी होना)

1 **be used to + noun (किसी वस्तु विशेष का आदी होना)**

subject	**+**	**(is, are, am)** **or** **(was, were)** **or** **(will be) etc.***	**+ used to**	**+**	**noun**

2 **be used to + v..ing (किसी क्रिया विशेष का आदी होना)**

subject	**+**	**(is, are, am) + used to + v..ing + ...** **or** **(was, were)** **or** **(will be) etc.**

☞ * इस स्थान पर सहायक क्रिया का चयन **'tense'** और **'mood'** के अनुसार होता है। नीचे दिए गए वाक्यों की सहायता से प्रयोग सीखें।

☞ यही वाक्य नकारात्मक करने के लिए सहायक क्रिया और **'used to'** के बीच में **'not'** का प्रयोग कीजिए।

☞ प्रश्नात्मक बनाने के लिए सहायक क्रिया शुरू में रखें।

■ **Present simple tense: (is, are, am) + used to + noun /activity**

aff.:	I am used to spicy food.	मुझे मसालेदार भोजन की आदत है।
	I am used to eating spicy food.	मुझे मसालेदार भोजन खाने की आदत है।
neg.:	I am not used to spicy food.	मुझे मसालेदार भोजन की आदत नहीं है।
	I am not used to eating spicy food.	मुझे मसालेदार भोजन खाने की आदत नही है।
int.:	Are you used to spicy food?	क्या आपको मसालेदार भोजन की आदत है?
	Are you used to eating spicy food?	क्या आपको मसालेदार भोजन खाने की आदत है?

■ Examples of habit - sentence formation in other tenses and modes. Follow the above given examples to make negative and interrogative sentences.

- **Past Habitual**

I was used to spicy (eating) food. — मुझको मसालेदार भोजन (खाने) की आदत थी।

- **Past simple**

I got used to (eating) spicy food. — मुझको मसालेदार भोजन (खाने) की आदत हो गई।

- **present perfect simple**

I have *gotten used to (eating) spicy food. — मुझको मसालेदार भोजन (खाने) की आदत पड़ गई है।

☞ * **gotten** के स्थान पर **got** भी लगा सकते हैं।

- **past perfect simple**

I had gotten used to (eating) spicy food.	मुझको मसालेदार भोजन (खाने) की आदत पड़ गई थी।

- **future simple**

I **will get** used to (eating) spicy food.	मुझको मसालेदार भोजन (खाने) की आदत पड़ जाएगी।

- **present compulsion structure**

I have to get used to (eating) spicy food.	मुझको मसालेदार भोजन (खाने)का/की आदी होना है।

- **past compulsion structure**

I had to get used to (eating) spicy food.	मुझको मसालेदार भोजन (खाने)का/की आदी होना पड़ा।

- **future compulsion**

I will have to get used to (eating) spicy food.	मुझको मसालेदार भोजन (खाने) का/की आदी होना होगा।

- **probability**

I may have to get used to (eating) spicy food.	हो सकता है मुझको मसालेदार भोजन (खाने) का/ की आदी होना पड़े।

- **advice**

You should get used to (eating) spicy food.	तुमको मसालेदार भोजन (खाने) का/की आदी होना चाहिए।

Compare and comprehend: used to + ininitive : used to v-ing

☞ वाक्य 1a., 2a. से बोध होता है कि व्यक्ति कोई कार्य पहले किया करता था लेकिन अब नहीं करता। (see past habitual structure pg. 39)

☞ वाक्य 1b., 2b. से बोध होता है कि व्यक्ति को कोई कार्य करने की आदत

है। वह पहले भी करता था, वर्तमान में भी करता है और भविष्य में भी करता रह सकता है।

1a. I used to work long hours.
मैं घण्टों काम किया करता था।

1b. I am used to working long hours.
मुझे घण्टों काम करने की आदत है।

2a. She used to live alone.
वह अकेली रहती थी।

2b. She is used to living alone.
उसको अकेली रहने की आदत है।

Ex.1: Change from the past habitual to habit structure as shown:

> **I used to live in a small house.**
> **=> I am used to living in a small house.**

1. I used to take part in debates.

....

2. She used to wear western dresses.

....

3. He used to swim in the river.

....

4. We used to climb up the mountains.

....

5. I used to do my work myself.

....

6. We used to get up early.

....

Ex. 2: Translate into English

1. मुझको रात को पढ़ने की आदत है। 2. हमें ज़मीन पर सोने की आदत है। 3. उन्हें मेहनत करने की आदत नहीं है। 4. उन्हें रेस्टारेण्ट में खाने की आदत

नहीं थी। 5. पहले मुझे खाना पकाने की आदत नहीं थी। शादी के बाद मुझे खाना पकाने की आदत हो गई। 6. मैंने सुना है तुम जापान जा रहे/रही हो। तुम्हें छोटे घर में रहने का आदी होना पड़ेगा। 7. कोई बात नहीं। वहाँ जा कर मैं छोटे घर में रहने का आदी हो जाऊँगा। 8. शायद आपको भारत जाकर ज़मीन पर बैठने की आदत डालनी पड़े।9. अमरीका में आपको अवश्य ही अपना काम अपने आप करने की आदत डालनी पड़ेगी। 10. व्यक्ति को अपने लिए निर्णय स्वयं लेने का आदी होना चाहिए।

Key 1

1. I am used to taking part in debates. 2. She is used to wearing western dresses. 3. He is used to swimming in the river. 4. We are used to climbing up the mountains. 5. I am used to doing my work myself. 6. We are used to getting up early.

Key 2

1. I am used to studying at night. . 2. We are used to sleeping on the floor. 3. They are not used to working hard. 4. They were not used to eating in a restaurant. 5. Formerly I was not used to cooking. After marriage I got used to cooking. 6. I have heard you are going to Japan. You will have to get used to living in a small house. 7. No problem; after going there I will get used to living in a small house. 8. You may have to get used to sitting on the floor after going to India. 9. In America you will certainly have to get used to doing your work yourself. 10. One ought to be used to taking decisions for oneself.

★★★★★

Vocabulary : Natural Calamities

1.	earthquake	अर्थ क्वेक	2.	hurricane	हरिकेन
3.	tornadoes	टोरनेडोज़	4.	volcano	वौलकेनो
5.	drought	ड्राउट	6.	famine	फ़ैमिन

1.भूकंप 2. तूफ़ान, भीण आंधी 3. प्रचण्ड आंधी 4. ज्वाला मुखी 5. सूखा
6. अकाल

29 must + inf.   have to + inf.

compulsion structure

In English compulsion is expressed in two ways:
(1) must + infinitive (2) have to + infinitive

■ **Use of must + infinitive**

Normally when compulsion is self imposed, 'must' is used:
सामान्यता स्वतः अपने पर लागू की गई अनिवार्यता की स्थिति में **must** का प्रयोग करते हैं।

☞ **first person** में **must** अनिवार्यता सूचक अर्थ में **have to** का पर्यायवाची हैं।

☞ **must** का प्रयोग **present** और **future** के लिए होता है।

☞ **must** का **past tense** नहीं होता। **past tense** में अनिवार्यतासूचक अभिव्यक्ति **'had to'** है।

☞ **he, she, it** के साथ **must** के साथ **'s'** नहीं जोड़ा जाता।

Examples:

1. We must leave now. — अब हमें जाना होगा।
2. I must reach home by 6 p.m. — मुझे आज शाम को छह बजे तक घर पहुँचना है।
3. I must help my children with their studies as their exams are drawing near. — मुझे अपने बच्चों को उनकी पढ़ाई में मदद करनी है क्योंकि उनकी परीक्षा पास आ रही है।

☞ नकारात्मक अनिवार्यतासूचक अर्थ में **must not** का प्रयोग ठीक नहीं। **external** और **internal** दोनों वर्ग की अनिवार्यता **don't have to** का प्रयोग करें।

Use of 'have to + infinitive'

1 When compulsion is imposed by some external force:
जब अनिवार्यता किसी बाह्य कारक के द्वारा लागू हो :

Language structure: have to + infinitive

aff.:	**subject + has to / have to + infinitive**
int.:	**Do / Does + subject + have to + infinitive**
neg.	**subject + do or does+ not + have to + infinitive**

☞ **negative of both 'have to + inf.' and 'must + inf.' ' is**
' don't have to' = 'need not'

Comprehension:

1. Even when I am not well, I have to cook for the family.	जब मेरी तबीयत ठीक नहीं होती, मुझे तब भी अपने परिवार के लिए भोजन बनाना पड़ता है।
2. We used to have to wear a uniform at the school.	हमें स्कूल में वर्दी पहननी पडती थी।
3. How much money did you have to spend on your daughter's wedding?	आपको अपनी बेटी के विवाह में कितना धन व्यय करना पड़ा?
4. Since I did not find a rickshaw, I had to walk home.	क्योंकि मुझे रिक्शा नहीं मिला, मुझे पैदल घर जाना पड़ा।
5. The tyre of my bicycle got punctured; I had to get it mended.	मेरी साइकिल का 'टायर' फट गया; मुझे इसे ठीक करवाना पडा।
6. The patient's condition is very	मरीज़ की हालत बहुत ख़राब है; आपको

'must not = ought not to (see pg. 185); inf. = i nfinitive

bad; you will have to take him to hospital immediately.	उसे तुरन्त अस्पताल ले जाना पड़ेगा।
7. She may have to be operated upon next week.	हो सकता है अगले सप्ताह उसका 'आपरेशन' करना पड़े।
8. You don't have to go out at this time. = You need not go out now.	तुम्हारे लिए इस समय बाहर जाना अनिवार्य नहीं। (परन्तु जाना चाहो तो जा सकते हो।)
9. You didn't have to meet him. = You did not need to meet him/her.	तुम्हारे लिए उसे मिलना अनिवार्य नहीं था। (परन्तु यदि मिल लिए, तो कोई हर्ज़ नहीं।)
10. You won't have to wear any formal dress to work .	तुम्हारे लिए काम पर कोई औपचारिक पोशाक पहनना अनिवार्य नहीं होगा। (परन्तु चाहो तो पहन सकते हो।)

2 **Also we use 'have to + infinitive' if there is compulsion to do an activity regularly.**

जो काम हमें अनिवार्यता नियमित अन्तराल पर करने पड़ते हैं, वहाँ भी **'have to + infinitive'** का प्रयोग होता है।

1. I have to dress this wound twice a day.	मुझे दिन में दो बार इस जख़्म की पट्टी करनी होती है।
2. I have to cook three times a day.	मुझे दिन में तीन बार खाना पकाना होता है।

Ex .1: Write compulsion structure sentennces in required tenses using the cues given below:

> **I / get up / 5 a.m. / every day.**
> **=> I have to get up at 5 a.m. every day.**

don't have to = need not

1. They / not / go so early.
2. You / be / 18 years / to drive in India.
3. We / waited / 2 hours for the bus.
4. She / will / make a phone call.
5. She / asked / several people for directions.
6. He / may / work under my supervision.
7. She / has worn / glasses since she was a little girl.
8. I / used to close / windows every evening.
9. I / work / very hard to support my family.
10. Administrators / confront difficult situations every day..

Ex. 2: Fill in the blanks with must / have to:

1. It is getting late. I .... go now.
2. It is getting late. I .... go now otherwise mother will be angry.
3. "Exams are coming near. I .... study hard.
4. I have run out of money. I .... go to the bank today.
5. I .... write this letter before I do anything.
6. You .... tell them the truth.
7. Do all Indian girls ....wear a saree after marriage?
8. In our country we don't .... learn English to study at the university.

Ex. 3: Translate into English:

1. मेरी निगाह कमज़ोर हैं। मुझे हर वक़्त ऐनक पहननी पड़ती है। 2. तीसरे सत्र के अन्त में आप सब को परीक्षा देनी पड़ेगी। 3. राबर्ट बहुत हिन्दी नहीं जानता।आपको उसके साथ बहुत धीरे बोलना होगा। 4. मैं आज सुबह बैंक गया था। मुझे कुछ पैसा निकालना था। 5. मुझे रोज़ सुबह बहुत जल्दी उठना पड़ता है। 6. आपको कितना समय मेरी प्रतीक्षा करनी पड़ी? 7. आपको ठीक कितने बजे जाना है? 8. मुझे तुरन्त जाना पड़ेगा। मुझे पन्द्रह मिनट के भीतर किसीको मिलना है। 9. तुम्हें डॉक्टर के पास कितने बजे जाना है? 10. उसे अपनी शिक्षा चालू रखने के लिए दो अल्पकालिक काम करने पड़ते हैं। 11. प्रबन्धकों को हर रोज़ मुश्किल हालात का सामना करना पड़ता है। 12. आपको कितनी दूर पैदल चलकर जाना पड़ा? 13. तुम्हें कितने बजे हवाई अड्डे पर होना था। 14. मुझे अगले सप्ताह दादा.दादी से मिलने जाना होगा।

Key 1

1. They don't have to go so early. 2. You have to be 18 years to drive in India. 3. We had to wait for 2 hours for the bus. 4. She will have to make a phone call. 5. She had to ask several people for directions. 6. He may have to work under my supervision. 7. She has had to wear glasses since she was a little girl. 8. I used to have to close windows every evening. 9. I have to work very hard to support my family. 10. Administrators have to confront difficult situations every day.

Key 2

1, 3, 4, 5 must ; 2, 6,7,8, have to

Key 3

1. My eyesight is weak. I have to wear glasses all the time. 2. At the end of the third semester, all of you will have to take a test. 3. Robert doesn't know much Hindi. You will have to speak with him very slowly . 4. I went to the bank this morning. I had to withdraw some money. 5. I have to get up very early every day. 6. How long did you have to wait for me? 7. What time exactly do you have to go? 8. I must leave immediately. I have to meet someone in fifteen minutes. 9. What time do you have to go to the doctor? 10. She has to do two part-time jobs to continue her education. 11. Managers have to confront difficult situations every day. 12. How far did you have to go on foot? 13. What time did you have to be at the airport? 14. I will have to visit my grandparents next week.

Let's Go To A Restaurant

Savita : Let's go out today?
Sudhir : That's fine. Let's go to a restaurant.
Savita : Which one?
Sudhir : How about 'Kesari'?
Savita : Kesari? Which one's that?
Sudhir : Don't you remember? The one that serves the most delicious 'missi-roti'. We went there once. It's at Gydolia.

30 had better It is time

☞ ध्यान दें – यद्यपि **'had'** **'have'** का **past tense** है, तो भी **had better** + **inf. without 'to'** का यह प्रयोग वर्तमान और भविष्य के अर्थ में होता है।

Aff.: **subj. + had better + infinitive without 'to'**

- You **had better go** by taxi. अच्छा हो कि आप 'टेक्सी' से जाएँ। (अर्थात आपको 'टेक्सी' से जाना चाहिए। ऐसा न करने से आपको परेशानी हो सकती है।)

Neg.: **subj. + had better + not + infinitive without 'to'**

- You **had better not go** by bus. अच्छा हो कि आप 'बस' से न जाएँ। (अर्थात आपको 'बस' से नहीं जाना चाहिए। बस से जाने से आपको परेशानी हो सकती है।)

☞ सामान्यता प्रश्नवाचक वाक्यों में had better का प्रयोग नहीं होता।

☞ परन्तु नकारात्मक प्रश्नवाचक (negative interrogative) वाक्यों में इसका प्रयोग होता है।

☞ **had better + infinitive** और **should** समानार्थी हैं। परन्तु प्रयोग में सुक्ष्म भेद है। **had better + infinitive** का प्रयोग उस स्थिति विशेष में करते हैं जब अभिप्राय कुछ ऐसा हो कि अमुक व्यक्ति के लिए अमुक कार्य अमुक समय पर करना या न करना ज़्यादा ठीक रहेगा (अन्यथा व्यक्ति को परेशानी हो सकती है।),

Comprehension:

1. You look very tired. You **had better not** go to school today. तुम बहुत थके लग रहे हो। अच्छा हो कि तुम आज स्कूल न जाओ।

2. You **had better not** have a late night party on the terrace. The neighbors will be disturbed.	तुम्हें देर रात तक छत पर दावत नहीं करनी चाहिए। पड़ोसियों को परेशानी होगी।
3. You **had better wash** the wound and put a bandage on it.	अच्छा हो कि तुम घाव धोकर उसपर पट्टी बाँध लो।
4. Rani is suffering from fever; she **had better** go to bed early tonight.	रानी को बुखार है। उसे आज रात को जल्दी सो जाना चाहिए।

■ इसी से मिलते जुलते अर्थ में एक और भाषा ढाँचा प्रयोग किया जाता है :

It is time X did Y (= It is time for X to do Y)

☞ *यहाँ भी* **past tense** *का प्रयोग* **future** *और* **present** *के लिए है,* **past** *के लिए नहीं।*

• **It is time** I went to sleep. = **it is time** for me to sleep.	अब मुझे सोना चाहिए।(अब मेरा सोने का समय हो गया है।)

☞ *यह सामान्यता शिकायत या आलोचना करते समय, या फिर चेताने के अर्थ में प्रयोग करते हैं*

• You are still at home ! **It is time** you went to office.
तुम अभी तक घर पर हो? अब तुम्हें दफ़्तर जाना चाहिए।
(= अब और देर नहीं करनी चाहिए।)

■ *जब शिकायत या आलोचना या फिर चेताने में सख़्ती का कुछ पुट हो, तो* **time** *से पहले* **high** *या* **about** *का प्रयोग करते हैं।*

- **It is + <u>high time</u> + X did Y.**
- **It is + <u>about time</u> + X did Y.**

Comprehension:

1. **It is high time** the Prime Minister did something to control prices.	अब तो प्रधानमंत्री को मँहगाई पर क़ाबू पाने को कुछ करना ही चाहिए।
2. **It is about time** you bought yourself a new coat.	अब तो तुम्हें अपने लिए नया कोट ख़रीद ही लेना चाहिए।
3. **It is high time** you visited us.	अब तो आपको हमारे यहाँ आना ही चाहिए।
4. **It is high time** you consulted some doctor.	अब तो आपको किसी डाक्टर से सलाह ले ही लेनी चाहिए।

Ex.1: Write sentences using 'had better + infinitive' and the cues given below as shown:

> **you / wear / that jacket**
> **=>You'd better wear that jacket.**

1. She / have / a haircut. ....
2. The typist / type / that letter. ....
3. You / dispose of / the old car. ....
4. I / go / bank. ....
5. You / smoke / less. ....
6. The children / go / bed early tonight. ....
7. The driver / move slowly. ....
8. The Korean athlete / run / faster. ....
9. He / phone / his father. ....
10. They / change / jobs. ....
11. You / repaint / doors and windows. ....
12. You / reserve seats / concert. ....
13. You / keep quiet ....
14. you / get up / now...

Ex. 2: Complete the sentences given below using 'had better + infinitive':

1. I haven't started cooking dinner yet.
   ....now
2. If you haven't reserved seats for the concert yet
   ....today
3. If she hasn't typed the letter yet.
   ....right away.
4. If you haven't fixed up an appointment with the dentist yet............
   ....soon
5. I haven't registered myself with the Foreigners' Registration Office yet. ....this week
6. You have not started preparing for the examination yet.
   ....right away
7. You are putting on weight .
   ....cut down on sugar
8. It is getting late . We ....go now.

Ex. 3: Rewrite the sentences given below using 'it's time, it's about time, it's high time' etc as shown:

> **My exams start next month and I haven't even begun studying yet.**
> **=> It's time I began studying for the exams.**

1. It is past midnight. We should sleep now.
   ....
2. It is the third week of June and we haven't had any rains.
   ....
3. It is ages since you wrote to your father. I think you should

write to him now.

....

4. Rising prices are making it difficult for the common man to make both ends meet. The Prime Minister should take some measures to control inflation.

....

5. Your coat is worn out and is covered in holes. You should buy yourself a new coat.

....

6. The train is already late by thirty minutes. If it does not come now, we will miss the connecting train.

....

7. Due to increasing pollution more and more people are suffering from breathing problems. The Health Minister should do something to control pollution.

....

8. The guests are arriving in an hour; you have'nt begun preparing food yet.

....

9. Monsoons are expected in about a week's time. Every time it rains, the ceiling of this room leaks.

....

10. She must reach Germany next month and she hasn't got her passport yet.

....

Ex. 4: Translate into English:

1. भारत में बारिश के मौसम में अच्छा हो कि आप पानी उबालकर पीएँ।
2. अगर तुम स्कूल में अनुपस्थिति नहीं चाहते तो ज़रा जल्दी करो।
3. अच्छा हो कि तुम धूम्रपान छोड़ दो। यह तुम्हारे स्वास्थ्य को हानि पहुँचा रहा है।

4. किसी गुरूद्वारे के अन्दर जाने से पहले सिर अवश्य ढकें।
5. अब हमें जाना चाहिए।
6. अब तो आपको छत ठीक करवा ही लेनी चाहिए।
7. अब तो उसे समझ लेना चाहिए कि जीवन की वास्तविकता कोई काल्पनिक कहानी से नहीं है।
8. अब तो हमें परीक्षा के लिए पढ़ना शुरू कर ही देना चाहिए। (अर्थात पहले ही बहुत देर हो चुकी है।)

Key 1

1. She had better have a haircut.
2. The typist had better type that letter.
3. You had better dispose of the old car.
4. I had better go to the bank.
5. You had better smoke less.
6. Children had better go to bed early tonight.
7. The driver had better move slowly.
8. The Korean athlete had better run faster.
9. He had better phone his father.
10. They had better change jobs.
11. You had better repaint the doors and windows.
12. You had better reserve seats for the concert.
13. You had better keep quiet.
14.` You had better get up now.

Key 2

1. I'd better start cooking now.
2. you'd better do it today.
3. she'd better type it right away.
4. you'd better do it soon.
5. I'd better do it this week.
6. You'd better start right away.
7. You'd better cut down on sugar.
8. We'd better go now.

Key 3

1. It is high time we slept.

2. It is high time it rained.
3. It is high time you wrote a letter to your father.
4. It is about time the Prime Minister took some measures to control inflation.
5. It is high time you bought yourself a new coat.
6. It is high time the train came.
7. It is high time the Health Minister did something to control pollution.
8. It is time you began preparing food .
9. It is about time the ceiling was repaired.
10. It is high time she got her passport.

Key 4

1. In India, during the rainy season, you had better drink boiled water.
2. You had better hurry up if you don't want to miss school.
3. You had better stop smoking; it is harming your health.
4. You had better cover your head before you enter a Sikh Temple.
5. We had better go now.
6. It is about time you had the ceiling repaired.
7. It is high time she realized the reality of life is not any fiction.
8. It is about time we started studying for the exams.

Wisdom from Grandma

- Blood is thicker than water.
- Honesty is the best policy.
- Silence is golden.
- Love is blind.
- Still waters run deep.

31 Keep on + v..ing

☞ **keep on = do something continuously or repeatedly.**

keep on की जगह **go on** का प्रयोग भी होता है।

☞ **go on** का प्रयोग एक प्रकार की हकारत लिए रहता है।

- He went on eating. वह खाता गया।
- She goes on talking. वह बोलती जाती है।

☞ (अर्थात उस का खाना, बोलना कुछ ज़रूरत से ज़्यादा था जो देखने, सुननेवाले को अखरा)

☞ **keep on** के साथ **on** का प्रयोग अनिवार्य नहीं, परन्तु अपने इस अर्थ में **go** के साथ **on** का प्रयोग अनिवार्य है।

■ **Present Indefinite** **keep / keeps on + v..ing**

aff.:	**subj. + keep / keeps on + v..ing + obj. (if any)**
int.:	**Do or Does + subj. + keep on + v..ing + obj. (if any)**
neg.:	**subj. + do or does + not + keep on + v..ing + obj. (if any)**

- He keeps on singing. वह गाता रहता है।
- Does he keep on singing? क्या वह गाता रहता है?
- He doesn't keep on singing. वह गाता नहीं रहता ।

Examples of sentence construction in other tenses. Follow the above given examples to make negative and interrogative sentences.

- **past habitual**

He used to keep on singing. वह गाता रहता था।

- **past simple**

He kept trying. वह प्रयास करता रहा।

- **future simple**

He will keep trying. वह प्रयास करता रहेगा।

- **advice: present tense**

He should keep studying. उसे पढ़ते रहना चाहिए।

- **advice: past tense**

He should have kept trying. उसे प्रयास करते रहना चाहिए था।

- **present compulsion**

She has to keep cooking. उसे खाना पकाते रहना पड़ता है।

- **past compulsion**

They had to keep digging all day. उन्हें दिन भर खोदते रहना पड़ता था।

- **future compulsion**

We will have to keep searching. हमें ढूँढते रहना पड़ेगा।

Will we have to keep searching? क्या हमें ढूँढते रहना पड़ेगा?

We will not have to keep searching. हमें नहीं ढूँढते रहना पड़ेगा।

- **Presumptive perfect**

They must have kept following the thief. वे चोर का पीछा करते रहे होंगे।

■ **Presumptive negative *और* interrogative *वाक्य रचना में* 'must' *के स्थान पर* 'could' *का प्रयोग करते हैं।***

int.: **could + subj. + have + kept on + v..ing + obj. (if any)?**

- Could they have kept on following the thief? क्या वे चोर का पीछा करते रहे होंगे?

neg.: **subj. + could not have + kept on + v..ing + obj. (if any)**

- They could not have kept वे चोर का पीछा नहीं करते रहे होंगे।

following the thief.

Ex. 1: Complete the sentences given below as shown . Use the verbs and tense given in the brackets.

They .... (visit).........us. (present simple tense) =>They keep visiting us.

1. It ....(rain)........ here from June to October. (present simple tense)
2. Please ....(explain).......this to me. (present simple tense)
3. He ....(tell).........me about his family all the time. (past habitual)
4. The baby ....(cry)............ all night. (past habitual)
5. Those men ....(work)............hard for several days. (past simple)
6. The old man ....(cough).................. (past simple)
7. Grandfather ....(.go, narrate) .... stories one after the other. (past simple)
8. We should ....(help)......... them. (advice)
19. We .... (study)............... until midnight. (past compulsion)
10. You ....(try).... ....(future compulsion)
11. Rani .... (drive)..... .... all night. (negative presumption)

Ex. 2: Translate into English:

1. मेरी छोटी बेटी मुझे काम करते हुए सदैव परेशान करती रहती है। 2. वह सबकी आलोचना करता रहता है। यह काफ़ी लज्जाजनक है। 3. वह बार-बार एक ही ग़लती करती रहती है। यह बहुत कुंठाकारी है। 4. माँ मुझे हमेशा बड़ों के प्रति मेरे फ़र्ज़ याद दिलाती रहती थीं। मुझे बहुत गुस्सा आता था। 5. माँ रात भर कपड़े सीती रहीं। 6. वे सब हँसते रहे। 7. मुझे लगता है, रात भर बारिश होती रहेगी। 8. लोग मंत्री जी से मिलने के लिए घास के मैदान में बैठे रहे। 9. आपको प्रयास करते रहना चाहिए। 10. आप सब को शरणार्थियों की मदद करते रहना चाहिए था। 11. हमें आधी रात तक जागते रहने पड़ा। 12. आपको लम्बे समय तक अभ्यास करते रहना पड़ेगा। 13. वह दिनभर इस बिस्तर पर लेटी रही। 14. वह रातभर उस कोने में बैठा रहा।

Key 1

1. keeps on raining
2. keep explaining
3. used to keep telling
4. used to keep crying
5. kept working
6. kept coughing
7. went on narrating
8. should keep helping
9. had to keep on studying
10. will have to keep on trying.
11. could not have kept driving

Key 2

1. My little daughter keeps disturbing me while I am working. 2. He keeps criticising everybody. It is pretty embarrassing. 3. She keeps making the same mistake again and again. It is very frustrating. 4. Mother used to keep reminding me of my duties towards elders. It was very annoying. 5. Mother kept stitching clothes all night. 6. All of them kept laughing. 7.I think, it will keep raining all night. 8. People kept sitting on the lawn to meet the minister. 9. You should keep on trying. 10. All of you should have kept helping the refugees. 11. We had to keep awake until midnight. 12. You will have to keep pracitising for a long time. 13. She kept lying on this bed all day.14. He kept sitting in that corner all night.

Vocabulary: Society, State

1. patriarchy	पैट्रिआर्की	2. matriarchy	मैट्रिआर्की
3. anarchy	अनार्की	4. oligarchy	ओलिगार्की
5. monarchy	मोनार्की	6. autarchy	औटार्की
7. democracy	डेमोक्रेसी		

1. पितृतन्त्र 2. मातृतन्त्र 3. अराजकता 4. अल्पतन्त्र, धनिक तन्त्र ....
5. राजतन्त्र 6. निरंकुश राजतन्त्र 7. गणतन्त्र, लोकतंत्र.

32 Want

The verb **'want'** can be used in two ways:

1. **To want to do something.** स्वयं कुछ करना चाहना
2. **To want someone to do something.** चाहना कि कोई दूसरा कुछ करे

■ **subj. + want / wants + to infinitive + object (if any)**

aff.	I want	to go out.	मैं बाहर जाना चाहता हूँ।
neg.	I don't want	to go out?	मैं बाहर नहीं जाना चाहता ।
int.	Do you want	to go out?	क्या आप बाहर जाना चाहते हैं?
int. neg.	Don't you want to go out?		क्या आप नहीं चाहते कि आप बाहर जाएँ?

■ **subj. + want / wants + object + to infinitive +**

aff.	I want	Seema to go out.	मैं चाहता हूँ कि सीमा बाहर जाए।
neg.	I don't want	Seema to go out.	मैं नहीं चाहता कि सीमा बाहर जाए।
int.	Do you want	Seema to go out?	क्या आप चाहते हैं कि सीमा बाहर जाए?
int. neg.	Don't you want	Seema to go out ?	क्या आप नहीं चाहते कि सीमा बाहर जाए?

☛ ध्यान रहे कि 'I' के स्थान पर we, you they के साथ भी वाक्य रचना उपरोक्त ही रहेगी। परन्तु यदि subject ' he, she, it' हो, तो wants, doesn't want आदि का प्रयोग करें। जैसे:

aff. He wants ......
neg. He doesn't want ......
int. Does he want ......
int.neg. Doesn't he want ......

Comprehension:

1a.	I want to be a doctor.	मैं डॉक्टर बनना चाहता हूँ।
1b.	Mother wants me to be a doctor.	माँ चाहती हैं कि मैं डॉक्टर बनूँ।
2a.	Rani wants to be a film actress.	रानी फ़िल्म अभिनेत्री बनना चाहती है।
2b.	Rani's father wants her to be a film actress.	रानी के पिता जी चाहते हैं कि वह फ़िल्म अभिनेत्री बने।
3a.	I want to marry Anil.	मैं अनिल से शादी करना चाहती हूँ।
3b.	My parents don't want me to marry Anil.	मेरे माता-पिता नहीं चाहते कि मैं अनिल से शादी करूँ।
4a.	Do you want to go abroad?	आप विदेश जाना चाहते हैं?
4b.	Does your husband want you to go abroad?	क्या आपके पति चाहते हैं कि आप विदेश जाएँ?
5a.	I don't want to drink tea.	मैं चाय नहीं पीना चाहती।
5b.	I don't want my children to drink tea.	मैं नहीं चाहती कि मेरे बच्चे चाय पीयें।
6a.	Don't you want to go to the cinema?	आप सिनेमा नहीं जाना चाहतीं?
6b.	Don't you want your hus-band to go to the cinema?	आप नहीं चाहती कि आपके पति सिनेमा जाएँ?

Ex. 1: Write sentences with the help of the cues given below and the verb 'want' as shown:

> **My sister / I / to help / her**
> **=> My sister wants me to help her**

1. The chldren / I / buy / they / ice-cream. (present simple tense)
2. My husband / I / learn / to drive. (present simple tense)
3. My friends / you / go / picnic. (present simple tense)
4. My teacher / I / write / essay on terrorism. (past simple tense)
5. Our servant / we / lend / he / some money. (present simple tense)
6. His doctor / he / go / hill station. (past simple tense)
7. Her music teacher / she / attend / the concert. (present simple tense)
8. I / they / know the truth. (present simple tense)
9. They / I / repeat. (past simple tense)
10. She /not / I / wait for her. (past simple tense)

Ex. 2: Translate into English:

1. मैं विदेश जाना चाहती हूँ। 2. आज शाम को हम आपके घर आना चाहते हैं। 3.तुम क्या करना चाहते हो? 4. सरकार कीमतें कम करना चाहती है। 5. सब विद्यार्थी छात्रवृत्ति चाहते थे। 6. मज़दूर वेतन में व द्धि चाहते थे। 7. निकट भविष्य में मेरे पिता जी कोई नया व्यापार करना चाहेंगे। 8. मैं चाहती हूँ कि तुम आधे घण्टे में लौट आओ। 9. मैं नहीं चाहती कि तुम मेरी प्रंतीक्षा करो। 10. तुम जो चाहो कर सकते हो। 11. वे जैसे चाहें रह सकते हैं। 12. जितनी जल्दी हो सके, मैं यह देश छोड़ना चाहता हूँ।

Key 1

1. The children want me to buy them an ice-cream.
2. My husband wants me to learn to drive.
3. My friends want you to go for a picnic.
4. My teacher wanted me to write an essay on terrorism.
5. Our servant wants us to lend him some money.
6. His doctor wanted him to go to a hill station.

7. Her music teacher wants her to attend the concert.
8. I want them to know the truth.
9. They wanted me to repeat.
10. She did not want me to wait for her.

Key. 2

1. I want to go abroad. 2. We want to come to your house this evening. 3. What do you want to do? 4. The government wants to reduce the prices. 5, All the students wanted scholarship. 6. The labourers wanted an increase in their wages. 7. In near future my father would want to start a new business. 8. I want you to be back in half an hour. 9. I don't want you to wait for me. 10. You may do what you want. 11. They may live as they want . 12. I want to leave this country as soon as possible.

Commonly-used Non-English Words 

1. ad nauseam (ऐडनॉज़िअम) घ णास्पद होने तक
2. ad valorem (ऐडवैलोरेम) यथा मूल्य
3. inter alia (इन्टर एलिया) अन्य विषयों में
4. locus standi (लोकस स्टैंडाई) घ णास्पद होने तक
5. par excellence (पार एक्सेलां) सर्वोत्कृष्ट
6. per se (पर सें) अपने आप में ; ***यथा स्थिति***
7. prima facie (प्रीमा फ़ेसी) प्रत्यक्षता
8. RSVP (French re'spondez s'il vous plait) (आर एस वी पी) कृपया उत्तर दें।
9. sans (साँ) बिना, बग़ैर
10. sine die (साइन डाई) अनिश्चित काल तक

33 Tell /Ask 'X' to do 'Y'

■ **subject + tell or ask + object + to inf. + object. (if any)**

aff.	**I tell my son to study.**	*मैं अपने बेटे को पढ़ने को कहता /कहती हूँ।*
neg.	**I don't tell my son to study.**	*मैं अपने बेटे को पढ़ने को नहीं कहता /कहती ।*
int.	**Do you tell your son to study?**	*क्या आप अपने बेटे को पढ़ने को कहते /कहती हैं?*

☞ *ध्यान रहे कि* **'I'** *के स्थान पर* **we, you they** *होने पर भी वाक्य रचना उपरोक्त ही रहेगी। परन्तु यदि कर्ता* **' he, she, it'** *हो तो* **tells, asks** *हो जाएगा।*

उपरोक्त उदाहरण **present tense** *में है। जिस काल विशेष में वाक्य रचना हो, उसी के अनुसार* **tell / ask** *से पहले सहायक क्रिया का प्रयोग करें।*

☞ *कुछ अन्य* **verbs** *जैसे* **persuade, advise, encourage, remind, order, enable etc.** *इसी रूपरेखा के अनुसार प्रयोग किए जाते हैं।*

Comprehension:

1. I told Kamla to walk slowly. **(past simple)** — मैंने कमला को धीरे चलने को कहा।
2. I have told the servant to bring fruit from the market. — मैंने नौकर को बाज़ार से फल लाने को कहा है।

(present perfect)

3. Father had told you to get some money from the bank. **(past perfect)**	पिता जी ने तुम्हें बैंक से कुछ पैसे लाने को कहा था।
4. Mother will ask you to cook the evening meal. **(future simple)**	माँ तुम्हें शाम का भोजन बनाने को कहेंगी।
5. The teacher may ask you to take part in the annual sports. **(subjunctive)**	हो सकता है अध्यापक तुम्हें वार्षिक खेलों में भाग लेने को कहें।

Ex.1: Write sentences using the cues given below in the required tense as shown:

> Doctor / tell / I / stop / smoking. (past simple)
> => Doctor told me to stop smoking.

1. She / ask / I / stay / with her. (past simple)
2. Who / ask you / go there? (past perfect)
3. She / persuade / I / accompany / she / to the exhibition. (past simple)
4. They / ask / she / speak slowly. (past simple)
5. Mother always / advised / I / never / waste time. (past habitual)
6. He / tell / I / meet you. (past simple)
7. She / advise / we / be careful. (present perfect)
8. My daughter / ask / I / keep lunch ready for her by 12 O 'clock. (past simple)
9. A passerby / tell / I / turn right at the first crossing.(past perfect)
10. I / tell / he / to phone / I / as soon as possible. (past simple)

Ex.2: Translate into English:

1. माँ ने मुझे गुस्सा न होने को कहा। 2. दादी ने मुझे उन्हें दस बजे से पहले फ़ोन करने को कहा। 3. अध्यापक ने शिष्यों को नकारात्मक सोच कभी न करने को कहा। 4. डॉक्टर ने मुझे दो दिन के अन्दर उसके पास फिर जाने को कहा। 5. उसने मुझे

जल्दी करने को कहा। 6. उसने मुझे वाहन धीरे चलाने को कहा। 7. उसने मुझे उत्तेजित न होने को कहा। 8. मैंने उसे मुझसे शादी करने को कहा। 9. उसने मुझे अपने लिए इन्तज़ार न करने को कहा। 10. सीमा शुल्क अधिकारी ने मुझे मेरा थैला खोलने को कहा। 11. माँ ने मुझे अपनी बरसाती इस्तेमाल करने की इजाज़त दी। 12. कृपया मुझे शाम को पाँच बजे सभा में जाना याद दिला देना। 13. उसने मुझे उसके बगल वाले पड़ोसियों पर कभी भी विश्वास न करने की चेतावनी दी। 14. मेरी पत्नी ने मुझे नया धन्धा स्वीकार करने को मजबूर किया। 15. मेरे मंगेतर ने मुझे तैरना सीखने के लिए प्रोत्साहित किया। 16. मेरी माता जी ने मुझे सोने में पूंजी निवेश करने को मजबूर किया। 17. उन्होने हमें दस दिन अपने साथ रहने की इजाज़त दी है।

Key 1

1. She asked me to stay with her.
2. Who had asked you to go there?
3. She persuaded me to accompany her to the exhibition.
4. They asked her to speak slowly.
5. Mother always used to advise me never to waste time.
6. He told me to meet you
7. She has advised us to be careful.
8. My daughter asked me to keep lunch ready for her by 12 O' clock.
9. A passerby had told me to turn right at the first crossing.
10. I told him to phone me as soon as possible.

Key 2

1. Mother told me not to get angry. 2. Grandmother told me to phone her before 10 p.m. 3. The teacher told the pupils never to think negative. 4. The doctor told me to go back to him in two days. 5. She told me to hurry up. 6. He asked me to drive slowly. 7. She told me not to be excited. 8. I asked her to marry me. 9. She told me not to wait for her. 10. The customs officer asked me to open my bag. 11. Mother allowed me to use her raincoat. 12. Please remind me to attend the meeting at 5 p.m. 13. He warned me never to trust his next door neighbours. 14. My wife persuaded me to accept the new job. 15. My fiance encouraged me to learn swimming. 16. My mother forced me to invest in gold. 17. They have permitted us to stay with them for 10 days.

34 Preferences

■ किसी वस्तु या कार्य को किसी अन्य वस्तु या कार्य से अधिक पसन्द करने के अर्थ में निम्नलिखित वाक्य रचनाओं का प्रयोग होता है।

1 **subj. + prefer + noun + to + noun**

• She prefers a saree to a salwar-kurta.	वह सलवार कुर्ते की तुलना में साड़ी अधिक पसन्द करती है।
• I prefer yoghurt to milk.	मैं दूध से दही अधिक पसन्द करती हूँ।

2 **subj. + prefer + v..ing + to + v..ing + ...**

• I prefer cooking at home to eating in a restaurant.	मुझे 'रेस्टोरेण्ट' में खाने की तुलना में घर पर पकाना अधिक पसन्द है।
• She prefers staying at home to going out.	उसको बाहर जाने से घर पर रहना ज़्यादा पसन्द है।

3 **subj. + prefer + to + v. inf. + rather than + bare inf.**

• I prefer to live on the university campus rather than live in the city .	मुझे शहर में रहने से विश्वविद्यालय परिसर पर रहना ज़्यादा पसन्द है।
• She prefers to stay up late at night rather than get up early in the morning.	उसे सुबह जल्दी उठने की बजाय रात को देर तक जागना ज़्यादा पसन्द है।

bare inf. = infinitive without 'to'

4	subj. + would prefer + to Inf. + obj. subj. + would prefer + v..ing + obj. subj. + would rather / would sooner + bare inf. + obj. subj. + would rather / would sooner + bare inf. + X than Y

Comprehension:

1a.	Would you prefer something hot or cold?	आप क्या पसन्द करेंगे, कुछ गरम या ठण्डा?
1b.	I would prefer to drink something hot.	मैं कुछ गरम लेना ज़्यादा पसन्द करूँगा।
=	I would prefer drinking something hot.	" " " " " "
=	I would rather have something hot.	" " " " " "
2a.	Shall we go to the movies?	सिनेमा देखने चलें?
2b.	I would prefer to stay at home.	मैं घर पर रहना ज़्यादा पसन्द करूँगा।
=	I would prefer staying at home.	" " " " " "
=	I would rather stay at home.	" " " " " "
3.	I would rather drink tea than coffee.	मैं कॉफ़ी की तुलना में चाय पीना कहीं अधिक पसन्द करूँगी ।
=	I would prefer drinking tea to drinking coffee.	मुझे चाय पीना कॉफ़ी पीने से अधिक पसन्द है।
4.	I would rather / sooner play football than cricket.	क्रिकेट से तो मैं फुटबॉल खेलना कहीं अधिक पसन्द करूँगी ।
=	I would prefer playing football to playing cricket	

☞ ध्यान दें कि समानार्थी होते हुए **'would rather'** और **'would prefer'** के प्रयोग में कुछ अन्तर हैं ।

1 **Would prefer** के बाद **noun** लगाया जा सकता है, **would rather** के बाद नहीं।

I would prefer tea to coffee (√) यह वाक्य रचना ठीक है।

I would rather tea to coffee. (X) यह वाक्य रचना ठीक नहीं है।

2 **Would rather** के बाद **bare infinitive** लगता है, **'to inf.'** नहीं।

I would **rather have** tea. **(√)**

or

I would **rather have tea** than (have) coffee. **(√)**

I would **rather to have** tea **(X)** यह वाक्य रचना ग़लत है।

3 **Would prefer** के बाद **'to inf.'** लगता है।

- I would **rather go** by air.
  = I would **prefer to go** by air.
- I would **rather read** e-books.
  = I would **prefer to read** e-books.
- I would **prefer to smoke** a cigar. मैं 'सिगार' पीना ज़्यादा पसन्द करूँगा।

= I would **rather smoke** a cigar.

- Do you want to watch the cricket match on television? क्या आप दूरदर्शन पर क्रिकेट 'मैच' देखना चाहेंगे?
- I would rather not. मेरे लिए न देखना ज़्यादा ठीक रहेगा।

=

- I would prefer not to.

4 **would prefer** के बाद **v..ing,** लगाया जा सकता है, **would rather** के बाद नहीं।

- I would **prefer staying** at home to going out **(√)** ***यह वाक्य रचना ठीक है।***
- I would **rather staying** at home to going out. **(X)** यह वाक्य रचना ग़लत है।

■ **would rather** का 'चाहना' के अर्थ में प्रयोग:

subj. + would rather + person object + past form of the verb

☞ *ध्यान दें :* • यद्यपि इस रचना में **past tense** का प्रयोग है, किन्तु अर्थ **present** या **future** से है।

1. I would rather you studied now. — मैं चाहूँगा कि अब तुम पढ़ो।
2. I would rather you did this work. — मैं चाहूँगा कि यह काम तुम करो।
3. I would rather you went to the bank and got me some money. — मैं चाहूँगा कि तुम बैंक जाकर मेरे लिए पैसे ला दो।
4. I would rather you turned off the TV. I want absolute silence in this room. — मैं चाहता हूँ कि तुम टी.वी.बन्द कर दो। मुझे इस कमरे में बिलकुल चुप्पी चाहिए।

■ **Preference in the past:**

Would rather/would sooner + have + past participle

☞ would rather/would sooner + have + past participle का प्रयोग भूतकाल में किसी वस्तु या कार्य की वरीयता दिखाने के लिए होता है।

1. I traveled by train but I would rather/sooner have traveled by air. — मैंने गाड़ी से यात्रा की; परन्तु मुझे हवाई जहाज़ से यात्रा करना ज़्यादा अच्छा लगा होता।
2. If I were in your place, I would rather/sooner have gone by taxi. — यदि तुम्हारी जगह मैं होता तो 'टेक्सी' से चला गया होता।

Ex.1: Rewrite the sentences given below as shown:

I prefer living in India to living in Pakistan.
=> I prefer to live in India rather than Pakistan.

1. I prefer reading crime stories to reading romantic stories.
=> ....
2. I prefer visiting people to writing letters.
=> ....
3. I prefer eating at home to eating in a restaurant.
=> ....
4. I prefer jogging to running.
=> ....
5. I prefer swimming to playing cricket.
=> ....
6. I prefer sending e-mails to writing long letters.
=> ....
7. I prefer watching TV serials to watching films.
=> ....
8.. I prefer reading e-books to reading hard copies..
=> ....

Ex.2: Translate into English:

1. बाहर जाने की अपेक्षा मुझे घर पर रहना ज़्यादा पसन्द है।
2. मैं गर्मी की तुलना में सर्दी ज़्यादा पसन्द करता हूँ।
3. उसे मत बताना। मैं चाहता हूँ कि उसे हमसे ख़बर न मिले।
4. वह चाहती हैं कि मैं बरतन धोऊँ।
5. आप चाहती हैं कि मैं उसे फ़ोन करूँ?

6. आप चाहती हैं कि मैं उसे स्वयम् जाकर मिलूँ?
7. मैं तो चाहता हूँ कि आप नकद दें।
8. मैं तो चाहता हूँ कि वह मुझे सप्ताहान्त पर मिले।
9. मेरी मानें तो दावत स्थगित न करें।
10. मैं तो चाहता हूँ कि तुम इस काम के लिए प्रबन्धक से स्वयम् मिलो।

Key 1

1. I prefer to read crime stories rather than romantic stories.
2. I prefer to visit my friends rather than write letters.
3. I prefer to eat at home rather than eat in a restaurant.
4. I prefer to jog rather than run.
5. I prefer to swim rather than play cricket.
6. I prefer to send e-mails rather than write long letters.
7. I prefer to watch TV serials rather than watch films.
8. I prefer to read e-books rather than read hard copies.

Key 2

1. I prefer staying at home to going out.
2. I prefer cold weather to hot.
3. Don't tell her. I would rather she didn't get the news from us.
4. She would rather I washed the dishes.
5. Would you rather I phoned her?
6. Would you rather I visited her personally?
7. I would rather you paid in cash.
8. I would rather he visited me at the weekend.
9. I would rather you didn't postpone the party.
10. I would rather you approached the manager yourself for the job.

Changing Dollars

Robert : I'd like to change these American dollars, please.
Clerk : How many dollars do you have?
Robert : One hundred. What is the exchange rate?
Clerk : Just a second. Let me check today's rate. Er....
It is Rs. 52.15 paisa for a dollar.

35 'Let' 'X' do 'Y'

इजाज़त देने के अर्थ में

☞ **let** के **present, past** और **past participle** तीनों रूप एक ही हैं।

☞ सिर्फ़ **Present indefinite** में **'he, she, it'** के साथ **'lets'** का प्रयोग होता है। शेष सब **tenses** में सदैव **'let'** *का प्रयोग होता है* **चाहे subject** *एक वचन में हो या बहुवचन में।*

■ **Present indefinite**

X + let / lets + y + bare inf. + obj. (if any)

aff.:	The parents let the children watch TV.	माता-पिता बच्चों को दूरदर्शन देखने देते है।
neg.:	The teacher doesn't let him play.	अध्यापक उसे खेलने नहीं देता।
int.:	Do you let your servant go to the cinema?	क्या तुम अपने नौकर को सिनेमा जाने देते हो?

Examples of sentence formation in different tenses and moods:

- **Past habitual**

They used to let us play in the evening.	वे हमें शाम को खेलने देते थे।

- **Present progressive**

The servant is letting the guests come in.	नौकर मेहमानों को अन्दर आने दे रहा है।

- **Past progressive**
- **Past simple**

Mother let us eat rice.	माँ ने हमें चावल खाने दिए।

- **Present perfect**

They have let us decide.	उन्होंने हमें निर्णय लेने दिया है।

- **Past perfect**

My parents had let me learn swimming.	मेरे माता-पिता ने मुझे तैराकी सीखने दी थी।

- **Future**

Mother will let us go by bus.	माँ हमें 'बस' से जाने देंगी।

- **Advice - present tense**

The Principal should let us play a football match.	प्रधानाचार्य को हमें 'फुटबाल मैच' खेलने देना चाहिए।

- **Advice - past tense**

The chairman should have let the interviewer ask the candidates easy questions.	सभापति को साक्षातकारक को उम्मीदवारों से सरल प्रश्न पूछने देने चाहिए थे।

- **Present compulsion**

Many times the parents have to let their children do what they want.	कई बार माता पिता को अपने बच्चों को जो वे चाहें करने देना पड़ता है।

- **Past compulsion**

Last week our teachers had to let us play during the study hour.	पिछले हफ़्ते हमारे अध्यापकों को हमें पढ़ाई के घण्टे में खेलने देना पड़ा।

- **Past habitual compulsion**

Whether I liked it or not, I used to have to let my children go out with friends.	चाहे मुझे अच्छा लगता न लगता, मुझे अपने बच्चों को उनके दोस्तों के साथ जाने देना पड़ता था।

- **Future compulsion**

The hostel warden will have to let the students go to the movies.	छात्रावास के संरक्षक को विद्यार्थियों को सिनेमा देखने जाने देना पड़ेगा।

- **probability**

We may have to let them go to the market.	*हो सकता है हमें उन्हें बाज़र जाने देना पड़े)*
• They may have to let their daughter-in-law wear western clothes.	*हो सकता है उन्हें अपनी बहू को पाश्चात्य परिधान पहनने देने पड़ें।*

- **presumption**

They must be letting their employees have long vacation.	वे अपने कर्मचारियों को लम्बी छुट्टी लेने देते होंगे।
• Mother must be letting you watch late night movies.	माँ तुम्हें देर रात वाली फ़िल्में देखने देती होंगी।

■ *'इजाज़त देना' के अर्थ में* **'let'** *के स्थान पर* **allow** *या* **permit** *का प्रयोग भी कर सकते हैं।* ☞ ध्यान दें -

- **let + bare infinitive'**
- **allow/permit + 'to' infinitive**

•	Mother let me go.	माँ ने मुझे जाने दिया।
=	Mother allowed me to go.	" " " " "
•	Father let me play.	पिता जी ने मुझे खेलने दिया।
	Father permitted me to play.	" " " " " "

Ex. 1: Rewrite the sentences given below. Change 'let' to 'allow or permit' as shown:

> • **We don't let strangers park in front of our house.**
> => **We don't allow strangers to park in front of our house.**

1. My parents would not let me go out alone in the evening.
2. My husband won't let me spend so much money on this dress.
3. Grandmother does not let any one sit on her bed.
4. They may have to let Sita live with them.
5. They must be letting their children twatch television.
6. The teacher has to let the students play cricket every day.
7. You will have to let me go abroad.
8. Mother had to let the servant go on vacation for one week .
9. They may have to let Sita live with them.
10. All parents should let their daughters study.
11. Are the security staff letting the people meet with the Prime Min ister?
12. Should the teacher have let the students go on strike?

Ex. 2: Translate into English:

1. मैं अपने बच्चों को शाम को बाग़ीचे में खेलने देती हूँ।
2. हम अपने बच्चों को आधी रात तक जगने नहीं देते ।
4. वेदांश अपने मित्रों को अपनी आलोचना करने देता है।
5. आंचल ने अपनी छोटी बहन को 'आइस क्रीम' खाने दी।
6. सौम्या ने अपने पिता को अपनी बैठक में धूम्रपान नहीं करने दिया।
7. पिता जी ने मुझको कई बार दोस्तों के साथ नौकाविहार करने जाने दिया है।
8. उन्होंने हमें गत रविवार को क्रिकेट मैच देखने दिया था।
9. मकान मालिक ने किराएदार को अपने बाग़ीचे में दावत करने दी।
10. मैं तुम्हें अपनी पुस्तक पढ़ने दूँगी।
11. क्या तुम मुझे अपने कैमरे का प्रयोग करने दोगे?
12. वे अपने बच्चों को दूरदर्शन देखने देते होंगे।
13. हमारे प्रधानाचार्य हमें प्रतिदिन मैदान में खेलने देते थे।
14. आपको मुझे विदेश जाने देना पड़ेगा।
15. माँ को नौकर को शाम को फ़िल्म देखने जाने देना पड़ा।
16. हो सकता है उन्हें अपनी बहन को अपने साथ रहने देना पड़े।
17. सब माता-पिता को अपने बच्चों को बोलने की आज़ादी देनी चाहिए।

18. आपको उसे समय व्यर्थ नहीं गँवाने देना चाहिए।

19. आपको अपनी बेटी को शोध (Ph.D) करने देना चाहिए था।

20. मुझे लगता है मुझे उसे जाने नहीं देना चाहिए था।

Key 1

1. My parents would not allow me to go out alone in the evening.
2. My husband won't permit me to spend so much money on this dress.
3. Grandmother does not allow any one to sit on her bed.
4. They may have to permit Sita to live with them.
5. They must be permitting their children to watch television.
6. The teacher has to allow the students to play cricket every day.
7. You will have to allow me to go abroad.
8. Mother had to permit the servant to go on vacation for one week.
9. They may have to permit Sita to live with them.
10. All parents should allow their daughters to study.
11. Are the security staff allowing the people to meet with the Prime Min ister?
12. Should the teacher have allowed the students to go on strike?

Key 2

1. I let my children play in the park in the evening. 2. We don't let our children stay up until midnight. 4. Vedansh lets his friends criticize him. 5. Anchal let her younger sister eat ice cream. 6. Saumya did not let her father smoke in her living room. 7. Father has let me go with my friends for a boat ride several times . 8. They had let us watch the cricket match. last Sunday. 9. The landlord let the tenant organize a party in his garden. 10. I will let you read my book. 11. Will you let me use your camera? 12. They must be letting their children watch television. 13. Our Principal used to let us play in the field every day. 14. You will have to let me go abroad. 15. Mother had to let the servant go to watch a movie in the evening. 16. They may have to let their sister live with them. 17. All parents should let their children have freedom of speech. 18. You should not let him waste time. 19. You should have let your daughter do research (PhD.). 20. I feel I should not have let him go.

36 Should Must

(चाहिए के अर्थ में)

☞ **Language Structure**

aff.:	**subject + should + bare inf. + obj. (if any)**	
I / We You, He He / They	should work hard.	
neg.:	**subject + should not + bare inf. + obj. (if any)**	
I / We /You / He/They	should not work hard.	
int. :	**Should + subj. + bare inf. + obj. (if any)?**	
Should	I / we / you he / they	work hard?
int. neg.:	**Should + subj. + not + bare inf. + obj. (if any)?**	
Should	I/ we / you, he, they	not work hard.?

☞ **should** की जगह **ought to** का समानार्थी प्रयोग होता है।

Comprehension:

• I should study now.	मुझे अब पढ़ना चाहिए।
• They should go abroad.	उन्हें विदेश जाना चाहिए।
• I should not play at this time.	मुझे इस समय खेलना नहीं चाहिए।
• You should not be lazy.	तुम्हें आलसी नहीं होना चाहिए।
• They should not be careless.	उन्हें लापरवाह नहीं होना चाहिए।
• Should I go there?	क्या मुझे वहाँ जाना चाहिए?
• Should he be lazy?	क्या उसे आलसी होना चाहिए?
• Should they be careless?	क्या उन्हें लापरवाह होना चाहिए?
• Should I not go there?	क्या मुझे वहाँ नहीं जाना चाहिए?
• Should they not be careful?	क्या उन्हें सावधान नहीं होना चाहिए?
Should they not be diligent.	क्या उन्हें मेहनती नहीं होना चाहिए?

■ should के प्रयोग:

[1] should का अनिवार्यताबोधक प्रयोग must की तरह होता है। परन्तु should में must की अपेक्षा अनिवार्यता की तीव्रता कम होती है।
See 'must' pg. 145

[2] सलाह, सुझाव, राय देने में should का प्रयोग ।

1. You **should go to bed** now. You have to get up early tomorrow.	अब आपको सो जाना चाहिए। आपको सुबह जल्दी उठना है।
2. The flat **should be** very modern.	'फ़्लैट' बहुत आधुनिक होना चाहिए।
3. **'Should we visit** her in the hospital?"	क्या हमें उसे अस्पताल में देखने जाना चाहिए।
"I think **we should.**"	मुझे लगता है हमें जाना चाहिए।
4. I think the banks **should not raise** the interest rate on home	मेरे विचार में बैंकों को गृह निर्माण हेतु उधार पर ब्याज की दर नहीं

loans. बढ़ानी चाहिए।

3 should का किसी बात के होने की उम्मीद, संभावना के लिए प्रयोग।

1. They **should be** here any moment.	वे किसी भी समय यहाँ होंगे।
2. She worked very hard. She **should be** successful.	उसने बहुत परिश्रम किया। वह अवश्य सफल होगी।
3. There are plenty of job opportunities in this country. It **should not be** difficult for you to find a good job.	इस देश में रोज़गार के अवसर बहुत हैं। अच्छी नौकरी मिलना कठिन नही होना चाहिए।
4. There are several good colleges in this city. It **should not be difficult** to get admission.	इस शहर में कई अच्छे कालिज हैं। प्रवेश मिलना कठिन नहीं होना चाहिए।
5. There are several monastries in this area. You **should be able to find** an inexpensive place to stay.	इस इलाके में कई मठ हैं। आप रहने के लिए कोई सस्ता स्थान ढूंढ़ पाएँगे।

4 कोई काम जो हुआ नहीं, लेकिन उसका होना हितकर होता, या जो हुआ, लेकिन उसका न होना हितकर होता, उसकी अभिव्यक्ति में **should / shouldn't + have + past participle** का प्रयोग करते हैं।

aff.: subject + should have + pp. + object (if any)

- You should have worked hard. तुम्हें परिश्रम करना चाहिए था।

neg.: subject + should not have + pp. + object (if any)

- You should not have worked so hard. तुम्हें इतना परिश्रम नहीं करना चाहिए था।

pp. =past participle

int.: Should + subject have + pp. + object (if any)?

- Should he have worked so hard? क्या उसे इतना परिश्रम करना चाहिए था?

Compare and comprehend

1. You ought to live peacefully. तुम्हें शान्ति से रहना चाहिए।
   - You ought to have lived peacefully. तुम्हें शान्ति से रहना चाहिए था।
2. You ought to rest. तुम्हें आराम करना चाहिए।
   - You should have rested. तुम्हें आराम करना चाहिए था।
3. He should not waste money. उसे पैसा बर्बाद नहीं करना चाहिए।
   - He should not have wasted money. उसे पैसा बर्बाद नहीं करना चाहिए था।
4. Children ought to do physical exercise. बच्चों को व्यायाम करना चाहिए।
   - The children ought to have done physical exercise. बच्चों को व्यायाम करना चाहिए था।

5 **"should"** ***का 'if ' के साथ शर्तबोधक प्रयोग :***
(use of 'should' in conditional "if" sentences)

	If + X	**+**	**should**	**+**	**bare infinitive ....**
=	**Should**	**+**	**X**	**+**	**bare infinitive ....**
=	**If**	**+**	**X**	**+**	**bare infinitive ....**

1. If he comes, tell him to wait. अगर वह आए, तो उसे इन्तज़ार करने को कहना।

= If he should come, tell him to wait.
= Should he come, tell him to wait.

☞ ये तीनों वाक्य समानार्थी हैं। "should" वाले वाक्य में सम्भावना अपेक्षाकृत कम हो जाती है।

☞ **'should' in passive voice** **see pg.302**

■ **Use of 'must'** '— के पक्ष में' सलाह **(advice)** देने के अर्थ में :

☞ अपने इस प्रयोग में **must** और **should** पर्यायवाची हैं। परन्तु **should** की तुलना में **must'** ज़्यादा सख़्त हिदायत के लिए प्रयोग होता है।

1. You must look after your old parents.	तुम्हें अपने बूढ़े माता पिता का ध्यान रखना चाहिए।
2. The teachers must pay special attention to the weaker studens.	अध्यापकों को कमज़ोर विद्यार्थियों को विशेष देना चाहिए।
3. You must behave well with your colleagues.	तुम्हें अपने सहकर्मियों के साथ अच्छा व्यवहार करना चाहिए।
4. You must meet him before 6 p.m. on coming Tuesday.	तुम्हें उसे हर हाल में मंगलवार को सांय छः बजे से पहले मिलना चाहिए।

■ **Use of 'must not' = should not / ought not** '— के विपरीत' अधिक सख़्त सलाह **(advice)** देने के अर्थ में :

1. You must not wear jeans to work.	तुम्हें काम पर जीन्स नहीं (किसी हाल में नहीं) पहनने चाहिए।
2. You must not stay up late tonight since you have to get up early tomorrow morning.	तुम्हें आज रात को देर तक नहीं (किसी हाल मे नहीं) जागना चाहिए क्योंकि तुम्हें कल सुबह जल्दी उठना है।
3. You must not forget to give him my message. It is very important.	तुम्हें उसे मेरा संदेश देना नहीं भूलना चाहिए। यह बहुत आवश्यक है।

Ex.1: Rewrite the sentences given below as shown:

> **If anyone should phone, tell them I shall be away for a week.**
> **=> Should anyone phone, tell them I shall be away for a week.**
> **=> If anyone phones, tell them I shall be away for a week.**

1. If it should rain, move all these things in the portico.

=> ....

=> ....

2. If there should be any problem, inform me immediately.

=> ....

=> ....

3. If they should come in my absence, look after them well.

=> ....

=> ....

Ex.2: Write sentences using the cues given below as shown:

> **you / lock house / go out**
> **=> You should lock the house before you go out**
> **=> You should'nt go out until you have locked the house.**
> **✶ Otherwise burglars might take everything away.**

1. wash feet / get on the bed.

....

....

2. pass driving test / drive a car.

....

....

3. look both ways / cross road

....

....

4. wash hands / cook.

....

....

5. prepare well / take an exam.

....

. ...

Ex.3: Rewrite the sentences as shown:

	You ought to be careful.
=>	**You ought to have been careful.**

1. He ought not to read this book.

=> ....

2. He ought not to waste money.

=> ....

3. All young people ought to go to gym every day.

=> ....

4. You should consult a doctor and take the necessary medicine.

=> ....

5. You should look both ways and then cross the road.

=> ....

Ex.. 4: Translate into English:

1. मेरे विचार में तुम्हें अब अपना धंधा बदल लेना चाहिए।
2. मेरे विचार में तुम्हें नया 'केमरा' ख़रीद लेना चाहिए।
3. क्या आपको लगता है कि मुझे यह साड़ी ख़रीद लेनी चाहिए?
4. क्या आपको लगता है कि हमें उन्हें मिलने जाना चाहिए था?
5. मेरी राय में तुम्हें उन्हें मिलने नहीं जाना चाहिए था।
6. क्या आपको लगता है कि मुझे हिन्दी के पाठ्यक्रम में दाख़िला लेना चाहिए?

7. मुझे नहीं लगता कि उन्हें देर रात वाली फ़िल्में देखनी चाहिए।
8. मुझे लगता है कि तुम्हें वाहन इतनी तेज़ नहीं चलाना चाहिए था।
9. मुझे लगता है कि तुम्हें इतना परिश्रम नहीं करना चाहिए था।
10. मुझे लगता है कि सरकार को महँगाई और जनसंख्या दोनों पर नियन्त्रण करना चाहिए।
11. मुझे नहीं लगता कि आपको इतना अकसर बाहर खाना चाहिए जितना आप खाते हैं।

Ex. 5: Translate into English:

1. मरीज़ को दवाई लेनी चाहिए।
 - मरीज़ को दवाई लेनी चाहिए थी।
2. कमला को नई 'कार' ख़रीदनी चाहिए।
 - कमला को नई 'कार' ख़रीदनी चाहिए थी।
3. विद्यार्थियों को अपनी पुस्तकें ध्यान से रखनी चाहिए।
 - विद्यार्थियों को अपनी पुस्तकें ध्यान से रखनी चाहिए थी।
4. आपको मेरे जनम दिन पर मुझे नए कपड़े ख़रीदकर देने चाहिए।
 - आपको मेरे जनम दिन पर मुझे नए कपड़े ख़रीदकर देने चाहिए थे।
5. आपको दफ़्तर समय पर आना चाहिए।
 - आपको दफ़्तर समय पर आना चाहिए था।
6. श्री शर्मा को निष्ठा से काम करना चाहिए।
 - श्री शर्मा को निष्ठा से काम करना चाहिए था।

Key 1

1. => Should it rain, move all these things in the portico.
   => If it rains, move all these things in the portico.
2. => Should there be any problem, inform me immediately.
   => If there is any problem, inform me immediately.
3. => Should they come in my absence, look after them well.

=> If they come in my absence, look after them well.

Key 2

1a. You should wash your feet before you get on the bed.
1b. You shouldn't get on the bed until you have washed your feet.
✶c. Otherwise the bedsheet will get dirty.

2a. You should pass the driving test before you drive a car.
2b. You shouldn't drive a car until you have passed the driving test.
✶c. Otherwise you might have an accident.
3a. You should look both ways before you cross the street.
3b. You shouldn't cross the street until you have looked both ways.
✶c. Otherwise you might get run over.

4a. You should wash your hands well before you cook.
4b. You shouldn't cook until you have washed your hands well.
✶c. Otherwise you and your family may fall sick.

5a. You should prepare well before you take an exam.
5b. You should not take an exam until you have prepared well.
✶c. Otherwise you will fail.

✶c is common to both (a) and (b)

Key 3

1. He ought not to have read this book.
2. He ought not to have wasted money.
3. All young people ought to have gone to gym every day.
4. You should have consulted a doctor and taken necessary medicine.
5. You should have looked both ways and then crossed the road.

Key 4

1. I think you should change jobs now.
2. I think you should buy a new camera.

3. Do you think I should buy this saree?
4. Do you think we should have gone to meet them?
5. In my opinion you ought not to have gone to meet them.
6. Do you think I should join a Hindi course?
7. I don't think they should go to late night movies.
8. I think you should not have driven so fast.
9. I think you should not have worked so hard.
10. I think the government should control both inflation and population.
11. I don't think you should eat out as often as you do.

Key 5

1. The patient should take medicine.
   - The patient should have taken medicine.
2. Kamla ought to buy a new car.
   - Kamla ought to have bought a new car.
3. Students ought to keep their books carefully.
   - Students ought to have kept their books carefully.
4. You should buy me new clothes on my birthday.
   - You should have bought me new clothes on my birthday.
5. You ought to come to your office on time.
   - You ought to have come to your office on time.
6. Mr. Sharma ought to work conscientiously.
   - Mr. Sharma ought to have worked conscientiously.

★★★★★

Vocabulary: Animal Life

1. amphibians	एम्फिबिअन्स	2. mammals	मैमल्स
3. aves	एव्स	4. reptiles	रैपटाइल्स
5. pisces	पाइसिज	6. vertebrates	वर्टिब्रेट्स

1. उभयचर पशु 2. स्तनधारी जीव 3. पक्षी 4. रेंगनेवाले जीव
5. जलीय जीव 6. मेरूदण्डी जीव

37 Conditionals

■ Conditional Sentences – probable cases

if + subj. + verb in the present simple tense + ...,
subj. + verb in the future simple tense + ...

☞ जब किसी शर्त पर आश्रित बात की पूर्ति की संभावना बहुत अधिक हो तो **'if'** ' से शुरू होने वाले गौण वाक्यांश में **present simple tense** और प्रधान वाक्यांश में **future simple tense** का प्रयोग होता है।

1. If I come to Delhi, I will visit you.	अगर मैं दिल्ली आऊँगा, तो तुम्हें अवश्य मिलूँगा।
2. If I find her telephone number, I will call her .	अगर मुझे उसका टेलीफ़ोन नम्बर मिलेगा, तो मैं उसे टेलीफ़ोन करूँगा।
3. If we have time, we will go to the movies today.	अगर हमें समय होगा, तो हम आज सिनेमा जाएँगे।

■ Conditional Sentences – improbable cases

if + subj. + verb in the past simple tense + ...,
subj. + verb in conditional (would) .....

☞ जब किसी शर्त पर आश्रित बात की पूर्ति की संभावना कुछ कम हो, या फिर मात्र काल्पनिक है तो **'if''** से शुरू होने वाले गौण वाक्यांश मे **past simple tense** और प्रधान वाक्यांश में **conditional (would)** का प्रयोग होता है।

1. If I came to Delhi, I would visit you.	अगर मैं दिल्ली आया, तो तुम्हें मिलूँगा।
2. If I found her telephone number,	अगर मुझे उसका टेलीफ़ोन नम्बर मिला,

I would phone her.	तो मैं उससे दूरभाष पर बात करूँगा।
3. What would you do if you saw a snake in your bed room?	अगर तुम्हे अपने शयनकक्ष में साँप दिखाई दिया, तो तुम क्या करोगे?
4. If we had time, we would go to the movies tonight.	अगर हमें समय हुआ, तो हम आज रात को सिनेमा जाएँगे।

■ Conditional Sentences – unrealistic cases

if + subj. + were + ..., subj. + verb in the conditional + ...

☞ ध्यान दें- काल्पनिक वाक्यों में प्रायः **'if'** से शुरू होने वाले वाक्यांश में **subject (sg./pl.)** के बाद **were** का प्रयोग होता है, और प्रधान वाक्यांश में **conditional** का प्रयोग होता है। **I, he, she** के बाद भी **were** का प्रयोग होता है।

1. If I were an orange, I would be spherical.	अगर मैं संतरा होऊँ/होती तो गोल होऊँ/होती।
2. If I were you, I would divorce him.	अगर मैं तुम्हारे स्थान पर होऊँ/होती, तो उसे तलाक दे दूँ//दे देती।
3. If wishes were horses, everyone would ride.	अगर इच्छाएँ घोड़े हों/होतीं, तो सभी उन पर सवार हों/होते।
4. If I were a fish, I would swim.	अगर मैं मछली होऊँ/होती तो तैरूँ।/तैरती।

■ Conditional Sentences – 3 (impossible cases)

if + sub + past perfect ......, sub + conditional perfect ....

☞ ध्यान दें- जब भाव कुछ इस प्रकार हो यदि भूतकाल में स्थिति जैसी थी उससे

भिन्न हुई होती, तो परिणामस्वरूप उसपर आश्रित स्थिति भी भिन्न हुई होती, तो **'if'** से शुरू होने वाले वाक्यांश में **past perfect tense,** और प्रधान वाक्यांश में **conditional perfect (would have +past participle)** का प्रयोग होता है।

1. If you had bought an air conditioner and a generator, you would have lived comfortably in Varanasi in summer.	यदि तुमने 'एयर कंडिशनर' और 'जेनरेटर' ख़रीद लिया होता, तो तुम गर्मी में बनारस में आराम से रही होतीं।
2. If she had spoken slowly, I would have been able to understand her.	अगर वह धीरे बोली होती, तो मैं उसे समझ पाई होती।
3. The match would have been played, if the weather had been good.	अगर मौसम अच्छा रहा होता, तो 'मैच' खेला गया होता।
4. If you had had a couple of dogs in your house, there would not have been this robbery.	यदि तुम्हारे पास अपने घर में एक-दो कुत्ते रहे होते, तो यह डाका न पड़ा होता।

Ex.1: Change the sentences given below from highly probable conditional to less probable conditional as shown:

> **I will tell you if I know it.**
> **=> I would tell you if I knew it.**

1. I will buy this house if I have the money.

   ....

2. She will come if you invite her.

   ....

3. If you don't pay her well, she will not work for you.

   ....

4. I will apply for this job if I have the necessary qualifications.

   ....

5. I will emigrate to Australia if I get a work permit.

   ....

Ex. 2: Change the sentences given below using the 'past perfect' in the 'if clause' and the 'conditional perfect' in the 'main clause' as shown:

> **As she was not very diligent, she could not complete this work.**
> **=> If she had been diligent, she would have completed the work.**

1. As she did not have a good ear for music, she could not learn it well.

   ....

2. As he did not confide in me, I could not help him.

   ....

3. As she had poor health, she was not given the job.

   ....

4. As she was very old, she did not climb up the mountain.

   ....

5. As she was not a conscientious worker, she lost her job.

   ....

Ex. 3: Change as shown replacing 'unless' with 'if... not':

> **You will miss the train unless you leave immediately.**
> **=> You will miss the train if you don't leave immediately.**

1. She is hard of hearing; she can't hear unless you speak loudly.

....

2. I don't go to the movies unless I have to.

....

3. You won't learn Hindi unless you socialise with Indians.

....

4. I won't go to their wedding unless I am formally invited.

....

5. I will be present tomorrow unless I am ill.

....

Ex.4: Change as shown:

> **An intelligent person would not accept this job.**
> **=> If he were an intelligent person, he would not accept this job.**

1. Such a thing happening in my house would lead to divorce.

....

2. Left to myself, I would not pass the exam.

....

3. To think of giving up a job at the moment would be rather foolish.

....

4. To hear him speak English, one would take him for an American.

....

Ex. 5: Rewrite the sentences as shown:

> **I phoned to my mother; otherwise she would have worried about me.**
> **=> If I had not phoned to my mother, she would have worried about me.**

1. Left to herself, she would have become even sicker.

   ....

2. I could have heard even a leaf move.

   ....

3. A real brother would not have cheated him.

   ....

4. Without the road map she would never have reached my house.

   ....

5. She went to the hospital; otherwise she would have become seriously ill.

   ....

Ex. 6: Translate into English: Conditional Sentences – probable case:

1. अगर मेरा 'वीसा' बढ़ा दिया जाएगा, तो मैं अप्रैल के अन्त तक भारत में रहूँगा। 2. यदि दाम कम कर दिया जाएगा, तो हम इसे ख़रीद लेंगे। 3. यदि वेतन अच्छा होगा, तो मैं यह नौकरी स्वीकार कर लूँगा। 4. यदि तुम्हारे पास आवश्यक योग्यताएँ होंगी, तो तुम्हे अवश्य यह काम मिलेगा। 5. अगर वह परिश्रम करेगी, तो चिकित्सा प्रवेश परीक्षा में उत्तीर्ण होगी। 6. अगर उसे अमरीका की नागरिकता मिलेगी, तो वह उससे विवाह करेगी। 7. अगर आप मुझे बुलाएँगे, तो मैं अवश्य आऊँगा/आऊँगी।

Ex. 7: Translate into English: Conditional Sentences— improbable case :

1. यदि तुम्हारा 'मोबाईल फ़ोन' खो गया, तो तुम क्या करोगी? 2. अगर तुम्हारे क्षेत्र में भूकम्प आ गया, तो तुम क्या करोगी? 3. अगर उसने परीक्षा दी, तो वह अवश्य उत्तीर्ण

होगा। 4. अगर हम मठ में रहे, तो बहुत महँगा नहीं पड़ेगा। 5. अगर हमने उन्हें सच्चाई नहीं बताई, तो वे हमें सज़ा देंगे। 6. अगर तुम्हें निमंत्रण मिला, तो क्या तुम उनके विवाह में जाओगे? 7. अगर तुम रोज़ जल्दी सोए, तो सारा समय थके नहीं रहोगे।

Ex. 8: Conditional Sentences — unrealistic cases:

1. अगर मैं भारत की प्रधान मंत्री होऊँ, तो रक्षा व्यय में कटौती करूँ। 2. अगर आप अपने देश की प्रधान मंत्री हों, तो आप क्या करें? 3. अगर आप विश्व के रचयिता हों, तो कौन-कौन से परिवर्तन लाएँ। 4. अगर मैं तुम्हारे स्थान पर होऊँ, तो राजनीति में भाग न लूँ। 5. अगर तुम करोड़पति होओ, तो क्या करो?

Ex. 9: Conditional Sentences —impossible cases:

1.यदि तुमने याद नहीं दिलाया होता, तो मैं कतई भूल गया होता। 2. अगर मेरे पास पैसे रहे होते, तो मैंने अवश्य तुम्हें उधार दे दिए होते। 3. अगर मेरे भाई ने मुझे पैसे उधार न दिए होते, तो मैं यह घर कभी न ख़रीद पाया होता। 4. अगर यात्रियों ने 'सीट पेटी' न बाँधी हुई होती, तो वे दुर्घटना में बुरी तरह घायल हुए होते। 5. अगर उसने समय से डॉक्टर की सलाह ली होती, तो इस समय इतना रोगी नहीं होता। 6. अगर स्नानगृह का फ़र्श ठीक से साफ़ किया गया होता, तो फिसलने से मेरी टाँग नहीं टूटी होती। 7. अगर मुझे पता होता कि तुम्हें जल्दी जागना है, तो मैंने तुम्हें समय पर जगा दिया होता।।

Key 1

1. I would buy this house if I had the money.
2. She would come if you invited her.
3. If you didn't pay her well, she would not work for you.
4. I would apply for this job if I had the necessary qualifications.
5. I would emigrate to Australia if I got a work permit.

Key 2

1. If she had had a good ear for music, she could have learnt it well.
2. If he had confided in me, I could have helped him.
3. If she hadn't had poor health, she would have been given the job.
4. If she had not been so old, she would have climbed up the

mountain.

5. If she had been a conscientious worker, she would not have lost her job.

Key 3

1. She can't hear if you don't speak loudly.
2. I don't go to the movies if I don't have to.
3. If you don't socialize with Indians, you won't learn Hindi.
4. I won't go to their wedding if I am not formally invited.
5. I will be present tomorrow if I am not ill.

Key 4

1. If such a thing happened in my house, it woud lead to divorce.
2. If I were left to myself, I would not pass the exam.
3. If you thought of giving up a job at the moment, you would be rather foolish.
4. If one heard him speak English, one would take him for an American.

Key 5

1. If she had been left to herself, she would have got even sicker.
2. Even if a leaf had moved, I would have heard it.
3. If he had been his real brother, he would not have cheated him.
4. If she hadn't had the road map, she would never have reached my house.
5. If she had not gone to the hospital, she would have become seriously ill.

Key 6

1. If my visa is extended, I shall stay in India until the end of April. 2. If the price is reduced, we will buy it. 3. If the salary is good, I will accept the job. 4. If you have the necessary qualifications, you will certainly get the job. 5. If she works hard, she will pass the medical entrance test. 6. If he gets American citizenship, she will marry him. 7. If you call me I will/shall come.

Key 7

1. What would you do if you lost your mobile phone? 2. What would you do if an earthquake came in your area. 3. If he took the test, he would

certainly pass. 4. If we stayed in a monastry, it would not cost us much. 5. If we did not tell them the truth, they would punish us. 6. Would you go to their wedding if you were invited? 7. If you went to bed early every night, you wouldn't be tired all the time.

Key 8

1. If I were the Prime Minister of India, I would curtail defence expenditure. 2. What would you do if you were the Prime Minister of your country? 3. If you were the creator of the universe, what changes would you make? 4.If I were you, I would not take part in politics. 5.What would you do if you were a millionaire?

Key 9

1. If you had not reminded me, I would have totally forgotten. 2. If I had had the money, certainly I would have lent it to you. 3. If my brother had not lent me the money, I would not have been able to buy this house. 4. If the passengers had not been wearing a seat belt, they would have been badly injured in the accident. 5. If he had consulted the doctor in time, he would not be so sick now. 6. If the bathroom floor had been cleaned properly, I wouldn't have slipped and fractured my leg. 7. If I had known that you have to get up early, I would have woken you up on time.

Vocabulary: —proof

1. childproof चाइल्ड प्रूफ़ 2. foolproof फूलप्रूफ़
3. earthquakeproof अर्थक्वेकप्रूफ़ 4. waterproof वॉटरप्रूफ़
5. fireproof फ़ायरप्रूफ़

1. वस्तुएँ जिन्हे इस प्रकार बनाया जाए कि वे बच्चों को क्षति न पहुँचा सकें।
2. उपकरण जिन्हें इस प्रकार बनाया जाए कि वे कभी ख़राब न हों।
3. भवन जिनके निर्माण ऐसा हो कि उन्हें भूकम्प से क्षति न पहुँचे।
4. वस्तुएँ जिन्हें पानी से क्षति न पहुँचे।
5. वस्तुएं जिन्हें आग से क्षति न पहुंचे।

38 Wish

■ **Uses of 'wish':** (**wish** के प्रयोग)

1 Good wishes: शुभकामनाएँ करते हुए:

1. I wish you good luck.	आप भाग्यवान हों।/ तुम सौभाग्यवती होओ।
2. Wish you a happy birthday.	आपको जनम दिन की बधाई हो।/ आपको जनम दिन मुबारक!
3. Wish you many happy returns of the day.	यह दिन आपके जीवन में खुशियाँ लेकर बार-बार आए।
4. Wish you a safe journey.	आपकी यात्रा मंगलमय हो।
5. Wish you a long life.	चिर जीव होओ!/ आप दीर्घायु हों।
6. Wish you a very happy married life.	आपका विवाहित जीवन बहुत सुखमय हो।

2 **To express the desire that things were different from what they are**

☞ *जब आप इच्छा करते हैं कि कोई बात जैसी वर्तमान में है, उससे भिन्न होती तो* **past tense** *का प्रयोग करें।*

1. I wish I could swim!	काश मैं तैर सकता/ सकती!
2. I wish all smokers could give up smoking!	काश सब धूम्रपान करनेवाले धूम्रपान करना छोड़ सकते!

3. I wish I were an American by birth	काश मैं जनम से अमरीका की नागरिक होती!
4. I wish I had more friends!	काश मेरे और अधिक मित्र होते !
5. I wish it wasn't so cold!	काश इतनी सर्दी न होती!
6. I wish she wasn't so forgetful !	काश वह इतनी भुलक्कड़ न होती!

☞ *जब आप इच्छा करते हैं कि कोई बात जैसी भूतकाल में थी, उससे भिन्न होती तो* **past perfect** *का प्रयोग करें।*

7. I wish I hadn't cooked so much food!	काश मैंने इतना भोजन न पकाया होता !
8. I wish I had not bought this house!	काश मैंने यह घर न ख़रीदा होता!
9. I wish it had been cooler!	काश इससे और ठण्डा रहा होता!
10. I wish I had gone to the Ganges on 'Makar Sankranti'.	काश मैं मकर संक्रान्ति पर गंगा गई होती!

☞ *जब आप इच्छा करते हैं कि कोई बात जैसी वर्तमान में है, भविष्य में उससे भिन्न हो तो* **conditional tense** *का प्रयोग करें।*

11. I wish I wouldn't miss the train!	काश मेरी गाड़ी न छूटे!
12. I wish it wouldn't be so foggy tomorrow morning!	काश कल सुबह इतनी धुंध न हो!

Ex. 1: Write sentences with the help of the cues given below 'making wishes' as shown based on :

> **cue : You are poor.**
> **=> If only I could win a lottery!**
> **=> I wish I could have a windfall!**
> **=> I wish I wasn't so poor!**

1. You can't find a house to live in.

....

....

....

2. You are missing your girlfriend.

....

....

....

3. You are unemployed.

....

....

....

4. You have fractured your leg.

....

....

....

5. You are stuck in a traffic jam.

....

....

....

6. You are the oldest in your family.

....

....

....

Ex .2: Translate into English:

1. काश मुझे अपने मंगेतर से रोज़ एक पत्र प्राप्त होता। 2. काश मुझे इतना परिश्रम न करना पड़ता। 3. काश मैं तुम्हारे प्रश्न का उत्तर जानता होता। 4. काश मैं आज अपनी बेटी के पास होती। 5. काश तुम्हारे साथ मेरी शादी न हुई होती। 6. काश वह हर समय न बोलती होती। 7. काश यह कुत्ता इस तरह न भौंकता। 8. काश

वह मेरे जन्मदिन की दावत में गाता। 9. काश मेरी माँ आज मुझे 'फ़ोन' करतीं। 10. काश वह घर पर होती। 11. काश मैं इतनी लम्बी न होती। 12. काश मैं वैदिक धर्म के बारे में कुछ जानती होती।

Ex. 3: Translate into English

1. काश मुझे कोई कुछ खाने को दे। 2. काश ये बच्चे शोर मचाना बन्द करें। 3. काश तुम सब दरवाज़े अन्दर से बन्द रखो। 4. काश लोग हमारे घर के सामने कूड़ा-करकट न फेंकें। 5. काश मेरे पड़ोसी सारी रात बिजली न जलाए रखें। 6. काश मेरी माँ मुझे दावत में पहनने के लिए अच्छा परिधान ख़रीदकर दें। 7. काश वे समय से पहुँच जाएँ। 8. काश वह हर वक़्त शिकायत करना बन्द कर दे। 9. काश मेरा मंगेतर अगले सप्ताह यहाँ हो। 10. काश मेरे पास अपना 'मोबाईल फ़ोन' हो!

Ex. 4: Translate into English

1. काश तुमने इस पद के लिए आवेदन पत्र दिया होता। 2. काश हमने अपना घर हल्का नीला रंगा होता। 3. काश मैं अपना दूरबीन लाया होता। 4. काश उन्होंने हमें पहले सूचना दे दी होती कि वे भारत आ रहे हैं। 5. काश हम अमरीका में और अधिक रहे होते। 6. काश हमने उसकी बात ध्यान से सुनी होती। 7. काश हमारे पास और लम्बी छुट्टी रही होती। 8. काश मैं बड़े शहर में पला-बड़ा हुआ होता।

Key 1

1. If only I could find a house to live in.
   I wish I could find a house to live in.
   I wish I wasn't homeless.
2. If only my girlfriend was here.
   I wish my girlfriend was here.
   I wish I wasn't so lonely.
3. If only I could get a job.
   I wish I could get a job.
   I wish I wasn't unemployed.
4. If only I could walk.
   I wish I could walk.
   I wish I hadn't fractured my leg.
5. If only I could fly over this traffic jam.
   I wish I could fly over this traffic jam.

I wish I wasn't stuck in a traffic jam.

6. If only I were the youngest in my family.
   I wish I were the youngest in my family.
   I wish I wasn't / weren't the oldest.

Key . 2

1. I wish I got a letter every day from my fiance!
2. I wish I did not have to work so hard!
3. I wish I knew the answer to your question.
4. I wish I were with my daughter today!
5. I wish I wasn't/weren't married to you!
6. I wish she didn't talk all the time!
7. I wish this dog didn't bark like that!
8. I wish he sang at my birthday party!
9. I wish mother phoned me today!
10. I wish she was at home!
11. I wish I was not so tall.
12. I wish I knew something about Vedic religion.

Key 3

1. I wish somebody would give me something to eat. 2. I wish these children would stop making noise. 3. I wish you would keep the doors locked from inside. 4. I wish people would not throw garbage in front of my house. 5. I wish my neighbours wouldn't keep the lights on all night. 6. wish my mother would buy me a nice dress to wear to the party. 7. We wish they would arrive in time. 8. I wish she would stop complaining all the time. 9. I wish my fiance would be here next week. 10. I wish I had my personal mobile phone.

Key 4

1. I wish you had applied for this post. 2. I wish we had painted our house light blue. 3. I wish I had brought my binoculars. 4. I wish they had informed us earlier that they were coming to India. 5. I wish we had lived longer in the US. 6. I wish we had listened to him. 7. I wish we had had longer vacation. 8. I wish I had grown up in a big city.

39 A, An, The

■ जब बातचीत में या लिखते समय पहली बार किसी चीज़ का ज़िक्र आता है तो **indefinite articles 'a'** या **'an'** का प्रयोग करते हैं। जो शब्द **'vowel'** से शुरू होते हैं उन से पहले **'an'** लगता है, अन्यथा **'a'** लगता है। परन्तु जब श्रोता या पाठक पहले से उस वस्तु से परिचित हो चुका होता है तो **definite article 'the'** का प्रयोग करते हैं।

Examples:

1.	It is **a good plan.**	यह अच्छी योजना है।
1a.	**The plan** that you suggested today is very solid.	जो योजना तुमने आज सुझाई, बड़ी ठोस है।
2.	I bought **a new necktie** today.	मैंने आज एक नई 'टाई' ख़रीदी।
2a..	**The necktie** that I bought today was for my brother.	जो 'टाई' मैंने आज ख़रीदी, मेरे भाई के लिए थी।
3.	She found **a good** job.	उसे एक अच्छी नौकरी मिल गई।
3a.	She found **the job** that she was looking for.	उसे वह नौकरी मिल गई जिसकी उसे तलाश थी।
4.	What **a lovely** saree!	कितनी सुन्दर साड़ी।
4a	**The saree** that she is wearing is very beautiful.	जो साड़ी वह पहने हुए है, बहुत सुन्दर सुन्दर है।
5.	He is **an engineer.**	वह एक अभियन्ता है।
5a.	**The engineer** who designed this gadget is my uncle.	जिस अभियन्ता ने इस उपकरण को तैयार किया, वे मेरे चाचा हैं।
6.	I have **an earache** today.	आज मेरे कान में दर्द है।
6a.	**The ENT doctor** I visited today is very good.	जिस कान के डॉक्टर के पास मैं आज गया था, वह बहुत अच्छा है।

■ किसी एक वचन संज्ञा शब्द का वर्णन करते हुए, 'क्या /कैसा है' बताने के लिए हम a/an का प्रयोग करते हैं। उदाहरण:

- He is an actor. — वह अभिनेता है।
- A cat is an animal. — बिल्ली एक जानवर है।
- She is a really nice person. — वह सच में बहुत अच्छी व्यक्ति है।
- Vinod is a pessimist. — विनोद निराशावादी है।
- Anita is not a good driver. — अनिता अच्छी वाहन-चालक नहीं है।

☞ *इनके बहुवचन रूप के साथ कोई* **article** *नहीं लगता। उदाहरण:*

- They are actors. — वे अभिनेता हैं।
- Cats are animals. — बिल्लियां जानवर हैं।
- They are really nice people. — वह सच में बहुत अच्छे व्यक्ति हैं।
- They are good drivers. — वे अच्छे वाहन-चालक हैं।
- We are optimists. — हम आशावादी हैं।

■ *निम्नलिखित के साथ* **'a'** का प्रयोग होता है।

- once **a** week — सप्ताह में एक बार
- twice **a** year — साल में दो बार
- ten times **a** month — महीने में दस बार
- four rupees **a** kilo — चार रुपए किलो
- in **a** day or two — एक दो दिन में

■ *जब हम किसी अपरिचित व्यक्ति की बात करते हैं, तो* **'a'** का प्रयोग होता है। जैसे:

- **A** Mr. Bhasin wants to talk to you. — कोई श्री भसीन आपसे बात करना चाहते हैं।

■ *किसी उद्योग विशेष की उत्पादित एक इकाई से पूर्व* **'a'** का प्रयोग होता है। जैसे:

- I bought **a** Maruti last week. — मैंने पिछले सप्ताह एक मारुति ख़रीदी।

■ *किसी व्यक्ति विशेष की विशिष्ट गुणवत्ता को ध्यान में रखते हुए उसका नाम आने पर उससे पूर्व* **'a'** का प्रयोग होता है। जैसे:

- He is a good cricket player, but he can never be **a** Sachin Tendulkar. — वह क्रिकेट का अच्छा खिलाड़ी है, परन्तु वह कभी भी सचिन तेंदुलकर नहीं हो सकता।

■ निम्नलिखित के साथ 'a' ***का प्रयोग नहीं होता है।***

- midnight अर्धरात्रि — midday मध्यान
- noon दोपहर

■ *यातायात के साधनों के साथ* **'a'** का प्रयोग नहीं होता है।

- by train गाड़ी से — by bus बस से
- by plane हवाई जहाज़ से — on / by foot पैदल
- by post डाक से — by email ई-मेल से
- by phone दूरभाष से

■ *निम्नलिखित के साथ* **'the'** का प्रयोग होता है।

- in the morning — सुबह
- in the evening — शाम को
- in the forenoon — पूर्वाह्न में
- in the afternoon — अपराह्न में

■ **'the'** is used when there is only one of something:

जब कोई संज्ञा शब्द अपनी प्रकार का एक ही होता है, तो 'the' का प्रयोग करते हैं। उदाहरण :

- the longest , the highest , the biggest , the most expensive, the cheapest etc.
- the sun, the moon, the earth, the equator
- at the top, at the bottom,

■ Generally article is used with plural uncountable nouns .

However **'the** is used when the reference is to specific groups.

सामान्यता बहुवचन अगणनीय संज्ञा शब्दों के साथ article का प्रयोग नहीं करते, परन्तु जब बात किसी विशेष सामूहिक संज्ञा की हो तो **'the'** का प्रयोग होता है। उदाहरण:

- **The Education Ministry** has announced to provide free books to school children
- **The books** for school children have just arrived.

■ **'the'** का प्रयोग

sky, sea, ground, country, environment, space (*स्थान विशेष के अर्थ में*) , **same** के साथ होता है।

- Look up at the eagles **in the sky.** — आकाश में बाज़ों को देखो।
- We prefer to live **in the country**? — हमें देहात में रहना ज़्यादा पसन्द है।
- We must do more to protect **the environment.** — हमें पर्यावरण-रक्षा हेतु और अधिक काम करना चाहिए।
- We arrived at **the same time.** — हम एक ही समय पर पहुँचे।
- I could not put my bag under **the berth**, because **the space** was not sufficient. — मैं अपना सामान शयिका के नीचे नहीं रख सका, क्योकि जगह काफ़ी नहीं थी।

☞ अपवाद : space (अंतरिक्ष, आकाश के अर्थ में) **'the'** का प्रयोग नहीं होता।

- There are millions of stars **in space.** — अन्तरिक्ष में लाखों तारे हैं।

■ सामान्यता **lunch, dinner, breakfast** से पहले **article** का प्रयोग नहीं होता।

- What do you normally have **for lunch**? — सामान्यता आप दिन के खाने में क्या खाते हैं?
- They had **breakfast** in a very nice restaurant. — उन्हों ने बहुत अच्छे 'रेस्तराँ' में नाश्ता किया।
- What time is **dinner**? — रात का भोजन कितने बजे है?

☞ अपवाद : ***यदि इन से पहले कोइ विशेषण हो तो* 'a' *या* 'the' *का प्रयोग करते हैं। उदाहरण:***

- We had **a very nice breakfast.** — हमने बहुत बढ़िया नाश्ता किया।

■ जब भाव किसी सिनेमा विशेष से न हो तो cinema, theatre से पहले 'the' का प्रयोग करते हैं।

- I go **to the cinema** a lot, but I have never been **to the theatre.**

■ सामान्यता **radio,** से पहले 'the' का प्रयोग करते हैं, परन्तु **television** से पहले नहीं करते। उदाहरण:

- **I listen to the radio** a lot. — मैं रेडियो बहुत सुनती हूँ।
- **I watch television** a lot. — मैं दूरदर्शन बहुत देखती हूँ।
- We heard the news **on the radio** . — हमने रेडियो पर ख़बरें सुनीं।
- We watched the news **on television.** — हमने दूरदर्शन पर ख़बरें देखीं।

☞ परन्तु दूरदर्शन यंत्र के अर्थ में television से पहले 'the' का प्रयोग करते हैं। उदाहरण:

- Can you turn on **the television,** please? — कृपया दूरदर्शन चला दीजिए।

■ *यदि किसी भवन के नाम के अन्त में* **s / 's** *आए तो* **'the'** *का प्रयोग नहीं होता है।*

- Macy's, Lloyds Bank

■ *बड़े-बड़े उद्योगों और हवाई सेवाओं के नाम से पहले* **'the'** *का प्रयोग नहीं होता है।*

- IBM, Sony, Indian Airlines, Samsung, Canon, Maruti

■ **(noun + number)** *से पूर्व* **'the'** *का प्रयोग नहीं होता।*

Room 18(होटल में), Platform 12 (रेल स्टेशन पर), Page 21 (पुस्तक में), Question 7 (परीक्षा पत्र में), Gate 11 (हवाई अड्डे पर)

■ **We don't use 'the' with names of the following:**

निम्नलिखित लोगों और जगहों के नाम के साथ **'the'** *का प्रयोग नहीं होता है।* उदाहरण :

- **continents** — Africa , Europe, South America
- **countries, states etc.** — France , India, Rajasthan Japan, China
- **cities, towns etc.** — New Delhi, New York, Seol

☞ **Exception:** The Hague (Netherlands

- **islands:** — Cicily, Bermuda

☞ किसी एक द्वीप के पहले **'the'** का प्रयोग:नहीं होता।

☞ **Exception:** द्वीप समूह के पहले **'the'** का प्रयोग होता है।

the Andaman Nicobar Islands, the Shetlands, the Bahamas, the Philippines,
New Delhi, New York, Seol

- **mountains** — Everest, Etna, Kilimanjaro

☞ किसी एक पर्वत **(mountains)** के पहले **the** का प्रयोग:नहीं होता।
Everest, Etna, Kilimanjaro

☞ **Exception:** पर्वतमाला **mountain ranges)** के पहले **the** का प्रयोग होता है। the Himalayas, the Alps

■ **'the' is used before the names with** Republic, Kingdom, States etc.:

☞ *जिन जगहों के नाम के साथ* Republic, Kingdom, States etc. *लगा हो, उनके साथ* **'the'** *का प्रयोग होता है।* उदाहरण:

the Czech Republic The United Kingdom (the UK)

- I have been to France several times but I have never been to the United Kingdom?

मैं कई बार फ्रांस गया हूँ, परन्तु इंगलैंड कभी नहीं गया।

■ **'the' is used with plural names of people and places:**

लोगों और जगहों के बहुवचन प्रयोग के साथ **'the'** *का प्रयोग होता है।* उदाहरण:

- the Kapoors, the Kumars
- the United States, the Netherlands
- the Canaries, the Bahamas

■ Use 'the' before nationality words:

राष्ट्रीयताबोधक शब्दों से पहले **'the'** *लगाएँ:*

- the Indians, the Japanese, the Chinese, the Italians, the Dutch, the Germans, the Americans, the British, the Spanish, the Swiss, the Canadians, the Greeks.

■ **'the' is used with words of direction such as north, south east, west.**

दिशा सूचक संज्ञा शब्दों के साथ **'the'** *का प्रयोग होता है।* जैसे कि:

- the north of India, the south of Pakistan, the east of Bangladesh, the west of Spain

☞ **But we don't use 'the' with northern, western etc**

दिशा सूचक विशेषण शब्दों के साथ **'the'** *का प्रयोग नहीं होता है।* उदाहरण:—:

- in northern India, in western Europe etc

☞ *यदि ये दिशा सूचक शब्द किसी भूस्थल का नाम हों तो* **'the'** *का प्रयोग नहीं होता है।*

- North America, South America

■ **'the' is used with the names of buildings:**

निम्न लिखित भवनों के नामों के साथ **'the'** *का प्रयोग होता है।*

- **hotels/ restaurants:** The Radison, The Taj Ganges
- **theaters/ cinemas:** the Regal, the Plaza , the Nagri Natak Mandli
- **museums/ art galleries:** the Fine Arts Academy, the National Museum.
- **Monuments:** the Kutub Minar, the Taj Mahal, the White House, the Red Fort

☞ *ध्यान दें :* **Banaras Hindu University, Indira Gandhi Airport, Kolkota Station** के पहले **'the'** का प्रयोग:नहीं है क्योंकि **university, airport, station** से पूर्व **proper noun** है।

■ *यदि किसी भवन के नाम में* **'of'** *आए तो* **'the'** *का प्रयोग होता है।*

- the Bank of Baroda, the Bank of England, the Gateway of India, the Great Wall of China.

■ *अधिकांश समाचार पत्रों और संस्थानों के नाम से पहले* **'the'** *का प्रयोग होता है।*

- The Hindustan, The Times of India, The Statesman,The BBC, The CNN, The Red Cross.

■ जब **' adj.'** का प्रयोग **noun** के लिए होता है, जिससे समूह विशेष का बोध होता है, और इसके पहले **'the'** लगता है।

e.g. the blind, the poor, the sick, the unemployed, the injured

1. Conditions for **the blind** are very inadequate in India.

2. The government should support **the unemployed**.
3. **The rich** ought to be kind to **the poor**.
5. **The elderly** sick are taken care of in my country.
6. The exact number of **the dead** is not known yet.
7. Much work needs to be done for **the deaf** and **the blind**.

■ नदियों, समुद्रों, नहरों, खाड़ियों, से पहले **'the'** का प्रयोग होता है:

The River Ganges, the Thames, the Rhine, the Bay of Bengal, the Gulf of Mexico, the Pacific Ocean, the Atlantic Ocean, the Black Sea, the Red Sea, the Panama Canal, the Suez Canal.

■ जब **'singular countable noun'** का प्रयोग जातिबोधक हो, तो उससे पूर्व **'the'** लगाएँ।

1. **The peacock** is the most beautiful of birds.	पक्षियों मे मोर सबसे सुन्दर है।
2. **The chrysanthemum** is my favourite flower.	गुलदावदी मेरा पसन्दीदा फूल है।
3. **The rasgulla** is supposed to be the king of Indian sweets.	रसगुल्ला भारतीय मिठाइयों का राजा माना जाता है।
4. I play **the sitar** but my sister plays **the violin.**	मैं सितार बजाती हूँ, परन्तु मेरी बहन वायलिन बजाती है।
5. **The tabla** is my favourite instrument.	तबला मेरा प्रिय वादन है।
6. **The cycle-rickshaw** is a very convenient means of transportation.	साइकिल-रिक्शा एक बहुत सुगम यातायात का साधन है।
7. Who invented **the aeroplane**?	हवाई जहाज़ का आविष्कार किसने किया?

■ *नीचे लिखी अभिव्यक्तियों में* **'the'** *नहीं लगता।*

1. The children are **in bed.**	बच्चे बिस्तर में हैं।
2. I will go **to bed** early tonight.	मैं आज जल्दी सोऊँगा/ सोऊँगी

3. I go **to work** six days a week. — मैं सप्ताह में छः दिन काम पर जाता हूँ/जाती हूँ।
4. We are **at work** by 8.45 in the morning. — हम सुबह पौने नौ बजे तक काम पर होते हैं।
5. We **start work** at 9 a.m. and finish work at 5 p.m. — हम सुबह नौ बजे काम शुरू करते हैं और पाँच बजे समाप्त करते हैं।
6. I **get home** round 7 p.m. — मैं लगभग सात बजे घर पहुँचती हूँ।
7. I am **at home** on Sundays. — मैं रविवार को घर पर रहती हूँ।
8. Shall we **go home** now? — अब घर चलें?

■ जब कोई स्थान किसीके द्वारा अपने यथोचित कार्य के लिए प्रयोग किया जाता है तो **'the'** नहीं लगता। देखें वाक्य **(1–6)**:

■ जब अन्य लोग किसी अन्य काम से इन संस्थाओं में आते हैं तो इनके पहले **'the'** लगता है। देखें वाक्य **(7–9)**:

Examples:

1. My daughter goes **to school** five days a week. — मेरी बेटी सप्ताह में पाँच दिन स्कूल जाती है।
2. Mother went to **the school** to attend a teacher-parent meeting. — माँ शिक्षकों एवम् अभिभावकों की बैठक में भाग लेने के लिए स्कूल गईं।
3. He was sent **to prison** for 6 months. — उसे छः महीने के लिए बन्दीगृह भेजा गया।
4. The jail inspector visited **the prison** to inspect the conditions there. — बन्दीगृह का निरीक्षक बन्दीगृह में निरीक्षण करने के लिए गया।
5. My mother goes **to church** every day. — मेरी माँ रोज़ गिरजाघर जाती है।
6. Many workers are repairing **the church.** — कई मज़दूर गिरजाघर की मरम्मत कर रहे हैं।

Ex. 1: Fill in the blanks 'a' or 'an' if required.

1. Orange is ....fruit.
2. She has ....sharp nose.
3. She has .....beautiful eyes.
4. Premchand is ....writer.
5. Lata Mangeshkar is ... singer.
6. Shilpa Shetty is ....actress / ...film star.
7. They are............. actors/singers/players.
8. Piush is ....travel agent/ ....employee of this bank / ....musician / .....electrician
9. He is ...... plumber / ......journalist / ......travel agent /...... ....interpreter.
10. These are..... vegetables/...... fruits/..... music instruments/ .... birds.

Ex. 2: Put in 'the' or 'a/an' where necessary.

1A: Where did you have .... dinner?
1B: We went to .... restaurant.
2A: Did you have ..... nice vacation?
2B: Yes, it was...... best vacation we've ever had.
3A: Where's .... nearest bank?
3B: There's one at........... beginning of this lane.
4A: Do you often watch........... television?
4B: No. I prefer to listen to .... radio.
5A: Would you like to travel in.......... space?
5B: Yes, I'd love to go to .... moon.
6A: Do you go to .... cinema very often?
6B: I don't go to the theator. I do watch some films sometimes on..... television.
7A: It is .... nice day today, isn't it?
7B: Yes, it is. Let's go out for...........walk
8A: What did you have for....... lunch ?
8B: Nothing. I did not have .... lunch.
9A: Excuse me, where is........ Room 34, please?
9B: It's on........third floor.
10A: We saved much money because we did not stay at...... most expensive hotel in town.
10B: Why did you stay at........ inexpensive hotel?

Ex. 3: Put in 'the' where required.

1. How often do you go to .... cinema.
2. Lie down on....... ground and look up at...... sky.
3. Suniti wasted much time watching....... television.
4. . ... television is on in her room all the time..
5. Lisa and I arrived at....... same time.
6. Have they had..... breakfast yet?
7. ...... information you need is at...... bottom of..... page 6.
8. What's .... capital city of Spain?
9. Her 'sari' is......same colour as yours.
10. These bags don't look ....same.
11. We are going out this evening after ...... dinner'.
12. It was not windy today and ....ocean was very still.
13. .... test was fairly easy; however I couldn't answer. question 2.
14. I'm going to......cinema tonight.
15. Usually I don't have time for .....lunch.
16. Shut ...gate please.

Ex. 4: Put in 'the' or 'a / an / the' where required.

1. The sun is ....star.
2. We used to llive in ....small village in .....country.
3. ......moon goes round ......earth every 27 days.
4. We are tired of doing........ same thing every day.
5. It was....... very cold day. It was..... coldest day of year.
6. I don't usually have dinner, but I eat ....good lunch.
7. If you live in .....foreign country, you should learn .... language.
8. They missed their train because they were waiting on . ....wrong platform.
9. Next train to Delhi leaves from....... Platform 2.
10. Flight AI 111 to Chicago is now boarding at ...Gate 19.
11. I forgot to shut ...gate last night.
12. .... test was pretty easy, but I couldn't answer question 6.

Ex. 5: Which is correct?

1. This is **the worst/ worst** earthquake of this century.
2. He is **best/ the best** student in class.
3. **The only/only** film I ever saw in a cinema hall was Anarkali.
4. Today was **the coldest** / **coldest** day of the year.
5. Write your address and date on **right/ the right** hand side at **the top/ top** of the page. Sign at **bottom/ the bottom** of the page.
6. Delhi is **capital/ the capital** of India.
7. **The earth / Earth** revolves round the sun.
8. **The moon / Moon** goes round the earth.
9. What is **the longest / longest** river in India?
10. Pollution in **space/ the space** is increasing.
11. **Space / The space** here is not enough to accommodate five hundred people.
12. Save **the world / world** and **the universe / universe** from pollution.
13. He lives at **the end /end** of the street.
14. **The book /book** is not very interesting at **the beginning / beginning**.
15. He always stays at **the most expensive/ most expensive** hotel.
16. I can't sleep on **the ground / ground**.
17. Birds are flying high in **the sky / sky**.
18. We lived near **the sea /sea** when I was young.
19. We were **at sea / at the sea** for ten days.
20. He lives in **the country /country**.
21. I prefer to live in **city / the city**.
22. Let us go to **the movies** / **movies** this evening.
23. Sometimes we go to **the theatre/theatre**
24. Are you listening to **the radio/ radio**?
25. I like to watch television in **the evening/ evening**.
26. I heard the news of a train accident on **the radio/ radio** this morning.
27. I discouraged the children from watching **television/ the television**.
28. Please turn **the television/television** in the living room on. It is time for **the serial/ serial** to begin.
29. What is for **lunch/ the lunch** today?
30. Where did you have **dinner/ the dinner** yesterday?
31. We always have stuffed Indian bread with yoghurt for **breakfast** / **the breakfast**.
32. I sometimes go out for meal / **a meal**.

33. I had **a nice lunch / nice lunch** today.
34. They served **a delicious/delicious dinner** on the boat last week.

Key 1

1. a	2. a	3. x	4. a	5. a
6. an, a	7. x	8. a,an,a,an		
9. a,a,a,an	10. x			

Key 2

1A. x	1 B. a	2A. a	2B. the	3A. the
3 B. the	4A. x	4 B. the	5A . x	5B. the
6 A. the	6B. x	7A. a	7B. a	8A. x
8B. x	9A. x	9B. the	10A. the	10B. an

Key 3

1. the	2. the, the	3. x	4. the	5. the
6. x	7. the, the, x	8. the	9. the	10. the
11. x	12. the	13. the, x	14. the	15. x
16. the				

Key 4

1. a	2. a, the	3. the,the	4. the
5. a, the	6. a	7. a, the	8. the
9 . x	10. x	11. the	12. the

Key 5

1. the worst	2. the best
3. The only	4. the coldest
5. the right, the top, the bottom	6. the capital
7. The earth	8. The moon
9. the longest	10. space
11. The space	12. the world , the universe
13. the end	14. The book , the beginning.
15. the most expensive	16. the ground
17. the sky	18. the sea
19. at sea	20. the country
21. the city	22. the movies
23. the theatre	24. the radio

25. the evening	26. the radio
27. television	28. the television, the serial
29. lunch	30. dinner
31. breakfast	32. a meal
33. a nice lunch	34. a delicious dinner

Holiday In Benares

Anil and Chitra spent a few days in Benares last year. They went by air and stayed in an expensive hotel by the River Ganges. They spent a lot of money. To their surprise one day they discovered they were almost broke. So they decided to return home. They could not hire a taxi and they could not now travel by air. Also they were not used to travelling by bus. They did not even know where the bus stop was! Chitra sulked; she hated walking.

Anil : 'Come on! Be a sport. It's just down the street'

Chitra : 'Oh, it's not funny! Ask someone how to get there.'

Anil : 'Okay, okay. Excuse me, could you tell me how to get to the bus station, please?

Stranger: Walk up this street and turn right at the first traffic lights. Then walk until you come to a big building made of red stone, where there is an underground passage. Use it to go across the street. Walk straight ahead one block. There is the bus station. You can't miss it!

Anil : I see. Thanks very much. Come, Chitra, Let's go.

Chitra : Walk twenty minutes with these heavy bags! Are you crazy? Oh, Anil, I can't walk an inch with these bags. They are too heavy for me to carry. The bus-stand is too far for me to walk with these. Call a taxi, please!

Anil : Don't worry. I shall carry both the bags. Ah well, you are right ! They are heavier than I thought. Let's call a taxi.

40 Nouns

■ Nouns can be classified into five categories:
अंग्रेज़ी में **nouns** को पाँच वर्गों में वर्गीकृत किया जा सकता है।

Class	Definition	Examples
Common	name of a class of people, place, or thing.	horse, girl, chair, city, country, river, mountain
Proper	name of a particular person, place, or thing: always begins with a capital letter	Kamla, Anil, Ganges, Kolkata, Banaras Hindu University
Collective	a group of people, places or things considered as a unit; normally they take a singular verb; but when the focus is not the collective unit but the individuals making the group, it takes a plural verb.	team, class, people, audience, committee, family, army, navy
Mass	names quantity of matter without reqular shape usually takes a singular verb.	time, space, dust, gold, silver, snow, water, rain sunshine, color
Abstract	name of some idea or quality	sweetness, bitterness, generosity, happiness, grief, hatred, courage, fear, justice, ideocy

Gender लिंग

- **In English there are three genders:**

अंग्रेज़ी में तीन प्रकार के लिंग होते हैं।

- masculine – man, boy, dog, horse.
- feminine – woman, girl, bitch, mare, country.
- neuter – tree, grass, baby, pencil, table, infant.

☞: **baby** and an **infant**, though animate are usually treated as neuter in English. In the singular, the pronoun 'it' is used for them.

'baby' और **'infant'** सप्राण होने पर भी अंग्रेज़ी में प्रायः नपुंसक लिंग माने जाते हैं, और इनके लिए सर्वनाम **'it'** का प्रयोग किया जाता है।

Country, though inanimate, is normally considered feminine and pronoun 'she' is used for it.

'country' निष्प्राण होने पर भी अंग्रेज़ी में प्रायः स्त्रीलिंग माना जाता है और इसके लिए **'she'** सर्वनाम का प्रयोग किया जाता है।

Some nouns

masculine	feminine	masculine	feminine
boy	girl	bachelor	spinster
bridegroom	bride	brother	sister
father	mother	hero	heroine
husband	wife	king	queen
nephew	niece	son	daughter
uncle	aunt	widower	widow
bull	cow	drone	bee
dog	bitch	drake	duck
gander	goose	horse	mare
lion	lioness	ram	ewe
stag	doe	tiger	tigress
actor	actress	heir	heiress
host	hostess	pig	sow

■ **Some nouns have the same form whether masculine or feminine.**

कुछ संज्ञा शब्दों का स्त्रीलिंग और पुलिंग रूप समान होता है।

baby	child	cousin	infant
friend	parent	patient	person
relative	scholar	scientist	student
spouse	teenager	artist	assistant
cook	dancer	driver	doctor
musician	pilot	singer	

Number वचन

■ **English has nouns in singular and plural. Normally 's' is added to a noun to pluralize it. Given below are some valuable hints to change singular nouns into their plural form.**

अंग्रेज़ी में संज्ञा एकवचन और बहुवचन में होती है। सामान्यता **'noun'** के साथ **'s'** लगाकर बहुवचन बनाते हैं। नीचे वचन परिवर्तन के लिए कुछ उपयोगी संकेत दिए गए हैं।

1 **'es' is added to words ending in 's', 'sh', 'ch', 'x' or 'z' to pluralize them.**

जिन शब्दों के अन्त में 's', 'sh','ch' 'x' अथवा 'z' होता हैं, उनमे बहुवचन बनाने हेतु 'es' जोड़ते हैं।

bus	buses	glass	glasses
dish	dishes	crash	crashes
sandwich	sandwiches	rich	riches
box	boxes	fox	foxes
quiz	quizzes	buzz	buzzes

2 **'es' is added to pluralize some nouns ending in 'o'**

जिन शब्दों के अन्त में **'o'** होता हैं, उनमे भी बहुवचन बनाने हेतु 'es' जोड़ते हैं।

potato	potatoes	echo	echoes
tomato	tomatoes	hero	heroes
negro	negroes		

☞ **Only 's' is added to some nouns of foreign origin.**

कुछ विदेशी भाषा से लिए शब्दों के साथ सिर्फ़ 's' जोड़कर बहुवचन बनाते हैं।

dynamo	dynamos	photo	photos
kimono	kimonos	piano	pianos
silo	silos		

3 **Singular nouns with 'consonant + y' ending change to 'ies'-ending when pluralized.**

जिन एकवचन **nouns** के अन्त में **'consonant + y'** हो, उनका बहुवचन बनाने के लिए **'y'** हटाकर **'ies'** जोड़ते हैं।

baby	babies	fly	flies
party	parties	ferry	ferries
lady	ladies	worry	worries
country	countries	mystery	mysteries
dictionary	dictionaries		

4 **Only 's' is added to pluralize singular nouns ending in 'vowel + y'.**

जिन एकवचन **nouns** के अन्त में **'vowel + y'** हो, उनका बहुवचन बनाने के लिए सिर्फ़ **'s'** जोड़ते हैं।

day	days	monkey	monkeys
donkey	donkeys	boy	boys
guy	guys	key	keys

5 **Usually singular nouns with 'f' or 'fe' ending when pluralized change to 'ves'.**

जिन एकवचन **nouns** के अन्त में **'f'** 'या **'f'e** 'हो, उनका बहुवचन बनाने के लिए **'f'** 'या **'f'e** ' हटाकर **'ves'** जोड़ते हैं।

calf	calves	half	halves
knife	knives	wife	wives
leaf	leaves	life	lives
loaf	loaves	self	selves
shelf	shelves	thief	thieves
wolf	wolves		

6 **some 'f" or 'f'e nouns have their plural form both with 's' or 'ves' endings.**

'f' 'या **'f'e** 'कें अन्त वाले संज्ञा शब्दों का बहुवचन दोनों प्रकार से, **'s'** या **'ves'** लगाकर बनता है, ।

hoof	hoofs, or hooves
scarf	scarfs, or scarves
wharf	wharf, or wharves
handkerchief	handkerchiefs/-chieves

7 **Some nouns with 'f' or 'fe' are pluralized by adding only 's' to them.**

कुछ **'f'** 'या **'f'e** 'कें अन्त वाले संज्ञा शब्दों का बहुवचन सिर्फ़ **'s'** लगाकर बनता है।

cliff	cliffs
safe	safes

8 **Examples of some nouns that have irregular plural forms are given below.**

निम्नलिखित उदाहरण कुछ अनियमित रूप से बदलनेवाले संज्ञा शब्दों के हैं।

man	men	woman	women
foot	feet	tooth	teeth
goose	geese	louse	lice
mouse	mice	child	children

- **Some nouns don't change when pluralized. They take singular or plural verb depending upon whether they are used as singular or plural noun. Given below are some examples and their usage.**

  कुछ **nouns** (संज्ञा शब्द) बहुवचन में नहीं बदलते। अर्थ के अनुसार उनके साथ एकवचन या बहुवचन क्रिया का प्रयोग होता है। कुछ उदाहरण प्रयोग सहित निम्नलिखित हैं।

- fish, sheep, deer, aircraft, counsel (barristers working in court).

1. There aren't many fish (pl.) in this pond.	तालाब में बहुत मछलियाँ नहीं हैं।
2. This fish (sg.) seems to be dead.	यह मछली मरी हुई लग रही है।
3. Sheep are grazing.	भेड़ें चर रही हैं।
4. This sheep is lame.	यह भेड़ लंगड़ी है।
5. Near my house several aircraft are visible flying in the sky every evening.	मेरे घर के पास प्रति शाम को बहुत हवाई जहाज़ उड़ते दिखाई देते हैं।
6. This aircraft was new and comfortable.	यह जहाज़ नया और आरामदेह था।
7. The counsel are considering this case.	वकील इस मामले पर विचार कर रहे हैं।
8. Who is your counsel?	आपका वकील कौन है?

Some 's' / 'es'- ending nouns in are singular and take a singular verb.

☞ अंग्रेज़ी में कुछ **'s'**-अन्त वाले **nouns** वास्तव में एक वचन में होते हैं।और उनके साथ **singular verb** का प्रयोग होता है।

billiards, draughts, measles, news, rabies, the United Nations, the United States:

1. Billiards is an interesting game. — 'बिलियर्डस' रोचक खेल है।
2. Is draughts a very difficult game? — क्या "ड्राफ़्ट्स' बहुत मुश्किल खेल है?
3. Measles is very common disease in India. — 'खसरा' भारत में बहुत प्रचलित रोग है।
4. Rabies is a fatal disease. — रेबीज़' घातक रोग है।
5. What is the news today? — आज क्या ख़बर है?

Normally 'ics' ending nouns such as athletics, gymnastics, politics, electronics, economics, mathematics, take a singular verb. However these can be used with plural verb too.

☞ **'ics'**-अन्त वाले **nouns** के प्रसंग अनुसार **singular /plural** दोनों प्रयोग होते हैं, और यथा आवश्यकता **singular /plural verb** का प्रयोग होता है।

- Mathematics is a useful subject. — गणित रोचक विषय है।
- **Ethics is** a very interesting subject. — नीतिशास्त्र बहुत रोचक विषय है।
- What **are the ethics** of this system of government? — इस शासन प्रणाली की आचार संहिता क्या है।
- Medical ethics in this country are going down day by day. — इस देश में चिकित्सा सम्बन्धी नैतिकता दिन प्रति दिन गिरती जा रही है।
- **Athletics is** an up and coming — 'एथलैटिक्स' शोध के लिए एक

subject for research.	उभरता विषय है।
• **Athletics play** an important role in the personality development of the youth.	युवा वर्ग के व्यक्तित्व-विकास में खेलकूद की भूमिका महत्त्वपूर्ण है।
• **Physics is** a science dealing with matter and energy.	'फ़िज़िक्स' पदार्थ और ऊर्जा से संबंधित विज्ञान है।
• **Physics** of the environment **are** slowly changing due to rapid industrialization and automation.	बढ़ते उद्योगीकरण और मशीनीकरण से धीरे-धीरे पर्यावरण में भैतिकी परिवर्तन हो रहे हैं।
• **Politics is** not as difficult as mathematics.	राजनीति उतनी कठिन नहीं जितना गणित।
• Local **politics here are** very dirty.	यहाँ स्थानीय राजनीति बहुत ख़राब है।

■ **Some 's' ending nouns always take a plural verb even though they refer to a singular object.**

कुछ **nouns** का **'s'** के बिना कोई विशेष **singular** रूप नहीं होता। परन्तु एकवचन में होने पर भी उनके साथ **plural verb** का प्रयोग होता है।

arms (आयुध) ; bellows (धौंकनी) ; binoculars (दूरबीन) ; glasses/ spectacles (ऐनक) ; pants, trousers, tights (पैण्ट), jeans (जीन्स), pyjamas पजामा) ; premises (परिसर) ; surroundings (परिवेश) ; proceeds आय प्राप्ति) ; pliers (चिमटी) ; scissors (कैंची) ; shears (कैंचा) statistics (आंकड़े) ; suds (झाग, फेन) ; thanks ((धन्यवाद) ; tongs (चिमटा) ; tweezers (एक प्रकार की चिमटी) scales (तराजु) ; out skirts of a city/ town (n.pl.) (बहिमार्ग, बाह्यांचलय) ; wares/goods (माल, सौदा) ; stairs (n. pl.) (सीढ़ियां) ; savings (n. pl.) (बचत) :

1. We have run out of arms.	हमारे आयुध ख़त्म हो गए हैं।
2. These bellows are not expensive.	यह धौंकनी महँगी नहीं है।

3.	The binoculars that she gave me are very expensive.	जो दूरबीन उसने मुझे दिया, बहुत महँगा है।
4.	My glasses have broken.	मेरी ऐनक टूट गई है।
5.	How much are these jeans?	यह 'जीन्स' कितने की है?
6.	Where are my pliers? I just put them here.	मेरी चिमटी कहाँ है? मैने अभी-अभी उसे यहाँ रखा था।
7.	The school premises are flooded with rain.	पाठशाला के परिसर में वर्षा का पानी भर गया है।
9.	The sale proceeds are very low this year.	इस वर्ष बिक्री से आय बहुत कम हुई है।
10.	These scissors are blunt.	यह कैंची खुण्डी है।
11.	Where did you buy these shears?	आपने यह कैंचा कहाँ ख़रीदा?

■ **Below given expressions always take a singular verb.**

निम्नलिखित कुछ **noun clauses** के साथ सदैव **singular verb** का प्रयोग होता है।

1. **a vote of thanks (*धन्यवाद ज्ञापन*)**

A vote of thanks was given to the chief guest at the end of the meeting.	सभा समापन पर मुख्यातिथि को धन्यवाद ज्ञापन दिया गया।

2. **a pair of glasses: (*ऐनक/चश्मा*)**

A new pair of glasses costs a lot of money.	नई ऐनक बहुत महँगी पड़ती है।

3. **a pair of pants; (*पैण्ट*), a pair of trousers; (*पैण्ट*) a pair of jeans etc. (*जीन्स*)**

I bought a pair of new jeans today. आज मैंने एक नई जीन्स ख़रीदी।

■ **Nouns given below have no 's'- / 'es'- ending plural form. They take a plural verb.**

निम्नलिखित **nouns** का **'s'- / 'es'** अन्त वाला कोई बहुवचन रूप नहीं होता। उसके साथ हमेशा **plural verb** का प्रयोग होता है।ग

- cattle (मवेशी) ; police (पुलीस) ; youth (युवावर्ग) ; people (लोग)

1. The cattle are grazing in the field. — मवेशी खेत में चर रहे है।
2. The police are looking for the thief. — 'पुलीस' चोर को ढूँढ रही है।
3. The youth in India are frustrated. — भारत का युवावर्ग कुण्ठाग्रस्त है।
4. The people of India are determined to make progress. — भारत के लोग प्रगति के लिए कृतसंकल्प हैं।

■ **Nouns given below have no 's'- / 'es'- ending plural form. They take a singular verb.**

निम्नलिखित **nouns** का **'s'- / 'es'- ending** वाला कोई बहुवचन रूप नहीं होता। उसके साथ हमेशा **singular verb** का प्रयोग होता है।

- hair (बाल) ; information (सूचना) ; furniture (फ़र्नीचर) ; swarm of flies (कीड़े-मकौड़े) ; parliament (संसद) ; fleet of ships (बेड़ा) ;

1. Her hair is grey. — उसके बाल सफ़ेद हैं।
2. All the information he gave was wrong. — उसने जो सब सूचना दी, वह ग़लत थी।
3. Furniture is very expensive these days. — आजकल 'फ़र्नीचर' बहुत महँगा है।
5. In the rainy season, a swarm of night flies makes study at night impossible. — वर्षा ऋतु में रात्रि के कीड़े-मकौड़े रात को पढ़ना असम्भव कर देते हैं।
6. Parliament is in session. — संसद सत्र चल रहा है।

7.	A fleet of ships from Japan is coming to India with food and medicines for the earth-quake victims.	जापान से जहाज़ों का एक बेड़ा भूकम्प पीड़ितों के लिए खाना और दवाइयाँ लेकर आ रहा है।

■ **Some nouns can take singular or plural verb depending upon whether they are treated as an impersonal group or as several individuals belonging to that group.**

कुछ **nouns** के साथ **singular** या **plural** दोनों ही **verbs** का प्रयोग हो सकता है, यह इस पर निर्भर करता है कि उन्हें सामूहिक रूप में लिया जा रहा है या समूह से जुड़ी इकाइयों के रूप में।

- audience (श्रोतागण) ; crowd (भीड़) ; committee (समिति) ; gang (गिरोह) ; jury (जूरी/पंच) ; team (दल) ; family (परिवार) ; government (सरकार) ;

1.	The **audience was** sitting spell-bound.	श्रोतागण मंत्रमुग्ध बैठे थे।
2.	The **audience were** running in utter confusion in every direction.	श्रोतागण बुरी तरह अस्त-व्यस्त सब ओर दौड़ रहे थे।
3.	The **committee is** meeting tomorrow at 4 p.m.	समिति की बैठक कल शाम चार बजे हो रही है।
4.	In the previous meeting the **committee were** at loggerheads over all matters.	पिछली बैठक में समिति के सदस्य सभी मुद्दों पर एक दूसरे के प्रतिकूल थे।
5.	That **is a** terrible terrorist **gang.**	यह उग्रवादियों का बड़ा ख़तरनाक गिरोह है।
6.	**The gang were** nearly all caught; only one managed to run away.	लगभग सभी गिरोही पकड़े गए; सिर्फ़ एक भाग निकला।
7.	The **jury is** in the committee room.	पंच समिति कक्ष में हैं ।
8.	The **jury were** unable to come to	पंच निर्णय पर एकमत नहीं हो पाए।

an agreement over the judgement.

9. At present the **government** at the center **is** not in a majority. — इस समय केन्द्र में सरकार बहुसंख्यक नहीं है।

10. The new **government are** committed to inflation control. — नई सरकार महँगाई रोकने को वचनबद्ध है।

The singular as well as plural of the words given below has 's' ending.

निम्नलिखित शब्दों की ओर ध्यान दें। उनके एकवचन और बहुवचन दोनों ही रूपों में **'s'** रहता है।

means (साधन) :

- What is the chief means of transportation in your country? — आपके देश में यातायात का प्रमुख साधन क्या है?
- There are several means of transportation in my country. — हमारे देश में यातायात के अनेक साधन हैं।

crossroads (चौराहा) :

- From the Durga Temple there are five crossroads before you turn to my house. — दुर्गा मंदिर से मेरे घर की ओर मुड़ने से पहले पाँच चौराहे हैं।
- The crossroads just before the railway junction is very dangerous. Be careful and drive slowly at this place. — रेलगाड़ियों के सन्धिस्थान से पहले वाला चौराहा बहुत ख़तरनाक है। वहाँ पर सावधान रहना और धीरे चलाना।

series (धारावाहिक) :

- A new T.V. series is beginning on Jan. 10, 2012. — दस जनवरी, २०१२ को दूरदर्शन पर एक नया धारावाहिक शुरू हो रहा है।
- The television series last year were better than this year's. — पिछले साल दूरदर्शन पर धारावाहिक इस साल से ज़्यादा अच्छे थे।

barracks (सेना निवास/बैरक) :

- The **barracks are** usually not good looking. सेना निवास प्राय: देखने में सुन्दर नहीं होते।
- The **barracks** in which he lives **is** quite comfortable. जिस सेना निवास में वह रहता है, वह काफ़ी आरामदेह है।

■ **When plural noun is the name of a single thing, a singular verb is used with it.**

जब बहुवचन संज्ञा किसी एक वस्तु का नाम हो, तो, एकवचन क्रिया का प्रयोग करते हैं।

Example:

Chaucer's 'Canterbury Tales' is a fascinating book.

Similarly:

The Gulliver's Travels. The Three Musketeers.
The United States. The United Nations.

■ **'Amount of money' and 'period of time' and 'distance' take a singular verb.**

धनराशि, समयावधि, किन्हीं दो स्थानों की दूरी के साथ एकवचन क्रिया का प्रयोग होता है।

1. **Sixty five years is** a long enough time for a country to improve economically. पैंसठ वर्ष एक देश की आर्थिक स्थिति को सुधारने के लिए पर्याप्त अवधि है।
2. **Ten years is** too short a time to settle all the border disputes with neighboring countries. दस वर्ष पड़ोसी देशों के साथ सीमान्त झगड़े निबटाने के लिए अति अल्प अवधि है।
3. **One thousand rupees** a month is too small a salary for anybody. एक हज़ार रुपए मासिक किसीके भी लिए बहुत कम वेतन है।
4. For me **sixty thousand rupees** is too much for one trip to America. मेरे लिए साठ हज़ार रुपए अमरीका की एक यात्रा के लिए अत्याधिक है।
5. **Ninety miles** is too much to commute everyday. नव्वे मील रोज़ाना सफ़र के लिए बहुत ज़्यादा हैं।

■ **noun + noun' construction where the first component acts like an adjective.**

दो संज्ञाओं के मेल से बने शब्दों में पहली संज्ञा विशेषण की भूमिका निभाती है।

matchbox	दिया सिलाई की डिबिया
toothbrush	दाँत साफ़ करने का बुरुश
well water	कुँए का पानी
chocolatebox	चाकलेट
cost price	लागत मूल्य
shoe mender	जूता ठीक करने वाला
baggage counter	सामान का 'काउण्टर'
book shop	पुस्तक की दुकान
wheat crop	गेहूँ की फ़सल
labour welfare	मज़दूरों का कल्याण
art gallery	कला भवन
room number	कमरे का नम्बर
platform number	प्लेट फ़ारम नम्बर

☞ **Noun preceded by a number though plural in meaning, is treated as singular and takes a singular verb.**

Noun के पहले संख्यावाचक शब्द लगने पर बहुवचन अर्थ होने पर भी यह **singular** रूप लेता है और उसके साथ **singular verb** का प्रयोग होता है।

a ten-rupee note.
a fifty-paisa stamp.
a six-foot boy.
a 75 year-old man
a six-day course
a two-week vacation.
a six-kilometer walk.
a twelve-inch ruler.
a 20-page article
200-year old temple

Ex. 1: Which is correct?

1. The jeans you gave Sarita don't/ doesn't fit her.
2. Physics were / was always my weakest subject.

3. Is this / Are these scissors sharp enough?
4. The news was / were bad indeed.
5. My family is / are in the US.
6. The police has not / have not arrested the killer yet.
7. Two weeks is / are too less time for a trip to India.
8. Where are / is your binoculars?
9. The people in my neighborhood are /is very unfriendly.
10. 15 degrees is / are too cold for us.
11. Is / Are gymnastics your favourite sport?
12. I like Vipul and Jigyasa. They are very nice people / persons.
13. Two hundred rupees isn't / aren't sufficient for this task.
14. My hair is / are turning grey.
15. Whose baggage is / are this/these?
16. More information / informations is / are needed to solve this case.
17. The suds are / is flowing out of the tub.
18. My thanks is / are due to the host.
19. How much are / is these tongs?
20. These is / are all my savings.
21. My kitchen scales has / have broken.
22. The outskirts of my city are / is a fascinating view.
23. All our wares were / was destroyed in the floods.
24. This / These stairs is / are very steep.
25. All this/these furniture/ furnitures is/are from China.

Ex. 2: Translate into English:

1. 'गेट' नम्बर	2. मौसम का पूर्वानुमान
3. कपड़ों की दुकान	4. आयुध प्रतिस्पर्धा
5. सीमा शुल्क अधिकारी	6. कक्षा
7. बैंक का प्रबन्धक	8. भौतिकी कार्यशिविर
9. तलने का बर्तन	10. कपड़े धोने की मशीन
11. भोजन कक्ष	12. तरण ताल
13. सब्ज़ी उद्यान	14 जीवनी

Key 1

1. don't	2. was	3. Are these	4. was
5. are	6. have not	7. is	8. are

9. are	10. is	11. Is	12. people
13. isn't	14. is	15. is, this	16. information, is
17. are	18. are	!9. are	20. are
21. have	22. are	23. were	24. These, are
25. this, furniture, is			

Key 2

1. gate number
2. weather forecast
3. clothes store
4. arms race
5. customs officer
6. class room
7. bank manager
8. physics workshop
9. frying pan
10. washing machine
11. dining room
12. swimming pool
13. vegetable garden
14 life story

Vocabulary: Shapes & Forms

1. rectangle	रैक्ट ऐङ्गल	2. square	स्क्वेअर
3. circle	सर्किल	4. pentagon	पेन्टागॉन
5. hexagon	हैक्सागॉन	6. octagon	आटॅक्टागॉन
7. oval	ओवल	8. triangle	ट्राइ ऐङ्गल
9. spiral	स्पाइअॅरल	10. sphere	स्फ़िअर
11. cube	क्यूब	12. pyramid	पिरामिड
13. cylinder	सिलिन्डर		

1.आयताकार 2.वर्गाकार 3. वत 4. पंचभुज 5. षट्कोण 6. अष्टकोण 7. अण्डाकार 8. त्रिकोण 9. चक्करदार, कुंडलि 11. घन, त्रिघात 10. आकाश -पिण्ड , गोला 12. कोणस्तूपाकार 13. रम्भ , बेलन के आकार का

41 Adjectives विशेषण

- **Adjectives qualify nouns; they give some information ragarding the noun.**

  'Adjectives' noun की विशेषता बताते हैं ; **noun** के बारे में कुछ अतिरिक्त विवरण देते हैं

- **In English, adjectives, unlike Hindi, have the same form irrespective of the number and gender of the noun. For example: good boy, good boys, good girl, good girls.**

☞ अंग्रेज़ी में वचन और लिंग कुछ भी हो, **adjective** का रूप एक ही रहता है। ***(यह हिन्दी से भिन्न है।)***

Classification	Examples	Placement	Use
Demonstrative	this, that, these, those, etc.	before noun	attributive
Possessive	my, our, your, his, her, its, their	–do–	–do–
Distributive	each, every, either, neither	–do–	–do–
Quantitative	numbers, some, any, little, few, many much	–do–	–do–
Interrogative	which, what, whose	–do–	–do–
Quality	good, bad, fat, thin,	before or after noun	attributive as well as predicative

☞ however, sometime the meaning changes depending upon the placement

■ **Adjectives are placed before the noun they qualify. But some adjectives awake (जगा हुआ), asleep (सोया हुआ), alone (अकेला), alive (जीवित), content (संतुष्ट), ill (बीमार), well (ठीक, स्वस्थ), lit (प्रकाशित), are placed after the verb.**

1. She is **wide awake.**	वह बिलकुल जगी हुई है।
2. I was **fast asleep** when the bell rang.	जब घण्टी बजी, मैं गहरी नींद में थी।
3. Is this dog **alive?**	क्या यह कुत्ता जीवित है?
4. I am **afraid.**	मैं भयभीत हूँ।
5. She seems **content.**	वह संतुष्ट प्रतीत होती है।
6. The house is well **lit.**	घर भली प्रकार प्रकाशित है।
7. He looks **ill.**	वह बीमार लगता है।
8. I am **quite well.**	मैं बिलकुल ठीक हूँ।

■ **Adjectives are used after sense verbs such as 'seem', 'look', 'appear', 'taste', 'feel', and 'smell'.**

Adjective अनुभूति क्रिया शब्दों **'seem, look, appear, taste, feel, smell'** आदि के बाद प्रयोग किए जाते हैं।

1. She **seems gloomy**.	वह उदास लगती है।
2. He **looked sick.**	वह बीमार दिखा।
3. Your violin **sounds good.**	तुम्हारे वायलिन की ध्वनि अच्छी है।
4. This dress **feels nice.**	यह पोशाक पहनने में मुलायम लग रही है।
5. It **tastes fresh.**	यह खाने में ताज़ा लग रहा है।
6. He **appeared happy.**	वह खुश लगा।

■ **Use of intransitive verbs like 'lie', 'sit', 'stand', 'turn', 'go', 'fall' etc. + adjective to describe the state or change of state of the subject and not his / her action.**

☞ **'lie', 'sit', 'stand', 'turn', 'go', 'fall' etc. + adjective** का कर्ता की अवस्था या अवस्था में परिवर्तन का वर्णन करने हेतु प्रयोग।

1. We **lay quie**t on the beach the whole afternoon.	हम अपराह्न भर समुद्र तट पर चुपचाप पड़े रहे।
2. He **stood still** for hours.	वह घण्टों बिना हिले-डुले खड़ा रहा।
3. He **fell unconscious** in the middle of the street.	वह बीच सड़क के बेहोश होकर गिर पड़ा।
4. She **goes mad** at small things.	वह मामूली बातों पर आपे से बाहर हो जाती है।
5. It **became dark.**	अंधेरा हो गया।
6. The milk **turned sour.**	दूध फट गया।
7. Fields **turn yellow** in autumn.	पतझड़ में खेत पीले हो जाते हैं।
8. In summer food **goes bad** without a refrigerator.	गर्मी में बिना 'रेफ्रिजरेटर' के भोजन ख़राब हो जाता है।
9. Her hair **turned grey.**	उसके बाल सफ़ेद हो गए।

■ **When several adjectives are used before a noun, it is not necessary to use 'and' between them. However if these adjectives tell about any one characteristic of the noun they qualify (i.e. if they tell about character of a person, colour of a thing, or the material it is made of), use of 'and' is possible.**

☞ जब **noun** के पहले एक से अधिक **adjectives** हों, तो उनके बीच **and** का प्रयोग आवश्यक नहीं। परन्तु यदि यह **adjectives** किसी एक ही **noun** के विशेष गुण के बारे में है, जैसे यदि वह किसी व्यक्ति के चरित्र के बारे में, किसी वस्तु के रंग के बारे में, या अमुक वस्तु किसी विशेष सामग्री की बनी

है आदि के बारे में, तो **'and'** का प्रयोग संभव है।

a kind and generous lady.	दयालु और उदार महिला
a tall and handsome man.	लम्बा और सुन्दर आदमी
red and black saree.	लाल और काली साड़ी
white and brown dog.	सफ़ेद और भूरा कुत्ता

■ **(noun + noun) is used where the first noun functions as adjective. (see page 231,233)**
अंग्रेज़ी में **'noun + noun'** का प्रयोग होता है जिसमें पहला **noun adjective** का काम करता है।

plum cake	wall paper	ear-ring
toe nail	car tyre	rain coat
school gate	apple pie	house work*

☞ **Almost always the first noun in this case is in the singular.**
लगभग हमेशा इस शब्द रचना में पहला **noun** एक वचन होता है।

■ **Present** participle और past participle दोनों adjective की तरह प्रयोग किए जा सकते हैं।

the crying baby	रोता हुआ बच्चा
the singing woman	गाती हुई औरत
the blossomed flower	खिला हुआ फूल
a tired horse	थका हुआ घोड़ा

■ **Adjectives can be classified as opinion adjectives (such as good, bad, ugly, handsome etc.) and fact adjectives such as big, small, new, old etc.)**
Normally opinion adjectives are placed before the fact adjectives. If there are more than one fact adjectives, these

may be arranged in the following order:

जब किसी एक वाक्य में, एक से अधिक **adjectives** हों तो निम्नलिखित क्रम रखें।

1. adjectives for shape, size, age, temperature
+
2. colour adjectives
+
3. adjectives giving information regarding place of origin
+
4. adjectives telling what this object is made of
+
5. adjectives telling the purpose of the object
+
6. noun

Comparatives

■ **comparative form of short adjectives and adverbs**

= base form of the adjective / adverb + 'er' + than.......

☞ छोटे **adjective** और **adverb** शब्दों के मूलरूप के साथ **'er' + than** लगाकर तुलनात्मक रूप बनाएँ जैसा कि नीचे दर्शाया गया है।

cheap	cheaper (than)	strong	stronger (than)
weak	weaker (than)	nice	nicer (than)
hot	hotter (than)	cold	colder (than)
thin	thinner (than)	hard	harder (than)
soft	softer (than)	lucky	luckier (than

1. This area **is quieter than** the rest of the city. — यह इलाक़ा बाकी शहर के मुक़ाबले शान्त है।
2. Their life **is simpler than** ours. — उनका जीवन हमारे जीवन से साधारण है।

3. She **is prettier than** her sister.	वह अपनी बहन से सुन्दर है।
4. This house is **cheaper than** that one.	यह घर उसवाले से सस्ता है।
6. Living in the country-side is **healthier than** living in big cities.	बड़े शहरों में रहने की तुलना में देहात में रहना कहीं अधिक स्वास्थ्यप्रद है।

☞ **Comparative form of longer adjectives**

= more / less + base form of the adjective) + 'than'

Adjectives शब्द बड़ा होने पर उनसे पहले **more** या **less** और बाद में **than +** जिस **noun** से तुलना की जा रही हो लगाकर तुलनात्मक रूप बनाएँ।

intelligent	more intelligent	generous	more generous
interesting	more interesting	serious	more serious

1. Houses in India **are less expensive than** they are in Europe.	भारत में घर यूरूप की तुलना में कम महँगे है।
2. He is **more intelligent than** his brother.	वह अपने भाई से अधिक बुद्धिमान है।
3. My uncle is **more generous than** my father.	मेरे चाचा मेरे पिता जी से अधिक उदार हैं।
4. Their problem turned out to be **much more serious than** I had anticipated.	उनकी समस्या जितना मैंने सोचा था उससे कहीं अधिक गंभीर निकली।
5. Health is **more valuable than** wealth.	स्वास्थ्य धन से कहीं अधिक मूल्यवान है।

'as + adj. / adv. + as'..	(उतना .... जितना)

1. I am not **as old as** her (she is). — मेरी उम्र उतनी नहीं जितनी उसकी।
2. Vipasha is not **as good** a student **as** Preeti — विपाशा उतनी अच्छी विद्यार्थी नहीं जितनी प्रीति।
3. Rashmi does **not work as much as** Keerti. — रश्मि उतना काम नहीं करती जितना कीर्ति।
4. Ram is **not as generous as** Neel. — राम उतना उदार नहीं जितना नील।

'not as + adj. + as'	(उतना .... नहीं + जितना)

1. Those shoes are not as expensive as these ones. — वे जूते उतने मँहगे नहीं जितने ये वाले।
2. That box is not as big as this one. — वह सन्दूक उतना बड़ा नहीं जितना यह वाला
3. Her mother does not cook as tasty food as she does. — उसकी माँ उतना स्वादिष्ट भोजन नहीं पकाती जितना वह।

'the same as...'	(वैसी ही . . . जैसी/'इतना . . . जितना)

1. This saree is the same price as that one. — इस साड़ी का दाम उतना ही है जितना उसवाली का।
2. She came here at the same time as me (I did). — वह उसी समय यहाँ आई जब मैं।
3. Her daughter is the same age as my daughter. — उसकी बेठी की उम्र ठीक उतनी ही है जितनी मेरी बेटी की।
4. Her car is exactly the same as mine in every respect. — उसकी कार हर प्रकार से वैसी ही है जैसी मेरी।

'v...ing + comparative + and + comparative' is used when there is continuous change (positive or negative) in something.

दिन प्रति दिन, साल दर साल स्थिति विशेष में परिवर्तन होते जाने पर:

1. Your Hindi is **getting better and better** every day.	आपकी हिन्दी दिन प्रति दिन बेहतर हो रही है।
2. These days it is **becoming harder and harder** to find domestic servants in India.	आजकल भारत में घरेलू नौकर मिलना दिन प्रति दिन और कठिन होता जा रहा है।
3. It is **becoming more and more difficult** to get admission into medical colleges.	चिकित्सा विद्यालयों में प्रवेश पाना दिन प्रति दिन और कठिन होता जा रहा है।

'the + comparative......., 'the + comparative' ....

जितना...................................... उतना.................

1. **The quicker** you do it, **the better** it will be.	आप जितनी जल्दी करेंगे, उतना अच्छा होगा।
2. **The more** you work, **the more** you will earn.	आप जितना ज़्यादा काम करेंगे , उतना ज़्यादा कमाएँगे।
3. **The more** people have, **the more** they desire.	जितना ज़्यादा लोगों के पास होता है, उतना ज़्यादा वे और इच्छा करते हैं।
4. **The colder** the weather, **the better**.	मौसम जितना ज़्यादा ठण्डा हो, उतना बेहतर।

Superlatives

■ **There are two ways to make adjectival and adverbial superlatives:**

☞ adjective या adverb की उत्तमावस्था दो तरह से बनती है।

(1) adjective +est.

nice	the nicest	easy	the easiest
cold	the coldest	old	the oldest
short	the shortest	large	the largest
rich	the richest	poor	the poorest

(2) most / least + adjective +than

valuable	the most valuable	boring	the most boring
famous	the most famous	known	the least known
comfortable	the most comfortable / the least comfortable		
expensive	the most expensive / the least expensive		
complicated	the most / the least complicated		

■ **'y'** में ख़त्म होने वाले शब्दों की उत्तमावस्था बनाते समय **'y'** को हटाकर **'iest'** जोड़ें या उससे पहले आवश्यकतानुसार **'most'** या **'least'** 'लगाएँ।

easy	easiest	happy	happiest;
crazy	craziest	heavy	heaviest
pretty	prettiest	healthy	healthiest

■ **Some irregular comparative and superlative forms: below:**

कुछ अनियमित तुलनात्मक और उत्तमावस्था के रूप :

bad	worse	worst
far	farther	farthest
good	better	best
little	less	least
many	more	most
much	more	most
old	older	oldest
old	elder	eldest

☞ **elder and eldest are used before a noun** (as comparative or superlative respectively) **within the family:**

- my **elder sister** (older is possible) मेरी बड़ी बहन
- her **eldest son** (oldest is possible) उसका सबसे बड़ा बेटा

☞ **elder than + noun is not possible.**

- She is older than Ram. (√) (right)
- She is elder than Ram . (X) (wrong)

Ex. 1: Complete the sentences using the words given in the brackets in comparative form (+ than) where required.

1. The problem with our car was .... we had expected. (serious)
2. We want a .... flat. We don't need so much space. (small)
3. I like to live in the suburbs. They are .... downtown.(peaceful)
4. Today the metro was .... usual. (crowded)
5. Vegetables are .... in the villages .... in big cities.(cheap)
6. A good map can help one find a place .... (easily)
7. He is .... in games...............in his studies. (more interested)
8. Education is .... wealth. (valuable)

Ex. 2: Complete the clauses given below with the adjectives given in the brackets arranged in proper order.

1. an .... bangle (oxidized silver, unusual)

2. an ....house (ugly, modern)
3. ....socks (woollen, red)
4. .... face (square, chubby, cute)
5. an .... Hindi movie. (old, interesting)
6. a .... .day . (rainy, pleasant).
7. a ....skirt (pink, lovely)
8. a.................................. passage (long, narrow)
9. an ....pullover (brown, torn, ugly)
10 a .... box. (brown, big, nice, wooden)
11. a... dog (white, little, fat, cute)
12. a .... raincoat. (blue and red, sleek, short)

Ex. 3: Translate into English:

1. बिलकुल सन्नाटा था। 2. उनकी हिन्दी धाराप्रवाह और दोषरहित थीं। 3. उसकी सफलता निरन्तर परिश्रम का परिणाम है। 4. मुझे परीक्षा से पहले हमेशा घबराहट होती है। 5. मैं बहुत परेशान हूँ ।

Ex. 4: Translate into English:

1. वह तुम से लम्बी है। 2. मैं उससे बड़ी हूँ । 3. वह मुझसे ज़्यादा बुद्धिमान है। 4. वह अपनी बहन से ज़्यादा अच्छा खाना बनाती है। 5. उनके पास हमसे ज़्यादा पैसा है। 6. वह तुमसे ज़्यादा तेज़ दौड सकता है। 7. मैं यहाँ उनसे ज़्यादा समय से हूँ । 8. हम आपसे जल्दी उठे। 9. राम अपने मित्र से धनी है। 10. रेल और हवाईजहाज़ से यात्रा साल दर साल और महँगी होती जा रही हैं। 11. आवश्यक वस्तुओं की गुणवत्ता दिन प्रति दिन बिगड़ती जा रही है।

Ex. 5: Translate into English:

1. अनिल के पास उतना पैसा नहीं जितना राम के पास है। 2. राम का मित्र उतना धनी नहीं जितना वह है। 3. मैं उतनी अच्छी नर्तकी नहीं जितनी मेरी बहन। 4. मैं उतनी अच्छी अंग्रेज़ी नहीं बोलती जितनी वह। 5. इस साल उतनी गर्मी नहीं जितनी पिछले साल थी। 6. मेरे इतने मित्र नहीं जितने आपके। 7. मैं उतना नहीं पढ़ सकता जितना तुम। 8. यह 'कैमरा' उतना महँगा नहीं जितना वहवाला। 9. मैं ठीक उतने बजे उठी जितने बजे मेरी माता जी उठीं। 10. हम इस साल उसी होटल में ठहरे जिसमें पिछले साल ठहरे

थे। 11. आपके जितने अधिक भारतीय मित्र होंगे, उतना शीघ्र आप हिन्दी बोलना सीखेंगे। 12.आप जितनी जल्दी यात्रा शुरू करेंगे, राजपथ पर उतनी कम भीड़ होगी और आप उतना जल्दी गन्तव्य पर पहुँचेंगे। 13. आप जितना कम बोलेंगे उतना अच्छा होगा।

Ex.6: Translate into English

1. तुम्हारे बालों का रंग मेरे बालों के जैसा है। 2. उनक का रहन सहन ठीक हमारे रहन सहन जैसा ही है। 3. उनकी शादी की वर्षगाँठ उसी दिन है जिस दिन हमारी। 4. वह ठीक मेरे जितना लम्बा है। 5 .मुझे ज़मीन पर सोना उतना ही आरामदेह लगता है जितना पलंग पर। 6. उसने इस बार भी वही ग़लती की है जो पिछले साल की थी।

Key 1

1. more serious than
2. smaller
3. more peaceful than
4. more crowded than
5. cheaper ....than
6. more easily
7. more interested...than
8. more valuable than

Key 2

1. an unusual oxidized silver bangle
2. an ugly modern house
3. red woollen socks
4. cute square chubby face
5. an interesting old Hindi movie
6. a pleasant rainy day
7. a lovely pink skirt
8. a narrow long passage
9. an ugly torn brown pullover
10 a nice big brown wooden box
11. a cute little fat white dog
12. a sleek, short, blue and red raincoat

Key 3

1. There was absolute silence. 2. Their Hindi was fluent and flawless. 3. Her success is the result of continuous hardwork. 4. I am always nervous before the exams. 5. I am terribly upset.

Key 4

1. She is taller than you. 2. I am older than her. 3. He is more intelligent

than me. 4. She cooks better food than her sister. 5. They have got more money than us. 6. He can run faster than you. 7. I have been here longer than them. 8. We got up earlier than you. 9. Ram is richer than his friend. 10. Rail as well as air travel has been **getting more and more expensive** over the years. 11. The quality of essential goods **is deteriorating day by day.**

Key 5

1. Anil does not have as much money as Ram has. 2. Ram's friend is not **as rich as** he is. 3. I am not **as good** a dancer **as** my sister is. 4. I don't speak English **as well as** she does (as well as her). 5. This year is not as hot as last year. 6. I don't have as many friends as you have. 7. I can't study as much as you can. 8. This camera is not as expensive as that one. 9. I got up at the same time as my mother. 10. We stayed at the same hotel this year as last year. 11. **The more** Indian friends you have, **the quicker** you will learn to speak Hindi. 12. **The earlier** you set out, **the less** crowded will the highway be and the sooner you will arrive at your destination. 13. **The less** you talk, **the better** it is.

Key 6

1. Your hair is the same color as mine. 2. Their life style is the same as ours. 3. Their wedding anniversary is the same day as ours. 4. He is just as tall as I am. 5. I find sleeping on the floor just as comfortable as sleeping on a bed. 6. He has made the same mistake this time as last year.

At The Bank **Opening an account**

Customer : May I come in?
Bank Officer : Come in. Please, take a seat. Now, what can I do for you?
Customer : I would like to open a bank account.
Bank Officer : What kind of account would you like to open, sir?
Customer : I am sorry, I must confess I am quite ignorant in

these matters. Could you please give me some information about the different services your bank offers.

Bank Officer : Well, you can have a saving account, a current account, a recurring deposit, or a fixed deposit.
In a saving account you can use your money whenever you please and at the same time earn some interest on it. The rate of interest is not very high, though.
If one has some money which one knows, for certain, one is not going to need in the near future, one can put it in the Money Multiplier Scheme. The rate of interest is reasonably good on these deposits. One could withdraw the interest every month, every three months or once at the end of the term. Recurring deposits are a good way of saving small amounts. You can deposit a certain sum every month for a certain period and at the end of the period receive all your money with added interest.

Customer : Thanks verymuch indeed for all this information. For now, I would like to open a saving account.

Bank Officer : One more thing, you need to have an introduction by somebody who is already an account holder at our bank.

Customer : I am afraid I am new to this place and I really don't know anyone so well here.

Bank Officer : Do you have a passport?

Customer : Yes, I do.

Bank Officer : Fill out this form please. Fill in your passport number, the date and the place where it was issued. We need your two passport size photos, Sir. Sign here. Fill out this deposit slip too. Deposit the money at the cash counter. Please come tomorrow to collect your pass book and account number, Sir.

Customer : Thank you very much. Goodbye!

Bank Officer : Goodbye.

42 Possession

my	our	your	his, her	their +		noun
मेरा	*हमारा*	*तेरा*	*उसका/इसका*	*उनका/इनका*	+	*संज्ञा*
		तुम्हारा				
		आपका				

Examples:

his friends	उसके दोस्त	her hobbies	उसकी अभिरुचियाँ
their complaints	उनकी शिकायतें	whose idea?	किसका विचार?
our boxes	हमारे सन्दूक	her college	उसका कॉलेज
your parents	तुम्हारे/ आपके माता-पिता		

Comprehension

1.	Do you know their address?	क्या आप उनका पता जानते हैं?
2.	My umbrella is very expensive.	मेरा छाता बहुत महँगा है।
3.	Their son is going to America.	उनका बेटा अमरीका जा रहा है।
4.	Her daughter is getting married next month.	उनकी बेटी की शादी अगले महीने हो रही है।
5.	I (m.) met his daughter at the party but I have forgotten her name.	मैं उनकी बेटी को दावत में मिला था परन्तु मैं उसका नाम भूल गया हूँ।
6.	That is her house.	वह उसका घर है।
7.	Take your umbrella; it might rain.	अपना छाता ले लो; हो सकता है बारिश आ जाय।
8.	Have you met her husband?	आप उसके पति से मिले हैं?
9.	Ram and his wife are doctors.	राम और उसकी पत्नी डॉक्टर हैं।

mine	ours	yours	his, hers	theirs
मेरा	*हमारा*	*तेरा/तुम्हारा/आपका*	*उसका/इसका*	*उनका/इनका*

■ **Possessive pronoun** *का यह रूप :—*

- *क्रिया से पहले या बाद में, दोनों तरह प्रयोग किया जाता है।*

  Examples 1,2

- *इसके के बाद कोई संज्ञा शब्द नहीं लगाया जाता।* **Examples 3,4**

1. Mine is overhere. — मेरी / मेरा यहाँ है।
2. This is mine — यह मेरा है।
3. That dog is ours. (√) — वह कुत्ता हमारा है।
4. That is ours dog. (X) — ***यह वाक्य ग़लत है।***
5. This house is yours. — यह घर तुम्हारा है।
6. These shops are hers. — ये दुकाने उसकी हैं।
7. These toys are theirs. — ये खिलौने उनके हैं।

☞ **his, whose** *दोनों तरह से, यानी* **noun** *के साथ और* **noun** *के बिना प्रयोग होते हैं।*

4. Those fields are his. (√) — वे खेत उसके हैं।
4. Those are his fields. (√) — वे खेत उसके हैं।
2. Whose is this ? (√) — यह किसका हैं?
2. Whose book is this ? (√) — यह किसकी किताब हैं?

☞ **Negative** (नकारात्मक) वाक्य में क्रिया के बाद 'not' लगाएँ।

1. This book is not mine. — यह किताब मेरी नहं है।

2. That dog is not ours. वह कुत्ता हमारा नहीं है।

☞ **Interrogative** (प्रश्नवाचक) वाक्य में क्रिया/प्रश्नसूचक शब्द वाक्य के आरम्भ में लगाएँ।

1. Is this book mine? क्या यह किताब मेरी है?
1. Which house is yours? कौन-सा घर आपका है?

Comprehension

1. This is ours.	यह हमारा/ हमारी है।
2. That field is theirs.	वह खेत उनका है।
3. These gloves are not **hers**; they are **his**.	ये दस्ताने उसके नहीं हैं; ये उसके हैं।
4. Her / His shoes are more comfortable than mine.	उसक जूते मेरे जूतों से ज़्यादा आरामदेह हैं।
5. My dress is pretty; hers is prettier than mine.	मेरी पोशाक सुन्दर है; उसकी मेरी वाली से ज़्यादा सुन्दर है।
6. Our camera is quite good but theirs is certainly much better than ours.	हमारा कैमरा काफ़ी अच्छा है, लेकिन उनका वाला हमारे वाले से निश्चित रूप से कहीं ज़्यादा अच्छा है।
8. My teeth are stronger than yours.	मेरे दाँत तुम्हारे दाँतों से ज़्यादा मज़बूत हैं।
9. Our culture is different from yours.	हमारी संस्कृति आपकी संस्कृति से भिन्न है।

■ **Use of apostrophe (= ' s) and 'of" in English:**

हिन्दी में सम्बन्ध कारक 'का, के, की' के लिए अंग्रेज़ी में उपरोक्त दो प्रयोग हैं।

1. **'of' ' + noun**
2. **apostrophe + s (= ' + s) + noun**

☞ **When the possessor is a plural noun with 's'- ending, put apostrophe after the 's'.**
यदि **plural noun** *में* **'s'** *हो तो सम्बन्ध कारक चिन्ह* **(') apostrophe 's'** *के बाद लगता है* **/ Examples 8, 9 below.**

1. Ram's son	son of Ram	राम का बेटा
2. Kamla's book	book of Kamla	कमला की किताब
3. dog's leg	leg of dog	कुत्ते की टाँग
4. bird's wings	wings of bird	चिड़िया के पंख
6. children's school	school of children	बच्चों का स्कूल
7. women's association	association of women	औरतों का संगठन
8. boys' sport	sport of boys	लड़कों का खेल
9. girls' uniform	uniform of girls	लड़कियों की वर्दी

☞ ध्यान दें।

1 सामान्यता प्राणीवाचक संज्ञा **(living nouns)** के साथ **apostrophe** और अप्राणीवाचक संज्ञा **(non living)** के साथ **of** का प्रयोग होता है।

2 जब अधिपति कोई संस्था हो तो सम्बन्ध कारक चिन्ह **apostrophe + s** कर सकते हैं, क्योंकि वास्तव में यह संस्थान सामूहिक व्यक्तिगण ही होते हैं।

1. India's most backward region.	भारत का सबसे पिछड़ा क्षेत्र।
2. World's most important problems.	विश्व की सबसे महत्वपूर्ण समस्याएँ।
3. America's largest river.	अमरीका की सबसे बड़ी नदी।
4. Varanasi's oldest temple.	वाराणसी का सबसे पुराना मंदिर।

5. Government's economic programme. — सरकार की आर्थिक योजना।

3 **If there are multiple nouns, use apostrophe after the final noun:**
एक से अधिक आधिपत्यसूचक संज्ञापद होने पर सम्बन्ध कारक चिन्ह **(apostrophe)** अंतिम संज्ञापद के बाद लगता है।

1. Rani and Ram's engagement. — रानी और राम की सगाई।
2. Savita, Sudhir and Sunil's problem. — सविता, सुधीर और सुनील की समस्या।
3. Pakistan and India's political relations. — पाकिस्तान और भारत के राजनैतिक सम्बन्ध।

4 **(apostrophe + s) is used with time expressions**
समयसूचक अभिव्यक्तियों के साथ भी **(apostrophe + s)** लगता है।

1. Yesterday's riots were horrible. — कल के दंगे बहुत भयंकर थे।
2. He is on a week's vacation. — वह एक सप्ताह की छुट्टी पर है।
3. Have you read today's news-paper? — आपने आज का अख़बार पढ़ा है?
4. We usually have two weeks' vacation at Diwali — हमें प्राय: दीवाली पर दो सप्ताह की छुट्टी होती है।
5. tomorrow's lecture — कल का भाषण।
6. evening's programme — आज शाम का कार्यक्रम।
7. two months' leave of absence — दो महीने की छुट्टी।
8. two minutes' walk — पैदल दो मिनट की दूरी।

■ noun + of + possessive pronoun

1. A friend of mine is coming today. — मेरा एक मित्र आज आ रहा है।

2. Anil is a relative of ours. अनिल हमारा रिश्तेदार है।

Ex. 1: Which is correct?

1. It is her/hers problem, not my/mine. 2. This is a good book. Is it your/ yours. 3. This is not my/mine pen. My/ mine is black. 4. I am eating out with mine/ my friends. 5. Our/ours house is bigger than your/yours. 6. These are not my/mine shoes. Those are my/mine. 7. This is not their/theirs house. That is their/theirs. 8. She gave me her/hers black jeans. 9. Whose camera is this? Is this her/hers? 10. This is your/yours work, not my/ mine.

Ex. 2: Complete the sentences using the appropriate word given in parentheses.

1. This is........ house. (our, ours)
2. Those books are......... (her, hers)
3. I wonder where.......... umbrella is. (my, mine)
4. That grey coat is......... (my, mine)
5. Is that........... dog? (your, yours)
6. No, it is........... (they, theirs)
7. This is....... idea (his, him)
8. This idea is........ (him, his)
9. She left......... moped in the portico. (her, hers)
10. We had.... lunch in the canteen (our, ours).

Ex. 3: Change as shown using the correct possessive pronouns:

1. This is my book.	This book is...............
2. That is their house.	That house is................
3. Those are our dogs.	Those..............
4. This is his car.	This car is ....
5. Is this your bag?	Is this bag.....?
6. This is not her umbrella	This umbrella is not ....
This is my umbrella.	This is ....
7. Is this his bicycle?	Is this bicycle ....?

Ex. 4: Change as shown using the correct possessive form:

> **I met one of your uncles.**
> => **I met an uncle of yours.**

1. She lent me one of her books.

....

2. He married one of his classmates.

....

3. We went for a picnic with some of our friends.

....

4. She invited a few of her friends to lunch.

....

5. I am going on vacation with one of my colleagues.

....

6. This tall man with a beard is my brother's friend.

....

7. It is Rani's idea to learn spoken English during the summer vacation.

....

Ex. 5: Translate into English- 1

1.यह मेरी चाची हैं। 2. क्या यह कमरा तुम्हारा है? 3. यह तुम्हारा है। 4. आपका नाम क्या है? 5. ये मेरे बेटे हैं। 6. यह तुम लोगों का कुत्ता है? 7. यह किसका है? 8. यह घर हमारा है। 9. यह मेरा है।10. यह समय की बर्बादी है।

Ex. 6: Translate into Englis-2

1. मेरी बेटी का जन्मदिन अट्ठाईस अप्रैल को है।
2. मेरे पिता जी का काम बहुत रोचक है।
3. मेरे बेटे का पसन्दीदा भोजन भुना हुआ मुर्गा है।
4. कृपया मुझे विभा का पता दीजिए।
5. मेरे भाई का कमरा हमेशा बहुत गन्दा होता है।
6. शहर का नाम और तारीख़ पृष्ठ के ऊपरी भाग में लिखें।
7. फ़रवरी और मार्च भारत में सबसे अच्छे महीने होते है।
8. मैं लड़ाई का कारण नहीं जानता/जानती।
9. मेरे स्कूटर के 'ब्रेक' ख़राब हो गए।

10. आधुनिक इमारतों की दीवारें बहुत पतली होती है।
11. ओबामा अमरीका के पहले काले राष्ट्रपति हैं।
12. क्या वह औरत आपकी मित्र है?
13. मैं तुम्हारे एक चाचा से दावत में मिला।
14. हम अपने कुछ दोस्तों के साथ 'पिकनिक' पर गए।
15. हम अपनी एक चाची के साथ फ़िल्म देखने गए।
16. उनकी एक बेटी अमरीका में है।

Ex. 7: Translate into Hindi:

1. वह अपने एक मित्र के साथ हवाई अड्डे पर गई। 2. मैं अपने कुछ सहकर्मियों के साथ नौका विहार पर गया। 3. वह अपने कुछ महमानों के साथ गंगा में स्नान करेगा। 4. मैंने अपने कुछ सहपाठियों के साथ फुटबॉल खेला। 5. वे अपने कुछ सहकर्मियों के साथ हमारे घर आए। 6. क्या वह आपकी रिश्तेदार है।

Key 1

1. her, mine 2. yours 3. my, mine 4. my
5. our, yours 6. my, mine 7. their, theirs 8. her
9. hers 10. your, mine.

Key 2

1. our 2. hers 3. my 4. mine
5. your 6. theirs 7. his 8. his
9. her 10. our

Key 3

1 .This book is mine.
2. That house is theirs
3. Those dogs are ours
4. This car is his.
5. Is this bag yours?
6. This umbrella is not hers. This is mine.
7. Is this bicycle his?

Key 4

1. She lent me a book of hers.
2. He married a classmate of his.
3. We went for a picnic with some friends of ours.
4. She invited a few friends of hers to lunch.

5. I am going on vacation with a colleague of mine.
6. This tall man with a beard is a friend of my brother's.
7. It is an idea of Rani's to learn spoken English during the summer vacation.

Key 5

1. This is my aunt. 2. Is this room yours? 3. This is yours. 4. What is your name? 5. They are my sons. 6. Is this your dog? 7. Whose is this? 8. This house is ours. 9. It is mine. 10. This is a waste of time.

Key 6

1. My daughter's birthday is on 28th April.
2. My father's profession is very interesting.
3. My son's favourite food is roasted chicken.
4. Give me Vibha's address please.
5. My brother's room is always very dirty.
6. Write the name of the town and the date at the top of the page.
7. February and March are the best months of the year in India.
8. I don't know the cause of the fight.
9. The brakes of my scooter failed.
10. The walls of modern buildings are very thin.
11. Obama is the first black President of America.
12. Is that woman a friend of yours?
13. I met an uncle of yours at the party.
14. We went for a picnic with some friends of ours.
15. We went to the movies with an aunt of ours.
16. One of his daughters is in America.

Key 7

1. She went to the airport with a friend of hers.
2. I went on a boat ride with some colleagues of mine.
3. He will have a bath in the Ganges with some guests of his.
4. I played football with some classmates of mine.
5. They came to our house with some colleagues of theirs.
6. Is she a relative of yours?

The Weather

Teacher : What was the weather like in Delhi last month?

Student : Last month it was very hot there. The maximum temperatur rose to 47^0 Celsius and the miniumum temperature never went below 30^{0}Celsius.

Teacher : What is the weather like in Varanasi these days?

Student : It is hot as well as humid.

Teacher : What will the weather be like in your city in November?

Student : In November it will be neither too cold nor too hot. It will be just the right weather to go round and visit places. The maximum temperature is usually about 28^0 to 30^{0}Celsius, and the minimum temperature oscillates between 15^0 and 20^{0}Celsius.

Teacher : What is the maximum temperature in Tokyo today?

Student : The maximum temperature in Tokyo today is 26^{0}Celsius.

Teacher : What is the minimum temperature is Sydney today?

Student : The minimum temperature is Sydney today is 9^{0}Celsius.

Teacher : What have the meteorologists predicted about the weather in India today?

Student : The meteorologists have predicted heavy rain in Assam, Orissa and Bengal; they have predicted cloudy skies with light showers accompanied by lightning and thunder for the plains of Uttar Pradesh.

Teacher : Which city had the highest maximum temperature today?

Student : Ahmedabad had the highest temperature today.

Teacher : Name the cities with the lowest minimum temperature in India today.

Student : Delhi and Bombay had the lowest minimum temperature today.

43 Reflexive Pronouns

■ my / your / his / her / its / our / their = *अपना, अपने, अपनी*

1. Tell me your address. — मुझे अपना पता बताइए।
2. Wash your hands before you eat. — खाने से पहले अपने हाथ धोओ।
3. Kamla gave me her address. — कमला ने मुझे अपना पता दिया।
4. I gave her my address. — मैंने उसको अपना पता दिया।
5. Father kept his money in his safe. — पिता जी ने अपने पैसे अपनी तिजोरी में रखे।
6. I will go to my house. — मैं अपने घर जाऊँगा/जाऊँगी।
7. He is reading his book. — वह अपनी किताब पढ़ रहा है।
8 Open your books. — अपनी–अपनी किताब खोलिए।

■ my/ your / his / her / its / our / their + own = *अपना, अपने, अपनी*

1. I live in **my own** house. — मैं अपने घर में रहता हूँ।
2. Is this **your own** car? — क्या यह आपकी अपनी कार है?
3. In this building every tenant has **his own** parking place. — इस भवन में सब किरायेदारों के पास अपनी कार रखने की जगह है।

■ * by oneself, by herself, by himself, by yourself, by them selves, by ourselves = *अपने-से/अकेले*

1. Do you go to school by yourself? — क्या तुम स्कूल अपने–से जाते हो?
2. My 90 years old grandmother — मेरी नव्वे वर्ष की नानी अपना सब

* **by** *का प्रयोग छोड़ा भी जा सकता है।*

does all her work by herself.	काम अपने–से करती हैं।
3. We painted our house ourselves.	हमने अपना घर अपने–से रंगा।
4. I often see her walking on the 'ghats' by herself.	मैं उसे अक्सर घाट पर अकेले घूमते देखता हूँ।

■ **oneself, herself, himself, yourself, themselves, ourselves**

अपना/ अपने/ अपनी + यथोचित कारक

1. She paid for herself.	उसने **अपने लिए** पैसे दिए।
2. They paid for themselves.	उन्होंने **अपने लिए** पैसे दिए।
3. He does not consider himself qualifiied for the job.	वह **अपनेको** इस काम के लिए योग्य नहीं समझता।।
4. He is very selfish. He only thinks of himself.	वह बहुत स्वार्थी है। वह सिर्फ़ **अपने बारे में** सोचता है।
5. Ask yourself!	**अपने से पूछो**।

Ex.1: Fill in the blanks with the appropriate reflexive pronouns such as oneself, myself, yourself etc.

1. One should do it by..........
2. I live by........... in this big house.
3. She cooked it by.............
4. They came here by.........
5. Can you do it all by............?
6. He sat by.................
7. It opened by...............
8. We arranged this exhibition all by............
9. Mother made all the arrangements for the party by........
10. He repairs his gadgets by............

Ex. 2: Fill in the blanks with the correct form of the pronoun given in the brackets:

1. If you look in the mirror, you see..... (your, yourself).
2. I believe in caring for....... (me, myself) and letting others care for...... (them, themselves).

3. Rani told me a poem which her mother had recited to...... (her, herself) last evening.
4. Students cannot understand everything by...... (them, themselves), so their teachers must help........ (them, themselves).
5. We enjoyed........ (us, ourselves) at the party.
6. The old couple lived in that big house by....... (them, themselves).
7. Society makes one corrupt; one doesn't become corrupt by.... (one, onself).

Ex. 3: Translate into English:

1.मैं यह भारी संदूक अपने–से नहीं ले जा पाऊँगा। 2. मैंने यह घड़ी अपने–से ठीक की। 3. वह अपना खाना अपने–आप बनाना चाहती है। 4. हर बात के लिए अपने को दोष न दो। 5. उसने मुझे अपनी कहानी सुनाई। 6. मैं अपना देश पसन्द करता हूँ/करती हूँ । 7. इस शहर में देर रात को अकेले बाहर जाना असुरक्षित है। 8. अगर तुम निष्ठा से काम करोगे, तो तुम अपने–से अपना लक्ष्य प्राप्त कर सकते हो।

Key 1

1. oneself	2. myself	3. herself
4. themselves	5. yourself	6. himself
7. itself	8. ourselves	9. herself
10. himself		

Key 2

1. yourself	2. myself, themselves	3. her
4. themselves, them	5. ourselves	6. themselves
7. oneself		

Key 3

1. I will not be able to carry this heavy box by myself. 2. I repaired this watch myself. 3. She wants to cook her dinner herself. 4. Don't blame yourself for everything. 5. She told me her story. 6. I like my country. 7. In this city it is unsafe to go out late in the night by oneself. 8. If you work sincerely, you can reach your goal yourself.

The Coldest Weather

A : It is too cold today.
B : It certainly is. This is the coldest weather I can remember.
A : The cold is not so bad. But the problem is the biting wind. My nose and ears seem to be freezing!.
B : Yes, the heavy snowfall yesterday just made it worse. Even though today the sky is clear and the sun is shining, it hasn't made us any warmer.
A : The meteorological department predicted a rise in temperature next week. It should feel warmer then.
B : I hope so. Let's go to a place where we can drink some hot coffee.
A : That's a good idea. Let's go.

The Hottest Summer

A : I find the heat these days almost unendurable. What has the temperature been like lately?
B : Everybody is finding it unendurable! Do you know this has been the hottest summer, in more than fifty years. In most cities, the mercury crossed 50°Celsius. In my city, there have been so many deaths due to heat that there wasn't enough space in the cremation grounds to burn the dead bodies. And to top it, the 'doms'* fled for the fear that they might fall a victim to heat stroke and die. Man, it's frightening. In any case I am moving to the mountains tomorrow morning.
A : So am I. I am leaving tonight!

* The supposedly lowest caste among the Hindus, burning dead bodies in cremation grounds.

44 Adverbs

some important classifications

■ **Adverbs qualify verbs, adjectives, adverbs and phrases, clauses or sentences.**

Classification	Examples
• Adverbs of manner — How a person does something.	courageously, sadly, happily, fast cheerfully, sharp, coldly, warmly.
• Adverbs of place—- where something happened.	up, down, near, far, here, there.
• Adverbs of time — When something happens.	now, then, today, tomorrow, still, yet.
• Adverbs of frequency—How often something happens	twice, 3-hourly, always, periodically sometimes, frequently, never, often.
• Adverbs of degree —	hardly, rather, quite, too, so, absolutely, barely, scarcely, entirely, almost, very.
• Adverbs of sentence —	surely, certainly, fortunately, definitely, actually, apparently.
• Interrogative adverbs —	how, when, why, where.
• Conjunctive adverbs — These join and relate independent clauses	accordingly, also, anyway, finally, furthermore, hence, however, incidentally, indeed, instead, meanwhile, moreover, nevertheless, nonetheless, now, otherwise.

Adverbs as qualifiers of verbs:

- It is snowing heavily. बहुत बर्फ़ पड़ रही है।
- Our school team played badly. हमारे स्कूल की टीम ख़राब खेली।
- I found your house easily. मुझे आपका घर आसानी से मिला।
- Please wait patiently. कृपया धैर्यपूर्वक प्रतीक्षा करें।

Adverbs as qualifiers of adjectives :

- He is seriously ill. वह गंभीर रूप से बीमार है।
- Their house is absolutely enormous. उनका घर बहुत बड़ा है।
- This street is unusually quiet today. आज यह सड़क असाधारण शान्त है।
- I find most TV serials unnecessarily long. मुझे दूरदर्शन के धारावाहिक अनावश्यक लम्बे लगते हैं।

Usually we can make an adverb by adding 'ly' to an adjective:

प्राय: **adjective** के साथ **'–ly'** लगाकर **adverb** बनाते हैं।

adjective		adverb	
easy	आसान	easily	आसानी से
angry	गुस्सा	angrily	गुस्से से
quiet	चुप	quietly	चुपके से
slow	धीरे	slowly	धीरे से
careful	सावधान	carefully	सावधानी से
foolish	मूर्खतापूर्ण	foolishly	मूर्खतापूर्ण ढंग से
reasonable	युक्तिसंगत, वाजिब	reasonably	वाजिब तौर पर
perfect	दोषरहित	perfectly	दोषरहित ढंग से
bad	बुरा	badly	बुरी तरह

☞ **However, it is not always possible to make an adverb like this.**

e.g. adverb of 'good' is 'well'.

याद रखें कि हमेशा **adverb** इस प्रकार नहीं बनाया जा सकता। जैसे कि **'good'** का **adverb 'well'** है।

• Robert's Hindi is very good. (adj.)	राबर्ट की हिन्दी बहुत अच्छी है।
• Robert speaks Hindi very well. (adv.)	राबर्ट हिन्दी बहुत अच्छी बोलता है।
• Robert is a good student. (adj.)	राबर्ट अच्छा विद्यार्थी है।
• He behaves well in class. (adv.)	वह कक्षा में अच्छी तरह व्यवहार करता है।

■ **Some '- ly' ending words such as cowardly, costly, deadly, friendly, likely, lonely, lovely, silly, ugly are adjectives and cannot be used as adverbs. Some other word is added to these to give an adverbial meaning.**

Cowardly, costly, deadly, friendly, likely, lonely, lovely, silly, ugly आदि कुछ **'- ly'** अन्त वाले शब्द **adverb** की तरह प्रयोग नहीं होते। उनकी **adverbial** अभिव्यक्ति कुछ और शब्द लगाकर बनाते हैं जैसे कि

adjective		adverb	
friendly	मैत्रीपूर्ण	in a friendly manner	मैत्रीपूर्ण भाव से
lovely	प्यारा	lovingly	स्नेहपूर्ण भाव से
silly	मूर्ख	in a silly manner.	मूर्खतापूर्ण ढंग से

■ **Some '-ly' ending words such as daily, yearly, monthly, weekly can be used both as adjectives and as adverbs.**

कुछ **'-ly'** अन्त के शब्द **adjective** और **adverb** दोनों का काम करते हैं जैसे कि, **daily, yearly, monthly, weekly etc.**

1. This is our daily routine.(adj.) यह हमारी दिनचर्या है।
2. I do this daily. (adv.) मैं यह रोज़ करता हूँ।

■ **Some words such as 'fast', 'hard', 'late', have the same form as adjective and adverb.**

कुछ शब्दों का **adjective** और **adverb** रूप एक ही होता है जैसे कि **fast, hard, late** । ☞**There is no such word as 'fastly'.**
(ध्यान दें कि **'fastly'** कोई शब्द नहीं।)

1. He is a fast reader. (adj.) वह तीव्र गति से पढनेवाला है।
2. He reads fast. (adv.) वह तीव्र गति से पढ़ता है।
3. The teacher gave a hard blow(adj.) अध्यापक ने उसे ज़ोर से घूंसा मारा।
4. She works hard. (adv.) वह मेहनत करती है।
5. She is a late comer. (adj.) वह सदैव देर से पहुँचनेवालों में से है।
6. She came late today. (adv.) वह आज देर से पहुँची।

■ **Some words have two adverbial forms, one exactly the same as 'adjective' the other with '-ly' ending. But usually the adverb with '-ly' ending has an entirely different meaning; e.g. late** देर से, **lately** हाल में।

☞ कई शब्दों के दो **adverb** रूप होते हैं एक तो **'adjective'** के जैसा, दूसरा **'-ly'** अन्तवाला। परन्तु दोनों का अर्थ बिलकुल भिन्न होता है।

Lately he has become very careless. हाल में वह बहुत लापरवाह हो गया है।

clean (adj.) साफ़ ; **(adv.)** पूर्ण रूप से
cleanly (adj.) साफ़ **(adv.)** अच्छी तरह

1. She keeps her house clean. (adv.). वह अपना घर साफ़ रखती है।

2. I like to have dogs as pets; they are clean animals (adj.).	मुझे कुत्ते पालना अच्छा लगता है। वे साफ़ जानवर होते हैं।
3. These scissors cut the cloth very cleanly (adv.).	यह कैंची कपड़ा बहुत अच्छा काटती है।(अर्थात इसकी धार बहुत तेज़ है।)
4. It clean (absolutely) slipped out of my mind to invite him to the party. (adv.).	उसे दावत में बुलाना मेरे दिमाग से ही निकल गया। (अर्थात मैं बिलकुल भूल गई।)
5. The robbers got clean away. (adv.).	चोर सफ़ा भाग गए। (अर्थात बिना कोई सुराग़ छोड़े भाग निकले।)

☞ **Use of 'clean + past participle' is possible as an adjective:**

1. It is a clean forgotten incident.	यह भूली बिसरी घटना है।
2. He used to have a beard but this morning I saw him clean shaven.	उसकी दाढ़ी हुआ करती थी, परन्तु आज सुबह मैंने उसे बिना दाढ़ी के देखा।

Close (adj.) घनिष्ठ; **(adv.)** नज़दीक
closely (adv.) निकटसे **closely + past participle(Ex. 5,6)**

1. We are **close** friends. (adj.)	हम ***घनिष्ठ*** मित्र हैं।
2. I sat **close to** him. (adv.)	मैं उसके ***नज़दीक*** बैठा।
3. Someone is running **close** behind us.(adv.)	कोई ***बहुत पास ही*** हमारा पीछा कर रहा है।
4. I always **watched closely** how my mother cooked. (adv.)	मैं हमेशा ***ध्यान से*** देखा करती थी मेरी माँ खाना कैसे पकाती थीं।
5. The terrorist activities are being **closely guarded.** (adv.).	उग्रवादी गतिविधियों पर ***कड़ी निगाह रखी*** जा रही है।
6. She took along two **closely**	वह अपने साथ दो ***ठूंस-ठूंस कर भरे***

packed boxes of clothes. (adj.). हुए कपड़ों के सन्दूक ले गई।

dead (adj.) मरा हुआ **(adv.)** पूर्ण रूप से

deadly (adj.) घातक, जानलेवा **(adv.)** घातक रूप से

1. Today I saw a **dead man** on my way back home. (adj.) — आज घर लौटते समय मैंने एक मरा हुआ आदमी देखा।
2. The train moved **dead slow**. (adv.) — गाड़ी बहुत धीरे चल रही थी।
3. I get **dead tired** after the day's work. (adv.) — मैं दिनभर के काम के बाद थक कर चूर हो जाती हूँ।
4. **Deadly hatred** prevails among the people of these tribes. (adj.) — इन जनजातियों में अत्यधिक घ णा प्रचलित है।

direct (adj.) सीधा, स्पष्ट **(adv.)** सीधे, प्रत्यक्षत:

directly (adv.) तुरन्त, स्पष्ट तौर पर

1. This bus goes **direct** to the station. (adv.) — यह बस सीधी स्टेशन जाती है।
2. The chairman left **directly** after the meeting. (adv.). — सभापति बैठक के तुरन्त बाद चले गए।
3. He gave a short and **direct** reply.(adj.). — उसने छोटा और सीधा उत्तर दिया।

high (adj.) ऊँचा, उच्च **(adv.)** बहुत ज़्यादा

highly (adv.) बहुत ज़्यादा

1. He jumped over the **high** wall with ease. (adj.) — वह ऊँची दीवार से आसानी से कूद गया।
2. If one aims **high** and fixes one's hopes high, one is bound to — यदि व्यक्ति ऊँचा लक्ष्य बनाता है, ऊँची उम्मीदें रखता है, तो निश्चित ही अपने

achieve one's goal. (adv,)	लक्ष्य को प्राप्त करता है।
3. He held his head **high** even when he was very poor. (adv.)	जब वह बहुत ग़रीब था, तब भी अपना सिर ऊँचा उठा रखता था।
4. The teachers thought very **highly** of him. (adv.)	अध्यापकों की राय उसके बारे में बहुत ऊँची थी।

loud (adj.) ऊँचा स्वर
(adv.) ऊँचे स्वर से

loudly (adv.) ऊँचे स्वर से, ज़ोर से
aloud (adv.) ऊँचे स्वर में

1. The teacher spoke in a **loud** and clear voice. (adj.)	अध्यापक ऊँचे और स्पष्ट स्वर में बोला।
2. A teacher should speak **loudly** and clearly. (adv.)	अध्यापक को ऊँचा और साफ़-साफ़ बोलना चाहिए।
3. She sang **aloud**. (adv.)	उसने उच्च स्वर में गाया।
4. She narrated her grievances **loudly.** (adv.)	उसने अपना दुखड़ा खुलकर बताया।

pretty (adj.) सुंदर

prettily (adv.) आकर्षक ढंग से

1. She is a **pretty** girl. (adj.)	वह बहुत सुन्दर लड़की है।
2. She is always **pretti**ly dressed. (adv.)	वह बहुत आकर्षक ढंग से तैयार होती है।
3. I am **pretty** tired of doing the same thing every day. (adv.)	मैं एक ही काम रोज़ करते-करते ऊब गया हूँ।
4. It is **pretty** expensive. (adv.)	यह काफ़ी मँहगा है।

right (adj.) ठीक, दायाँ, उपयुक्त

(adv.) ठीक से

rightly (adv.) ठीक ही, उचित रीति से

1. He made the **right** decision.(adj.)	उसने ठीक फ़ैसला लिया।

2. I hurt my right hand. (adj.) — मेरे दाहिने हाथ में चोट लग गई।
3. Do it right away. (adv.) — इसे तुरन्त करो।
4. Rightly so. (adv.) — बिलकुल ठीक।
5. Serve him right. (adv.) — उसके साथ ऐसा ही होना चाहिए।

round (adj./adv.) गोल, वर्तुल — **roundly (adv.)** साफ़-साफ़

1. I like **round** mirrors. (adj.) — मुझे गोल दर्पण पसन्द हैं।
2. Run **round** the corner. (adv.) — नुक्कड़ पर दौड़ो।
3. She told me **roundly** that she could not help me. (adv.) — उसने मुझे साफ़-साफ़ कह दिया कि वह मेरी मदद नहीं कर पाएगी।

sharp (adj.) तेज़, पैना, उच्च (स्वर) — **sharply (adv.)** तेज़ी से, कठोरता से

1. Cut it with a **sharp** knife. (adj.) — इसे तेज़ धार के चाकू से काटो।
2. She has very **sharp** features. (adj.) — उसके नयन-नक्श बहुत तीखे हैं।
3. Meet me at 9 O' clock **sharp** tomorrow morning. (adv.) — मुझे कल सुबह ठीक नौ बजे मिलो।
4. She sings rather **sharp.** (adv.) — वह कुछ ऊँचे स्वर में गाती है।
5. He spoke **sharply** to me. (adv.) — वह मुझसे कठोरता से बोला।

tight (adj.) तंग, कसी हुई — **tightly** (adv.) ठसाठस, मज़बूती से, कस के

1. These jeans are **tight** for me. (adj.) — यह जीन्स मेरे लिए तंग हैं।
2. Pack it **tight**. (adv.) — इसे कस कर बाँधो।
3. She sent me a **tightly** packed box of chocolates. (adj.) — उसने मुझे ठसाठस भरा हुआ चाकलेट का डब्बा भेजा।

4. She stayed tight lipped. वह बिलकुल चुप रही।

Position of adverbs

■ **Adverbs can be placed at the beginning, in the middle, or at the end of a sentence. However, all adverbs cannot go in all three positions.**

☞ **The adverbs of manner follow the verb.**

- He played badly. (adv.) वह बहुत ख़राब खेला।
- She organized the inaugural function very well. (adv.) उसने उद्‌घाटन समारोह का इन्त-ज़ाम बहुत अच्छी तरह किया।
- She decorated the house nicely. (adv.) उसने घर की सजावट बहुत भली प्रकार की।

☞ **Adverbs of place come before the adverb of time.**

- I go to school everyday. मैं रोज़ स्कूल जाती हूँ।।
- We arrived at the station at 5 O'clock. हम स्टेशन पाँच बजे पहुँचे।

■ **Word order if a sentence has several adverbs of place: (1) the adverb referring to the smaller place + (2) the adverb referring to larger place and so on.**

यदि एक वाक्य में एक से अधिक **adverbs of place** हों तो वाक्य लिखते या बोलते समय क्रम से छोटे स्थान से शुरू करके बड़े की ओर जाएं।

उदाहरण:

- I used to live at Jodhpur colony on the BHU campus in Varanasi in India.

मैं भारत में बनारस में बनारस हिन्दु विश्वविद्यालय के परिसर पर जोधपुर कलौनी में रहती थी।

■ **Word order if a sentence has several types of adverbs:**

(1) adverbs of manner + (2) adverbs of place and (3) adverbs of time.

☞ यदि एक वाक्य में एक से अधिक विभिन्न **adverbs** हों तो वाक्य लिखते या बोलते समय क्रम से **adverbs of manner + adverbs of place** और अंततः **adverbs of time** रखें। उदाहरण:

- I went to Delhi last week. — मैं पिछले सप्ताह दिल्ली गया।
- He came to my house at 2 p.m. — वह अपराह्न दो बजे मेरे घर आया।
- The Indian team played well in Australia yesterday. — भारत की 'टीम' कल ऑस्ट्रेलिया में अच्छा खेली।
- She organized an exhibition at the Arts Auditorium last month. — उसने पिछले महीने 'आर्ट्स ऑडि-टोरियम' में एक प्रदर्शनी का आयोजन किया।

☞ **With verbs of movement like ' come',' go', 'run', 'reach', 'arrive', use the adverb of place before the adverb of manner.**

- He drove on the highway slowly. — उसने राजपथ वाहन पर धीरे चलाया।
- She went to her office quickly. — वह अपने दफ़्तर जल्दी से गई।
- She arrived in Delhi by plane. — वह दिल्ली जहाज़ से पहुँची।

■ **Adverbs are placed after the verb 'is, are, am. was. were.'**

- They are always on time. — वे हमेशा समय पर आते हैं।
- She is never late. — वह कभी देर से नहीं आती।
- This street is usually very noisy. — इस सड़क पर सदैव शोर रहता है।

■ **Adverbs are usually placed before the one word verb.**

- He always comes home late. — वह हमेशा देर से घर आता है।
- She never travels by air. — वह हवाईजहाज़ से यात्रा कभी नहीं करती।

3. He hardly watches Hindi films. — वह कभी-कभार हिन्दी फ़िल्म देखती है।

4. They rarely use the internet.	वह कभी-कभार 'इन्टरनैट' पर काम करती है।

☞ **Don't put 'never' and 'always' at the beginning of a sentence.**

■ **When a sentence has both an auxiliary verb and a main verb, put adverb after the auxiliary verb.**

1. She has always worked hard.	उसने हमेशा बहुत परिश्रम किया है।
2. I have never enjoyed this work.	मुझे कभी भी इस काम में आनन्द नहीं आया।
3. I am definitely eating out today.	मैं आज निश्चित ही बाहर खाऊँगी।
4. She has always been kind to us.	वह हमारे साथ सदैव दयालु रही है।
5. I might never have met my fiance if I had not travelled by Indian Airlines.	यदि मैंने एयर इण्डिया से यात्रा न की होती, तो मैं अपने मंगेतर से कभी न मिली होती।

■ **Adverbs such as 'always', 'often', 'also', 'never', are placed before 'have to.'**

1. I always have to get up early.	मुझे सदैव जल्दी उठना पड़ता है।
2. Mother always has to cook for us all.	माँ को हमेशा हम सब के लिए खाना पकाना पड़ता है।
3. She often has to send money to her parents.	उसे अकसर अपने माता पिता को पैसा भेजना पड़ता है।

■ **In a negative sentence 'probably' is placed before a negative.**

1. I probably won't come to the party.	शायद मैं दावत में नहीं आऊँगी।

=

I will probably not come to the party.

Ex. 1: Fill in the blanks with the suitable frequency adverbs:

> I go to the temple... (Monday, Saturday)
> => I go to the temple twice a week.

1. She washes her hair........ (Sunday).
2. Mother cooks meals........ (morning, evening).
3. The washerman does washing...... (Monday, Tuesday, Wednesday, Thursday, Friday, Saturday, Sunday).
4. The children play cricket....... (5 p.m.)
5. I go to the office by car......... (Tuesday, Thursday, Saturday).
6. She changes jobs......... (1988, 1992, 1996)
7. The patient should take medicine..... (8 a.m., 2 p.m., 8 p.m., 2 a.m.)
8. We take a shower...... (morning, afternoon, late in the evening)
9. I pay for the newspaper...... (1st of every month).
10. This magazine is published...... (7th, 21st of every month).
11. I learn English..... (Monday, Wednesday, Friday).
12. The doctor visited the patient........ (8 a.m., 10 a.m., 12 a.m.)
13. We go to Mussoorie..... (in June every year).
14. We have Navaratri....... (in April, in October).

Ex.2: Place the words in the parentheses in the right place.

1. We were on vacation in India. (all)
2. You are very kind. (always)
3. Mother has to start her day very early in the morning. (usually)
4. I don't have to cook for the family. (normally)
5. Do you go to temple in the morning? (always)
6. Robert is learning Hindi; he is learning Sanskrit. (also)
7. We can assist them. (probably)
8. They can't do this. (probably)
9. This house is not very expensive. (probably)
10. This house costs a lot to rent. (probably)

Ex.3: Fill in the blanks using the words in parentheses in correct order:

1. I .... phone numbers. (can/ remember/ never)
2. She .... tea without sugar. (usually/ takes)

3. I .... slow in the forenoon. (usually, am)
4. She .... to the post office. (probably/ has/ gone)
5. He is a good singer. He ....very well. (dance/also/ can)
6. Our dog .... at innocent people. (often/ barks)
7. Mother .... while watching television. (often/ sleeps)
8. We live in the same colony, but we .... each other. (never/visited/ have)
9. I .... get up very early. (have to/ always/ get up)
10. Children .... in the playground. (still/ are / playing)
11. I .... irritated at this time of the day. (am/ always)
12. I .... the exam this year. (won't take/ probably)
13. We .... to Mumbai next week. (go/ probably/ will)
14. She .... for the US next month. (be/ probably/ leaving/ will)

Ex.4: Which is correct?

1. It was a **fatal / fatally** accident.
2. He was **fatal / fatally** injured.
3. There was **continuous / continuously** rain for a week.
4. It rained **continuous / continuously** for a week.
5. Her English is **flawless / flawlessly.**
6. He speaks English **flawless/ flawlessly**.
7. He is a **carefully / careful** worker.
8. He works **careful / carefully.**
9. She narrated to me an **incredibly / incredible** experience of hers.
10. The car was **bad / badly** damaged.
11. It was a **terribly / terrible** collision.
12. The prices here are **reasonably / reasonable** and the food is **terrific.**
13. We waited **patiently/ patient** for the rain to stop.
14. India lost the cricket match because our team played **very bad / badly.** (adv.)
15. He didn't hit you **intentionally / intetional.**

Ex.5: Translate into English:

1. रेस्टोरेण्ट बेहद महँगा था। 2. बाढ़ में इस इमारत को बहुत नुकसान पहुँचा। 3. खजुराहो

बेहद सुन्दर था। 4. यह रेस्टोरेण्ट काफ़ी सस्ता है। 5. कल हमने मोती महल में खाया। खाना बहुत स्वादिष्ट था। 6. मेरे माता-पिता मेरे परिणाम से अत्यधिक निराश होगें। 7. कृपया धीरे बोलिए। 8. छुट्टियाँ बहुत जल्दी बीत गईं। 9. मैं यहाँ विशेषकर आपसे मिलने आया। 10. यह 'जीन्स' तुम्हें बिल्कुल ठीक आई हैं। 11.उसने अंग्रेज़ी लगातार पाँच साल सीखी। अब वह धाराप्रवाह और एक दम परिशुद्ध बोलती है। 12. मौसम अचानक बदल गया।

Ex. 6: Translate into English:

1. बाज़ार उतना पास नहीं था जितना मैंने सोचा था। 2. आजकल मैं फ़िल्म उतना अकसर नहीं देखता जितना पहले देखता था। 3. वह मुझे इतनी अच्छी तरह नहीं जानता जितना उसकी माता जी। 4. वह जितनी जल्दी हो सका यहाँ पहुँची। 5. वे जब तक चाहें हमारे यहाँ रह सकते हैं। 6. जितनी जल्दी हो सके यह काम ख़त्म कर दो। 7. अब मुझे अंधेरे से उतना डर नहीं लगता जितना पहले लगता था। 8. आप वहाँ पहुँचते ही फ़ोन कीजिएगा। 9. 'मेट्रो' की तुलना में बसें ज़्यादा चलती हैं। 10. हवाई जहाज़ की तुलना में रेलगाड़ी से ज़्यादा समय लगता है।

Key 1

1. once a week
2. twice a day/two times a day
3. every day
4. every evening
5. thrice a week / three times a week.
6. every four years
7. every six hours / four times a day.
8. thrice a day / three times a day
9. monthly / once a month
10. bi-weekly
11. on alternate days / every other day
12. every two hours.
13. once a year
14. twice a year

Key 2

1. We were **all** ....
2. You are **always** ....
3. Mother **usually** has to
4. I don't **normally** have to ....
5. Do you always go ....
6. ....he is also learning..........
7. We can probably ....
8. They probably can't ....
9. This house is probably not.......
10. This house probably costs .....

Key 3

1. can never remember
2. usually takes
3. am usually
4. has probably gone
5. can also dance
6. often barks
7. often sleeps
8. have never visited
9. always have to
10. are still playing
11. am always
12. probably won't take
13. will probably go
14. will probably be leaving

Key 4

1. fatal
2. fatally
3. continuous
4. continuously
5. flawless
6. flawlessly
7. careful
8. carefully
9. incredible
10. badly
11. terrible
12. reasonable
13. patiently
14. badly
15. intentionally

Key 5

1. The restaurant was **extremely** expensive.
2. This building was **badly** damaged in the floods.
3. Khajuraho was **incredibly** beautiful.
4. This is a **reasonably** inexpensive restaurant.
5. Last evening we ate at The Moti Mahal; the food was **extremely** delicious.
6. My parents will be **bitterly** disappointed by my result.
7. Please speak **slowly.**
8. The vacation passed **very quickly.**
9. I came here specially to meet you.
10. These jeans fit you **perfectly**.
11. She learnt English continuously for 5 years. Now she speaks **fluently** and **flawlessly.**
12. The weather changed **suddenly**.

Key 6

1. The market was not as near as I had thought.

2. These days I don't watch movies as often as I used to.
3. He does not know me as well as his mother.
4. She came here as quickly as she could.
5. They may stay with us as long as they want.
6. Finish this task as soon as possible.
7. I am not as afraid of darkness now as I used to be.
8. Phone me as soon as you arrive there.
9. Buses run more frequently than metro.
10. It takes longer by train than by air.

Customer Satisfaction Is Our Motto

Neela bought a new VCR last week. There is something wrong with it. She has just entered into the service centre of the BPL.

SE : Good morning, Miss Patel. What can we do for you?

Neela : I am afraid there is something wrong with this VCR. It makes funny creaking sounds.

SE : I am sorry to hear this, madam. Can you leave it with us for a day or two? We'd better have a look at it.

Neela : Much though I dislike it, I suppose I'll have to. Do you think it might be something serious?

SE : We don't usually get complaints. BPL is known for perfection.

Neela : I certainly hope not. I need to use it tomorrow. Do you think it will be ready by then?

SE : It should be. But honestly it depends upon what the trouble is. Customer satisfaction is our motto.

Neela : It is very kind of you indeed. Thanks so much. Goodbye.

SE : Goodbye.

SE = Servicing engineer

45 Prepositions

Use of prepositions in the English language is baffling for a foreign student. There aren't many well defined rules. One should learn the expressions separately e.g. by car, by bus, by train but on foot; ; in the morning, in the evening but at night.
Then there are prepositional phrases. The same word followed by a different preposition has an entirely different meaning. For details refer to my book 'Prepositions and Prepositional Phrases'.

Prepositions of time

■ In, on, at

- at 5 a.m. / at 11.30 p.m. etc सुबह पाँच बजे / रात को साढ़े ग्यारह बजे।
- at the weekend(s) सप्ताहान्त पर
- at the moment / at present इस वक़्त
- at noon, at midnight दोपहर को / आधी रात को।

☞ at night / in the night रात को / रात में

1. I don't go out at night. मैं रात को बाहर नहीं जाता/जाती।
2. There was a bank robbery in the night.
रात में बैंक में डाका पड़ा।

- on Monday/ on Tuesday etc सोमवार को / मंगलवार को आदि।
- on Monday morning / on Tuesday afternoon etc. सोमवार को सुबह / मंगलवार को अपराह्न में आदि।
- on Diwali day / on Christmas day यहाँ अभिप्राय दिन विशेष से है।

☞ at Diwali / at Christmas / at Holi etc.

यहाँ अभिप्राय त्योहार के साथ जुड़े हुए अवकाश काल से है।

- in the morning(s) / in the evening(s) / in the afternoon(s),
- in summer / in winter / in autumn / in spring.
  गर्मी / सर्दी / पतझड़ / बसन्त में।

☞ in / during the summer / winter holidays गर्मी / सर्दी की छुट्टियों में।

- in January / in February / in 2012 / in the 21st century etc.
  जनवरी में / फ़रवरी में / सन् 2012 में / इक्कीसवीं सदी में।
- in the Middle Ages मध्यकाल में/ in the Modern Age आधुनिक काल में।
- in two days / in two days time दो दिनों में / दो दिनों के भीतर
- in a couple of days एक-दो दिनों में।
- in a week / in a week's time एक सप्ताह में / एक सप्ताह के भीतर।

■ **in time / in good time** समय से, पर्याप्त समय रहते

just in time लगभग देर हो जाना, देर होते होते बचना

on time ठीक समय पर **in no time** तुरन्त

- They arrived on time. वे ठीक समय पर पहुँचे।
- We arrived at the station **in time** for the train. हम गाड़ी चलने से कुछ पहले ही स्टेशन पर पहुँचे।
- We arrived at the station **just in time** for the train. हम लगभग गाड़ी चलने के ऐन वक़्त पर ही स्टेशन पर पहुँचे। (हमारी गाड़ी छूटते छूटते बची।)

■ **for, since** 'से'

☞ हम हिन्दी भाषी कालावधि (period of time) और कालबिन्दु (point of time) सम्बन्धी अभिव्यक्तियों में एक ही कारक 'से' का प्रयोग करते हैं, परन्तु अंग्रेज़ी में period of time के साथ for और point of time के साथ since का प्रयोग करते हैं। जैसे:—

- for years सालों से for the time being अभी के लिए

- since Tuesday मंगलवार से — since last week पिछले हफ्ते से
- since 9 O'clock नौ बजे से — since the morning सुबह से
- She has been learning English for two months / since January. — वह ***दो महीनों से/जनवरी से*** अंग्रेज़ी सीख रही है।

during 'के दौरान'

- during the night रात्रिकाल मे; during the film फ़िल्म के दौरान;
- during the speech भाषण के बीच मे;
- I learnt cooking during the summer holidays — मैंने गर्मी की छुट्टियों में खाना बनाना सीखा।

by + time expression अमुक समय के भीतर ही, उसके बाद नहीं

- It will be ready by 5 O' clock / by Monday / by January.

  यह पाँच बजे तक / सोमवार तक / जनवरी तक तैयार हो जाएगा।

until + time expression अमुक समय तक, उससे पहले नहीं

- Wait for me until 6 p.m. — छः बजे तक मेरी प्रतीक्षा कीजिएगा।

from... to... से ... तक...

- from 9 a.m. to 4 p.m. — सुबह नौ बजे से शाम को चार बजे तक।
- from January 2012 to December 2013

  जनवरी दो हज़ार बारह से दिसम्बर दो हज़ार तेरह तक

Preposition is not used with the following:
निम्नलिखित के साथ preposition नहीं लगता।

- last week / last month / last year etc. पिछले हफ़्ते/-महीने/-साल
- next week / next month / next year etc. अगले हफ़्ते/-महीने/-साल
- this week / this month / this time / every time / what time? etc.

  इस हफ़्ते/महीने ; इस बार / हर बार /, कितने बजे?
- today/ tomorrow / the day after tomorrow / yesterday / the

day before yesterday etc. आज, कल (आगामी) , परसों (आगामी),
कल (गत), परसों (गत)

- these days, those days. आज-कल /इन दिनों, उन दिनों।

Prepositions of place In, on, at,

■ in a building भवन के अन्दर

☞ at the front / at the back of a building भवन के सामने / पीछे (बाहर)

■ in an office / in a department / in a room दफ़्तर / विभाग/ कमरे में

■ in a cupboard / -a drawer / - a box अलमारी/दराज़/सन्दूक़ में

■ in town / in a village / in a country / in the world.
शहर / गाँव / देश / दुनिया ।

■ in a row / in a line / in a queue पंक्ति / क़तार में
in the newpaper / -magazine / -bookअख़बार / पत्रिका /पुस्तक में

- All the important papers are in this drawer. सब आवश्यक काग़ज़ इस दराज़ में हैं।
- Stand in a queue. पंक्ति में खड़े हो जाओ।
- Towels are in this cupboard. तौलिए इस अलमारी में हैं।
- The garage is at the back of the building. गराज भवन के पिछवाड़े में है।

■ **in prison** बन्दी का बन्दीगृह में होना **/ in hospital** रोगी का अस्पताल में होना

- He was in prison for two months. वह दो महीने बन्दीगृह में था।
- She is in hospital these days. वह आजकल अस्पताल में है।

■ at sea समुदी यात्रा पर होना / in sea समुद्र में (तैरना या गोता लगाना)

- **on a table, on a shelf, on a list**

- Buy everything that is on this list. जो सब इस सूची में है, ख़रीद लेना।
- Put this book on the top shelf. इस पुस्तक को ऊपर की ताक पर रखो।
- The dictionary is **on** the table. शब्दकोश मेज़ पर है।

- **on a page; at the top / at the bottom of a page**

- Write **at** the top of the page. पृष्ठ के ऊपरी भाग में लिखो।
- Answer to this question is **given on** page 15. इस प्रश्न का उत्तर पृष्ठ १५ पर दिया हुआ है।

- **on the right (hand side), on the left (hand side) ; in the center**

- They drive **on the right** in the US. अमरीका में लोग वाहन बायीं ओर चलातें हैं।
- They sat **in the center** of the hall. वे कमरे के मध्य में बैठे।
- **Sign at** the bottom of the page **on** the left hand side. पृष्ठ के नीचे के भाग में, बायीं ओर हस्ताक्षर कीजिए।

- **at the door; at the window; at the gate etc.**

- Someone is at the door. कोई द्वार पर है।
- I saw her standing at the window. मैंने उसे खिड़की पर खड़े हुए देखा।

- **at platform + number, on the platform**

- The train is **at platform 7**. गाड़ी प्लेटफ़ार्म संख्या ७ पर है।
- The passengers are **on the platform.** यात्री प्लेटफ़ार्म पर हैं।

- **in the park, in the garden, in the field, in the sky:**

- The children are playing **in the field.** — बच्चे मैदान में खेल रहे हैं।
- Birds are flying **in the sky**. — पक्षी आकाश में उड़ रहे हैं।

■ **on the (first) floor; on the ground /ground floor; on the balcony/ terrace:**

- The children lay **in the sun on the terrace.** — बच्चे छत पर धूप में लेटे थे।
- we live on the 2nd floor. — हम दूसरी मंज़िल पर रहते हैं।

■ **in** an arm chair, **on** a stool / bench / chair without arms:

- Don't sit **in this armchair.** — इस आराम कुर्सी पर मत बैठो।
  Sit on that stool. — उस तिपाई पर बैठो।

■ **on + a river / a coast / the beach.**

- Varanasi is **on the river** Ganges. — वाराणसी गंगा नदी पर(स्थित) है।
- Mumbai is **on the West Coast.** — मुम्बई पश्चिमी तट पर है।

■ **in the street, in a lane , on the road**

- I think their house is **in this street.** — मेरा ख़याल है उन का घर इस सड़क पर है।
- Our house is **on the road** to station. — हमारा घर स्टेशन जाने की सड़क पर है।

☞ **along the street** सड़क के साथ-साथ,

☞ **up and down the road** सड़क पर इधर से उधर

- Keep walking **along the street.** — सड़क के साथ-साथ चलते जाओ।

- Stop walking **up and down the road.** सड़क पर इधर से उधर चक्कर लगाना बन्द करो।

■ **in front of the car/behind the car** कार के आगे/ कार के पीछे; **in the front of the car/in the back of the car** कार के अन्दर सामनेवाले भाग में/ कार के अन्दर पीछेवाले भाग में।

- The bus is **in front of** the car. बस कार के आगे है।
- The rickshaw is **behind** the car. रिक्शा कार के पीछे है।
- I shall sit **in the front of** the car. मैं 'कार' में सामनेवाले भाग में बैठूँगा।
- You sit **in the back** of the car. तुम 'कार' में पीछे की 'सीट' पर बैठो।

■ **in + country / city ; at + smaller place like a locality/area in a town / city**

- I live in India in Varanasi at Godoliya. मैं भारत में, वाराणसी में गदोलिया पर रहता/रहती हूँ।

☞ कभी-कभी **city** के साथ भी **at** लगता है।

- We changed trains at Lucknow. हमने लखनऊ में गाड़ी बदली।

■ **arrive, reach** पहुँचना

☞ **arrive** के साथ **in /at** लगता है।

- They arrived in Delhi at 5 p.m. वे शाम को पाँच बजे दिल्ली पहुँचे।

☞ **arrive home** में **home** से पूर्व **preposition** नहीं लगता। जैसे :

- Yesterday evening I arrived home very late. कल शाम को मैं घर देर से पहुँचा/ पहुँची।

☞ **reach** के साथ **preposition** नहीं लगता।

- They reached Delhi on Monday morning. — वे सोमवार सुबह दिल्ली पहुँचे।

■ **at the cinema, at the theatre, at the station, at the conference, at the airport, at dinner.**

- How many people were there at the party? — दावत में कितने लोग थे?
- I met your uncle at the meeting. — मैं सभा में तुम्हारे चाचा से मिला।

■ किसी भवन के साथ **at** और **in** लगते हैं। जब ध्यान भवन की ओर हो तो **in** और जब ध्यान भवन में हो रही घटना (जैसे दावत, गोष्ठी खेल, तमाशा आदि) पर हो तो **at** लगाएँ।

- We were **at** Radhika's house on Saturday. — हम शनिवार को राधिका के घर पर थे।
- There are many rooms **in** her house. — उस के घर में कई कमरे हैं।

■ स्कूल, कालिज के साथ **at** और **in** दोनों लगते हैं।
जब किसी स्कूल, कालिज का नाम लेकर बात करें, तो **at** लगाएँ।

- I studied **at** Francis Girls' High School. — मैं फ्रांसिस गर्लस हाई स्कूल में पढ़ती थी।
- My children are **at** school just now. — मेरे बच्चे इस समय स्कूल में हैं।
- My son is **in** college but my daughter is still **in** school. — मेरा बेटा महाविद्यालय में पढ़ता है, परन्तु मेरी बेटी अभी स्कूल में पढ़ती है

■ **by, near, near to, close to, next to** 'के पास होना' के अर्थ में

☞ **by** का प्रयोग बहुत पास होने के अर्थ में करते हैं।

- She sat by me. वह मेरे बगल में बैठी।
- They live by the post office. वे डाकघर के पास रहते हैं।

☞ **near, near to, close to** का प्रयोग बहुत दूर न होने के अर्थ में करते हैं।

- Meerut is near Delhi. मेरठ दिल्ली के पास है।
- We live close to the bank. हम बैंक के पास रहते हैं।

☞ **next to** से अगलावाला

- Their house is next to ours. उनका घर हमारे से अगलावाला है।

■ **above, over; below, under**

☞ **above / over** = के ऊपर; **below / under** = के नीचे;

सामान्यता **above / over, below / under** पर्यायवाची है। ध्यान दें कि जहाँ समानान्तर गति **(horizontal movement)** हो, तो **above** या **below** नहीं, **over** या **under** का प्रयोग होता है।

- Birds flew over the valley. पक्षी घाटी के ऊपर से उड़े।
- There is a picture above / over the window. खिड़की के ऊपर एक तस्वीर है।
- She stood at the window below / under the picture. वह तस्वीर के नीचे खिड़की पर खड़ी थी।
- The cat ran under the table. बिल्ली मेज़ के नीचे दौड़ी।

Some more uses of prepositions

■ **inform by post / by e-mail** डाक/ ई-मेल द्वारा सूचित करना

■ **announce on the radio / on television** रेडियो/टेलीवियन पर

सूचना प्रसारित करना

■ **speak by phone / speak on the phone** 'टेलीफ़ोन' पर बात करना।

■ **by car, by bicycle, by aeroplane, by ship, by bus etc.**

☞ सामान्यता यात्रा के साधनों के साथ **by** का प्रयोग करते हैं। इनके साथ article **'the'** नहीं लगता।

- I don't like to travel **by** air. — मुझे हवाई जहाज़ से सफ़र पसन्द नहीं।

☞ **on one's bicycle / on the bus / on the boat / on the train etc.**

किसी विशेष साधन से यात्रा कर रहा होना।

- I came here on my bike. — मैं यहाँ अपनी साइकिल से आया।

☞ **in a car / in a taxi** 'कार' से/ 'टेक्सी' से

- They went in their car. — वे अपनी 'कार' से गए।
- We came in a taxi. — हम टेक्सी से आए।

☞ **on foot / by foot** पैदल चलना

■ **to get on the bus/plane/train etc.** बस, हवाई जहाज़, गाड़ी में चढ़ना।

to get off the bus /plane/ train etc. बस, हवाई जहाज़, गाड़ी से उतरना।

☞ **get into / get out of a car / taxi** 'कार' में चढ़ना/-से बाहर निकलना

■ **at / on the corner of the street** सड़क की नुक्कड़ पर

☞ **in the corner of the room** कमरे के अन्दर कोने में

☞ **round the corner** सड़क के मोड़ पर

- There is a bakery at the — सड़क के मोड़ पर एक

corner of this street. 'बेकरी' है।

- Put this television in the corner of the room. यह दूरदर्शन कमरे में कोने में रखो।
- He ran round the corner of the lane. वह गली के मोड़ पर से दौड़ा।

■ **to be in the way** रास्ते में रुकावट के रूप में होना।

■ **to be on the way** कहीं जाते हुए रास्ते में होना।

to do on the way कहीं जाते हुए रास्ते में होना करना।

- Remove this chair from here. It is **in the way.** यह कुर्सी यहाँ से हटा दो। यह रास्ते में आ रही है।
- **On my way to** America, I stopped at Frankfurt. अमरीका जाते समय मैं फ्रैंकफ़र्ट में ठहरा/ठहरी।

■ **write in pen / ink** पैन/स्याही से लिखना

write in pencil सिक्के की पेन्सिल से लिखना

☞ परन्तु यदि संकेत किसी विशेष पेन/पेन्सिल से हो, तो **with** का प्रयोग करें।

- I wrote this letter **with** your pen

■ **pay by cheque / credit card / bank draft etc.** चैक, कैडिट कार्ड, बैंक ड्राफ़्ट आदि से भुगतान करना

☞ **pay cash / pay in cash** नकदी देना

■ **at the end** आख़िर में **in the end** अंतत:

- The post office is at the end of this street. डाकघर इस सड़क के अंत में है।
- They offered me a job at the end of the interview. साक्षातकार के अंत में उन्हों ने मेरें सामने काम का प्रस्ताव रखा।
- I could not improve the मैं अपने पुरानेवाले घर के इर्द-गिर्द

surroundings of our old house and in the end sold it off.	सुधार नहीं पाई, और अंततः उसे बेच दिया।

■ through, across

• The train went **through** a long dark tunnel.	गाड़ी लम्बी अन्धेरी सुरंग में से निकलकर गई।
• Breathe **through** the nose.	नाक द्वारा श्वास लो।
• Don't run **across** the street.	सड़क के पार दौड़ कर मत जाओ।
• Look on your left and right before you go **across** the street.	सड़क पार करने से पहले अपनी दाय -बाय ओर देखो।

Ex. 1: Fill in the blanks with the appropriate prepositions:

1. Put the TV... ....the corner of the room.
2. She stood... .... the corner of the street.
3. We ran... .... the corner.
4. The post office is... ....the corner of this road.
5. Who is... ....the door?
6. It is very cool.... .... my office.
7. Which film is on... ....the Regal?
8. Let us meet ... . the College gate.
9. I had a busy day... .... the office today.
10. Let's meet .... Vidushi's house.

Ex.2: Fill in the blanks with appropriate prepositions:

1. I don't go out alone .... night.
2. They are coming here .... the end of this month.
3. They entered the hall .... the same time.
4. I work .... weekends.
5. She is usually home .... the weekend.
6. I am not free .... the moment.
7. We visit each other .... Diwali.
8. Children have fun .... Diwali day.

9. Today I got up .... 4 O'clock .... the morning.
10. Sign .... the bottom of this page .... the right side.
11. I usually watch television .... the evening.
12. They will be here .... about 10 minutes.
13. The airplane will land .... a few minutes.
14. They arrived .... the station .... time.
15. The musician arrived .... the concert just .... time.
16. She is never .... time.
17. Swati was born .... 30 April 1974.
18. Meet me .... Tuesday morning.
19 This temple was constructed .... the MIddle Ages.
20. I usually stay home.............. Sundays.

Ex. 3: Fill in the blanks with the appropriate prepositions:

1. The flight arrives .... 9 a.m. Can you meet me .... the station?
2. They came to our house .... foot, but went back .... their friend's car.
3. Do you know which film is on .... the cinema tonght?
4. My daughter is still .... school.
5. I have a haircut .... the Beauty Parlour round the corner.
6. My friend's father had an accident. He is .... hospital.
7. The train was delayed. We waited .... the station .... nearly six hours.
8. We enjoyed the journey .... Taj Express. Particularly the food .... train was excellent.
9. Jigyasa's husband works .... ships. She is .... sea with him most of the time.
10. I stayed .... a very nice hotel when I was .... Delhi.
11. There were 21 rooms .... our old house.
12. I saw an exhibition .... Pragati Maidan .... New Delhi .... India.
13. She lives .... Jaipur. She is a professor .... Jaipur University.
14. I liked the city. But it was too cold .... the hotel.
15. I saw Shveta .... the writers' conference last month.

Ex.4: Complete the sentences using 'since' or 'for':

1. She hasn't seen him....... .... Diwali.
2. We haven't met... .... last year.
3. They have lived in Bombay... .... 10 years.
4. I have'nt bought any new dress.... ....ages.
5. There hasn't been a flood here... ....1979.
6. Mother hasn't written to me.... .... 6 months.
7. You have cooked the same food.... ....one week.
8. She has been in hospital... .... Monday.
9. I haven't driven a car... ....more than a year.

Ex.5: Complete the sentences using 'since' or 'for':

1. She works .... a factory.
2. The boy is standing .... the corner of the street.
3. Please put the new television set .... the corner of the living room.
4. I can see a dog .... the top of the ladder.
5. Our cat likes to sit .... the back of the car.
6. The bank is .... the left hand side of the street.
7. My office is across from the bank .... the right hand side of the street.
8. We were quite late and had to sit .... the back.
9. Write your address .... the front of the envelope.
10. My dahughter is not .... this photograph.
11. I usually stay .... bed until 6 a.m.
12. We have a lawn .... the front and a small kitchen garden .... the back of our house.
13. There is a temple of Lord Hanuman .... the end of this road.
14. I could not find your house .... this map.
15. Our flat is.......... the 2nd floor .... that red building.
16. In India we drive .... the left.
17. I want to hear the teacher clearly and see the blackboard well. Therefore I prefer to sit .... the front of the class.
18. What is the oldest religion .... the world?

Ex. 6: Fill in the blanks using the prepositions in, on ,by.

1. I met her .... chance .... the cinema.

2. She took my book .... mistake.
3. Wash this scarf .... hand.
4. I don't normally like to pay .... credit card. I prefer to pay .... cash.
5. Do you go to work .... bus or .... your car?
6. Usually I go to work .... foot. Sometimes I go .... bike.
7. Sometimes I have to travel .... air. Personally I prefer to travel .... train.
8. Godan is a novel .... Premchand.
9. They went round the city .... a taxi.
10. We travelled in Europe .... ship.

Ex. 7: Translate into English:

1. धूप में मत बैठो। छाया में बैठो। **2.** कलम से लिखो। पेन्सिल से मत लिखो। **3.** पानी १०० अंश सेलसियस पर उबलता है। **4.** वह सौ मील प्रति घण्टा की रफ़्तार से चला रहा था। **5.** हवाई जहाज़ नौ सौ किलोमीटर प्रति घण्टा की रफ़्तार से बारह हज़ार मीटर की उंचाई पर उड़ रहा था। **6.** राम व्यापार के सिलसिले में बाहर गया है। **7.** हम तीन साल पहले विश्व भ्रमण पर गए। **8.** जब वे लौटे, उन्होंने देखा कि उनके घर में आग लगी हुई थी। **9.** मैंने जानबूझ कर उन का दिल नहीं दुखाया। **10.** जब मैं बारह साल का था, मैंने भारत भ्रमण किया। यात्रा हमारे स्कूल के द्वारा आयोजित की गई थी।

Ex. 8: Translate into English:

1. गाड़ी सुबह सात बजे तक दिल्ली में होगी। **2.** मुझे रात के भोजन के समय तक घर पर होना होता है। **3.** जब तक हम वहाँ पहुँचे, गोष्ठी शुरू हो चुकी थी। **4.** जब तक तुम घर आओगे, भोजन तैयार हो चुका होगा। **5.** जब तक वो दावत में आया, उसके अधिकाँश घनिष्ठ दोस्त जा चुके थे। **6.** बैंक दोपहर दो बजे तक खुला होता है। अब तक बन्द हो गया होगा। **7.** मुझे शाम के पाँच बजे तक स्टेशन पहुँचना होगा। **8.** हमें हर महीने की पाँच तारीख़ तक घर का किराया देना होता है। **9.** इस महीने के अन्त तक घर की मरम्मत अवश्य हो जाएगी। **10.** सामान्यता मैं रात के दस बजे तक दूरदर्शन देखता हूँ।

Key 1

1. in	2. at	3. round/to	4. on/at
5. at	6. in	7. at	8. at
9. at	10. at		

Key 2

1. at	2. at	3. at	4. at
5. at	6. at	7. at	8. on
9. at, in	10. at , on	11. in	12. in
13. in	14. at, on	15. at, in	16. on
17. on	18. on	19. in	20. on

Key 3

1. at , at	2. on in	3. at	4. at
5. at	6. in	7. at ,for	8. by , on
9. at, in	10. at, in	11. in	12. at ,in, in
13. in , at	14. in	15. at	

Key 4

1. since	2. since	3. for	4. for
5. since	6. for	7. for	8. since
9. for			

Key 5

1. in	2. at	3. in	4. on
5. in	6. on	7. on	8. at
9. on	10. in	11. in	12. at ,at
13. at	14. on	15. on, in	16. on
17. at	18. in		

Key 6

1. by, at	2. by	3. by	4. by , in / x
5. by , in	6. on, on	7. by, by	8. by
9. in	10. by		

Key 7

1. Don't sit in the sun. Sit in the shade.

2. Write in ink. Don't write in pencil.
3. Water boils at 100^0 s celcius.
4. He was driving at 100 miles an hour.
5. The airplane was flying at 900 kilometers an hour and at an altitude of 12000 meters.
6. Ram is away on business.
7. We went on a world tour three years ago.
8. When they came back, they saw their house was on fire.
9. I did not hurt her on purpose.
10. When I was 12 years old, I went on a trip to India . The trip was organized by our school.

Key 8

1. The train will be in Delhi by 7 a.m.
2. I have to be home by dinner time.
3. By the time we got there, the seminar had already started.
4. By the time you come home, lunch will be ready.
5. By the time he came to the party, most of his friends had left.
6. The bank is open until 2 p.m. It must be closed by now.
7. I will have to be at the station by 5 p.m.
8. We have to pay the house rent by 5th of every month.
9. The house will certainly be repaired by the end of this month.
10. I usually watch TV until 10 p.m.

You Look Tired!

Sudhir :	Hello, Anil. You look very tired.
Anil :	Yes, we have been very busy. I have been working very hard.
Sudhir:	I think you should take a holiday.
Anil :	I know. But it is not possible. We have to supply some urgent orders. All of us are working fourteen hours a day.
Sudhir :	Fourten hours! You are kidding! You will kill yourself. Why don't you quit this job?
Anil :	Well, I reallycan't. I need the money. It is not easy to get another job!

46 Active-/Passive Voice

- **In English language the use of passive voice is relatively less compared to Hindi.**
  Passive voice is particularly used when the doer of the action is unknown or when it is not important to know who the doer is, i.e. we use passive voice when the emphasis is on activity and not on the identity of the doer .

☞ **The subject of an active sentence is the agent of a passive sentence; 'by' precedes the agent. However it is not always necessary to mention the agent.**

☞ **The object of an active sentence becomes the grammatical subject of a passive sentence.**
Given below are some passive language structures :

अंग्रेज़ी भाषा में passive voice का प्रयोग हिन्दी की तुलना में कम होता है। अंग्रेज़ी में passive voice विशेष रूप से वहाँ प्रयोग करते है जहाँ कर्म कर्ता से अधिक महत्व रखता हो। जैसे कि 'New road is being laid'. यहाँ सड़क का डाला जाना ज़्यादा महत्व रखता है न कि किसने सड़क डाली। प्राय: ऐसे वाक्यों में active voice में कर्ता के स्थान पर 'they' लगाते हैं।

☞ कर्त वाच्य का कर्ता कर्मवाच्य में agent होता है, जिससे पहले by होता है। 'by + agent' का प्रयोग वाक्य में सदैव अनिवार्य नहीं।

☞ कर्त वाच्य का कर्म, कर्मवाच्य में व्याकरणिक कर्ता होता है। कुछ कर्मवाच्य प्रयोग नीचे दिए गए हैं।

- **Present Simple Passive**

subject + is / are / am + pp + by + agent

A: Mother cooks food.	माँ भोजन पकाती हैं।
P: Food is cooked by mother.	माँ के द्वारा भोजन पकाया जाता है।
A: The servant cleans the house.	नौकर घर साफ़ करता है।
P: The house is cleaned by the servant.	नौकर के द्वारा घर साफ़ किया जाता है।

■ Present Simple Progressive Passive

subject + is / are / am + being + pp + by + agent

A: Mother is cooking food.	माँ भोजन पका रही हैं।
P: Food is being cooked by mother.	माँ के द्वारा भोजन पकाया जा रहा है।
A: The gardener is mowing the lawn.	माली 'लॉन' छील रहा है।
P: The lawn is being mowed by the gardener.	माली के द्वारा 'लॉन' छीला जा रहा है।

■ Present Perfect Simple Passive

subject + has / have + been + pp + by agent

A: Mother has cooked food.	माँ ने भोजन पकाया है।
P: Food has been cooked by mother.	माँ के द्वारा भोजन पकाया गया है।
A: They have built a new bridge in our town.	हमारे शहर में एक नया पुल बना है।
P: A new bridge has been built in our town.	हमारे शहर में एक नया पुल बनाया गया है।

Present Perfect Progressive Passive

subject + has / have + been + being + pp + by + agent

A: Mother has been preparing lunch since the morning.	माँ सुबह से भोजन पका रही हैं।
P: Lunch has been being prepared by mother since the morning.	माँ के द्वारा सुबह से भोजन पकाया जा रहा है।
A: She has been writing this book for a year.	वह साल भर से यह पुस्तक लिख रही हैं।
P: This book has been being written by her for a year.	यह पुस्तक साल भर से उसके द्वारा लिखी जा रही हैं।

Past Habitual Passive

subject + used to be + pp + by + agent

A: Mother used to cook food.	माँ भोजन पकाया करती थीं।
P: Food used to be cooked by mother.	माँ के द्वारा भोजन पकाया जाता था।
A: She used to sew clothes for a living.	वह जीविका हेतु कपड़े सीती थी।
P: Clothes used to be sewn by her for a living.	उसके द्वारा जीविका हेतु कपड़े सीए जाते थे।

Past Simple Passive

subject + was / were + pp + by + agent

A: Mother cooked food.	माँ ने भोजन पकाया ।
P: Food was cooked by mother.	माँ के द्वारा भोजन पकाया गया।
A: He started a new business.	उसने नया कारोबार शुरू किया।

Present perfect progressive passive, यह ढाँचा बोलचाल की भाषा में विशेष प्रयोग में नहीं आता।

A: = Active; P: = Passive; pp = past participle

P: A new business was started by him.	उस के द्वारा नया कारोबार शुरू किया गया।

■ Past Perfect Passive

subject + had + been + pp + by + agent

A: Mother had cooked food.	माँ ने भोजन पकाया था।
P: Food had been cooked by mother.	माँ के द्वारा भोजन पकाया गया था।
A: The cobbler had repaired the shoes.	मोची ने जूतों की मरम्मत की थी।
P: The shoes had been repaired by the cobbler.	मोची के द्वारा जूतों की मरम्मत की गई थी।

■ Past Perfect Progressive Passive

subject + had + been + being + pp + by + agent

A: They had been selling sweets for ten years.	वे दस वर्षों से मिठाइयाँ बेच रहे थे।
P: Sweets had been being sold by them for ten years.	उनके द्वारा दस वर्षों से मिठाइयाँ बेची जा रही थीं।
A: He had been smuggling trucks all his life.	वह जीवनभर ट्रकों की तस्करी करता रहा था।
P: Trucks had been being smuggled by him all his life.	उसके द्वारा जीवन भर ट्रकों की तस्करी की जा रही थी।

■ Future Simple Passive

subject + will + be + pp + by + agent

past perfect progressive passive, यह ढाँचा बोलचाल की भाषा में विशेष प्रयोग में नहीं आता।

A: Mother will cook food. — माँ भोजन पकाएँगी।

P: Food will be cooked by mother. — माँ के द्वारा भोजन पकाया जाएगा।

A: They will hold a meeting tomorrow. — वे कल एक बैठक करेंगे।

P: A meeting will be held by them tomorrow. — उनके द्वारा कल एक बैठक की जाएगी।

■ Future Progressive Passive

subject + will + be + being + pp + by + agent

A: Tomorrow at 11 a.m. mother will be cooking food. — कल ग्यारह बजे माँ भोजन पका रही होंगी।

P: Tomorrow at 11 a.m. food will be being cooked by mother. — कल ग्यारह बजे माँ के द्वारा भोजन पकाया जा रहा होगा।

A: Mr. Bhalla will be training Anil in archery at 4 p.m. on Mondays. — प्रति सोमवार को शाम को चार बजे श्री भल्ला अनिल को धनुर्विद्या सिखाएँगे।

P: Anil will be being trained by Mr. Bhalla in archery at 4 p.m. on Mondays. — प्रति सोमवार को शाम को चार बजे श्री भल्ला के द्वारा अनिल को धनुर्विद्या सिखाई जा रही होगी।

■ Future Perfect Passive

subject + will + have + been + pp + by + agent

A: Mother will have prepared lunch by 1 p.m. — माँ एक बजे तक भोजन पका चुकी होंगी।

P: Lunch will have been prepared by 1 p.m. by mother. — माँ के द्वारा एक बजे तक भोजन पकाया जा चुका होगा।

A: They will have constructed a — वे दिसम्बर तक नया घर बना चुके

new house by December. — होंगे।

P: By December a new house will have been constructed by them. — उन के द्वारा दिसम्बर तक नया घर बनाया जा चुका होगा।

■ Future Perfect Progressive Passive

subj. + will + have + been + being + pp + by + agent

- This book will have been being written for seven years in January. — जनवरी में यह पुस्तक सात सालों से लिखी जा रही होगी।
- Next week I will have been being taught archery by this coach for five years. — अगले हफ़्ते मुझे इस प्रशिक्षक के द्वारा पाँच सालों से धनुर्विद्या सिखाई जा रही होगी।

■ Ability structure in passive

subject + can be + pp + by + agent

- Most disputes can be settled out of court. — अधिकाँश झगड़ों का निपटारा कचहरी के बाहर किया जा सकता है।
- An amicable agreement can be reached in this matter. — इस मामले में सौहार्दपूर्ण समझौता किया जा सकता है।

subject + could be + pp + by + agent

- The patient could not be cured. — मरीज़ ठीक नहीं किया जा सका।
- The students could be trained. — विद्यार्थी प्रशिक्षित किए जा सके।

■ Present compulsion structure in passive

subject + has / have + to be + pp + by + agent

future perfect progressive यह ढाँचा बोलचाल की भाषा में विशेष प्रयोग में नहीं आता।

• These clothes have to be washed today.	ये कपड़े आज धोए जाने हैं।
• Those boys have to be taught a lesson.	उन लड़कों को सबक सिखाया जाना हैं।

Past compulsion structure in passive

subject + had to be + pp + by + agent

• The children had to be brought home today.	आज बच्चों को जल्दी घर लाया जाना पड़ा।
• Our dog had to be taken to the veterinarian (vet) today.	आज हमारे कुत्ते को पशुचिकित्सक के पास ले जाया जाना पड़ा।

Future compulsion structure in passive

subject + will have to be + pp + by + agent

• The defence budget will have to be curtailed.	रक्षा बजट काटा जाना होगा।
• Inflation will have to be controlled.	मँहगाई पर नियन्त्रण किया जाना होगा।

Compulsion structure + subjunctive passive

subject + may / might + have to be + pp + by + agent

• The price of gas may have to be raised after the budget.	हो सकता है बजट के बाद गैस का दाम बढ़ाया जाना पड़े।
• She may have to be operated upon next month.	हो सकता है अगले महीने उसका 'ऑपरेशन' किया जाना पड़े।

Probability in passive

subject + may / might + be + pp + by + agent

- More funds may be spent on defence. — हो सकता है रक्षा पर अधिक धनराशि खर्च की जाय।
- The number of students might be curtailed to improve academic standards. — हो सकता है शिक्षा का स्तर ऊपर उठाने हेतु विद्यार्थियों की संख्या कम की जाय।

Advice in passive

subject + should or ought to + be + pp + by + agent

- Less money should be spent on defence. — रक्षा पर कम धनराशि खर्च की जानी चाहिए।
- More funds should be allocated for education and social welfare. — शिक्षा एवम् समाज कल्याण के लिए अधिक धनराशि नियत की जानी चाहिए।

Ex. 1 : Write sentences in present simple passive using the cues given below.

1. My house / clean / twice a day. ....
2. Parking / not allow / here. ....
3. 'Dosa' and 'idli' / make / from rice. ....
4. Clothes / wash / washerman. ....
5. Where/ sell / milk? ....
6. Our house / repaint / every year. ....
7. How many languages / speak / in India?. ....
....
8. You / invite / party? ....

Ex. 2: Write sentences in past simple passive using the cues given below.

1. This building / make /last year. ....
2. My wallet / steal / last week. ....
3. We / wake / loud music. ....
4. The letter / send / wrong address? ....
5. Bank / rob / last night. ....
6. When / radio / invent? ....
7. This film / make / 1984. ....
8. How / break / window? ....

Ex. 3: Write sentences in present simple continuous passive using the cues given below.

1. My house / paint. ....
2. Our garage / repair. ....
3. A new road / built / in front of our house. ....
4. New jobs / create / the government. ....
5. Crops / harvest. ....
6. Preparations / make / for mid term elections. ....
7. Large sums of money / donate / many people. ....

Ex.4: Complete the sentences in present simple passive using the verbs given in brackets

1. Lunch........................ by mother. (prepare)
2. The lawn........................ by the gardener. (mow)
3. The house .... by the servant. (clean)
4. The students........................ ancient history by Mr. Sharma.(teach)
5. A meeting .... usually.............. in this field in the evening.(hold)
6. Dogs .... here. (train)

7. The main gate .... at 10 p.m. (lock)
8. Mostly fatal accidents........................ by careless driving. (cause)

Ex.5: Complete the sentences in present simple progressive passive using the verbs given in brackets

1. Food .... by mother. (serve)
2. The students .... by the teacher. (teach)
3. A new dress .... by the tailor. (make)
4. The plants .... by the gardener. (water)
5. A cardigan...................... .... for me by my sister. (knit)
6. A new road .... to connect Varanasi with Ramnagar. (lay)
7. I think I .... by some people. (follow)
8. My computer...................... .... by somebody today (repair)

Ex.6: Complete the sentences in present perfect passive simple using the verbs given in brackets

1. All educational institutions....................... . for three weeks. (close)
2. The lawns .... (mow)
3. The bridge .... (build)
4. Our house .... recently (repaint)
5. She ....the President of the Ladies' Club. (make)
6. The mail .... not .... yet. (deliver)
7. This story .... by my friend. (write)
8. ....the books .... to the library?(return)

Ex. 7: Rewrite the sentences given below using the appropriate passive form:

1. They will send you the certificate by speed post.

   ....

2. The teachers will hold a meeting during the lunch hour tomorrow.

   ....

3. She will have been teaching me English for three years in January 2012.

   ....

4. The employees should do their work conscientiously.

....

5. They may have to cancel the trains because of fog.

....

6. They might lay new roads in this area before the rains start.

....

7. I have to return this book to the library by tomorrow.

....

8. I had to postpone the meeting for ten days.

....

9. The teacher will have to complete the course by next week.

....

10. He cannot repair this clock.

....

11. They could not decorate the house by Diwali.

....

Ex. 8: Rewrite the sentences given below as shown:

> **It is said that she has a computer memory.**
> **=>She is said to have a computer memory.**

1. It is said that he is 140 years old.

....

2. It is believed that the killer of the chief of the company escaped to the Middle East.

....

3. It is alleged that he robbed the bank.

....

4. It is reported that a mother burnt herself along with her two children to death.

....

5. It is known that Mr. Bhalla was a very good surgeon.

....

6. It is expected that the new director will join the office tomorrow.

....

7. It is believed that the robbers came in through the basement.

....

8. It is reported that two terrorists were killed in the encounter.

....

9. It is reported that thousands of people died in the earthquake.

....

10. It is believed that he was the mastermind behind most of the recent scams in India.

....

Ex.9: Translate into English

1. माता के द्वारा बच्चों की देखरेख की जाती है। 2. दादा जी के द्वारा किराना, फल सब्ज़ियाँ आदि ख़रीदे जाते हैं। 3. वह बहुत बुद्धिमान माना जाता है। 4. उसे बहुत सम्मान दिया जाता है। 5. हमें सदैव धोखा दिया जाता है। 6. वह मूर्ख कहलाती है। 7. बिजली मिस्त्री के द्वारा 'कूलर' ठीक किया जा रहा है। 8 .रंग साज़ों के द्वारा घर रंगा जा रहा है। 10. उग्रवादियों के द्वारा दस आदमी मारे गए हैं। 11. जनवरी से नई भूमिगत नालियाँ डाली जा रही हैं। 12. मेरी घड़ी दो घण्टों से ठीक की जा रही हैं। 13 वह अपने अध्यापकों के द्वारा प्रतिभाशाली माना जाता था। 14. वह सब के द्वारा सलाहकार माना जाता था। 15. हमारे द्वारा उन्हें रसद और दवाइयाँ आदि भेजी जाती थीं। 16. मेरा बटुआ किसी सहयात्री के द्वारा चुरा लिया गया। 17. हमें उसके द्वारा रसायन शास्त्र पढ़ाया गया था। 18. ज़ंजीर खींचकर गाड़ी रोकी गई थी।19. उसके द्वारा सन् 1975 से विदेशियों को हिन्दी पढ़ाई जा रही थी। 20. पुलीस के द्वारा घण्टों चोर का पीछा किया जा रहा था।

Ex. 10: Translate into English

1. उसके द्वारा यह पुस्तक प्रतिदिन सुबह चार बजे से छ: बजे तक लिखी जाएगी। 2.

आज खेल के घण्टे में विद्यार्थियों के द्वारा खेल के मैदान में 'फुटबाल' का अभ्यास किया जाएगा। 3. अगले महीने तक उसके द्वारा 'कम्प्यूटर' चलाना अच्छी तरह सीखा जा चुका होगा। 4. कल से दूरदर्शन पर नया धारावाहिक शुरू किया जाएगा। 5. इस उग्रवादी को बन्दी बनाने के लिए बहुत बड़ा पुरस्कार देने का वचन दिया जाना पड़ा। 6. उसके जन्म का प्रमाण पत्र प्राप्त करने के लिए बड़ी रिश्वत दी जानी पड़ी। 7. अग्नि स्थल पर छः दमकल तुरन्त भेजे जाने पड़े। 8. भीड़ पर काबू पाने के लिए आँसू गैस छोड़ी जानी पड़ी। 9. बेरोज़गारों को सहारा दिया जाना होगा। 10. हो सकता है निर्णय लेने से पूर्व और जानकारी प्राप्त की जानी पड़े। 11. हो सकता है यह दवाई आयात की जानी पड़े। 12. हो सकता है राजनीतिक कारणों से बन्दी उग्रवादी को छोड़ दिया जाना पड़े। 13. हो सकता है मध्यावधि चुनाव जल्दी ही कराए जाने पड़ें। 14. दीवार में कील नहीं ठोके जाने चाहिए।

Key 1

1. My house is cleaned twice a day.
2. Parking is not allowed here.
3. 'Dosa' and 'idli' are made from rice.
4. Clothes are washed by the washerman.
5. Where is milk sold?
6. Our house is repainted every year.
7. How many languages are spoken in India?
8. Are you invited to the party?

Key 2

1. This building was made last year.
2. My wallet was stolen last week.
3. We were woken up by loud music.
4. Was the letter sent to the wrong address?
5. The bank was robbed last night.
6. When was radio invented?
7. This film was made in 1984.
8. How was the window broken?

Key 3

1. My house is being painted.
2. Our garage is being repaired.

3. A new road is being built in front of our house.
4. New jobs are being created by the government.
5. Crops are being harvested.
6. Preparations are being made for the mid term elections.
7. Large sums of money have been donated by many people.

Key 4

1. is prepared
2. is mowed
3. is cleaned
4. are taught
5. is ..... held
6. are trained
7. is locked
8. are caused

Key 5

1. is being served
2. are being taught
3. is being made
4. are being watered
5. is being knitted
6. is being laid
7. am being followed
8. is being repaired

Key 6

1. have been closed
2. have been mowed.
3. has been built.
4. has been repainted
5. has been made
6. has .... been delivered
7. has been written
8. Have.............been returned

Key 7

1. The certificate will be sent to you by speed post.
2. A meeting will be held by the teachers during the lunch hour tomorrow.
3. I will have been being taught English by her for three years in January 2012.
4. Work should be done by the employees conscientiously.
5. Trains may have to be cancelled because of fog.
6. New roads might be laid in this area before the rains start.
7. This book has to be returned to the library by tomorrow.
8. The meeting had to be postponed by me for ten days.
9. The course will have to be completed by the teacher by next week.
10. This clock cannot be repaired by him.
11. The house could not be decorated by Diwali.

Key 8

1. He is said to be 140 years old.
2. The killer of the chief of the company is believed to have escaped to the Middle East.
3. He is alleged to have robbed the bank.
4. A mother is reported to have burnt herself along with her two children to death.
5. Mr. Bhalla is known to have been a good surgeon.
6. The new director is expected to join the office tomorrow.
7. The robbers are believed to have come in through the basement.
8. Two terrorists are reported to have been killed in the encounter.
9. Thousands of people are reported to have died in the earthquake.
10. He is believed to have been the mastermind behind most of the recent scams in India.

Key 9

1. Children are taken care of by mother. 2. Groceries, fruit and vegetables etc. are bought by grandfather. 3. He is considered very intelligent. 4. She / He is highly respected. 5. We are cheated all the time. 6. She is called stupid. 7. The cooler is being repaired by the electrician. 8. The house is being painted by the painters. 10. Ten men have been killed by the terrorists. 11. New underground water pipes have been being laid since January. 12. My watch has been being repaired for two hours. 13. He used to be considered a genius by his teachers. 14. He used to be regarded as mentor by everybody. 15. Provisions and medicines etc. used to be sent to them by us. 16. My wallet was stolen by some co-traveler. 17. We had been taught chemistry by him. 18. The chain had been pulled and the train stopped. 19. Hindi had been being taught by her to foreigners since 1975. 20. The thief had been being chased by the police for several hours.

Key 10

1. This book will be written by him / her every morning from 4 a.m. to 6 a.m. 2. Today during the games hour, football will be practised by students in the playground . 3. By next month computer operation will have been mastered by him. 4. A new TV serial will be started tomorrow. 5. A big reward had to be promised to arrest this terrorist. 6. A big bribe had to

be given to get his / her birth certificate. 7. Six fire-engines had to be rushed to the site of the fire. 8. Tear gas had to be released to control the mob. 9. The unemployed will have to be supported. 10. More information may have to be obtained before taking any decision. 11. This medicine may have to be imported. 12. The arrested terrorist may have to be freed for political reasons. 13. Mid-term elections may have to be held soon. 14. Nails should not be hammered into the wall.

At The Indian Airlines

Passenger	:	Where can I get a ticket please?
Clerk	:	Right here, sir. Where are you going?
Passenger	:	To Bombay. How much is it?
Clerk	:	Rs. two thousand and two hundred.
Passenger	:	When does the plane leave?
Clerk	:	At 11.15 a.m.
Passenger	:	What time do I have to check in?
Clerk	:	One hour before the scheduled flight time, sir. Today the flight is delayed because of bad weather.
Passenger	:	What time will the plane leave today?
Clerk	:	Your flight will be announced half an hour before the departure time.
Passenger	:	What do I do with the luggage?
Clerk	:	Put it on the scales at the Indian Airlines counter over there.
Passenger	:	What about the little bag? Does this have to be weighed too?
Clerk	:	No. You can carry it on the plane and put it under your seat.
Passenger	:	Will they serve a meal on the plane?
Clerk	:	I am afraid not. Meals are not served on short distance flights.
Passenger	:	That's all I want to know. Thank you.
Clerk	:	I hope you enjoy flying with us, sir. Goodbye.

47 Relative Clauses

■ **In English the same words 'who', 'whose', 'which', 'what', 'when','where', etc. are used both as interrogative as well as relative pronouns / relative adverbs.**
As interrogatives these are placed at the beginning of the sentence whereas when used as relative pronouns they are placed after the noun or the clause they refer to. This is different from Hindi, which has a special group of words ' जो, जिस, जिन, जब, जहाँ' **etc.used as relative pronouns / relative adverbs.**

☞ **When a relative clause describes 'which / what kind of a person or thing' is referred to by the speaker, we use 'who / that for a person, and 'that / which for a thing'.**

☞ **Sometimes 'which person or thing' is already known, and a relative clause only gives 'more information about a noun or pronoun already mentioned by the speaker; we use only 'who' for a person and only 'which' for a thing.**
See examples on page 316.

■ **Use of 'who', 'which', 'that' as a relative pronoun used for he, she, they ,it :**

☞ 'who' is used for a person. 'who' cannot be used for things.

☞ 'which' is used only for things.

☞ 'that' can be used both for a person or a thing

'who' as relative pronouns

1a. A boy is playing over there. एक लड़का वहाँ खेल रहा है। वह

	He is very naughty.	बहुत शैतान है।
1b.	The boy **who** / **that** is playing over there is very naughty.	जो लड़का वहाँ खेल रहा है, वह बहुत शैतान है।
2a.	I have several students. They are from different countries.	मेरे अनेक विद्यार्थी हैं। वे विभिन्न देशों से हैं।
2b.	I have several students **who / that** are from different countries.	मेरे अनेक विद्यार्थी हैं जो विभिन्न देशों से हैं।
3.	That is the boy **who / that** likes to play cricket.	वह लड़का है जो क्रिकेट खेलना पसन्द करता है।
4.	You are the first person **who / that** has come up with a practical proposal.	आप पहले व्यक्ति हैं जिन्होंने एक उपयोगी सुझाव दिया है।

'which' and 'that' as relative pronouns

1a.	I have a few books. I read them again and again.	मेरे पास कुछ पुस्तकें हैं। मैं उन्हें बार-बार पढ़ता हूँ / पढ़ती हूँ।
1b.	I have a few books **which / that** I read again and again.	मेरे पास कुछ पुस्तकें हैं जिन्हें मैं बार-बार पढ़ता हूँ / पढ़ती हूँ।
2a.	He asked for a magazine. It was not in the library.	उसने एक पत्रिका माँगी। यह पुस्तकालय में नहीं थी।
2b.	He asked for a magazine **that / which** was not in the library.	उसने एक पत्रिका माँगी जो पुस्तकालय में नहीं थी।
3.	I like novels **that / which** have happy endings.	मुझे वे उपन्यास अच्छे लगते हैं जो सुखान्त हों।
4.	I work for a factory **that / which** manufactures air-coolers.	मैं एक कारख़ाने में काम करता/करती हूँ जो वातानुकूलन यंत्र बनाता है।

☞ **Use of 'who', 'which' and 'that' as relative pronouns** is not

obligatory when used as object:

1. Are these the keys **(that)** you were looking for?	क्या यही चाभियाँ हैं जिन्हें आप ढूँढ रहे थे?
2. I don't like the people **(who)** I work with.	मैं जिन लोगों के साथ काम करता हूँ, वे मुझे अच्छे नहीं लगते।
3. She is one such person **(who)** you can trust in time of need.	वह एक ऐसी व्यक्ति है जिसपर आप ज़रूरत के समय भरोसा कर सकते हैं।
4. Who is that young lady **(that)** I saw with you at the cinema?	वह युवती कौन है जिसे मैंने सिनेमा घर में आपके साथ देखा था।

'whom' as relative pronoun

☞ **When a person is the object of a relative clause, 'whom' can be used instead of who'**

1a. That is the man. I met him on a train last week.	वही आदमी है। मैं उसे पिछले सप्ताह गाड़ी में मिली थी।
1b. That is the man **whom** I met on a train last week.	वही आदमी है जिसको मैं पिछले सप्ताह गाड़ी में मिली थी।
2a. That is the teacher. They are planning to send her abroad for special training.	वह अध्यापिका है। वे उसे विशिष्ट प्रशिक्षण हेतु विदेश भेजने की सोच रहे है।
2b. That is the teacher **whom** they are planning to send abroad for special training.	वह अध्यापिका है जिसे वे विशिष्ट प्रशिक्षण हेतु विदेश भेजने की सोच रहे है।
3. She is the only writer **whom** I know very well.	वही एक मात्र लेखिका है जिसे मैं अच्छी तरह जानती हूँ।
4. She is the beautiful woman **whom** every young man at college wanted to befriend.	यही वह सुन्दर औरत है जिससे कॉलिज का प्रत्येक युवक मैत्री करना चाहता था।

'where' as relative adverb

1. My daughter is working in the hospital **where** she was born.	मेरी पुत्री उसी अस्पताल में काम कर रही है जहाँ उसका जन्म हुआ था।
2. This is the Bodhi tree **where** Lord Budha got enlightenment.	यही वह 'बोधि वृक्ष' है जहाँ भगवान बुद्ध को ज्ञान प्राप्त हुआ था।
3. I have never been to the village **where** I grew up.	मैं उस गाँव में कभी नहीं गया जहाँ मैं पला बड़ा हुआ था।
4. I would like to build a house **where** there is no noise.	मैं ऐसी जगह घर बनाना चाहता हूँ जहाँ शोर न हो।
5. This is the playground **where** we practise cricket every evening.	यह खेल का मैदान है जहाँ हम हर शाम को क्रिकेट का अभ्यास करते हैं।
6. Is there a shop nearby **where** one could buy a Hindi newspaper?	क्या यहाँ पास में कोई दुकान है जहाँ व्यक्ति हिन्दी का अख़बार ख़रीद सके?

'what' as a relative pronoun :

☞ **'What' as a relative pronoun = the thing that / the things which:**

1. **What** I would want for my birthday this year is a yellow sapphire.

=. **The thing that** I would want on my birthday this year is a yellow sapphire.

जो मुझे इस साल अपने जन्मदिन पर चाहिए, वह है पुखराज।

2. Is this **what** they want us to do?

=. Is this **the thing that** they want us to do?

क्या यही है जो वे चाहते हैं कि हम करें?

3. They cannot comprehend **what** I teach.

=. They cannot comprehend **the matter that** I teach.

जो मैं पढ़ाता हूँ वे समझ नहीं सकते।

4. While leaving India she gave me **what I needed.**
=. While leaving India she gave me **the things which** I needed.
भारत छोड़ते समय उसने मुझे वह दिया जो मुझे चाहिए था।

More examples:

1. We love all what is pretty. — वह सब, जो सुन्दर है, हमें प्रिय है।
2. Did you agree with what they said? — उन्होंने जो कहा, क्या आप उससे सहमत थे ?
3. What she said was not true. — जो उसने कहा, सत्य नहीं था।
4. What I do is nobody's business. — मैं जो करता हूँ इससे किसीको कोई मतलब नहीं।

'whose' as a relative pronoun

■ 'Whose' as a relative pronoun can be used for people as well as things.

In a relative clause 'whose' is used instead of his, her, their etc.= जिसका, जिसके, जिसकी

☞ संबंधकारक सर्वनाम के रूप में **'whose'** का प्रयोग his, her, their etc आदि के स्थान पर व्यक्ति और वस्तु दोनों के लिए प्रयोग हो सकता है।

संबंधकारक वाक्यांश में **'whose = his, her, their'**

1. I saw a man. **His** hand was bleeding. — मैंने एक आदमी को देखा। उसके हाथ से खून निकल रहा था।
=. I saw a man **whose** hand was bleeding. — मैंने एक आदमी को देखा जिसके हाथ से खून निकल रहा था।
2. I know a woman. **Her** husband is the education minister. — मै एक औरत को जानती हूँ। उसका पति शिक्षा मंत्री है।
=. I know the woman **whose** husband is the education — मैं उस औरत को जानती हूँ जिसका पति शिक्षा मंत्री है।

	minister.	
3.	What is the name of the young man **whose** father had died in an accident?	उस युवक का नाम क्या है जिसके पिता की मृत्यु दुर्घटना में हो गई थी?
4.	Who is that leader in front of **whose** house the crowd was shouting slogans?	वह नेता कौन है जिसके घर के सामने भीड़ नारे लगा रही थी?

■ **Relative clauses giving some more information about the person or thing already mentioned:**

Use 'who' for person, 'which' for thing:

1.	They have two daughters. They both became doctors.	उनकी दो बेटियाँ हैं। वे दोनों डॉक्टर बनीं।
=.	They have two daughters, **who** became doctors.	उनकी दो बेटियाँ हैं जो डॉक्टर बनीं।
2.	I have a friend from Maharashtra. She lives in Japan these days.	मेरी एक महाराष्ट्र से मित्र हैं। वह आजकल जापान में रहती है।
=.	I have a friend from Maharashtra, **who** lives in Japan these days.	मेरी एक मित्र महाराष्ट्र से हैं , जो आजकल जापान में रहती है।
3.	He showed me a photograph of his mother, **who** is a writer.	उसने मुझे अपनी माता का चित्र दिखाया, जो लेखिका हैं।
4.	I have known Kamla, **who** is my best friend, since childhood.	मैं कमला को, जो मेरी सबसे अच्छी सहेली है, बचपन से जानती हूँ।
5.	The milk van, **which** is usually on time, was late today.	दूध की गाड़ी, जो प्राय: समय पर आती है, आज देर से आई।
6.	She introduced me to several people, **most of whom** were not worth remembering.	उसने मुझे बहुत लोगों मिलाया जिनमें से अधिकांश याद रखने लायक नहीं थे।
7.	He gave me two watches, **neither of which** worked.	उसने मुझे दो घड़ियाँ दीं जिनमें एक भी ठीक नही थी।

8. There were many people in the meeting, quite **a few of whom** I had never met before.

बैठक में बहुत लोग थे जिनमें से कइयों को मैं पहले कभी नहीं मिली थी।

Ex.1: Which is correct?

1. The students **who / that** were injured in the riots are out of danger.
2. A medical doctor is someone **who / that** cures the patients.
3. There is a lane behind this house **who / that** leads to the temple.
4. The woman **who / that** answered the phone said she would come to the party.
5. The nurse **that / who** looked after me in the hospital was very rude and unkind.
6. The advice **that / who** he gave me was very good.
7. The picture **who / that** he showed me was of his wife.
8. Police arrested the students **that / who** had incited the communal tension.
9. The woman **who / that** lives upstairs is very rich.
10. The boy **that / who** is running towards us is very intelligent.
11. Earth is believed to be the only planet **who / that** can sustain life.
12. What happened to the calendar **that / who** was on this wall.

Ex.2: Change as shown using the relative pronoun 'where':

	Next month I am going to Delhi. My parents live there.
=>	**Next month I am going to Delhi where my parents live.**

1. Next to my house is a playground. Children play there in the evening.

   ....

2. We had a picnic by the river. Our teachers took us there.

   ....

3. I know a guest house at Rajiv Chowk. You can stay there comfortably at a reasonable price.

....

4. I know a shop. You can buy imported perfumes there.

   ....

5. This is the Red Fort. The Prime Minister of India hoists the national flag here and addresses the nation on Indepndence Day every year.

   ....

Ex. 3: Change as shown using the relative pronoun 'which':

	She is always traveling in connection with her work. This makes it very difficult to contact her when necessary.
=>	She is always traveling in connection with her work, **which** makes it difficult to contact her when necessary.

1. He left the house without paying three months' rent. This was a shame.

   ....

2. It is very noisy where I live. This makes it impossible for us to concentrate on anything.

   ....

3. She didn't thank them for their generous hospitality. In my opinion this was very rude.

   ....

4. The railway strike lasted three days. It was called off this morning.

   ....

5. He told me his phone number. I immediately noted it down in my diary.

   ....

Ex.4: Change as shown using the relative pronoun 'whose':

> **He took me to a temple. Now I don't remember its name.**
> **=> He took me to a temple whose name (= the name of which) I don't remember now.**

1. They have set up a branch office in India. Its job is to give prompt service to the customers.

   ....

2. This is my sister's father-in-law. I could not have got this job without his help.

   ....

3. This is Mr. Sharma. His son got the 'Young Scientists Award' last week.

   ....

4. That is Dinesh. His brother died in the air crash last week.

   ....

5. This is my maths teacher. I could not have passed the exam without his encouragement.

   ....

6. It was an opportunity. Its importance did not occur to me then.

   ....

Ex. 5: Translate into English:

1. यही वह अभिनेत्री है जिसके बारे में मैंने सुबह बात की थी। 2. क्या यही वह बिजली मिस्त्री है जिसे आपने आज बुलाया था? 3. यही वह औरत है जिसे लोग देखते ही पसन्द करते हैं। 4. मुझे एक स्थान पता है जहाँ आप घण्टों चुपचाप शान्ति सें बैठ सकते हैं। 5. मठ वह स्थान है जहाँ भिक्षु रहते हैं। 6. मैं ऐसे देश में काम करना चाहूँगी जहाँ सदैव ठण्ड रहती हो। 7. क्या आप यहाँ पास में कोई स्थान बता सकते हैं जहाँ मैं बाल कटवा सकूँ। 8. क्या इस इलाके में कोई दवाई की दुकान है जहाँ दिन-रात दवाई मिलती हो। 9. अनिल परीक्षा में असफल रहा, जिससे सभी को निराशा हुई। 10. अपनी योग्यताओं

के बावजूद उसे नौकरी नहीं मिल पाई, जो सच में खेद की बात थी। 11. इस वर्ष अक्तूबर का महीना बहुत गर्म था, जिसकी मुझे पहले से कोई प्रत्याशा न थी। 12. अमरीका के दूतावास ने मुझे 'वीसा' नहीं दिया जिससे मेरा अपनी बहन के पास पहुँचना असम्भव हो गया है। 13. उन्होंने मुफ़्त खाना और रहने को आवास देने की बात कही, जो पर्याप्त नहीं था। 14. रूपा की माँ, जो ब्यासी वर्ष की हैं, प्रतिदिन योगाभ्यास करती हैं। 15 नया ' प्रेक्षाग ह ', जिसमें पाँच हज़ार लोग बैठ सकते हैं, आगामी सप्ताह तैयार हो जाएगा। 16. सिद्धान्त, जो मेरा मामा है, मुझसे पाँच साल छोटा है। 17. उसने मुझे दो चाकलेट के डब्बे डाक से भेजे, जिनमें से एक भी मुझे अभी तक नहीं मिला। 18. कई विद्यार्थियों ने इस पाठ्यक्रम के लिए आवेदन भेजा, जिनमें से अंततः किसीको भी प्रवेश नहीं मिला। 19. भूमि ने दूरदर्शन के एक 'रिएलिटी शो' में दस लाख रुपए जीते, जिसमें से अधिकांश उसने दान में दे दिया। 20. सविता के पाँच भाई बहन हैं, जिनमें सभी अमरीका में बसे हैं। 21. मैंने लगभग आधी दर्जन पोशाकें पहन कर देखीं, जिनमें से कोई भी ठीक माप की नहीं थी। 22. दो युवक, जिनमें से किसीको भी मैंने पहले नहीं देखा था, मेरे अध्ययन कक्ष में घुस आए। 23. गाड़ी में मैं एक लड़की को मिली जिसकी माता मेरी माता की सहपाठिन थी। 24. वे लोग कहाँ हैं जिनके घर में पिछली सर्दी में चोरी हुई थी? 25. वह औरत अब कैसे है जिसके पति हाल में सांप्रदायिक दंगों में मारे गए थे। 26. आज छात्रों द्वारा आयोजित एक प्रदर्शन था जिस का ध्येय स्वयं छात्रों को भी नहीं मालूम था। 27. यह एक ऐसी सूचना है जिसका असली मूल्य तुम बाद में जानोगे। 28. लेखक को एक लाख रुपए नकद पुरस्कार मिला, जो सारे का सारा उन्होंने भूकम्प पीड़ितों के सहायता कोश में दान कर दिया। 29. मेरे पास बहुत से रसोई घर के उपकरण हैं जिनमें आधे से ज़्यादा मैं कभी प्रयोग नहीं करती।

Key 1

1. who/that	2. who/that	3. that	4. who /that
5. who/that	6. that	7. that	8. who/that
9. who /that	10. who/that	11. that	12. that

Key 2

1. Next to my house is a playground where children play in the evening.
2. We had a picnic by the river where our teachers took us.

3. I know a guest house at Rajiv Chowk where you can stay comfortably at a reasonable price.
4. I know a shop where you can buy imported perfumes.
5. This is the Red Fort where the Prime Minister of India hoists the national flag and addresses the nation on the Independence Day every year.

Key 3

1. He left the house without paying three months' rent, which was a shame.
2. It is very noisy where I live, which makes it impossible for us to concentrate on anything.
3. She didn't thank them for their generous hospitality, which in my opinion was very rude.
4. The railway strike, which lasted three days, was called off this morning.
5. He told me his phone number, which I immediately noted down in my diary.

Key 4

1. They have set up a branch office in India whose job (= the job of which) is to give prompt service to the customers.
2. This is my sister's father-in-law without whose help I could not have got this job.
3. This is Mr Sharma, whose son got the 'Young Scientists Award' last week.
4. That is Dinesh, whose brother died in the air crash last week.
5. This is my maths teacher, without whose encouragement I could not have passed the exam.
6. It was an opportunity whose (= of which the) importance did not occur to me then.

Key 5

1. This is the actress of **whom** I spoke this morning. 2. Is this the electrician **whom** you had called today? 3. She is the woman **whom** people like at first sight. 4. I know a place **where** you can sit quietly in peace for hours. 5. A monastry is a place **where** monks live. 6. I would like to work in a country **where** it is always cold. 7 Could you suggest a place near here **where** I could have a hair cut? 8. Is there a drug store in this locality

where medicines are available day and night? 9. Anil failed in the examination, **which** disappointed everybody. 10. In spite of his qualifications he couldn't get the job, **which** was a pity. 11. This year the month of October was very hot, **which** I had not anticipated. 12. The U.S. Embassy didn't grant me a visa, **which** has made it impossible for me to go to my sister. 13. They offered to provide me with free boarding and lodging, **which** was not enough. 14. Rupa's mother, **who** is 82 years old, practises yoga every day. 15. The new auditorium, **which** can accommodate 5000 people, will be ready next week. 16. Siddhant, **who** is my maternal uncle, is five years younger than I am. 17. She sent me two boxes of chocolates by post, **neither of which** I have received yet. 18. Several students applied for this course, **none of whom** finally got admission. 19. Bhoomi won Rs. ten lacs in a Reality Show on TV, **most of which** she gave away in charity. 20. Savita has five siblings, **all of whom** are settled in the USA. 21. I tried about half a dozen dresses, **none of which** was the right size. 22.Two young men, **none of whom** I had met before, broke into my study room. 23. On train I met a young lady **whose** mother had been my mother's classmate. 24. Where are those people **whose** house was burgled last winter? 25. How is that woman now **whose** husband was killed in the communal riots recently? 26. There was a students' demonstration today, **whose** purpose (= the purpose of which) was not known even to the students themselves. 27.This is a piece of information **whose** real worth you will know later. 28. The writer was awarded a cash prize of Rs. one lac, **all of which** he donated to the earthquake relief fund. 29. I have many kitchen gadgets, **more than half of which** I never use.

Wisdom from Grandma 

- Once bitten, twice shy.
- Attack is the best defence.
- A stitch in time saves nine.
- What cannot be cured must be endured.
- Strike while the iron is hot.
- A bad workman always blames his tools.

48 Direct / Reported Speech

■ If A wants to tell B what C told him, in English language there are two possibilities.
यदि कोई व्यक्ति एक आदमी से सुनी हुई बात किसी अन्य व्यक्ति को बताना चाहता है, तो अंग्रेज़ी भाषा में दो तरीके हैं।

1 **Direct speech reproduces verbatim what somebody said:**
(= *सुनी हुई बात को अक्षरश: दोहराना:*) **For example:**

- Rani said, **'I am going** to America **next month**'.
  रानी ने कहा, ' मैं अगले महीने अमरीका जा रही हूँ ।'

2 **Reported or indirect speech rewords the story, changing the tense and person.**
(= *सुनी हुई बात का* **tense** *और* **person** *बदलकर बात बताना ।*)

- Rani told me that **she was going** to America **the following month.**
  रानी ने मुझे बताया कि वह अगले महीने अमरीका जा रही है।

☞ **In the above example :**

- I => she
- am going => was going
- next month => the following month

☞ **Normally the changes given below take place while reporting direct speech.**

Present tense	=>	**Past tense**
• is/am	=>	was
• are	=>	were
• Is / am / are + v..ing	=>	was / were + v....ing

=> = changes to

- do, does => did
- has, have => had
- this => that
- here => there
- tomorrow => the following day
- yesterday => the day before

past form of the verb **or** **has/have + past participle**	=> **had + past participle**

Dir. : She said, 'I **studied** eighteen hours yesterday'.
Rep : She told me that she **had studied** eighteen hours the day before.
Dir : He said, 'I **have read** this book'.
Rep. : He told me that he **had read** that book.

Present perfect continuous	=> **past perfect continuous**
has/have + been + v..ing	=> **had + been + v...ing**

Dir : She said, 'I have been cleaning the house since the morning'
Rep: She told me that she had been cleaning the house since the morning.

Similarly:

- will => would
- will be + v.. ing => would be + v .. ing
- will have + pp => would have + past participle
- can => could
- may => might

=> = changes to; Dir. = direct speech; Rep. = reported speech

	Direct speech	Reported speech
1.	She said, 'if I have a lot of money, I will go round the world'	She said that she would go round the world if she had a lot of money.
2.	She said, 'I will be cruising next week'.	She told us that she would be cruising the following week.
3.	She said, 'I can speak six languages".	She told us (that) she could speak six languages.
4.	She said, 'I may go to Delhi tomorrow'.	She told me she might go to Delhi the following day.

☞ **'Would, should, ought to, must, might, could' remain unchanged.**

■ **If the situation does not change while reporting, the verb need not necessarily change.**

यदि परिस्थिति में कोई परिवर्तन न हो तो tense में परिवर्तन अनिवार्य नहीं।

	Direct speech	Reported speech
1.	Kamla said, 'I like Sudhir'.	Kamla told me she liked (or likes) Sudhir.
2.	Kamla said, 'Sudhir works very hard'.	Kamla told me Sudhir worked (or works) very hard.
3.	Kamla said, 'He is enjoying his present job'.	Kamla told me he was (or is) enjoying his present job.
4.	Kamla said, 'He wants to be a famous scientist'.	Kamla told me that he wanted / wants to be a famous scientist.
5.	Kamla said, 'He is coming to the party this evening'.	Kamla told me he was/is coming to the party this evening.
6.	Kamla said, 'we are considering getting married soon'.	Kamla told me they were / are considering getting married soon.

=> = changes to

Reporting questions

1 Reporting questions the answer to which is 'yes' or 'no' :
(जिन प्रश्नों का उत्तर 'हाँ' या 'न' में हो।)

Reporting verb + 'if' or 'whether' + subject + verb.

Direct: Are you going to watch TV tonight?
Reported : He asked whether I was going to watch TV that night.

2 Reporting all other questions with 'when, where, why, what, how' etc : (अन्य प्रश्न)

Reporting verb + interrogative pronoun + sub. + verb

Dir. question: How did you do it?
Rep. question: He asked how I had done it.

☞ **The word order of a reported question is not the same as the word order of a direct question.**

Remember:

- In direct question, the verb precedes the subject.
- In reported question, the verb follows the subject like in a state ment in direct speech.
- There is no question mark at the end of a reported question.

Comprehension — direct vs reported:

	Direct	**Reported**
1.	He asked, "Are you happy here?"	He asked if / whether I was happy there.
2.	He asked, "Did you go to the movies yesterday?"	He asked if I had gone to the movies the day before.
3.	She asked, "Do you always wear	She asked if I always wore a

	a saree?"	saree.
4.	He asked, "Are the mangoes ripe?"	He asked if the mangoes were ripe.
5.	He asked, "Have my shoes been cleaned?"	He asked if his shoes had been cleaned.
6.	He asked, "How much does it cost?"	He asked how much it cost.
7.	He asked, "What are you upto ?"	He asked what I was upto.
8.	He asked, "How is the pain at this time?	He asked how the pain was at that time.
9.	He asked, "How did you do it?"	He asked how I had done it.

While reporting suggestions, advice, commands, requests etc., 'to infinitive' Is used. (सुझाव, सलाह, आदेश, निवेदन आदि।)

	Direct : He said,	**Reported :**
1.	"Don't watch TV all day.'	He advised me not to watch TV all day.
2.	"Eat home cooked food as far as possible.'	He suggested to me to eat home cooked food as far as possible.
3.	"While you are in India, don't go out alone at night.'	He advised me not to go out alone at night while I am in India.
4.	"Always plan your expenses within your income."	He advised me to plan my expenses within my income.

Ex.1: Rewrite the sentences in indirect speech:

Prashant said to me:

1. "I don't like my present job, so I am thinking of changing it. "

   ....

2. "I sold my old car."

   ....

3. "I have asked the bank for a loan."

....

4. "I will buy a new car next month."

....

5. "I may buy a new house too."

....

6. "I want to go abroad for further study."

....

7. "My brother got married last week."

....

8. "I went to a music concert yesterday. It was really good."

....

9. "I seldom go out to eat.".

....

Ex. 2: Change the questions given below into reported speech:

> **She said, "How will you come to the party?"**
> **=> She asked how I would go to the party.**

Kamonica asked me:

1. "When did you come?"..
2. "What would you like to eat?"..
3. "Where are you planning to eat?"..
4. "Why didn't you lock the house?"..
5. "How did you do it?"..
6. "Why did you learn astrology?"..
7. "Do you like India?"..
8. "Are Ankita and Ankur married?"..
9. "Was any one injured in the car accident?"................................

....

10. "Is your brother coming to stay with you?"..

....

11. "Do you smoke?"..

12. "Can you come with us for a picnic?"...

Ex. 3: Change the sentences given below into indirect speech: He / She said to you:

1. "Don't listen to the radio after 10 p.m."..
2. "Please be home by 8 p.m. for dinner"...
3. "Take your umbrella with you. It is likely to rain"..............................

   ....

4. "Save some money and build a house while you are young".....

   ....

5. "Be careful while bathing in the Ganges. There are strong whirlpools as well as crocodiles"...

   ....

6. "Meet me on Monday at 10 a.m."..
7. "Don't worry. All will be well."..
8. "The customs officer said, "Open the boxes and show me the contents"......... ....

   ....

Ex. 4: Change to reported speech

The Chief Minister said, " Population figures have been going up. Prices have been soaring high. The previous government is responsible for this state of affairs in the country. The situation will not improve without joint efforts by all. We are inviting suggestions and proposals from various political and social agencies. I shall raise the issue in Parliament. I am sure the centre will support our views. We hope to get a majority in the coming elections. We will make every possible effort to control population as well as prices. We wiill bring prosperity to the country.

....

....

....

....

....

....

....

Ex. 5: Translate into English

1. उसने कहा कि उसको भूख नहीं थी।
2. कमला ने कहा कि उसे इसकी बहुत आवश्यकता थी।
3. उन्होंने कहा कि मैं इसे अपने पास रख सकती हूँ।
4. मेरे मित्र ने कहा कि वह मुझे हर हफ़्ते पत्र लिखेगा।
5. दादी ने कहा वे दूरदर्शन देखेंगी।
6. पियूष ने कहा वह आकाशवाणी पर ख़बरें सुनेगा।
7. उसने मुझे बताया कि वह व्रत नहीं रखेगी।
8. मेरे भाई ने मुझे वचन दिया कि वह मुझे सप्ताह में दो बार टेलीफ़ोन करेगा।
9. उसने मुझे बताया कि उसकी माँ अमरीका गई हैं।
10. माँ ने मुझे राम से शादी करने से मना किया।
11. सीमा शुल्क अधिकारी ने मुझे मेरा 'बैग' खोलने को कहा।
12. उन्होंने उसे अपने काम से काम रखने को कहा।
13. मैंने उसे धूम्रपान करने से मना किया।
14. मैंने अपने बेटे को रोज़ अख़बार पढ़ने को कहा।
15. आनन्द ने मुझे बताया कि उसे अभी नौकरी नहीं मिली।

Key 1

Prashant told me that:

1. he doesn't like his present job, and so he is thinking of changing it.
2. he had sold his car.
3. he had asked the bank for a loan.

4. he would buy a new car the following month.
5. he might buy a new house too.
6. he wanted to go abroad for further study.
7. his brother had gotten married the week before.
8. he had gone to a music concert the day before. It had been really good.
9. he seldom goes out to eat.

Key 2

Kamonica asked me,

1. when I had come.
2. what I would like to eat.
3. where I was planning to eat.
4. why I hadn't locked the house.
5. how I had done it.
6. why I had learnt astrology.
7. if I liked India,
8. if Ankita and Ankurj were married.
9. if any one had been injured in the car accident.
10. if my brother was coming to stay with me.
11. if I smoked.
12. if I could go with them for a picnic.

Key 3

1. He advised me not to listen to the radio after 10 p.m.
2. He requested me to be home for dinner by 8 p.m.
3. He advised me to take my umbrella with me as it was likely to rain.
4. He advised me to save some money and build a house while I am young.
5. He advised me to be careful while bathing in the Ganges and told me about the strong whirlpools and crocodiles in it.
6. He ordered me to meet him on Monday at 10 a.m.
7. He told me not to worry and assured me that all would be well.
8. The customs officer asked me to open the boxes and show him the contents.

Key 4

The Chief Minister admitted that the population figures had been going up and that the prices had been soaring high. He added that the previous government was responsible for this state of affairs in the country. He said the situation would not improve without joint efforts by all. He told us that they are inviting suggestions and proposals from various political and social agencies. He promised to raise the issue in Parliament. and was sure the centre would support their views. They hoped to get a majority in the coming elections. He assured the audience that they would make every possible effort to control population as well as prices and bring prosperity to the country.

Key 5

1. He /She said he /she was not hungry. 2. Kamla said she needed it very much. 3.They said I could keep it with me. 4. My friend said that he would write to me every week. 5. Grandmother said she would watch television. 6. Piush said he would listen to news on the radio. 7. She told me that she would not observe a fast. 8. My brother promised to phone me twice a week. 9. She told me that her mother has gone to the US. 10. Mother forbade me to marry Ram. 11.The customs officer told me to open my box. 12. They told him to mind his own business. 13. I advised him not to smoke. 14. I suggested to my son to read the newspaper every day. 15. Anand told me he had not got the job yet.

Wisdom from Grandma 

- Beauty is but skin deep.
- Don't count your chickens before they are hatched.
- Look after the pennies and the pounds will take care of themselves.
- It is no use crying over spilt milk.
- Barking dogs seldom bite.
- Might is right.

49 Enough..... to, too... to

☞ अंग्रेज़ी में enough.... to... का प्रयोग किसी चीज़ की पर्याप्तता के लिए
और
too......to... का प्रयोग किसी चीज़ की अत्याधिकता के लिए होता है।

■ **enough + noun**

- Is there **enough sugar** in your tea? — क्या चाय में पर्याप्त चीनी है?
- There isn't **enough space** in my office — मेरे कार्यालय में पर्याप्त जगह नहीं है।

■ **adjective + enough**

- This is not **strong enough.** — यह पर्याप्त मज़बूत नहीं है।
- Is the coffee **hot enough?** — क्या कॉफ़ी पर्याप्त गरम है?
- My office is not **spacious enough.** — मेरा कार्यालय पर्याप्त लम्बा-चौड़ा नहीं है।

■ **adjective + enough + to + infinitive**

- You are not **old enough to go out alone.** — तुम अकेले बाहर जाने लायक बड़े नहीं हुए।
- This house is **big enough to accommodate** fifty guests. — यह घर पचास महमानों को ठहराने के लिए पर्याप्त है।

■ **too + adjective / adverb**

- This house is **too small.** — यह घर बहुत ज़्यादा छोटा है।
- This shirt is **too big.** — यह कमीज़ बहुत ज़्यादा बड़ी है।

• There were **too many people.**	वहाँ बहुत ज़्यादा लोग थे।
• She drove **too fast.**	उसने वाहन बहुत तेज़ चलाया।

■ **too + adjective / adverb + for X + to infinitive**

• This house is **too small for us to live** comfortably.	हमारे आराम से रहने के लिए यह घर बहुत ज़्यादा छोटा है।
• This dress is **too big for me.**	यह परिधान मेरे लिए बहुत ज़्यादा बड़ा है।

Ex. 1: Rewrite the sentences given below using 'enough.... to' as shown:

> **She is very intelligent. She can understand it.**
> **=> She is intelligent enough to understand it.**

1. The volume of the Radio is loud. I can hear from here.

=> ....

2. I am not very strong. I cannot carry it alone.

=> ....

3. This dress is very good. I can wear it to a party.

=> ....

4. This food is quite tasty. I can eat it.

=> ....

5. His voice was quite loud and clear. Everybody could hear and understand it.

=> ....

6. The water was not very deep. One could not swim in it.

=> ....

7. Today it was very hot outside. One could roast a lamb.

=> ....

8. This book is very easy; you can read it.

=> . ...

9. The children were very hungry; they could eat an elephant.

=> ....

10. I am not very rich; I cannot always travel by aeroplane.

=> ....

11. He is very honest; we can trust him.

=>...

Ex. 2: Rewrite the sentences given below using 'too... to' and 'so... that' structures as shown:

> **It is very dark; I can't see anything.**
> **=> It is too dark for me to see anything.**
> **=> It is so dark that I cannot see anything.**

1. This dress is very small; it won't fit you.

=>..

=> ....

2. This book is very difficult; I cannot understand it.

=> ....

=> ....

3. This house is very expensive; we cannot buy it.

=> ....

. =>...

4. This city is very hot in summer; they won't be able to live here.

=> ....

=> ....

5. This tea is very hot; I cannot drink it quickly.

=> ....

=> ....

6. I am very weak, I cannot move.

=> ....

=> ....

7. She is very lazy. She cannot do it.

=> ....

=> ....

8. English language is very difficult. I cannot learn it.

=> ....

=> ....

9. The flower vase is very high. I cannot reach it.

=> ....

=> ....

10. She is very young; she cannot marry.

=> ....

=> ....

Key 1

1. The volume of the Radio is loud enough for me to hear from here.
2. I am not strong enough to carry it alone.
3. The dress is good enough for me to wear to a party.
4. This food is tasty enough for me to eat.
5. His voice was loud and clear enough for everybody to hear and understand.
6. The water was not deep enough to swim in.
7. Today it was hot enough outside to roast a lamb.
8. The book is easy enough for you to read.
9. The children were hungry enough to eat an elephant.
10. I am not rich enough to always travel by aeroplane.
11. He is honest enough for us to trust.

Key 2

1. This dress is too small to fit you.
   This dress is so small that it won't fit you.
2. This book is too difficult for me to understand.
   This book is so difficult that I cannot understand it.
3. This house is too expensive for us to buy.
   This house is so expensive that we cannot buy it.
4. This city is too hot in summer for them to live .
   This city is so hot in summer that they won't be able to live here.
5. This tea is too hot for me to drink quickly.
   This tea is so hot that I cannot drink it quickly.
6. I am too weak to move.
   I am so weak that I cannot move.
7. She is too lazy to do it.
   She is so lazy that she cannot do it.
8. English language is too difficult for me to learn.
   English language is so difficult that I cannot learn it.
9. The flower vase is too high for me to reach.
   The flower vase is so high that I cannot reach it.
10. She is too young to marry.
    She is so young that she cannot marry.

Wisdom from Grandma 

- While there is life there is hope.
- All that glitters is not gold.
- Make hay while the sun shines.
- Don't judge a book by its cover.
- Don't put all your eggs in one basket.
- A drowning man will catch a straw.

50 there it

to begin a sentence

Language Structure

There	Is, are, was, were, has been, have been, had been, will be, may be, can be, could be etc.
It	Is, was, has been, had been, will be, may be, can be, could be etc.

■ किसी ऐसी चीज़ का होना बताने हेतु, जिसका कोई पूर्व संदर्भ न हो, वाक्य के शुरू में 'There' का प्रयोग करते हैं।

- There are three boys at the gate. — फाटक पर तीन लड़के हैं।

☞ यहाँ लड़कों के बारे में पूर्व जानकारी नहीं है।

- The three boys are at the gate. — फाटक पर तीन लड़के हैं।

☞ *यहाँ लड़कों के बारे में पूर्व जानकारी है।*

Examples: 'There'

1. There is a big hole in your saree. — तुम्हारी साड़ी में एक बड़ा छेद है।

2. There are several mango trees in our garden. — हमारे बाग़ में कई आम के पेड़ हैं।
3. There was much traffic in the city yesterday. — कल शहर में बहुत 'जाम' लगा था।
4. There was a bank robbery last week. — पिछले हफ़्ते बैंक में डाका पड़ा।
5. There will be a good film on television next Sunday. — अगले रविवार को दूरदर्शन पर एक अच्छी फ़िल्म होगी।
6. There are about fifteen thousand students **at this** university. — इस विश्वविद्यालय में लगभग पन्द्रह हज़ार विद्यार्थी हैं।
7. There are two flights daily from Varanasi to Delhi — बनारस से दिल्ली के लिए रोज़ दो उड़ानें हैं।
8. Is there any mail for me today? — क्या आज मेरे लिए कोई डाक है?
9. Have there been any visitors this morning? — क्या आज सुबह कोई मिलनेवाले आए थे?
10. There may be snowfall tomorrow. — शायद कल हिमपात हो।

■ समय, दूरी, मौसम सूचक वाक्यों को और अवैयक्तिक, भाववाचक या शब्दों के जोड़ से बने subject वाले वाक्यों को प्राय: It से शुरू करते हैं।

Examples: ' It'

1. It is 2 O' clock. — दो बजे हैं।
2. It was past midnight when we reached there. — जब हम वहाँ पहुँचे, आधी रात बीत चुकी थी।
3. Is it very far? — बहुत दूर है क्या?
4. No it isn't very far. In fact it is quite near. — नहीं, बहुत दूर नहीं है। वास्तव में बहुत पास है।
5. It was long time ago. — यह बहुत समय पहले की बात हैं।
6. It is very foggy today. — आज बहुत धुंधनुमा है।
7. It is raining cats and dogs. — मूसलाधार बारिश हो रही है।

8. It is a sin to tell a lie.	झूठ बोलना पाप है।
9. It is not wise to spend more than one's income.	आय से अधिक ख़र्च करना बुद्धिमानी नहीं है।
10. It is unrealistic to imagine that India is a country of saints.	यह कल्पना हक़ीक़ी नहीं है कि हिन्दुस्तान साधु-सन्तों का देश है।
11. It might rain tomorrow.	शायद कल बारिश हो।
12. It will take us three days to reach there.	हमें वहाँ पहुँचने में तीन दिन लगेंगे।

☞ ध्यान दें: वाक्य संख्या आठ में 'to tell a lie' subject है, जो एक शब्द न हो कर शब्दों का समूह है। व्याकरण की दृष्टि से 'To tell a lie is a sin' ग़लत नहीं है। परन्तु अंग्रेज़ी भाषा में सामान्यता ऐसे बाक्यों में subject को पीछे खिसका कर वाक्य को It से शुरू करने की प्रथा है। हिन्दी में इसका कोई सटीक अनुवाद नहीं मिलता।

■ यह आवश्यक नहीं कि प्रत्येक वाक्य को It और There दोनों से बनाया जा सके।

☞ आम तौर पर there से शुरू होने वाले वाक्य में noun और It से शुरू होने वाले वाक्य में adjective या gerund का प्रयोग होता है।

1. There is fog.	2. It is foggy.
3. There is rain.	4. It is raining.
5. There is humidity.	6. It is humid.
7. There is snow.	8. It is snowing

Ex.1: Fill in the blanks with 'there', 'it' and the suitable form of the verb 'to be'

1. .... a good film on TV yesterday.
2 .... always a lot of traffic in this street.
3. .... several visitors this morning.
4. ....a painting exhibition at Bharat Kala Bhavan next week.
5. ....12 O' clock.

6 ....foggy yesterday.

7 ....raining since the morning.

8 ....not too far to walk.

9. ....late.

10 ....take you at least three years to learn Korean.

11. .... many children playing in the park.

12. ....a course of desk top publication next week.

Ex. 2: Translate into English:

1. कल दिल्ली में वस्त्र-प्रदर्शनी थी?
2. बहस जारी रखने में कोई अर्थ नहीं।
3. इतना गुस्सा होने की कोई जरूरत नहीं थी।
4. मुझसे इसके बारे में बात करने का कोई मतलब नहीं।
5. और कहने या करने को बचा ही क्या है।/शायद ही कुछ बचा है।
6. उसके बाद बहुत हंगामा हुआ।
7. उसके साथ कोई बात तो थी।
8. क्या घर में कुछ खाने को कुछ है?
9. बहुत ज़्यादा धुंध थी।
10. मूसलाधार बारिश हो रही है।
11. किसीको बुरा भला कहना ग़लत बात है।
12. तालाब में कई लोग तैर रहे थे।
13. संस्थान के प्रमुख फाटक के सामने एक बड़ा ट्रक खड़ा था।
14. क्या आपके साथ कोई और भी रह रहा है?

Key 1

1. There was
2. There is
3. There have been / were
4. There will be/ is
5. It is
6. It was
7. It has been
8. It is
9. It is
10. It will
11. There were
12. There is

Key 2

1. There was a textile show in Delhi yesterday.
2. There is no point in continuing the discussion.
3. There was no need to get so angry.
4. There seems to be no sense in talking with me about it.
5. There is hardly anything more to be said or done.
6. There followed a big commotion.
7 There was something the matter with her.
8. Is there anything to eat in the house?
9. It was very foggy.
10. It is raining cats and dogs.
11. It is wrong to offend somebody.
12. There were many people swimming in the lake.
13. There is a big truck parked in front of the main gate of the Institute.
14. Is there anybody else staying with you?

Time expressions

- a.m./A.M. (Latin शब्दों ante meridiem का संक्षिप्त रूप) रात्रि के बारह बजे के बाद से ले कर दिन के बारह बजे तक का समय।
- दोपहर के बारह बजे 12 a.m
- p.m./P.M. (Latin शब्दों post meridiem का संक्षिप्त रूप) दोपहर के बारह बजे के बाद से ले कर रात्रि के बारह बजे तक का समय।
- रात्रि के बारह बजे 12 p.m
- O' clock = complete hour (O' = of)
- 1 O' clock, 2 O'clock etc.

51 Question tags

■ **Question tags are put at the end of a negative or positive sentence. Sometimes the speaker actually expects a 'yes' or 'no' answer. Sometimes he just expects the other person's agreement with what he says.**

☞ **The auxiliary verb which is used in the main sentence is also used in the question tags.**

- You have been to the bank, haven't you? — आप बैंक हो आए हैं न?
- They will go to Kashmir, won't they? — वे काश्मीर जाएँगे न?

☞ **If the main sentence has present simple or past simple form of the verb, 'do', 'does', or did are used in the question tags.**

- You eat rice, don't you? — आप चावल खाते हैं न?
- He likes football, doesn't he? — वह 'फुटबाल' पसन्द करता है न?
- She passed the test, didn't she? — वह परीक्षा में सफल हुई न?

☞ **If the main sentence is negative, the question tag is positive.**

- She isn't rich, is she? — वह धनी नहीं है न?

☞ **If the main sentence is positive, the question tag is negative.**

- They will be here in the evening, won't they? — वे शाम को यहाँ होंगे न?

☞ **When the main sentence begins with "let's", the question tag is 'shall we'?**

- Let's eat, shall we?
- Let's watch TV, shall we?

☞ **When the main sentence is imperative , the question tag is 'will you'?**

- Sit down, will you?
- Turn off the light, will you?

☞ *ध्यान दें कि प्रत्येक* **question tag** *युक्त वाक्य का सटीक अनुवाद संभव नहीं। हिन्दी में प्राय: वाक्यान्त में 'है न' या 'न' लगा देते हैं। अंग्रेज़ी में यह प्रयोग नियम बद्ध है। जिस सहायक क्रिया का प्रयोग प्रधान वाक्य में होता है, उसी का प्रयोग* **question tag** *में भी होता है।*

Ex. 1: Complete the sentences with the appropriate question tag:

- **You are a student, aren't you?**
- **She has gone, hasn't she?**
- **They aren't Indians, are they?**
- **He won't come, will he?**

1. That isn't her house,..?
2. He doesn't drink,..?
3. She hasn't met her fiance..?
4. You will be on time, ...?
5. Mother didn't go to the temple,...?
6. Father returned from the office,.. ?
7. That dress is beautiful,... ?
8. She has written several books,.. ?

9. He can't drive,.. ?
10. Your brother isn't going abroad,.. ?
11. You slept well last night,.. ?
12. He teaches Hindi literature,.. ?
13. Your daughter phoned you last week,.................................... ?
14. You enjoyed your vacation in Italy,......................................?
15. The music concert wasn't good,... ?
16. You want to study philosophy,..?
17. He should apologise to you,.. ?
18. They needn't go so soon,.. ?
19. He is a kleptomaniac,.. ?
20. He is as good as gold,.. ?
21. Let's go to the concert,...?
22. Let's sleep, ... ?
23. Let me work now, ... ?
24. Let the dog out, ...?
25. Let him go to the cinema,.. ?

Ex. 2: Translate into English:

1. यह आपके लिए बिलकुल ठीक है न?
2. वह शाकाहारी है न?
3. आप लोग पिछले महीने छुट्टी पर गए थे, गए थे न?
4. उनके पास 'लैपटॉप' नहीं है न?
5. वह आपसे पहले कभी नहीं मिली थी न?
6. वह आपको पैसा उधार नहीं दे पाया न?
7. आपको देर तो नहीं होगी न?
8. तुम विदेशी पंजीकरण कार्यालय में हो आए हो न?
8. तुम्हें दूरदर्शन देखना अच्छा लगता है, न?
10. आप अण्णा हज़ारे की भ्रष्टाचार के खिलाफ़ मुहिम के समर्थक हैं, हैं न?
11. चला जाए, चला जाए क्या?
12. मुझे देर हो गई है न?

Key 1

1. .... is it?
2. . ..does he?
3. .. has she?
4. ... won't you?
5. ... did she?
6. ... didn't he?
7. .... isn't it?
8. ...hasn't she?
9. ... can he?
10. . .. is he?
11. ... didn't you?
12. ...doesn't he?
13. . ... didn't she?
14. ... didn't you?
15. ... was it?
16. . ... don't you?
17. ....shouldn't he?
18. . need they?
19. ..... isn't he?
20. ... isn't he?
21. .....shall we?
22. ....shall we?
23. ....will you?
24. ...will you?
25. .... will you?

Key 2

1. This is just right for you, isn't it?
2. She is vegetarian, isn't she?
3. You went on vacation last month, didn't you?
4. They don't have a laptop, do they?
5. She had never met you before, had she?
6. He couldn't lend you money, could he?
7. You won't be late, will you?
8. You have been to the foreigners' registration office, haven't you?
9. You like to watch television, don't you.
10. You support Anna Hazare's anticorruption movement, don't you?
11. Let's go, shall we?
12. I am late, ain't I

Vocabulary : Journalism

1. journalist जॅरनलिस्ट
3.editor ऐडिटर
4. columnist कालमिस्ट
5.publisher पबलिशर
6. critic. क्रिटिक
7.proof-reader प्रूफ़रीडर
8.reporter. रिपोर्टर
2.foreign correspondent फ़ौरेन कौरसपौण्डैण्ट

1. पत्रकार. 2. सम्पादक 3. स्तम्भ लेखक,स्तम्भकार 4. प्रकाशक

5.आलोचक 6. प्रूफ़ शोधक 7.संवाददाता 8. विदेशी संवाददाता

52 Questions with negative connotation

☞ **Sometimes Interrogative speech is used to convey a negative idea.**

1.	What use is life without literacy?	साक्षरता के बिना जीवन का क्या लाभ है?
=>	Life is no use without literacy.	साक्षरता के बिना जीवन का कोई लाभ नहीं।
2.	What good is crying over spilt milk?	गिरे हुए दूध पर रोने से क्या लाभ?
=>	It is no good crying over spilt milk.	गिरे हुए दूध पर रोने से कोई लाभ नहीं।
3.	What good is a government that cannot ensure law and order?	ऐसी सरकार किस काम की जो कानून और व्यवस्था न दे सके?
=>	A government that cannot ensure law and order is no good.	ऐसी सरकार जो कानून और व्यवस्था न दे सके, किसी काम की नहीं।
4.	What use is helping those who do not help themselves?	उन लोगों की मदद करने से क्या लाभ, जो अपनी मदद खुद नही करते?
=>	It is no use helping those who do not help themselves.	उन लोगों की मदद करने से कोई लाभ नहीं, जो अपनी मदद खुद नही करते।

★★★★★

53 Contractions

It's	(It is)	I'm	(I am)
he's	(he is, he has)	she's	(she is, she has)
you're	(you are)	you've	(you have)
they're	(they are)	they've	(they have)
we're	(we are)	we've	(we have)
who's	(who is, who has)	what's	(what is)
I'll	(I will)	I'd	(I would, I had)
you'll	(you will)	you'd	(you would, you had)
they'll	(they will)	they'd	(they would, they had)
we'll	(we will)	we'd	(we would, we had))
he'll	(he will)	he'd	(he would, he had)
she'll	(she will)	she'd	(she would, she had)
am not	(ain't)		
is not	(isn't)	wasn't	(was not)
aren't	(are not)	weren't	(were not)
hasn't	(has not)	haven't	(have not)
hadn't	(had not)		
won't	(will lnot)	wouldn't	(would not)
can't	(can not)	couldn't	(could not)
sha'nt	(shall not)	shouldn't	(should not)
doesn't	(does not)	don't	(do not))
mustn't	(must not)	needn't	(need not)

Getting To The Post Office

A: Excuse me, is there a post office near here?
B: Yes, there is.
A. Is it very far from here?
B. No, not really. Turn left at the first traffic light. It is on the right.
A. Thanks very much.
B. You are welcome.

At The Post Office

Customer : Please give me five stamps of ten paise each and twenty stamps of fifty paise each. Also give me ten aerogrammes and fifteen inland letters.
Clerk : Here you are, sir. Anything else?
Customer : No, thank you. How much does it come to?
Clerk : Mmm.... ten times five is fifty paise, fifty times twenty is ten rupees, ten times six-fifty is sixty-five rupees and fifteen times seventy-five is eleven rupees and twenty five paise. All together it is eighty-six rupees and seventy-five paise.
Customer : One more thing. Can I open a savings acount here?
Clerk : Yes, you can. Also we have several other saving schemes. You can invest your money for a fixed period and earn interest. If you are an income tax payee, you get income tax rebate on national savings certificates.
Customer : Thanks for the information. Goodbye.
Clerk : Goodbye.

Related Vocabulary:

postmaster postman registered letters/parcels
express delivery speed post insured letters/parcels
bookpost money order post-box letter box

54 Usages

while	while + a clause (i.e. subject + verb)
during	during + noun

Use of 'while' — जिस समय, जब

- While the guests were eating, children were making much noise. — जिस समय महमान खा रहे थे, बच्चे बहुत शोर मचा रहे थे।
- While father was watching TV, mother was preparing lunch. — जिस समय पिता जी दूरदर्शन देख रहे थे, माँ भोजन बना रही थीं।
- While I was listening to the news on the radio, my wife was teaching the children. — जिस समय मैं रेडियो पर समाचार सुन रहा था, मेरी पत्नी बच्चों को पढ़ा रही थी।
- While I was in Canada, I met several interesting people. — जब मैं कनाडा में था / थी, मैं कई रोचक लोगों से मिला/ मिली।

Use of 'during' — *के दौरान*

- During my stay in Canada, I did several interesting things. — अपने कनाडा में प्रवास के दौरान मैंने अनेक रोचक कार्य किए।
- During the lunch hour, I quickly went to the bank and got some money. — भोजन अन्तराल के दौरान मैं जल्दी से बैंक जाकर कुछ पैसे निकाल लाया/लाई।

- They did not ask me anything during the interview. — उन्होंने मुझे साक्षात्कार के दौरान कुछ नहीं पूछा।
- There were many interruptions during the lesson. — आज पाठ के दौरान बहुत रुकावटें आईं।

Ex.1: Fill in the blanks with 'during'or 'while':

1. It started to snow ....we were on the highway.
2. The postman came.......................I was having lunch.
3. We ate potato wafers and drank Coca Cola........intermission.
4. I could not visit my friends ....my stay in Delhi.
5. She fell off the chair................she was putting up the curtains.
6. Anil hurt his leg.................playing cricket.
7. Our neighbors looked after our dog................we were away.
8. I went to the bank ....the lunch hour.
9. ....my stay in Germany, I learnt German.
10. Your sister-in-law called..............you were in the bathroom.
11. I visited several museums.................. my stay in New York.
12. There was pin drop silence .... the Prime Minister's speech on the Republic Day.
13. .... the time I have been away from India, many changes have taken place.
14. He cut himself ....chopping onions.
15. She burnt herself ....cooking.
16. My husband usually reads the newspaper ....I watch TV.
17. He worked as a journalist.................... his stay in India.
18. The doorbell rang several times .... the night.
19. I got the news .... I was driving.

Key 1

1, 2, 5, 6, 7, 10,14, 15 16, 19	while
3, 4, 8, 9, 11, 12, 13, 17, 18.	during

In case, lest — कहीं ....न ; If — यदि

☞ जब व्यक्ति किसी बात के होने की आशंका या अंदेशा होने पर उसके ख़राब प्रभाव से बचने हेतु पहले से कोई क़दम उठाने की सोचे, तो 'in case' clause / 'lest' clause का प्रयोग करते हैं।

☞ जब व्यक्ति किसी परिस्थिति विशेष के पनपने के बाद कोई क़दम उठाने की सोचे, तो 'if ' clause का प्रयोग करते हैं।

• Don't sit in the sun **in case / lest** your skin gets burnt.	धूप में मत बैठो, कहीं तुम्हारी त्वचा न जल जाए।
• Wear your hat **in case / lest** you catch cold.	टोपी पहन लो, कहीं तुम्हें ठण्ड न लग जाए।
• I will visit you **if** I come to India.	अगर मैं भारत आया तो तुम्हें मिलूँगा।
• You should phone the police **if** there is a robbery in the house.	अगर घर में चोरी हो जाए, तो पुलीस को सूचना कर देना।

Ex. 1: Translate into English:

1. टेक्सी ले लीजिए, कहीं आपकी गाड़ी न छूट जाए।
2. नौ बजे के पहले फ़ोन करना, कहीं मुझे नींद न आ जाए।
3. तुम्हें अपने घर में पुरावस्तुओं का बीमा करवा लेना चाहिए, कहीं चोरी न हो जाए।
4. अपना छाता ले जाइए, कहीं बारिश न आ जाए।
5. अगर बारिश आ जाए, तो अपनी बरसाती पहन लेना।
6. अगर तुम्हें चोट लग जाए तो तुम्हें यह मरहम लगानी चाहिए।
7. तुम्हें यह मरहम हमेशा अपने पास रखनी चाहिए, कहीं चोट न लग जाए।

Key 1

1. Take a taxi in case/ lest you miss the train.
2. Phone me before 9 p.m. in case / lest I go to bed.
3. You ought to insure the antiques in your house in case / lest there is a robbery.
4. Take your raincoat in case it rains.
5. You wear your raincoat if it begins to rain.
6. You should apply this ointment if you get injured.
7. You should always keep this ointment with you in case you get injured.

in spite of / despite — के बावजूद
although, though — यद्यपि

Although / Though + subject + verb......
In spite of / Despite + noun / pronun / v... ing ....

■ अधिकांशतया **although / though** ये दोनों शब्द एक ही अर्थ में प्रयोग किए जा सकते हैं। परन्तु ध्यान दें कि -

☞ though के पूर्व even लगा सकते हैं although के पूर्व नहीं।
'though' conjunction और adverb दोनों तरह प्रयोग किया जाता है। जब 'though' adverb का काम करता है, तो वाक्य के मध्य या अन्त में भी आ सकता है।

☞ although सिर्फ़ conjunction के रूप में प्रयोग किया जाता है।

- In spite of / Despite the Principal's warning, the students did not attend the lecture. — प्रधानाचार्य की चेतावनी के बावजूद छात्रों ने व्याख्यान नहीं सुना।

• In spite of / Despite her impudent behaviour, everybody was kind to her.	उसके उद्दण्ड व्यवहार के बावजूद उसपर सबकी कृपा थी।
• In spite of / Despite having a lot of money, they are unhappy.	बहुत धन होने के बावजूद वे नाखुश हैं।
• Although it was very hot, they did not use a cooler.	यद्यपि बहुत गर्मी थी, उन्होंने 'कूलर' का प्रयोग नहीं किया।
• Although I had vowed never to live in Varanasi during the summer, I could not go out this year.	यद्यपि मैंने गर्मी में बनारस में न रहने की शपथ ली थी, मैं इस वर्ष बाहर नहीं जा पाई।
• Although they played well, they did not win the match.	यद्यपि वे बहुत अच्छा खेले, वे मैच जीत नहीं पाए।

Ex. 1: Rewrite the sentences given below as shown:

> **Although she is very rich, she is very humble.**
> **In spite of / Despite being very rich, she is very humble.**

1a. Although it snowed heavily, we enjoyed our stay in the mountains.
1b. In spite of / Despite ....
2a. Although she was highly qualified, she was not given the job.
2b. In spite of / Despite ....
3a. Although mother was very tired, she cooked a big meal for us.
3b. In spite of / Despite ....
4a. Although he is wealthy, he is very miserly.
4b. In spite of / Despite ....
5a. Although we are poor people, we are content and happy.
5b. In spite of / Despite ....

Ex. 2: Translate into English.

1a. यद्यपि वातानुकूलन यंत्र चालू था, कमरा ठण्डा नहीं था।
1b. वातानुकूलन यंत्र चालू *होने के बावजूद /होते हुए भी* कमरा ठण्डा नहीं था।

2a. यद्यपि मैं बहुत थका हुआ था, मुझे नींद नहीं आई।

2b. बहुत थका हुआ ***होने के बावजूद /होते हुए भी*** मुझे नींद नहीं आई।

3a. यद्यपि यातायात बहुत ज़्यादा था, हम समय से पहुँचे।

3b. बहुत ज़्यादा यातायात ***होने के बावजूद /होते हुए भी*** हम समय से पहुँचे।

4a. यद्यपि वेतन बहुत कम था, उसने नौकरी स्वीकार कर ली।

4b. वेतन कम ***होने के बावजूद /होते हुए भी*** उसने नौकरी स्वीकार कर ली।

5a. यद्यपि वे एक ही इलाक़े में रहते हैं, वे एक दूसरे को नहीं जानते।

5b. एक ही इलाक़े में ***रहने के बावजूद /रहते हुए भी*** वे एक दूसरे को नहीं जानते।

Key 1

1b. In spite of / Despite heavy snow, we enjoyed our stay in the mountains.

2b. In spite of / Despite her being highly qualified, she was not given the job.

3b. In spite of / Despite being very tired, mother cooked a big meal for us.

4b. In spite of / Despite being wealthy, he is very miserly.

5b. In spite of / Despite being very poor, we are content and happy.

Key 2

1a. Although the air-condtioner was on, the room wasn't cool.

1b. In spite of / Despite the air-condtioner being on, the room wasn't cool.

2a. Although I was very tired, I could not go to sleep.

2b. In spite of / Despite being very tired, I could not go to sleep.

3a. Although there was heavy traffic, we reached on time.

3b. In spite of / Despite heavy traffic, we reached on time.

4a. Although the salary was low, she accepted the job.

4b. Despite / In spite of the low salary, she accepted the job.

5a. Although they live in the same neighborhood, they don't know each other.

5b. Despite / In spite of living in the same neighborhood, they don't know each other.

be supposed to — *माना जाना, अपेक्षित होना*

■ अमुक व्यक्ति, वस्तु , परिस्थिति के बारे में लोगों की आम धारणा अथवा आम अपेक्षा की अभिव्यक्ति में सामान्यता **passive** भाषा ढाँचे **'be supposed to' / 'expected to' etc** का प्रयोग होता है।

1. Varanasi is supposed (= is said) to be the most ancient city in the world. (अर्थात ऐसी आम धारणा है।)
   बनारस को विश्व का सबसे पुराना शहर माना जाता है।
2. The aeroplane was supposed to (=was scheduled to) land at 7 a.m. but it landed at 7.45 a.m.
   हवाई जहाज़ सुबह सात बजे आने को था, परन्तु पौने आठ बजे आया।
3. He is supposed (= said to be) to have been a good football player when he was young. (अर्थात लोग ऐसा कहते है।)
   कहते हैं जब वह युवा था, वह फुटबाल का बहुत अच्छा खिलाड़ी था।
4. You are not supposed to (= not allowed to) eat sweets.
   आपको मिठाई नहीं खानी चाहिए (= मिठाई खाना आपके लिए हानिकारक है।)
5. I didn't mean to hurt you. It was supposed (intended) to be a joke.
   मेरा आपको दुखी करने का इरादा नहीं था। मैंने मज़ाक में कहा था।
6. Anil was supposed to (= expected to) come to the party. What happened?
   अनिल को दावत में आना था। क्या हुआ?
7. You are supposed to be studying at this time, not watching TV
   इस समय तुम्हें पढ़ रहा होना चाहिए, न कि दूरदर्शन देखना।
8. You are not supposed to smoke here. It is a public place.
   तुम्हें यहाँ धूम्रपान नहीं करना चाहिए। यह सार्वजनिक स्थान है।
9. You are not supposed to go out of the country.
   तुम्हें देश से बाहर जाने की इजाज़त नहीं।

10. Oh God! I was supposed to meet my boss, but it completely slipped out of my mind.
हे भगवान! मुझे तो अपने अधिकारी से मिलना था, लेकिन मेरे दिमाग से बिलकुल निकल गया।

11. I want to listen to his speech. It is supposed to be (expected to be) really good.
मैं उसका भाषण सुनना चाहती हूँ। यह बहुत अच्छा होना चाहिए।

few, a few, the few, little, a little, the little

■ Few का प्रयोग countable nouns के साथ और little का प्रयोग uncountable nouns के साथ होता है; अर्थात few संख्या और little मात्रा के लिए प्रयोग होता है।

few — लगभग न के बराबर (ज़रूरत से कहीं कम) संख्या
little — लगभग न के बराबर (बहुत कम) मात्रा
few and little have negative connotation. (बिना article के few और little का संकेत नकारात्मक अर्थ में होता है।)

- I have **few** acquaintances in this city. — इस शहर में मेरी जानपहचान लगभग न के बराबर है ।
- Robert learnt Hindi for several years. He makes **few** mistakes. — राबर्ट ने कई साल हिन्दी सीखी। वह लगभग ग़लती नहीं करता।
- I have **little** time for myself. — मेरे पास अपने लिए समय नहीं।
- She is diabetic. She takes **little** sugar. — वह मधुमेह की मरीज़ है। वह चीनी लगभग नहीं लेती।

positive connotation

थोड़ी संख्या या मात्रा, परन्तु शून्य से अधिक के अर्थ में

a few — थोड़े से, कुछ

a little — थोड़ी सी मात्रा

- I have **a few** stamps . I have to buy some more. — मेरे पास **कुछ** टिकट हैं। मुझे कुछ और ख़रीदने हैं।
- We are going on vacation **for a few days.** — हम ***कुछ दिनों के लिए*** छुट्टी पर जा रहे हैं।
- I can speak **a little** German. — मैं थोड़ी-सी जर्मन भाषा बोल सकती हूँ।
- We have **a little time** before the film starts; let us have some coffee. — हमारे पास फ़िल्म शुरू होने से पहले कुछ समय है। आओ, कुछ कॉफ़ी पी लें।

positive connotation.

the few — किसी विशेष थोड़ी संख्या, जिसका ज़िक्र पहले आ चुका हो, की ओर संकेत।

the little — किसी विशष थोड़ी मात्रा, जिसका ज़िक्र पहले आ चुका हो, की ओर संकेत।

- He knows **very little** Hindi, but **the little** that he speaks, is absolutely without mistakes. — उसे हिन्दी बहुत कम आती है; परन्तु जो थोड़ी बहुत वह बोलता है, उसमें कतई गलतियाँ नहीं होतीं।
- **The few weeks** I spent in India has been the best time in my life. — जो थोड़े से हफ़्ते मैंने भारत में बिताए, वह मेरी ज़िन्दगी का बेहतरीन वक़्त था।

Ex.1: Translate into English:

1. आजकल शाम को सड़कों पर लोग दिखाई नहीं देते। अधिकांशत: वे घर पर बैठकर दूरदर्शन देखते हैं।
2. वह हिन्दी बहुत कम बोलती थी, इसलिए उसे भारत में बहुत कठिनाई हुई।
3. आज मेरे घर में पनीर बहुत कम है (लगभग बिल्कुल नहीं)।
4. पिछले आतंकी हमले के बाद इस शहर में पर्यटक लगभग नहीं आते।
5. माँ को आज **कुछ पत्र** मिले।
6. मैं कुछ-एक बार अमरीका हो आई हूँ।

Key 1

1. These days one sees **few** people in the streets in the evening. Mostly they sit at home and watch TV.
2. She spoke **little** Hindi, so she had a lot of difficulty in India.
3. There is **little** cheese in my house today.
4. **Few** tourists visit this city after the last terrorist attack.
5. Mother received **a few letters** today.
6. I have been to America **a few times.**

plenty a lot of lots of many much

☞ **'plenty'** *और* **'a lot of '** *का प्रयोग दोनों* **countable** *और* **uncountable nouns** *के साथ* होता है। प्राय: 'a lot of', 'plenty of' का प्रयोग positive वाक्यों में होता है।

'plenty' = जितना चाहिए, उससे ज़्यादा।

Gautam has	plenty of / a lot of	money. ideas. things.

much + uncountable nouns	many + countable plural nouns
much wealth much food much happiness	many women many flowers many ideas

☞ **much** *का प्रयोग अधिकांशत: प्रश्नवाचक या नकारात्मक* **(interrogative, negative)** *वाक्यों में होता है;* **positive** *वाक्यों में आम तौर पर* **much** *का प्रयोग न करके* **a lot of** *का प्रयोग करते हैं।*

- Hurry up! We don't have **much** time. — जल्दी करो। हमारे पास बहुत समय नहीं है।
- She didn't say **much**. — उसने अधिक कुछ नहीं कहा।
- She said **a lot.** — उसने बहुत कुछ कहा।
- We have **a lot of** time. — हमारे पास बहुत समय है।

☞ **many / a lot of** *का प्रयोग तीनों तरह के वाक्यों* **(positive, negative, interrogative)** *में करते हैं।*

- My husband **has many / a lot of** friends. — मेरे पति के बहुत मित्र हैं।
- There were **many / a lot of** people at the concert. — गोष्ठी में बहुत लोग थे।
- Do you have **many / a lot of** friends? — क्या आपके बहुत मित्र हैं?
- I do**n't** have **many / a lot of** friends. — मेरे बहुत मित्र नहीं हैं।

☞ **We say 'many' + hours, days, weeks, months or years.**

☞ **We don't say ' a lot of' + hours, days, weeks, months or years.**

Ex. 1: Which is correct?

1. My husband uses the phone **a lot / much.**
2. There is always **much / a lot of** traffic in the morning.
3. I need **much / a lot of** money to start business.
4. I drink **much / a lot** of coffee.
5. I don't drink **much / a lot of** coffee.
6. Get ready soon. You haven't got **much / a lot of** time.
7. Don't make haste. You have **much / plenty of** time.
8. They have got **much / plenty of** money. They can easily travel by air.
9. I always take **much / a lot of / lots of** photographs when I travel.
10. She will accompany you. She hasn't got **much / a lot** to do these days.
11. You can come with us in my car. There is **much / plenty of** room.
12. There are **plenty of / lots of** inexpensive hotels near the station.
13. I don't know **a lot of / much** Hindi, just a few words.

Key 1

1. a lot	2. a lot of	3. a lot of
4. a lot of	5. much	6. much
7. plenty of	8. plenty of	9. a lot of / lots of
10. much	11. plenty of	12. plenty of/ lots of
13. much		

some any

■ **'Some' and 'any' are used with uncountable as well as plural countable nouns.**

some rice, some advice, some men, some people

☞ सामान्यता **some** का प्रयोग **positive** (सकारात्मक) और **'any** का प्रयोग **interrogative** (प्रश्नवाचक) वाक्यों में होता है।

- Please take **some** medicine. कृपया कुछ दवाई ले लीजिए।
- There is **some** milk in the रसोईघर में कुछ दूध है।

kitchen.

- Have you ever had **any** antibiotic? — क्या आपने कभी कोई ऐण्टिबायोटिक लिया है?

☞ **Interrogative** (प्रश्नवाचक) वाक्यों में **some** का प्रयोग तब होता है जब उत्तर में स्वीकारोक्ति की अपेक्षा हो। जैसे:—

- You don't look well. Is something the matter? — तुम कुछ ठीक नहीं लग रहे हो। कोई बात है क्या?

(उपरोक्त पहले वाक्य में प्रश्नकर्ता जानता है कि ज़रूर कुछ ठीक नहीं है, और उत्तर 'हाँ' में ही मिलेगा।)

- Can I have some milk from the refrigerator? — क्या मैं 'रेफ्रीजरेटर' से कुछ दूध ले सकता हूँ।

(इस वाक्य में प्रश्नकर्ता जानता है कि दूध वहाँ है।)

■ **some** का प्रयोग हम किसी ऐसे व्यक्ति या वस्तु के सन्दर्भ में करते हैं जिसके होने की हमें पूर्व जानकारी हो, या जिसकी मौजूदगी में हमें विश्वास हो। जैसे: —

- There is someone at the gate. — दरवाज़े पर कोई है।

(इस वाक्य से किसी की मौजूदगी का पूर्व बोध होता है।)

■ **We use 'some' in interrogative sentences both (1) when we offer something to somebody as well as (2) when we ask someone for something.**

किसीको कुछ पेशकश करते हुए, या किसीसे कुछ याचना करते हुए **'some'** का प्रयोग करते हैं।

- Would you like **some** tea? — आप कुछ चाय लेंगे?
- Would you like **something** to drink? — आप कुछ पीएँगे?
- Could you lend me **some** money? — आप मुझे कुछ पैसा उधार दे पाएँगे?
- Could I have **some** salt please? — कृपया मुझे कुछ नमक दीजिए।

'some' + singular countable noun' to express indifference, sometimes even contempt.
उदासीनता या हकारत की स्थिति में

- She lives in **some small village** in U.P. — वह उत्तर प्रदेश के किसी छोटे-से गाँव में रहती है।
- He works for **some soap factory** in Delhi. — वह दिल्ली में किसी साबुन के कारख़ाने में काम करता है।

'some + number' used in the sense of 'about' — कोई, लगभग

- She has **some two thousand** sarees. — उसके पास कोई दो हज़ार साड़ियाँ हैं।
- Badhohi exported **some fifty lac** carpets this year. — बदोही ने इस वर्ष कोई पचास लाख ग़लीचे निर्यात किए।

■ **'Any' is used in negative** (नकारात्मक) **and interrogative** (प्रश्नवाचक) **sentences.**

☞ **any** का प्रयोग हम किसी ऐसे व्यक्ति या वस्तु के सन्दर्भ में करते हैं जिसकी मौजूदगी की हमें कोई जानकारी न हो। जैसे: —

- She doesn't need **any** medicine. — उसे कोई दवाई नहीं चाहिए।
- Does she need **any** medicine.? — क्याा उसे कोई दवाई चाहिए?
- There isn't **any** milk in the kitchen. — रसोईघर में दूध बिलकुल नहीं है।
- Isn't there **any** milk in the kitchen? — क्या रसोईघर में दूध बिलकुल नहीं है?

any — कोई सा-, कोई से-, कोई सी-

1. Which story do you want me to narrate?	आप मुझसे कौन-सी कहानी सुनना चाहते हैं?
• **Any.**	कोई सी।
2. Which train shall I take?	मैं कौन सी गाड़ी लूँ?
• **Any.** All trains go via Allahabad.	कोई-सी भी। सब गाड़ियाँ इलाहाबाद से गुज़रती हैं।
• What time shall I call you?	मैं आपको कितने बजे 'फोन करूँ?
• **Any time.** I shall be home all day	किसी भी समय। मैं दिन भर घर पर होऊँगी /होऊँगा?

If any / anyone — अगर कोई /कुछ के अर्थ में

• If **anyone** wants to meet me today, tell them I am sick.	यदि आज मुझसे कोई मिलना चाहे, तो उसे कह देना कि मैं बीमार हूँ।
• Bring **some** grapes **if** you see **any** at the fruit shop	अगर फल की दुकान पर अंगूर दिखाई दे जाएँ तो कुछ ले आइएगा।

anything, anywhere, any time etc — कुछ भी, कहीं भी, कभी भी आदि

• You may wear **anything.**	तुम ***कुछ भी*** पहन सकते हो।
• You may visit **anybody**.	तुम ***किसीसे भी*** मिलने जा सकते हो
• You may phone me **any day any time.**	तुम मुझे किसी भी दिन, किसी भी समय फ़ोन कर सकते हो।
• You can travel by **any train**.	तुम किसी भी गाड़ी से यात्रा कर सकते हो।

- You can study any subject. तुम कोई भी विषय पढ़ सकते हो।

'some' and 'any' — as pronouns

1: Would you like more coffee? आप और कॉफ़ी लीजिएगा?

- No thanks, I have got **some.** जी नहीं, मेरे पास अभी है।

2: Did you bring some butter? तुम कुछ मक्खन लाए?

- No they didn't have **any.** नहीं, दुकान पर (मक्खन) कतई नहीं था।

Ex.1: Which is correct?

1. She didn't buy **some / any** dresses here.
2. She bought **some / any** books in Delhi.
3. He visited us with **some / any** friends last week.
4. Did you go to **any / some** museum in India?
5. I would like **any / some** milk and sugar in my coffee.
6. **Some / Any** birds cannot fly.
7. I want to buy **some / any** clothes.
8. Mary speaks **some / any** Hindi.
9. I watched **any/ some** good movies in the US.
10. This morning it snowed in **some / any** places.

Ex. 2. Fill in the blanks with one of the following words. anything, somebody, something, anybody, any, some:

1. He was too shocked to say ....
2. .... is knocking at the door,
3. I had .... stomach problem, so I did not eat ....
4. You must be thirsty. Would you like........................... to drink?
5. Mother seemed disturbed, but she did not tell ....
6. Hindi is a very easy language. .... can learn it very quickly.
7. There was hardly .... in the market.
8. We didn't buy .... gift.
9. Next week we are going to Kanyakumari with .... friends of ours.
10. I haven't seen ....movie lately.

11. I can't have .... milk in my tea.
12. I couldn't get .... information about him.
13. I needed a dictionary to understand.................. words in this article.

Ex. 3: Translate into English:

1. मरीज़ ने कोई दवाई लेने से इनकार कर दिया।
2. इस हादसे के बारे में किसीको कुछ न बताना।
3. क्या तुम कहीं अस्पताल के आस-पास रहते हो?
4. क्या तुमने कभी कोई किताब लिखी है?
5. वह आज सुबह से बहुत चुप और उदास है। उसका कुछ खो गया लगता है?
6. अगर कोई दरवाज़ा खटखटाए, तो उन्हें अन्दर न आने देना।
7. अगर कभी कोई तुमसे मदद माँगे, तो 'न' कभी मत कहना।
8. अगर कल रात के डाके के बारे में किसीको कुछ भी पता लगे, तो हमें तुरन्त सूचना दें।
9. क्या तुमने इनमें से कोई फ़िल्म देखी है?
10. मैंने तो कोई नहीं देखी, परन्तु मेरी बहन ने कुछ देखी हैं।
11. वह किसीसे बिना कुछ कहे बाहर चला गया।
12. उसने मुझे अपनी कार दी और कहीं भी, किसी भी समय जाने की इजाज़त दी।

Key 1

1. any
2. some
3. some
4. any
5. some
6. some
7. some
8. some
9. some
10. some

Key 2

1. anything
2. somebody
3. some ; ..... anything
4. something
5. anyone, anything
6. anybody
7. anybody
8. any
9. some
10. any
11. any
12. any.
13. some

Key 3

1. The patient refused to take any medicine.
2. Don't tell anyone anything about this incident.
3. Do you live anywhere near the hospital?
4. Have you ever written any book?
5. She has been very quiet and sad since the morning. She seems to have lost something.
6. If anyone knocks at the door, don't let them in.
7. If ever anyone asks you for help, never say 'no' to them.
8. If anyone comes to know anything about the robbery last night, inform us immediately.
9. Have you watched any of these movies?
10. I have'nt seen any, but my sister has seen some.
11. He went out without saying anything to anybody.
12. She gave me her car and allowed me to go any time anywhere.

as	**like**

as + adj. + as —	*उतना............जितना..................*
not as + adj. + as —	*उतना नहीं ....जितना............*
the same as X—	*ठीक उतना ही...... जितना.............*
	X *के जितना ही ....*

• This house is **almost as big as** that one.	यह घर *लगभग उतना ही बड़ा है* जितना वह वाला।
• She is **just as clever as** her sister.	वह *उतनी* ही होशियार *है जितनी* उसकी बहन।
• She is **the same age as** I am.	वह मेरी उम्र की है।
• She gets **the same salary** as I do.	वह *उतना ही* वेतन *पाती है जितना मैं*।

see pg. from adj chapter

as if — जैसे कि

- It looks **as if** he will jump into the well. — ऐसा लगता है ***जैसे कि*** वह कुएँ में कूदेगा।
- You look **as** if you have seen a ghost. — आप ***ऐसे*** लग रहे हैं ***जैसे*** कि आपने कोई भूत देखा हो।

as — के रूप में

- We think of him **as** a generous person. — हम उसे एक उदार व्यक्ति के रूप में मानते है।
- Many adjectives can be used **as** nouns. — बहुत से विशेषण संज्ञा की तरह प्रयोग किए जा सकते हैं।

as — क्योंकि

- **As** yesterday was a national holiday, all schools were closed. — क्योंकि कल राष्ट्रीय छुट्टी थी, सब स्कूल बन्द थे।
- **As** I had forgotten to wear my watch, I had no idea of time. — क्योंकि मैं अपनी घड़ी पहनना भूल गया था, मुझे समय का कोई अंदाज़ नहीं था।

as — जब, जिस समय

- She got burnt **as** she was making bread. — जिस समय वह रोटी बना रही थी, जल गई।
- The boy slipped **as** he was getting off the bicycle. — जब लड़का साइकिल से उतर रहा था, उसका पैर फिसल गया।

just as — जैसे ही

- Just **as** I lay down, someone knocked at our door. — जैसे ही मैं लेटी, किसीने हमारा दरवाज़ा खटखटाया।
- Just **as** we came out, it began to snow. — जैसे ही हम बाहर आए, बर्फ़ पड़ने लगी।

As if / as though — जैसे कि ☞ use of कि is not obligatory

- In spite of the bomb blast, the minister continued his speech **as if / as though** nothing had happened. — बम विस्फोट के बावजूद मंत्री ने अपना भाषण ऐसे जारी रखा जैसे कुछ हुआ ही न हो।
- Why are you looking at me **as if / as though** I were some crazy clown. — तुम मुझे ऐसे क्यों देख रहे हो जैसे मैं कोई सिरफिरा गँवार होऊँ ।
- She ate **as though / as if** she had never eaten anything for ages. — उसने ऐसे खाया जैसे उसने सदियों से कभी कुछ न खाया हो।
- They look after me **as if** I were their own daughter. — वे मेरा ऐसे ख़्याल रखते हैं जैसे मैं उनकी अपनी बेटी होऊँ ।

as + someone or something — के समान, की तरह

- He works as the Headmaster of this Institute. — वह इस संस्थान के प्रधानाचार्य की हैसियत से काम करता है।(=वह प्रधानाचार्य है।)
- Once upon a time, I used to work **as** a salesman. — एक समय की बात है, मैं विक्रेता की हैसियत से काम किया करता था। (=मैं विक्रेता था।)

Like = similar to (*के जैसा, के समान*) preposition *है।* *इसके बाद* noun / pronoun / v..ing *का प्रयोग होता है।*

• They live in a big mansion. It is **like some old castle.**	वे बहुत बड़े भवन में रहते हैं। यह किसी पुराने क़िले के जैसा है।
• Robert is a doctor **like me.**	राबर्ट मेरी तरह डॉक्टर है।
• I don't wear glittering clothes **like these.**	मैं इस तरह के भड़कीले कपड़े नहीं पहनती।
• It was **like walking on** a bed of **dry leaves.**	यह सूखे पत्तों की क्यारी पर चलने जैसा था।
• There were sounds **like pigs grunting and jackals howling.**	सूअरों और सियारों के रोने-चिल्लाने जैसी आवाज़ें थीं।
• The floor is very cold. It feel **like a block of ice. (actually not so)**	फ़र्श बहुत ठण्डा है। बर्फ़ की सिल्ली की तरह / के जैसा लग रहा है।

Compare and comprehend prepositional use of:	
like + noun/ pronoun	**as + noun**
• She runs **like an athlete.** **(actually not an athelete)** वह खिलाड़ी के जैसी दौड़ती है। (=वह वास्तव में खिलाड़ी नहीं है।)	• He works **as Headmaster.** (is actually a headmaster) वह प्रधानाचार्य की हैसियत से काम करता है।(= और वह वास्तव में प्रधानाचार्य है।)
• Their house is **like a muse-. um. (but actually it is not a museum)** उनका घर संग्रहालय जैसा है। (=परन्तु वास्तव में संग्रहालय	• During the riots this building was used **as shelter** home. **(the building was actually a shelter home)** दंगों में यह भवन आश्रय गृह

नहीं है।)	की तरह प्रयोग किया जाता था। (=यह वास्तव में आश्रय-ग ह था।)

Some fixed expressions with 'as' are:

- **As** you already know — जैसा कि आप पहले से जानते हैं :
- **As** I said — जैसा कि मैंने कहा
- **As** they expected — जैसी उन्हें उम्मीद थी
- **As** we think — जैसा कि हम सोचते हैं

Like = ***जैसेकि/उदाहरणार्थ***

- Some animals **like** snakes and scorpions can be very dangerous. — कुछ जानवर, ***उदाहरणार्थ*** साँप और बिच्छू बहुत ख़तरनाक हो सकते हैं।
- Some sports **like** ice skating can cause injury. — कुछ खेल ***जैसेकि*** 'आइस-स्केटिंग' चोट पहुँचा सकते है।

Ex.1: Complete these sentences using ' like' or 'as' + any of the following.

his father.	her mother,
a beginner.	some temple.
you are	wedding gift.
elephants and tigers	chief nurse
they like	you

1. He looks..
2. ...., she has big and beautiful eyes.
3. She has been playing the guitar for seven years, but she still plays ....
4. That building over there looks ....

5. You needn't change. Just come ....
6. She gave me this car ....
7. Some animals ....can be very dangerous.
8. I have been working .... in this hospital since 2005.
9. Children should be allowed to spend their time ....
10. I wish I could speak Hindi................ you.

Ex.2: Which is correct?

1. They have several animals. Their house is almost **as / like** a mini zoo.
2. **As / like** I told you, I am planning to change places.
3. On Sunday, I visited my parents **like / as usual.**
4. He was gloomy **like / as always.**
5. Don't waste time doing things **like** / **as** playing cards or flyings kites.
6. I wish I had a house **as / like** yours.
7. Trying to convince him of something is **as / like** breaking your head against the wall.
8. He talks nonsense. I cannot tolerate people **as / like** him.
9. It is too hot for the month of December. It is almost **like / as** the month of June.
10. Do **like / as advised** by your parents.
11. Plan your life **as / like** you like.
12. He has adventurous hobbies **as / like** diving and flying.
13. **As / like** you can imagine, I was very bored sitting and waiting for their train to arrive.

Ex. 3: Translate into English:

1. वह अपनी नानी ***के जैसी*** दिखती है।
2. उसके कन्धें अपने पिता जी की तरह चौड़े हैं।
3. वह दस वर्ष से हिन्दी सीख रही है, लेकिन अभी भी नौसिखिए की तरह बोलती है।
4. जल्दी करो ! जैसे हो वैसे ही आ जाओ।
5. मैंने उसे यह 'मोबाईल फ़ोन' उसके जन्म दिन के उपहार स्वरूप दिया।

6. कुछ जानवर, ***उदाहरणार्थ*** घड़ियाल और हाथी बहुत ख़तरनाक हो सकते हैं।
7. वह इस बैंक में 2008 से प्रमुख प्रबन्धक ***की हैसियत से*** काम कर रहा है। (= वह वास्तव में प्रमुख प्रबन्धक है)
8. देश के राष्ट्रपति की हैसियत से उसे बहुत से अप्रिय फ़ैसले करने पड़ते है। (= वह वास्तव में राष्ट्रपति है)
9. वे देश के उप राष्ट्रपति है। राष्ट्रपति की तरह उन्हें भी बहुत-से अप्रिय फ़ैसले करने पड़ते है। (= वह वास्तव में राष्ट्रपति नहीं है)
8. बच्चों को ***जैसे*** वे चाहें ***वैसे*** काम करने दिया जाना चाहिए।
9. काश मैं ***आपकी तरह*** विश्व भ्रमण कर सकता।

Ex. 4: Translate into English:

1. उनके पास बहुत-सी पुरावस्तुएँ हैं। उनका घर तक़रीबन एक छोटे संग्रहालय ***जैसा*** है।
2. ***जैसा कि*** उसने मुझे बताया, वह काम बदलने की सोच रहा है।
3. रविवार को मैं हमेशा ***की तरह*** समुद्रतट पर गया।
4. वे हमेशा ***की तरह*** खुश दिखे।
5. आज हमने बाहर खाना खाया ***क्योंकि*** मेरा खाना पकाने का मन नहीं था।
6. ***क्योंकि*** मैं दूरदर्शन ज़्यादा नहीं देखती, मैंने उसे एक दोस्त को दे दिया।
7. ***क्योंकि*** मेरी तबीयत अच्छी नहीं लग रही थी, मैंने आज छुट्टी ले ली।
8. वह ***ऐसे*** आचरण करती है ***जैसे*** वह धरती पर सबसे बुद्धिमान व्यक्ति हो।
9. उसकी बातों से ***ऐसे*** लग रहा था ***जैसे*** उसकी 'लॉटरी'निकली हो।
10. ***ऐसे*** लग रहा है ***जैसे*** बर्फ़ पड़ने वाली है।
11. उसका वेतन ***मेरे जितना*** है।
12. यह पोशाक ***उतनी*** महंगी ***नहीं जितनी*** आप सोचते हैं।
13. इस साल ***उतनी*** गर्मी ***नहीं जितनी*** पिछले साल थी।

Key 1

1. like his father
2. like her mother
3. like a beginner.
4. like some temple.

5.	as you are.	6.	as a wedding gift.
7.	like elephants and tigers	8.	as chief nurse
9.	as they like.	10.	like you.

Key 2

1, 5, 6,7, 8, 9 , 12	like
2, 3, 4, 10, 11, 13	as

Key 3

1. She looks **like** her grandmother.
2. He has broad shoulders **like** his father.
3. She has been learning Hindi for ten years, but she still speaks **like** a novice.
4. Hurry up! Just come **as** you are.
5. I gave her this mobile phone **as** her birthday gift.
6. Some animals **like** alegators and elephants can be very dangerous.
7. He has been working **as** chief manager in this bank since 2008.
8. **As President** of a country, he has to make many unpleasant decisions.
9. He is the Vice President of the country. **Like the President** he has to make many unpleasant decisions too.
10. Children should be allowed to work **as** they like.
11. I wish I could travel round the world **like** you.

Key 4

1. They have several antiques. Their house is almost **like** a mini museum.
2. **As** he told me, he is planning to change jobs.
3. On Sunday, I went to the beach **as usual.**
4. They seemed happy **as always.**
5. We ate out today **as** I was not in a mood to cook.
6. **As** I don't watch TV much, I gave it away to a friend.

7. **As** I was feeling unwell, I took a day off.
8. She behaves **as if** she were the most intelligent person on earth.
9. He sounded **as if** he had won a lottery.
10. It looks as if it is going to snow.
11. Her salary is **the same as** mine.
12. This dress did not cost me **as much as** you think (it did)
13. This year it is not **as hot as** it was last year.

nothing but	**but for**
last but one	**next but one**

1. She drinks **nothing but milk.**	वह दूध के अतिरिक्त और कुछ नहीं पीती।
2. My brother lives **next door but one.**	मेरा भाई एक घर छोड़कर अगलेवाले में रहता है।
3. Nobody but himself could accomplish this task.	उसके अतिरिक्त यह काम और कोई नहीं कर सकता था।
4. Ruchika lives in **the last house but two** in this street.	रुचिका इस सड़क पर आखिर से दो घर पहले रहती है।
5. Turn at the **next crossing but two** from here.	यहाँ से दो चौमुहानी छोड़कर अगली वाली पर से मुड़ो।
6. Who **but the present finance minister** could change the Indian economy?	वर्तमान वित्तमंत्री के अतिरिक्त और कौन भारत की अर्थव्यवस्था को बदल सकता था? (=अर्थात सिर्फ़ वर्तमान वित्तमंत्री ही ऐसा कर सकता था।
7. **But for your support** and encouragement, I would not be what I am.	आपके सहारे और प्रोत्साहन के बिना, मैं वह न होता, जो हूँ।

Ex.1: Rewrite the sentences following the models given below:

> **Paavani thinks only of eating all the time.**
> **=>Paavni thinks of nothing but eating all the time.**

1. You think only of going to the movies.
   ....
2. He thinks only of learning English.
   ....
3. She thinks only of good clothes and jewellery.
   ....

> **Only hard work can bring you success.**
> **=>Nothing but hardwork can bring you success.**

4. Only honesty can earn you esteem in society.
   ....
5. Only a feeling of brotherhood can make this world worth living in.
   ....
6. Only goat's milk satisfies her.
   ....

> **This place is not at all safe.**
> **=>This place is anything but safe.**

7. He is not at all diligent.
   ....
8. Bhaskar is not at all a genius.
   ....
9. This is not at all Indian food.
   ....

Key 1

1. You think of **nothing but** going to the movies.
2. He thinks of **nothing but** learning English.
3. She thinks of **nothing but** good clothes and jewellery.
4. **Nothing but** honesty can earn you esteem in society.
5. **Nothing but** a feeling of brotherhood can make this world worth living in.
6. **Nothing but** goat's milk satisfies her.
7. He is **anything but** diligent.
8. Bhaskar is **anything but** a genius.
9. This is **anything but** Indian food.

seldom, rarely, scarcely, hardly, never

विरले ही, यदा-कदा, मुश्किल से, कभी-कभार कभी नहीं

• **Never** would she listen to my advice.	वह कभी मेरी सलाह नहीं मानती।
= She would never listen to my advice.	
• **Seldom** have I seen such a beautiful woman.	मैंने विरले ही ऐसी सुन्दर औरत देखी होगी।
= I have seldom seen such a beautiful woman.	
• **Hardly** had I gone a few metres on the highway when my car broke down.	मैं मुश्किल से कुछ ही मीटर राजपथ पर गया था कि मेरी कार ख़राब हो गई।
= I had hardly gone a few metres on the highway when my car broke down.	
• **Rarely** do we have communal quarrels in our village.	हमारे गाँव में विरले ही कभी साम्प्रदायिक झगड़े होते हैं।

= We rarely have communal quarrels in our village.

- **Scarcely** had we set out when it began to snow. — हम बाहर निकले ही थे कि बर्फ़ पड़ने लगी।

= We had scarcely set out when it began to snow.

- **Little** did she realize how good her parents were. — उसे बिलकुल एहसास नहीं था कि उसके माता-पिता कितने अच्छे हैं।

= She **little** realized how good her parents were.

no sooner......... than.........
= had only just + pp.......when..........

☞ जैसे ही कोई व्यक्ति काम शुरू करे, वैसे ही किसी अन्य अप्रत्याशित बात के घटने पर उपरोक्त ढाँचे का प्रयोग करते हैं।

- No sooner had I turned the TV on than the lights went out.

= I had only just turned the TV on when the lights went out.
मैंने टी.वी. चलाया ही था कि बिजली चली गई।

- No sooner had the bank opened than a gang of robbers broke into the building and took away all the cash.

= The bank had only just opened when a gang of robbers broke into the building and took away all the cash.
बैंक खुला ही था कि डाकुओं का दल भवन में घुस कर सारा नकद ले गया।

- No sooner had he found a new job than he fell very ill.

= He had just only found a new job when he fell very ill.
उसे नई नौकरी मिली ही थी कि वह बहुत बीमार हो गया।

- No sooner had mother begun cooking than the gas finished.

= Mother had only just begun cooking when the gas finished.
माता जी ने खाना पकाना शुरू किया ही था कि गैस ख़त्म हो गया।

Ex. 1: Rewrite the sentences given below using 'had only just.... when' instead of 'no sooner... than' as shown:

> **No sooner had I lain in bed than the doorbell rang.**
> **=> I had only just lain in bed when the doorbell rang.**

1. No sooner had we set out than our car broke down.

   ....

2. No sooner had I sat down to study than the lights went out.

   ....

3. No sooner had the train moved than someone pulled the chain and it stopped again.

   ....

4. No sooner had she arrived in America than her father died and she had to come back.

   ....

Ex. 2: Translate into English:

1. मैं बिस्तर पर लेटा ही था कि किसीने दरवाज़े पर खटखटाया।
2. हवाई जहाज़ उड़ा ही था कि इंजिन में ख़राबी आ गई और उसे फिर नीचे आना पड़ा।
3. मैंने खाना खाया ही था कि मुझे चक्कर आने लगे।
4. माँ गई ही थीं कि बच्चा रोने लगा।

Key 1

1. We had only just set out when our car broke down.
2. I had only just sat down to study when the lights went out.
3. The train had only just moved when someone pulled the chain and it stopped again.
4. She had only just arrived in America when her father died and she had to come back.

Key 2

1. No sooner had I lain in bed than someone knocked at the door.
- I had only just lain in bed when someone knocked at the door.
2. No sooner had the airplane taken off than the engine trouble started and it had to land again.
- The plane had only just taken off when the engine trouble started and it had to land again.
3. No sooner had I eaten the meal than I began to feel dizzy.
- I had only just eaten the meal when I began to feel dizzy.
4. No sooner had the mother left than the child began to cry.
- Mother had only just left when the child began to cry.

so	**such**
so + adjective / adverb इतना, बहुत ज़्यादा **so + adj / adv. + that** इतना कि	**such + a / an + adj. + noun** बहुत ज़्यादा **such + a / an + adj. + noun + that** इतना कि

☞ **so** और **such** अपने इस प्रयोग में **adjective** को और सशक्त बनाते हैं

1a.	I don't like him. He is **so** foolish.	मैं उसे पसन्द नहीं करती। वह इतना (= बहुत ज़्यादा) मूर्ख है।
1b.	I don't like him. He is **such** a foolish person.	मैं उसे पसन्द नहीं करती। वह इतना/बहुत ज़्यादा मूर्ख आदमी है।
2a.	This dress is **so expensive.**	यह परिधान बहुत ज़्यादा महँगा है।
2b.	This is **such an expensive** dress.	यह इतना ज़्यादा महँगा परिधान है।

Ex.1: Fill in the blank spaces 'so' or 'such .'

1. It took you .... long to do it.
2. It took you.................... long t ime long to do it.
3. I didn't know they lived.....................far from the Airport.
4. I didn't know they lived ....long way from the Airport.
5. Who could anticipate .... many problems!
6. Who could anticipate .... lot of problems.
7. They were......................friendly.
8. They were .... friendly people.
9. Teaching profession is .... boring.
10. Teaching is......................boring profession.
11. Life is ....expensive in this city.
12. This is .... expensive city.
13. The concert was .... boring.
14. It was .... boring concert that we left it half way.
15. The dinner she served was...................... delicious. I have never eaten ....delicious food.
16. The boat ride was .... enjoyable. It is ....pity that you were not with us.
17. She was .... shocked at the news that she just stood speechless.
18. It has been .... long time since I went to my village.

Ex.2: Translate into English:

1. यह भूदृश्य बहुत सुन्दर हैं। 2. यह इतना सुन्दर भूदृश्य हैं। 3. भारतीय बहुत अच्छे हैं। 4. भारतीय बहुत अच्छे लोग हैं। 5. वर्षा इतनी ज़्यादा हुई कि सड़कें दस मिनट के भीतर घुटनों तक गहरे पानी में थीं। 6. इतनी तेज़ वर्षा थी कि सड़कें दस मिनट के भीतर घुटनों तक गहरे पानी में थीं। 7. सड़क इतनी संकुल है कि उसपर चलना कठिन है। 8. यह इतनी ठसा-ठस भरी हुई सड़क है कि इस पर चलना कठिन है। 9. हमारा कुत्ता इतना खूँखार है कि कोई हमारे फाटक के पास आने की हिम्मत नहीं कर सकता। 10. हमारे पास इतना खूँखार कुत्ता है कि कोई हमारे फाटक के पास आने की हिम्मत नहीं कर सकता।

Key 1

1. so	2. such a	3. so	4. such a
5. so	6. such a	7. so	8. such
9. so	10. such a	11. so	12. such an
13. so	14. such a	15. so ... such	16. so.......such a
17. so	18. such a		

Key 2

1. This landscape is **so beautiful.**
2. This is **such a beautiful** landscape.
3. Indians are **so nice.**
4. Indians are **such nice people.**
5. It rained **so heavily that** the roads were knee deep in water within ten minutes.
6. It was **such heavy rain** that the roads were knee deep in water within ten minutes.
7. The street is **so congested** that it is difficult to move on.
8. It is such a **congested** street that it is difficult to move on.
9. Our dog is **so wild** that no one dare come near the gate.
10. We have such a wild dog that no one dare come near the gate.

so much , so many — इतना, इतने, इतनी

☞ **so much .... used with singular uncountable nouns.**

☞ **so many .... used with plural countable nouns.**

- I had just **so much money** left. — मेरे पास सिर्फ़ इतना ही पैसा बचा था।
- She has collected **so many antiques** that she doesn't have enough space to store — उसने इतनी ज़्यादा पुरावस्तुएँ एकत्रित कर ली हैं कि उसके पास उन्हें रखने की पर्याप्त जगह नहीं है।

them.

- She used to waste **so much** of my **time** every day. — वह रोज़ मेरा इतना (=बहुत ज़्यादा) वक़्त बर्बाद किया करती थी।
- **So many** of her **antiques** have have been damaged. — उसकी इतनी (= बहुत ज़्यादा) पुरा वस्तुएँ नष्ट हो गई हैं।

> - **so as + to infinitive' / so that = *ताकि***
> **= in order + 'to' infinitive**
> ☞ **These expressions express purpose of the activity.**

- I shall work very hard during the summer vacation **so as to be able to go** skiing in the winter. — मैं ग्रीष्म अवकाश में बहुत परिश्रम करूँगा ***ताकि*** मैं सर्दी के मौसम में 'स्की' करने जा सकूँ।
- One ought to save while one is young **so as to enjoy** one's old age. — जब व्यक्ति युवा हो, उसे बचत करनी चाहिए ***ताकि*** बुढ़ापे में आनन्द ले सके।
- They are learning Hindi **so that** they can work in India — वे हिन्दी सीख रहे हैं ताकि वे भारत में काम कर सकें।
- He went by taxi **so that** he wouldn't miss the train. — वह टेक्सी से गया ताकि उसकी गाड़ी न छूट जाए।

> **so** — इसलिए ; **since** — क्योकि

1a: I did not have enough money **so** I did not buy it. — मेरे पास पर्याप्त पैसा नहीं था, ***इसलिए*** मैंने उसे नहीं ख़रीदा।

1b: **Since** I did not have enough money, I did not buy it. — ***क्योंकि*** मेरे पास पर्याप्त पैसा नहीं था, मैंने उसे नहीं ख़रीदा।

2a: The children have summer — बच्चों की गर्मी की छुट्टियाँ हैं,

vacation, **so** they are at home these days. — *इसलिए* वे आजकल घर पर हैं।

2b: **Since** the children have summer vacation, they are at home these days. — *क्योकि* बच्चों की गर्मी की छुट्टियाँ हैं, वे आजकल घर पर हैं।

'say(s)+ so' to avoid repetition of the words already used

A: "India will win". — भारत जीतेगा।

B: "Everybody **says so**" — सभी ऐसा कहते (कह रहे) हैं।

A: "You will certainly get the job". — आपको अवश्य नौकरी मिलेगी।

B: "Who **says so**"? — किसने ऐसा कहा?

subject + told + you + so — चेतावनी के अर्थ में
= subject warned you about the consequences

1. "Mother, I am suffering from fever". — माँ मुझे बुख़ार है।

- "**I told you so;** you shouldn't have gone out without your raincoat on". — मैंने तो तुम्हें पहले ही कहा था; तुम्हें बिना बरसाती पहने बाहर नहीं जाना चाहिए था।

so + adj. + as / as + adj. + as — उतना.....जितना....(नकारात्मक अर्थ में)
as + adj. + as, — उतना.............जितना (सकारात्मक अर्थ में)

☞ **In comparison of positive equality we use 'as + adj. + as' structure.**

☞ **In comparison of negative equality , we can use both 'not as + adj. + as', 'not + so + adj. + as' constructions.**

1a. He works **as hard as** his brother.	वह उतना ही परिश्रम करता है जितना उसका भाई।
1b. He doesn't work **so / as** hard as his brother.	वह उतना परिश्रम नहीं करता जितना उसका भाई।
2a. She is **as intelligent as** her mother.	वह उतनी ही बुद्धिमान है जितनी उसकी माँ।
2b. She is not **so/ as intelligent** as her mother.	वह उतनी बुद्धिमान नहीं है जितनी उसकी माँ।

Use of 'so' in some negative as well as positive expressions with verbs such as hope, think , believe, suppose, expect etc.

1. Is she doing well at school?	क्या वह स्कूल में ठीक चल रही है?
• **It doesn't seem so.**	***ऐसा लगता तो नहीं।***
2. It won't cost much, will it?	इसमें बहुत लागत तो नहीं आएगी न?
• **I don't suppose so.**	***मुझे लगता तो नहीं।***
3. It didn't rain here, did it?	यहाँ बारिश तो नहीं हुई, हुई क्या?
• **I don't think so.**	***मेरा खयाल है नहीं हुई।***
4. Can I get a work permit in your country easily?	क्या मुझे तुम्हारे देश में काम करने का अनुज्ञापत्र आसानी से मिल जाएगा?
• **I expect so.**	***उम्मीद तो करता हूँ।***
5. Will you have to pay a lot of customs duty on this camera?	क्या तुम्हें इस 'कैमरे' पर बहुत सीमाशुल्क देना होगा?
• **I am afraid so.**	***मुझे खेद है, मगर हाँ देना तो होगा।***
6. Do you think we will have	क्या आपको लगता है इस साल

the monsoons in time this year?	मानसून समय पर होंगे?
• **I should think so.**	***लगता तो है।***
• **I hope so.**	***उम्मीद तो है।***
7. Is that the Prime Minister over there?	क्या वहाँ वे प्रधान मंत्री हैं?
• **I think so.**	***लगता तो है।***
8. He looks very pale. Has he been ill?	उसका चेहरा उतरा हुआ लग रहा है। क्या वह बीमार था?
• **I guess so.**	***मुझे भी लगता तो है।***

so + verb + subject" = X को भी / X भी।

1. I like indian philosophy.	मुझे भारतीय दर्शन पसन्द है।
• **So do I.**	***मुझे भी।***
2. The boys misbehaved in class.	लड़कों ने कक्षा में बद्तमीज़ी की।
• **So did the girls.**	***लड़कियों ने भी।***
3. I will have some tea.	मैं कुछ चाय लूँगी।।
• **So will I.**	***मैं भी।***
4. I am going to the dentist.	मैं दाँत के डॉक्टर के पास जा रही हूँ।
• **So am I.**	***मैं भी।***

so + subj. + verb' to express surprised agreement:

1. It is snowing.	बर्फ़ पड़ रही है।
• **So it is!**	***पड़ तो रही है।***
2. They left their house keys here.	वे अपने घर की चाबियाँ यहाँ भूल गए।

- Really! **So we did** once and it caused us much inconvenience

  सच! एक बार हम ने भी ऐसा ही किया था, और इससे हमें बहुत परेशानी हुई थी।

Ex. 1: Fill in the blanks with one of the expressions given below:

so as to	so	since

1. I am learning Sanskrit .... be able to read our scriptures.
2. We are building a high wall round the house .... stop burglars from breaking in.
3. She likes classical music, ... she must go to this music concert.
4. .... she likes classical music, she must go to this music concert.
5. India is a large country, ... it has many problems.
6. .... India is a large country, it has many problems.

Ex. 2: Translate into english:

1. वह हमेशा अपनी 'गन' साथ रखता है ***ताकि*** ख़राब लोगों को डरा सके।
2. वह आज दफ़्तर से जल्दी निकली ***ताकि*** रास्ते में कुछ ख़रीदारी कर सके।
3. आप कभी भारत में रहे नहीं, इसलिए आप भारतीयों को नहीं समझ सकते।
4. क्योकि आप कभी भारत में रहे नहीं, आप भारतीयों को नहीं समझ सकते।
5. वह कभी स्कूल नहीं गई, इसलिए उसे पढ़ना-लिखना नहीं आता।
6. क्योकि वह कभी स्कूल नहीं गई, उसे पढ़ना-लिखना नहीं आता।
7. मैं कभी विदेश नहीं गया, इसलिए मैं विदेशी रिवाज और संस्कृति नहीं जानता।
8. क्योंकि मैं कभी विदेश नहीं गया, मैं विदेशी रिवाज और संस्कृति नहीं जानता।
9. उनके बच्चे नहीं हैं, इसलिए वे उन्हें पालने से जुड़ी समस्याओं को नहीं समझते।
10. क्योकि उनके बच्चे नहीं हैं, वे उनके पालने से जुड़ी समस्याओं को नहीं समझते।

Ex.3: Translate into English:

1. सड़क पर इतना ज़्यादा यातायात था ! मुझे घर पहुँचने में इतना समय कभी नहीं लगता जितना आज लगा।
2. तुमने इतने छोटे कमरे में इतना सामान क्यों जमा कर रखा है?
3. तुम्हारे पास इतना 'फ़र्नीचर' और इतनी किताबें क्यों हैं?
4. यह पोशाक उतनी महँगी नहीं है जितनी वह वाली।
5. दिल्ली कभी बनारस के जितनी गर्म नहीं होती।
6. भूदृश्य इतना सुन्दर था; मैं उस पर से अपनी दृष्टि हटा ही नहीं पाया।
7. कमरा इतना छोटा और गन्दा था कि हम वहाँ रह नहीं सके।
8. प्रकाश इतना कम था कि हमें कुछ भी दिखाई नहीं दिया।
9. वाराणसी में इतनी गर्मी थी कि मैं बिलकुल बाहर नहीं जा सका/सकी।
10. यह किताब इतनी रोचक है कि मैं एक क्षण भी इसे पढ़ना नहीं छोड़ सकती।
11. भारत में हमारा समय इतना अच्छा बीता कि हम वहाँ हमेशा के लिए रहना चाहते थे।
12. वह स्पेनी भाषा इतनी धाराप्रवाह बोलती है जैसे वह जन्म से स्पेनी हो।
13. मुझे अपने गाँव गए बहुत समय हो गया है।
14. क्या तुम हमेशा इतनी जल्दी सोकर उठते हो।

Key 1

1,2	**so as to**	**3,5**	**so**
4,6	**since**		

Key 2

1. He always carries his gun with him **so as to** be able to frighten bad people.
2. She left the office early today **so as to** be able to shop on the way.
3. You have never lived in India, **so** you cannot understand Indians.
4. **Since** you have never lived in India, you cannot understand

Indians.

5. She never went to school, **so** she does not know how to read and write.
6. **Since** she never went to school, she does not know how to read and write.
7. I have never been abroad, **so** I don't know foreign customs and cultures.
8. **Since** I have never been abroad, I don't know foreign customs and cultures.
9. They don't have children, **so** they don't understand the problems connected with binging them up.
10. **Since** they don't have children, they don't understand the problems connected with binging them up.

Key 3

1. There was **so much traffic** on the road! It never takes me so long to reach home as it did today.
2. Why have you accumulated **so many things** in such a small room?
3. Why have you got **so much furniture** and **so many** books?
4. This dress isn't **so / as expensive as** that one.
5. Delhi never gets **so / as hot as** Varanasi.
6. The landscape was **so beautiful**; I couldn't take my eyes off it.
7. The room was **so small and dirty** that we could not live there.
8. The light was **so dim** that we could not see anything.
9. It was **so hot** in Varanasi that I could not go out at all.
10. This book is **so interesting** that I can't stop reading it even for a minute.
11. We had **such a** good time in India that we wanted to stay there for good.
12. She speaks Spanish **so fluently** as if she were Spanish by birth.
13. It has been **such a long time** since I went to my village.
14. Do you always get up **so early**?

have have got

■ **Use 'has'/ 'have' ; 'has got'/ 'have got' with:**

1. **ailments** (*बीमारियाँ*) such as a backache, sore throat, fever, a cold, a toothache, the flu etc.
2. **things** (*वस्तुएँ*) जैसे television set, laptop, furniture,
3. **relatives** (*सगे-संबंधी*) जैसे brothers, sisters, uncle etc,
4. **body limbs** (*शरीर के अंग*) जैसे eyes, legs, hair etc

subject	**+**	**has / have**	**+**	**ailment**
		or		**things, relatives,**
		has got / have got		**body limbs, etc**

- You have / have got a cold. — तुम्हें जुकाम है।
- I have / have got a headache . — मुझे सिर दर्द है।
- I have / have got many friends. — मेरे बहुत दोस्त हैं।
- We have / have got two houses. — हमारे दो मकान हैं।
- I have / have got two daughters. — मेरी दो बेटियाँ हैं।
- She has / has got jet black hair. — उसके बाल काले स्याह हैं।
- **Has she got** many friends. — क्या उसके बहुत दोस्त हैं?

= **Does she have** many friends.

- **I haven't got** many friends. — मेरे बहुत दोस्त नहीं हैं?

= **I don't have** many friends.

- I had a sever headache yesterday . — मुझे कल बहुत ज़्यादा सिर दर्द था।

☞ present tense में उपरोक्त प्रयोग में **has / have , has got / have got** दोनों सही और समानार्थी हैं।

☞ past tense में उपरोक्त प्रयोग में **had** के साथ **got** *का प्रयोग नहीं होता।*)

I had many friends. (सही)	I had got many friends. (ग़लत)
I had not got many friends (ग़लत)	I didn't have many friends. (सही)

■ **Use only has / have with actions** जैसे **shower, bath, lunch, dinner, meal etc.** (*यहाँ* **got** *का प्रयोग संभव नहीं।*)

subject	+	has / have	+	a shower, a bath a meal, breakfast, lunch, dinner

- I have a shower/ a bath every morning. — मैं रोज़ सुबह स्नान करता हूँ।
- I have breakfast at 9 a.m. — मैं सुबह नौ बजे नाश्ता करता हूँ।
- They used to have a party every month. — वे हर महीने दावत किया करते थे।
- We had dinner in a restaurant. — हमने रेस्टोरेंट में भोजन किया।
- Let's have a cup of tea. — चलिए , एक प्याला चाय पी जाए।

■ **Some other everyday uses of 'have' :**

- Have a safe journey! — आपकी यात्रा मंगलमय हो।
- Have a good weekend! — आपका सप्ताहान्त मंगलमय हो।
- We had a lot of fun. — हमने बहुत मौज की।
- We had a really enjoyable vacation. — हमारी छुट्टी बहुत आनन्दमय थी।
- She doesn't have a job at present. — इस समय उसके पास काम नहीं है।
- We had a lovely boat ride last weekend. — हमने पिछले सप्ताहान्त पर बहुत ही मनोहर नौका विहार किया।
- I don't have time for all this. — मेरें पास इस सब के लिए समय नहीं ।

- She had a baby last night	कल रातको उसको बच्चा हुआ।

Ex. 1: Which is correct?

1. I **don't have / haven't got** a car.
2. We **didn't have / had not got** our raincoats.
3. I **didn't have / had not got** any cheese in my house.
4. She **doesn't have / hasn't got** any furniture.
5. He **didn't have / had not got** an Ipod.
6. They **don't have / haven't got** a laptop.

Ex. 2: Translate into English:

1. हमारी हवाई यात्रा बहुत अच्छी थी।
2. वे नाश्ता कर रहे हैं।
2. हम चाय पी रही हैं।
4. वे मौज कर रहे हैं।
5. मैं संतरे का रस पी रहा हूँ।
6. उसके पास लाल 'कार' है।
7. क्या तुम्हारे सिर में दर्द है?
8. लगता है उसके दाँत में दर्द है।
9. मेरे पास न छाता है न बरसाती।
10. उनके पास पर्याप्त पैसा नहीं है।
11. अगले महीने उनके यहाँ पोती या पोता होगा।
12. क्या उनके पास बहुत पैसा है?

Key 1

1. don't have / haven't got
2. didn't have
3. didn't have
4. doesn't have / hasn't got
5. didn't have
6. don't have / haven't got

Key 2

1. We had a very good flight. 2. They are having breakfast. 3. We are having tea. 4. They are having fun. 5. I am having orange juice. 6. He has a red car. 7. Do you have a headache? 8. It seems he has a toothache. 9. I have neither an umbrella nor a raincoat. 10. They don't have enough money. 11. Next month they will have a grandchild . 12. Have they got a lot of money?

Yet	still अभी भी/ अभी-तक
just *अभी-अभी*	already *पहले से ही*

Yet (यैट) अभी तक (= बात पूछने या बताने के समय तक) जब किसी काम के होने की अपेक्षा होती है तो:

- यह पूछते समय कि अमुक कार्य अभी तक (= प्रश्न पूछने के समय तक) हुआ है या नहीं, **yet** का प्रयोग करते हैं।
- यह बताते समय कि अमुक कार्य अभी तक (= प्रश्न पूछने के समय तक) नहीं हुआ हैं, **yet** का प्रयोग करते हैं।

☞ ध्यान दें- **'yet'** का प्रयोग **negative** (नकारात्मक) और **interrogative** (प्रश्न वाचक) वाक्यों में होता है। इस अर्थ में **'yet'** को वाक्य के अन्त में रखते हैं।

☞ ध्यान दें- प्राय: ब्रिटिश अंग्रेज़ी में यह प्रयोग **present perfect tense** और अमरीकन अंग्रेज़ी में **past simple** में होता है। उदाहरणों से समझें।

1. I haven't told my parents my exam result **yet.**	मैंने अभी तक अपने माता-पिता को अपना परीक्षाफल नहीं बताया।
• I didn't tell my parents my exam result yet.	
2. Has it stopped raining **yet?** (= प्रश्न पूछने के समय तक)	क्या बारिश बन्द हो गई है।
• Did it stop raining **yet?**	
3. Have you seen the film 'Khalnayak' ***yet?**	क्या तुमने 'खलनायक' फ़िल्म देखी है?
• Did you see the film 'Khalnayak' **yet?**	
4. Have you met your fiancé **yet?**	क्या तुम (अब तक)अपने मंगेतर से मिली हो?

5. Has the mail come **yet?** — क्या डाक (अब तक) आ गई है?
6. It hasn't come yet. — अभी तक नहीं आई।
7. He hasn't finished **yet**. — उसका काम अभी तक ख़त्म नहीं हुआ।
8. The concert hasn't started yet. — गोष्ठी अभी शुरू नहीं हुई।

Uses of 'still' अब तक, तिस पर भी, तो भी

1 जब कोई काम कभी पहले शुरू होकर अभी तक भी चल रहा हो, तो **still** का प्रयोग कीजिए। इस का प्रयोग **affirmative, interrogative** और **negative** तीनों प्रकार के वाक्यों में होता है।

☞ वाक्यों में **still** को प्राय: **verb** के पास रखते हैं।

1. He is still unemployed. — वह अभी भी बेरोज़गार है।
2. She is still single. — वह अभी भी अविवाहित है।
3. They are still living in India. — वे अभी भी भारत में रह रहे हैं।
4. They are still upstairs. — वे अभी भी ऊपर हैं।
5. We still go for a morning walk every day. — हम अभी भी प्रतिदिन सुबह सैर करने जाते हैं।
6. The clock alarm is still ringing. — घड़ी का 'अलार्म' अभी भी बज रहा है।
7. I still think the opposition party was wrong. — मुझे अभी भी लगता है कि विपक्षी दल ग़लत था।
8. Will you still be here when I come back? — क्या मेरे लौटने तक अभी तुम यहीं होगे?

2 *प्राय:* ***negative*** *वाक्य में* ***still*** *(स्टिल) का प्रयोग तब करते हैं जब कोई काम प्रयास के बावजूद भी अमुक समय तक ख़त्म न हुआ हो, और वक्ता की अभिव्यक्ति से विस्मय या क्षोभ का बोध होता है।*

1. You **still** don't understand! — तुम्हें अभी भी समझ में नहीं आया!

'Khalnayak' = villain(of a film or story)

2. He **still** hasn't found a job.	उसे अभी भी नौकरी नहीं मिली।
3. It is **still** not clear to you!	तुम्हें अभी भी स्पष्ट नहीं हुआ!
4. She left a week ago and **still** hasn't written to us.	उसे गए हुए एक सप्ताह हो गया है, लेकिन उसने अभी तक हमें पत्र नहीं लिखा।

☞ *यहाँ* **still** *के प्रयोग से एक प्रकार की कटुता, क्षोभ या अधीरता का आभास होता है। जैसे कि ' उसे पत्र लिखना चाहिए था परन्तु लिखा नहीं।'*

☞ *यदि वाक्य रचना कुछ इस प्रकार होती* **'She hasn't written to us yet.'**
तो भाव कुछ इस प्रकार होता : ('उसने अभी तक पत्र नहीं लिखा, लेकिन लिख सकती है।)'

3 **'still'** *'और ज़्यादा', 'और भी', 'फिर भी' के अर्थ में।'*

1. This would be **better still** or This would still be better.	यह तो ***और भी*** अच्छा होगा।
2. That would be **cheaper still.** or This would still be cheaper.	यह तो और भी सस्ता पड़ेगा।

Use of 'not anymore', 'no more', 'no longer':

☞जब कोई काम आप पहले करते थे परन्तु अब नहीं करते या नहीं करना चाहते, तो **' not anymore', 'no more', 'no longer',** का प्रयोग कीजिए।

1a. She used to eat meat and eggs.	वह मांस और अण्डे खाया करती थी।

1b. She **still** eats eggs but does not eat meat **anymore.**	वह अभी भी अण्डे तो खाती है परन्तु अब मांस नहीं खाती।
2a. He was a doctor practising surgery.	वह डाक्टर था और शल्य चिकित्सा किया करता था।
2b. He is **still** a doctor but does **not** practise surgery **anymore.**	वह अभी भी डाक्टर है लेकिन अब शल्य चिकित्सा नहीं करता।
3. He **no longer** works in a bank.	वह अब 'बैंक' में काम नहीं करता।
4. She **no longer** teaches.	वह अब नहीं पढ़ाती।

Already — पहले से ही , अपेक्षा से पहले किसी काम का पूरा हो चुका होना।

1. The train has **already** arrived.	गाड़ी आ चुकी है।
2. She has **already** gone to bed.	वह सो गई है।

Just — अभी-अभी

1. She has **just** arrived.	वह अभी-अभी पहुँची है।
2. We have **just** had lunch.	हमने अभी-अभी खाना खाया है।
3. They have **just** gone out.	वे अभी-अभी बाहर गए हैं।
4. She **just** called.	उसने अभी-अभी 'फ़ोन' किया।
5. I **just** met them.	मैं अभी-अभी उनसे मिला।
6. They have **just** been to the temple.	वे अभी-अभी मंदिर होकर आए हैं।
7. I am **just** going to make coffee for all of us.	मैं सब के लिए कॉफ़ी बनाने ही वाला हूँ।

Just as ठीक उसी समय

1. I shut my eyes **just as** he took the photograph.
मेरी आँख ठीक उसी समय बन्द हो गई जब उसने तस्वीर खींची।

2. **Just as** we got on the boat, it began to rain.
ठीक उसी समय जब हम नाव में बैठे, बारिश होने लगी।

3. I got a phone call **just as** the story came to the climax.
जब कहानी अपनी चरमावस्था पर पहुँची, ठीक उसी समय मुझे किसी का 'फ़ोन' आ गया।

4. **Just as** I was going to lie down, someone knocked at the door.
ठीक उसी समय जब मैं लेटने जा रहा था, किसीने द्वार पर खटखटाया।

Ex.1: Fill in the blanks with 'yet', 'still'.

1. The doctor hasn't come..............
2. I haven't decided........... what course to study.
3. The children haven't returned from the playground.......
4. The film hasn't finished.............
5. I haven't taken the exam.........
6. Are you........ in Delhi?
7. Does she..... want to go abroad?
8. Is India....... an underdeveloped country?
9. The bridge is........ under construction.
10. My refrigerator...... makes a lot of noise.
11. Hasn't she finished writing the book....?
12. Not...... she is....... working on it.
13. Father hasn't finished with the newspaper .... He is ....reading it.
14. Are they.............. living in their old house? Haven't they moved to their new house ....?
15. The train is .... waiting for the signal. It hasn't left the platform.........
16. Their dog suddenly disappeared last week. They haven't found it ....They are .... looking for it.

Ex. 2: Translate into English: Use 'still', 'yet'.

1. वह अभी तक नहीं समझा। (= वह बाद में समझ सकता है।)
2. मैं अंग्रेज़ीं सीख रहा हूँ परन्तु अभी धाराप्रवाह बोल नहीं सकता।
3. 'गैस' बन्द मत करो; 'सूप अभी तैयार नहीं हुआ।
4. क्या कपड़े अभी तक नहीं सूखे?
5. वे अभी तक सोए नहीं हैं।
6. वह अभी भी छात्रा है।
7. माँ अभी भी पूजा कक्ष में है।
8. क्या वह अभी भी वायुसेना में भर्ती होना चाहता है?
9. क्या वह अभी भी जीवन बीमा निगम में काम करता है?
10. पिता जी अभी भी सोए हुए हैं।
11. वह अभी कविता याद कर रही है। उसे अभी याद नहीं हुई।
12. उन्होंने नाश्ता समाप्त नहीं किया। वे अभी भी मेज़ पर बैठे हैं।
13. हम कई वर्ष भारत में रहे। वहाँ अभी भी हमारे बहुत मित्र हैं।
14. कुछ महीने पहले उसकी नौकरी चली गई थी। उसे नया काम मिल गया है या वह अभी भी बेरोज़गार है?
15. मुझे जल्दी काम पर लौटना है। क्या अभी भोजन तैयार नहीं हुआ?
16. जब मैं पिछली बार उससे मिला था, वह किसी डाकघर में काम कर रही थी। क्या उसने काम बदल लिया है या अभी भी डाकघर में ही काम कर रही है।
17. अनु धनी है परन्तु नीला और ज़्यादा धनी है।
18. तुम बहुत जवान तो नहीं हो; लेकिन तुम अभी-भी बहुत कुछ कर सकते हो।

Ex. 3: Translate into English: use 'still', 'no more', 'not any more':

1a. वह क्रिकेट खेलता था और 'टीम' का सर्वश्रेष्ठ बल्लेबाज़ हुआ करता था।

1b वह अभी भी क्रिकेट खेलता है लेकिन अब वह 'टीम' का सर्वश्रेष्ठ बल्लेबाज़ नहीं है।

2a. मैं संस्कृत और 'जर्मन' भाषा पढ़ाया करता था।

2b. मैं अभी भी 'जर्मन' पढ़ाता हूँ, लेकिन अब मैं संस्कृत नहीं पढ़ाता।

3a. आज सुबह उसे थकान और बुख़ार लग रहा था।
3b. उसे अभी भी थकान लग रही है, लेकिन अब उसे बुख़ार नहीं लग रहा।
4a. उसका स्वास्थ्य अच्छा और रंग गोरा हुआ करता था।
4b. उसका रंग अभी भी गोरा है, लेकिन अब उसका स्वास्थ्य अच्छा नहीं है।
5. वह अब 'बैंक' में काम नहीं करता।
6. यह कमीज़ मुझे अब पूरी नहीं आती।
7. जब मैं अन्दर आया, मुझे बहुत प्यास लगी हुई थी। ***अब*** मुझे प्यास ***नहीं*** है।
8. ***अब*** उसे हिन्दी-फ़िल्में देखने में रुचि ***नहीं*** रही।
9. वह ***अब*** उतना सफ़र ***नहीं*** करता जितना पहले करता था।

Ex. 4: Translate into English: use 'already'

1. मैं अपने बेटे को स्कूल से ला चुका हूँ।
2. मैंने हम सब के लिए पहले से ही पैसा दे दिया है।
3. पिता जी दफ़्तर से लौट चुके हैं और दूरदर्शन देख रहे हैं।
4. पियूष को नया काम मिल गया है।
5. मेरी पत्नी ने रात का खाना पकाना शुरू कर दिया है।
6. मैं खाना खा चुका हूँ।
7. क्या आप लोग पहले मिल चुके हैं?
8. उसकी शादी हो चुकी है।
9. मैं पहले से इस संगठन का सदस्य / की सदस्या हूँ।

Key . 1

1, 2, 3, 4, 5, 11	yet
6, 7, 8, 9, 10	still
12, 13. 16	yet, still
14, 15	still, yet

Key . 2

1. He hasn't understood **yet.**
2. I am learning English but I can't speak fluently **yet**.
3. Don't turn the gas off; the soup is not ready yet.
4. Aren't the clothes dry **yet**?

5. They haven't gone to bed **yet.**
6. She is **still** a student.
7. Mother is **still** in the prayer room.
8. Does he **still** want to join the air force?
9. Does he **still** work for the Life Insurance Corporation?
10. Father is **still** asleep.
11. She is **still** memorizing the poem. She hasn't memorized it yet.
12. They haven't finished with the breakfast yet. They are **still** at the table.
13. We lived in India for many years. We **still** have many friends there.
14. She lost her job a few month ago. Has she found a new job yet or is she **still** unemployed?
15. I have to get back to work soon. Isn't the lunch ready **yet**?
16. When I met her last time, she was working in some post office. Has she already changed jobs or is she **still** working for the post office.
17. Anu is rich but Neela is **richer still**.
18. You are not very young; but you can **still** do a lot.

Key 3

1a. He used to play cricket and was the best batsman of the team.
1b. He still plays cricket but he is not the best batsman **anymore.**
2a. I used to teach Sanskrit and German.
2b. I still teach German but I don't teach Sanskrit **anymore.**
3a. This morning she was feeling exhausted and feverish.
3b. She is **still** feeling exhausted but she is **not feeling feverish anymore.**
4a. He used to have good health and a fair complexion.
4b. He **still** has a fair complexion but does **not** have good health **anymore**.
5. He **no longer** works in a bank.
6. This shirt doesn't fit me **anymore.**
7. I was very thirsty when I came in. I am **no more** thirsty.
8. He is not interested in Hindi movies **anymore.**
9. He **no longer** travels as much as he used to.

Key 4

1. I have **already** brought my son from school.
2. I have **already** paid for all of us.
3. Father has **already** come back from the office and is watching television.
4. Piush **already** found a new job.
5. My wife has **already** begun to cook dinner.
6. I have **already** eaten.
7. Have you guys met **already**?
8. She is **already** married.
9. I am **already** a member of this association.

been	**gone**
कहीं जाकर लौट आने पर	*कहीं गया होना*

☞ जब कोई व्यक्ति कहीं जाकर वापस लौट चुका हो, या अमुक स्थान उसका देखा हुआ हो, तो **'been'** का प्रयोग करते हैं । परन्तु जब कोई व्यक्ति कहीं गया है और अभी लौटा न हो, तो **'gone'**का प्रयोग करते हैं।

1. Kamla has gone to Mumbai. — कमला मुम्बई गई हुई है।(अर्थात इस समय कमला मुम्बई में है)
2. Kamla has been to Mumbai — कमला मुम्बई गई हुई है।(अर्थात मुम्बई कमला का देखा हुआ है)
3. Mother has gone to the bank. — माँ बैंक गई हुई है।(अर्थात इस समय माँ बैंक में है)

4. Mother has been to the bank. — माँ बैंक हो आई है।(अर्थात इस समय माँ बैंक जाकर लौट चुकी है)

A. Have you ever been to India? — क्या आप कभी भारत गए/गई हैं?

B. I have never been to India. — मैं भारत कभी नहीं गया/गई।

Ex. : Complete the sentences with 'been' or 'gone'.

1. Mr Kapoor is on vacation. He has ....to Mauritius.
2. She has just ......to the bank. She has deposited the checks.
3. Anil is not at his table at the moment. He has .... to the canteen to have lunch.
4. Are you going to the post office? No, I have already............ to the post office.
5. She has ....to a lot of places.
6. I have . ...to America several tmes.
7. Have your children ever .... to the Appu Ghar?
8. I am afraid, they have never .... to the Appu Ghar.

Key

1, 3 gone — 2, 4, 5, 6, 7, 8 been

as soon as

1. As soon as I get up, I drink a cup of tea. — मैं सुबह उठते ही एक प्याला चाय पीता/पीती हूँ।
2. As soon as the teacher left the classroom, the boys — अध्यापक के कक्षा से निकलते ही लड़के शोर मचाने लगे।

began to make a noise.

3. As soon as the sun rises, the birds begin to chirp.	सूर्य निकलते ही चिड़ियाँ चहकने लगती हैं।
4. As soon as the newspaper man comes, our dog begins to bark.	अख़बारवाले के आते ही हमारा कुत्ता भौंकने लगता है।

Ex. 1: Translate into English:

1. कमला बिस्तर पर लेटते ही सो जाती है।
2. वर्षा ऋतु शुरू होते ही वह बीमार हो जाता है।
3. मेरी आँख लगते ही टेलीफोन की घण्टी बजने लगी।
4. माँ के अन्दर आते ही बच्चा खुश हो जाएगा।
5. अपना काम ख़त्म करते ही मैं आपके पास आ जाऊँगा।
6. आप जैसे ही निर्णय ले लें, हमें बता दीजिएगा।
7. अमरीका पहुँचते ही मैं आपसे सम्पर्क करूँगा।
8. अवकाश से लौटते ही मैं आपको बताऊँगा।

Key 1

1. Kamla falls asleep as soon as she lies on bed.
2. He falls sick as soon as the rainy season begins.
3. As soon as I fell asleep, the telephone started ringing.
4. The child will become happy as soon as the mother comes in.
5. I will come to you as soon as I finish my work.
6. Let's know as soon as you have decided.
7. I will contact you as soon as I arrive in the US
8. As soon as I get back from vacation, I shall let you know.

about to do X..............X *करनेवाला होना*

1. I am about to sleep. — मैं सोनेवाला हूँ।
2. They were about to go. — वे जानेवाले थे।
3. Guests were about to arrive. — महमान पहुँचने वाले थे।
4. I was about to go to the bank when my friends arrived. — जब मेरे मित्र पहुँचे, मैं बैंक जाने ही वाला था ।

both	**either**	**neither**
दोनों	दोनों में से कोई भी	दोनों में से कोई भी नहीं

☞ **both , either , neither** *का प्रयोग किन्हीं दो व्यक्तियों, वस्तुओं की बात करते समय होता है।*

1. I visited two Hindu temples this morning. **Both** looked alike to me. — मैं आज सुबह दो हिन्दु मंदिरों में गया / गई। मुझे दोनों एक-से लगे।
2. First I learnt Korean, and later Japanese. **Neither** language was easy to learn. — मैंने पहले कोरिया की और फिर जापान की भाषा सीखी। दोनो में से कोई भी सीखना आसान नहीं था।
3. There are two routes from here to the Airport. You could go by **either.** — यहाँ से हवाई अड्डे जाने के दो रास्ते हैं। तुम दोनों में से किसीसे भी जा सकते हो।
4. Do you like the green one or — आपको हरावाला पसन्द है या

the blue one?	नीलावाला?
• I like **both.**	मुझे दोनों पसन्द हैं।
• **Either** would do.	कोई-सा भी चलेगा।
• I don't like **either.**	मुझे दोनों में से कोई भी पसन्द नहीं हैं।
• **Neither.**	दोनों में से कोई भी नहीं।

'Neither .... nor........' 'न...........न...........'

1. **Neither** Rama **nor** Sheila is present today.	आज न रमा उपस्थित है न शीला।
2. I can eat **neither** fried food **nor** sweets.	मैं न तला हुआ भोजन खा सकता / सकती हूँ न मिठाइयाँ।

☞ ध्यान दें : — ऊपर दिए गए वाक्यों में singular subject है। प्राय: **neither ....nor** से बने वाक्यों में **singular subject** के साथ **singular verb** होता है; परन्तु अनौपचारिक बोलचाल में **plural verb** लगाया जाता है।

'either... ....or...........' 'या...........या...........'

1. You can either study **or** enjoy yourself.	तुम या तो पढ़ सकते हो या मौज कर सकते हो।
2. One can either eat the cake **or** save it.	व्यक्ति या तो 'केक' खा सकता है, या बचा सकता है।

neither + singular noun + singular verb
'either + singular countable noun'

1. **Neither parent** gave time	माँ और बाप दोनों में से किसीने

	to the children.	भी बच्चों को समय नहीं दिया।
2.	**Neither doctor** was ready to do the operation.	दोनों में से कोई भी डॉक्टर ऑपरेशन करने को तैयार नहीं था।
3a.	Shall I meet you on Saturday or Sunday?	मैं आपको शनिवार को मिलूँ या रविवार को?
3b.	**Either day** is okay for me.	कोई-सा भी दिन मेरे लिए ठीक है।

neither **either** **both**	**+**	**of**	**+**	**determiner** **possessive,** **demonstrative,** **article**	**+**	**plural noun**	**+**	**verb** **(should be sg.)** **but can be** **plural in informal spoken** **English)**

☞ **both** *के साथ* ***'of'*** *का प्रयोग अनिवार्य नहीं।*

- I like **both of these** houses. = I like **both these** houses.
- **Both of** her daughters / **Both her daughters** live in the US.

☞ **either/neither** *के साथ* ***'of'*** *का प्रयोग अनिवार्य है।* उसके बिना वाक्य ग़लत होगा। उदाहरण के लिए आगे दिए गए वाक्य देखें।

☞ **either of / neither of + plural noun/pronoun** के साथ **singular verb** लगता है।

• **Neither of** my brothers is married yet.	मेरे दोनों भाइयों में से अभी किसीकी भी शादी नहीं हुई।
• **Neither of** his parents was present at his wedding.	उसके माता-पिता दोनों में से कोई भी उसकी शादी में उपस्थित नहीं था।
• **Either of** the students can do it.	इन (दोनों) में से कोई भी विद्यार्थी इसे कर सकता है।

- **Either of** these women is qualified to do this job. — इन (दोनों) में से कोई भी औरत इसे करने की योग्यता रखती है।

☞ **negative** वाक्य में बोलचाल की भाषा में **plural verb** भी लगाया जा सकता है। उदाहरण :—

- I don't think either of us **are / is going** to the movies tonight.
(is, are दोनों का ही प्रयोग यहाँ ठीक है।)

'neither' as pronoun	कोई भी नहीं
'either' as pronoun	कुछ भी, कोई-सा भी

A: Which one would you like to buy? — तुम कौन-सा वाला ख़रीदना चाहोगे।

B: **neither** — कोई भी नहीं।

A. Would you like to have tea or coffee? — आप चाय लेंगे या काफ़ी?

B. **Either.** — कुछ भी।

A. Shall I give you this one or that one? — मैं आपको यह वाला दूँ या वह वाला?

B. **Either.** I like both. — कोई-सा भी। मुझे दोनों पसन्द हैं।

- **Neither.** I don't like any. — दोनों ही नहीं। मुझे कोई-सा भी पसन्द नहीं।

both / either / neither + of + the pronouns 'you', 'them', 'us.'

- **Both of them** were strangers to me. — वे दोनों मेरे लिए अजनबी थे।
- **Neither of these** buildings is new. — इन दोनों इमारतों में से कोई भी नई नहीं हैं।

- Can **either of them** speak Hindi? — क्या उन दोनों में से कोई भी हिन्दी बोल सकता है?

neither / nor + verb + subject = भी नहीं

☞ इस रचना का प्रयोग छोटे उत्तर देने में होता है । यहाँ neither और nor दोनों समानार्थी हैं।

1a.	I can't cook.	मैं खाना नहीं पका सकती।
1b.	**Neither / Nor** can I.	मैं भी नहीं।
2 a.	My parents did not like the music concert yesterday.	मेरे माता-पिता को कल संगीत गोष्ठी अच्छी नहीं लगी।
2b.	**Neither / Nor** did my parents.	मेरे माता-पिता को भी नहीं।

Use of 'subject + not + either' in negative short answers:

1a.	I don't like horror films.	मुझे डरावनी फ़िल्में पसन्द नहीं।
1b.	I don't **either.**	मुझे भी नहीं।
2a:	I haven't read Kalidas.	मैंने कालीदास नहीं पढ़ा।
2b.	I haven't **either.**	मैंने भी नहीं पढ़ा।

'either' to mean 'both' — दोनों

☞ इस अर्थ में प्राय: side (ओर) end (छोर) bank (किनारा) आदि शब्दों के साथ प्रयोग होता है।

1. There were people **on either side** of the river. — नदी के दोनों ओर लोग थे।
2. **On either side** of the college gate — कॉलिज के फाटक के दोनों ओर

students waited for the Principal. छात्र प्रधानाचार्य की प्रतीक्षा कर रहे थे।

Compare and comprehend:				
Neither / Nor	**+**	**verb**	**+**	**subject**
= Subject	**+**	**negative auxiliary verb**	**+**	**either**

1. **Neither / Nor** do I. मैं भी नहीं।
 = I don't either.
2. **Neither / Nor** could we. हम भी नहीं (कर सके।)
 = We couldn't either
3. **Neither / Nor** did my parents. मेरे माता-पिता भी नहीं।
 = My parents didn't either.

neither + noun ..... nor + noun	neither + verb..... nor+ noun

1a. I like **neither** tea **nor** . coffee

1b. I **neither** like tea **nor** coffee

2a. She trusts **neither** her friends **nor** her relatives.

2b. She **neither** trusts her friends **nor** her relatives.

☞ 1b. और 2b. ग़लत नहीं हैं। परन्तु 1a. और 2a. ज़्यादा अच्छे हैं।

Ex.1: Change as shown using 'neither.... nor':

> My brother didn't go to the bank, and I didn't either.
> => Neither my brother nor I went to the bank.

1. Ram was not wrong, and Savita was not either.

 ....

2. I didn't find the book in America, and I didn't find it in Europe either.

....

3. I can't speak Spanish, and I can't speak Swedish either.

....

4. She didn't sleep, and she didn't work either.

....

5. He did not go to hospital, and he didn't take any medicine either.

....

6. She is not studying, and she is not working either.

....

Ex. 2: Translate into English:

1. आजकल न छात्र काम में रुचि रखते हैं न अध्यापक।
2. न वह आया न उसने टेलीफोन किया।
3. मैं न रेडियो सुनता हूँ न दूरदर्शन देखता हूँ
4. न प्रशँसा न अपमान उसे परेशान करता है।

5a. मुझे बिलकुल फुरसत नहीं।
5b. मुझे भी नहीं।

6a. हम आज सुबह मंदिर नहीं जा सके।
6b. हम भी नहीं ।

7a. आप डबलरोटी लेंगे या चावल?
7b. कुछ भी। मुझे दोनो पसन्द हैं।

8a. इस समय कितने बजे हैं, चार या पाँच?
8b. दोनों ही नहीं। साढ़े चार बजे हैं।

9. उन दोनों में से किसीका भी चयन नहीं हुआ।

10. तुम में से कोई भी सिनेमा न जाए।
11. घर के दोनों ओर खजूर के पेड़ हैं।
12. इन दोनों हरे केलों में से कोई भी 'कटलेट' बनाने के काम आ सकता है।
13. आप मेरे दोनों बड़े कमरों में से कोई भी दावत के लिए प्रयोग कर सकते हैं।
14. उसका नाम या छवि है या सारा।
15. तुम इसे या आज कर देना या कल।

Ex. 3: Complete the sentences with either, neither, both.

1. What would you like, tea or coffee?
   .... I like ....
2. Do you go to school by rickshaw or by bus?
   .... I go by car.
3. Savita has two daughters and a son. I have met her son, but I have not met .... of her daughters.
4. Which dress would you like to wear, the red one or the green one?
   I don't like .... I prefer pastel.
5. Last week I visited Frankfurt and Berlin. I liked .... the cities very much.
6. The shopkeeper showed me two picture frames. I didn't like ....
7. It was an interesting cricket match. .... teams played well.
8. They invited my friend and me to their anniversary. .... of us could go.
9. My bedroom has two doors. It is very cold and I shut

.... of them at night.

10. My sister and I play the sitar, but .... of us is really good at it.

Ex. 4: Translate into English:

1. वे दोनों बहुत मेहनती हैं।
2. वे दोनों तैरना पसन्द करते हैं।
3. ये दोनों इमारतें बहुत पुरानी हैं।
4. आज राम और रानी दोनों बीमार हैं।
5. मैं इन दोनों में से किसी के भी अन्दर नहीं गया।
6. उन दोनों में से कोई भी नृत्य नहीं कर सकता।
7. उन दोनों को खेलों में रुचि है।
8. जीवन में सफलता के लिए धन और समय, दोनों की आवश्यकता होती है।
9. उन दोनों में से किसी को भी खाना बनाने में रुचि नहीं।
10. पिछले सप्ताह मेरे इलाक़े में दो अच्छी संगीत गोष्ठियाँ थीं, लेकिन मैं एक में भी नहीं जा पाया।

Key 1

1. Neither Ram nor Savita was wrong.
2. I found the book neither in America nor in Europe.
3. I can speak neither Spanish nor Swedish.
4. She neither slept nor worked.
5. He neither went to hospital nor took any medicine.
6. She is neither studying nor working.

Key 2

1. Neither the students nor the teachers are interested in work these days.
2. He neither came nor called.
3. I neither listen to the radio nor watch TV.
4. Neither praise nor humiliation bothers him.

5a. I don't have any free time.
5b. Neither / Nor do I.
6a. We couldn't go to the temple this morning.
6b. Neither/nor could we.
7a. Do you want bread or rice?
7b. Either. I like both.
8a. What time is it now? 4 or 5 O' clock?
8b. Neither. It is 4:30.
9. Neither of them was selected.
10. Neither of you may go to the movies.
11. There are palm trees on either side of the cottage.
12. Either of these green bananas can be used for making cutlets.
13. You may use either of my big rooms for the party.
14. Her name is either Chavi or Sara.
15. You may do this either today or tomorrow.

Key 3

1. Either, both	2. Neither	3. either
4. either	5. both	6. either
7. Both	8. Neither	9. both
10. neither		

. **Key 4**

1. Both of them are very hardworking.
2. Both of them like swimming.
3. Both of these buildings are very old.
4. Both Ram and Rani are sick today.
5. I have not been inside either of these.
6. Neither of them can dance.
7. Both of them are interested in sports.

8. One needs both time and money to be successful in life.
9. Neither of them is interested in cooking.
10. There were two good music concerts in my neighborhood last week, but I could not go to either.

rather	pretty	quite

■ **rather** का एक प्रयोग **preference structure** में देखें। **(pg.171)**

■ **'rather'** का एक और प्रयोग **adjective / adverb / noun** के साथ **adverb of degree** के रूप में होता है, जिससे किसी गुण विशेष के बहुत ज़्यादा और बहुत कम के बीच के दरजे का (यानी **very** से कम और **a little /a few** से कुछ ज़्यादा) होने से होता है। उदाहरण :

- She drives rather fast. — वह कुछ तेज़ ही चलाती है।

☞ इस वाक्य से यह बोध होता है कि अमुक व्यक्ति वाहन कुछ तेज़ तो चलाता है, परन्तु बहुत ज़्यादा तेज़ नहीं।

☞ **rather** का प्रयोग सामान्यता कुछ नकारात्मक पुट लिए रहता है।

• This is **rather unshapely**.	यह कुछ बेढंगा ही है।
• I have had a **rather busy** day at work. I am exhausted.	आज काम पर मेरा दिन कुछ ज़्यादा ही व्यस्त था। मैं थक के चूर हो गया हूँ।
• I find my new job **rather boring.**	मुझे अपना नया काम काफ़ी उबाऊ लगता है।
• The novel was pretty good but **rather long**.	उपन्यास बहुत अच्छा था परन्तु कुछ ज़्यादा ही लम्बा ।

■ जब **rather** का प्रयोग सकारात्मक हो तो कुछ हैरानगी, असाधारण और अप्रायिक का बोध होता है।

rather + adjective

- This sweets-shop is rather good! Who told you about it? — यह मिठाई की दुकान काफ़ी अच्छी है! तुम्हें इसके बारे मे किसने बताया?
- This place was rather clean. — यह स्थान काफ़ी साफ़ था।

rather + noun

- Indians are rather peace loving people. — भारतीय काफ़ी शान्तिप्रिय लोग हैं।
- It is a rather amusing film. — यह काफ़ी मनोरंजक फ़िल्म है।

rather + adverb

- She did rather well in the examination. — उसने परीक्षा में काफ़ी अच्छा किया।

2. The annual function was rather well organized — वार्षिक समारोह काफ़ी सुव्यवस्थित था।

rather + verb

1. We **rather like** him. — हम उसे बहुत पसन्द करते हैं।
2. We **rather enjoy** watching films on television. — हमें दूरदर्शन पर फ़िल्में देखकर ज़्यादा आनन्द आता है।

rather...... comparatives

1. I am feeling **rather better** today. आज मैं पहले से काफ़ी अच्छा महसूस कर रहा हूँ ।
2. This house is **rather more** expensive than I had anticipated. यह घर जितना मैंने सोचा था, उससे कुछ ज़्यादा ही महँगा है।

■ **rather** से मिलते-जुलते अर्थ में **pretty, quite** का भी **adjective / adverb / noun** के साथ प्रयोग होता है।

☞ **pretty** और **quite** का प्रयोग समानार्थक और सकारात्मक है। **pretty** का प्रयोग अनौपचारिक बोलचाल में होता है।

ठीक इसी अर्थ मे **fairly** का प्रयोग भी होता है। परन्तु **fairly** में **adjective / adverb** की गुणवत्ता का दरजा **quite** की अपेक्षा कुछ कम होता है।

She drives quite fast.

= She drives pretty fast.

quite + adjective / adverb / verb

1. Give the children something to eat. They seem to be **quite hungry**. बच्चों को कुछ खाने को दो। वे बहुत भूखे लग रहे हैं।
2. Haven't you heard of him. He is **quite famous** here. तुमने उसके बारे में नहीं सुना। वह यहाँ काफ़ी मशहूर है।
3. Her new collection of short stories is **quite good.** I enjoyed reading it. उसका कहानियों का नया संग्रह बहुत अच्छा है। मुझे उसे पढ़कर बहुत आनन्द आया।

4a. Perhaps this food was too spicy for you. शायद यह भोजन आपके लिए बहुत ज़्यादा मसालेदार था।

4b. Not at all; **I quite like** spicy बिलकुल भी नहीं। बल्कि मैं तो

food.	मसालेदार भोजन काफ़ी पसन्द करता हूँ।
A I am sorry. We have run out of gas and we are having to cook on a kerosene stove today. The whole house smells of kerosene.	मुझे खेद है। आज हमारा गैस ख़त्म हो गया है। और हमें 'केरोसीन' पर खाना बनाना पड़ रहा है। घर-भर में 'केरोसीन' गमक रहा है।
B. No problem, **I quite like t**he smell of kerosene.	कोई समस्या नहीं। मुझे तो कैरासीन की महक काफ़ी पसन्द है।

quite + a + adj. + noun

1. She often sings at the temple meetings. She has **quite a melodious voice.**	वह अक्सर मंदिर की सभाओं में गाती है। उसकी आवाज़ बहुत मधुर है।
2. I am sorry to be late. There was **quite a lot of traffic.**	मुझे खेद है कि मुझे देर हो गई। बहुत ज़्यादा यातायात था।

Ex. 1: Translate into English: Use 'rather' where required:

1. रानी कुछ मूर्ख़ है।
2. वह कुछ अशान्त दिखी।
3. शहर में स्थिति काफ़ी तनावग्रस्त है।
4. उपन्यास कुछ ज़्यादा ही उबाऊ है।
5. आज कुछ ज़्यादा ही उमस है।
6. वह काफ़ी क्रूर है।
7. प्रधानाचार्य ने मेरे साथ कुछ ज़्यादा ही रूखा बोले।
8. भोजन कुछ ज़्यादा ही मसालेदार है।
9. वह वाहन कुछ ज़्यादा ही तेज. चलाती है।
10. उसने काफ़ी ज़्यादा मेहनत की।
11. उसने हमारी अपेक्षा से काफ़ी अच्छा किया।
12. यह काफ़ी मँहगी पोशाक है।

Ex. 2: Translate into English: Use 'quite.....' / quite a ......'as required.:

1. आज काम पर मेरा दिन बहुत दिलचस्प था।
2. पिछले महीने उन्होंने भारत में बहुत बढ़िया समय बिताया।
3. मुझे यहाँ आने के लिए बहुत लम्बा रास्ता पैदल चलना पड़ा।
4. वह काफ़ी शर्मीला व्यक्ति है।
5. सूप काफ़ी स्वादिष्ट है।
6. मुझे उनके रूखे व्यवहार से कुछ निराशा ही हुई।
7. रानी की आवाज़ बहुत मधुर है।
8. यह कुछ ज़्यादा ही परेशानीज़दा है।

Key 1

1. Rani is rather foolish. 2. She seemed rather restless. 3. The situation in the city is rather tense. 4. The novel is rather boring. 5. It is rather humid today. 6. He is rather cruel. 7. The Principal was rather rude to me. 8. The food is rather spicy. 9. She drives rather fast. 10. He worked pretty hard. 11. She did rather better than we expected from her. 12 This is a rather (rather an) expensive dress.

Key 2

1. I had **quite an interesting day** at work today.
2. They had **quite a nice time** in India last month.
3. I had to walk **quite a long distance** to come here.
4. He is **quite a shy** person.
5. The soup is quite delicious.
6. I was rather disappointed by their rude behaviour.
7. Rani has quite a melodious voice.
8. This is rather a nuisance.

•••

Each Every

■ **each, every** दोनों का प्रयोग countable noun, singular verb के साथ होता है।

each / each one = प्रत्येक, प्रति,, जब ध्यान दो या दो से अधिक इकाइयों के समूह में की हर अलग इकाई पर होता है।

every / every one = प्रत्येक, प्रति,, जब ध्यान तीन या तीन से अधिक इकाइयों के समूह में की सब इकाइयों पर होता है।

- There were four students in the class.Each / Every student was very keen to learn.

☞ जब समूह में दो ही इकाइयाँ हों तो हर हाल में सिर्फ़ each का प्रयोग होता है, every का नहीं।

- Each team performed well. √
- Every team performed well. X

■ **each** का प्रयोग **pronoun** की तरह सम्भव है, **every** का नहीं।

- Each was keen to learn. (correct) √
- Every was keen to learn. (incorrect) X

■ **each , every** दोनों के साथ one लगा सकते हैं।

every one (दो शब्द) = व्यक्ति और वस्तु दोनों के लिए।

everyone (एक शब्द) = सिर्फ़ व्यक्ति के लिए।

- I had seventy classmates. I was friends with **every one of them.**
- **Each student** has a different nationality. I am friends with **each one of them.**
- **Each side** of the hexagon is of a different color.
- **Every chair** in the hall was occupied.

every = frequency indicator (बारम्बारता सूचक प्रयोग)

■ every two hours, every other day, every four fours.

1. Take this medicine every four hours.
2. How often do you watch a Hindi movie?

• Every two weeks.

■ Each of + the, these, those, them etc ... √

Every of + the, these, those, them etc ... X

Each one / Every one of + the, these, those, them etc ... √

EX.1: Complete the sentences using each, every, everyone etc :

1. The bananas are three rupees ....
2. My sister and I have one house ....
3. .... driver should wear a seat belt.
4. I went to her house twice last week. .... time she was not there.
5. They had a great vacation. They enjoyed .... minute of it.
6. These greeting cards are Rs. 25/- ....
7. The food was pretty inexpensive. Both of us paid Rs 50 ....
8. I was invited to several concerts last week and I went to .... of these.
9. The interviewer asked me many questions. I could answer .... without difficulty.
10. He is very kind and friendly. .... praises him.
11. Elections in India are held .... five years.
12. .... mother does her best for her child.
13. We eat out .... Sunday.
14. I have four classmates. .... is from Europe.
15. This book has six parts: each of them has ten subdivisions.

Key 1

1. each 2. each. 3. Every 4. Each 5. every
6. each 7. each 8. everyone 9. everyone 10. Everyone
11. every 12. Every 13. every 14. Everyone 15. each

Even भी

■ अप्रायिक, आश्चर्यजनक बात में बलाघात हेतु even का प्रयोग करते हैं।

even

- She always has a bath with cold water, **even** in cold weather.
  वह हमेशा ठण्डे पानी से स्नान करती है, सर्दी के मौसम में ***भी***।
- No one came to his funeral, not **even** his own family.
  उसकी अन्तयेष्टि में कोई नहीं आया, उसके बच्चे ***भी*** नहीं।

even if, even though etc

- He will never be pleased, **even if** I gave up my life for him.
  वह कभी खुश नहीं होगा, चाहे मैं उसके लिए जान ***भी*** दे दूँ।
- Even after having lived in India for five years, she can't speak Hindi fluently.
  भारत में पाँच साल रहने के बाद ***भी*** वह धाराप्रवाह हिन्दी नहीं बोल सकती।
- **Even when** she is traveling, she stays in touch with her children by phone.
  जब वह यात्रा ***भी*** कर रही होती है, वह अपने बच्चों के साथ दूरभाष से सम्पर्क में रहती है।
- **Even though** she doesn't swim now, she goes to the swimming pool every evening.
  यद्यपि वह अब नहीं तैरती , वह रोज़ शाम को तरणताल पर जाती है।

even + comparative

- I slept quite late, but my friend slept **even** later.
  मैं काफ़ी देर से सोया, परन्तु मेरा मित्र ***और भी*** देर से सोया।
- He arrived earlier. His friends arrived **even** earlier
  वह जल्दी पहुँचा, परन्तु उसके मित्र ***उससे भी*** जल्दी पहुँचे।

Ex.1: Complete the sentences using even even if, even though etc.

1. Her dress sense is aweful. .... our maid servant has better dress sense.
2. She doesn't know cooking. She can't .... make a cup of tea.
3. She is very well off. She .... has her own airplane.
4. Her handwriting is very bad. .... she herself cannot read what she writes.
5. She has an air conditioner in every room, ... one in her kitchen..
6. .... I did not learn Hindi script, I learnt to speak the lan guage fluently.
7. The train leaves in 15 minutes. We will not be able to catch the train .... we go by cab.
8. This building is very old, but that one over there is .... **older.**
9. All in my team plady badly, but I played .... **worse.**

Key

1, 2, 3, 4, 5 ,8,9 **even** .

6 **Even though**

7. **even if**

Simile — उपमा

Some commonly used similes in English are:

1. as pale as a ghost/death. — डरे हुए या मानसिक आघातग्रस्त व्यक्ति के लिए ।
2. as slim as a reed. — बहुत दुबली पतली औरत के लिए।
3. as light as a feather. — बहुत कम वज़न की वस्तु के लिए
4. as round as a barrel. — बहुत मोटे व्यक्ति के लिए।
5. as merry as a cricket. — बहुत खुशमिज़ाज व्यक्ति जिस की
6. as red as fire/a beetroot. — गालें गुस्से या धूप से लाल हों।

7. as slippery as an eel.	धूर्त बौर चालाक व्यक्ति, ऊपर से कुछ और, अन्दर से कुछ और।
8. as ugly as a scarecrow/	बहुत बदसूरत
9. as bold as brass.	बहुत साहसी
10. as brown as a berry.	धूप में त्वचा का रंग बदल जाने पर
11. as cool as a cucumber.	बहुत शान्त
12. as blind as a bat.	जिसे बिलकुल दिखाई न दे
13. like a bear with a sore head	बहुत ख़राब मिज़ाज व्यक्ति के लिए
14. to sleep like a log	बहुत गहरी नींद सोना ।
15. like a red rag to a bull	उस व्यक्ति के लिए जो अवश्य दूसरे को गुस्सा दिलाएगा
16. to have a head like a sieve	कमज़ोर यादाश्त वाला व्यक्ति
17. to eat like a horse and drink like a fish	बहुत ज़्यादा खाना पीना
18. like a bull in a china shop	गँवार असंस्कारी व्यवहार वाला आदमी
19. like a fish out of water	असहनीय तकलीफ़ महसूस करना
20. eyes like a hawk	तुरन्त परिस्थिति को समझने में सक्षम व्यक्ति
21. like a whirlwind	बहुत तेज़ गति और मेहनत से काम करने वाला व्यक्ति
22. to work like a dream	कोई योजना सहज निर्विघ्न समाप्त होना
23. a memory like an elephant	बहुत अच्छी स्मरण-शक्ति वाला
24. like an oven	बहुत गरम स्थान
25. like a dog with two tails	ऐसा व्यक्ति जो किसी बात को ले कर बहुत गर्वित महसूस कर रहा और बहुत प्रसन्न हो
हो	
26. like water off a duck's back	चिकना घड़ा जिस पर किसी की

	चेतावनी, सलाह, आलोचना का कोई प्रभाव न हो
27. to have eyes like a ferret.	क्रूर आंखों वाला

Binomial expressions

English uses several binomial expressions, which are compounds of two similar-meaning words to convey a fixed idea.

1. odds and ends	कुछ फुटकर/ ग़ैरज़रूरी चीज़ें
2. be sick and tired of	से ऊब जाना/ से तंग आ जाना
3. to be a hit and miss	आकस्मिक संयोग से
4. sooner or later	देर-सवेर
5. slowly but surely	धीरे, मगर अवश्य
6. rough and ready	कम गुणवत्तावाले
7. first and foremost	सर्वोपरि प्राथमिकता
8. prim and proper	औपचारिक और गंभीर
9. up and down	एक सिरे से दूसरे सिरे तक
10. here and there	यहाँ-वहाँ
11. rest and recreation	विश्रान्ति, मनबहलाव
12. on and off	रह-रह कर
13. wine and dine	का मनोरंजन करना
14. rant and rave	क्रोधपूर्वक चिल्लाना
15. in leaps and bounds	तेज़ गति से
16. rack and ruin	जीर्णावस्था में होना
17 part and parcel	ज़रूरी हिस्सा
18. pick and choose	भरपूर चयन संभव होना

55 Letter writing

- पृष्ठ के ऊपर दायीं ओर अपना पता और उसके नीचे तारीख़ लिखें।
- औपचारिक (formal, business) letters में इसके नीचे, बायीं ओर जिस को पत्र भेजा जा रहा हो, उसका पूरा नाम और पता लिखें।
- निजी पत्रों को Dear के बाद व्यक्ति का नाम लिखकर सम्बोधन करें e.g. Dear Anil, Dear Rani, Dear Mother, Dear Uncle etc.
- औपचारिक पत्रों में Dear के बाद Sir, Sirs, Madam आदि लिखें।
- औपचारिक पत्र समाप्त होने पर दायीं ओर या बायीं ओर Yours sincerely, Yours faithfully, Yours truly आदि लिखकर अपना नाम लिखें।
- निजी पत्रों में Yours, Yours affectionately, Love आदि लिखकर अपना नाम लिखें।

Informal letter to a friend

29 Hiran Magri
Udaipur
Nov. 20, 2012

Dear Sunita,

Thanks for putting me up during my stay in Delhi. It was good to see you and everybody in the family after a long time. One thing, I have a feeling I left my wrist watch on the study table in your room. Just check. In case you find it, keep it safely. I shall take it from you when I come to Delhi the next time.

Thanks again,
Yours sincerely,
Sudha

Applying for a job

29, Gandhi Nagar
Jaipur – 302004
Nov. 3, 2012

The Head, Economics Department
University of Delhi
Delhi – 110 007

Dear Sir:
My advisor Prof. A.K. Singh has informed me that you are interested in hiring a part-time teacher. I obtained a master's degree in economics from Rajasthan University last year and am presently doing a Ph.D. My special paper in M.A. was labour economics. I took some private computer courses and have a fairly good command on its use. their use. I feel my academic background qualifies me for this work and would enable me to make a valuable contribution to your department.
A resume is enclosed for your kind perusal. I look forward to hearing from you.

Sincerely yours,

Sudhir Pandey

Vocabulary: Plants

1.	shrub	श्रब	2.	vine	वाइन
3.	creeper	क्रीपर	4.	plant	प्लान्ट
5.	tree	ट्री	6.	fern	फ़र्न
7.	annuals	ऐन्युअल्स	8.	biennials	बाइ एनिअल्स
9.	perennials	पैरिनिअल्स	10.	deciduous	डेसिड्युअस
11.	evergreen	ऐवर गीन			

1. झाड़ी 2. बेल 3. लता 4. पौधा 5. पेड़ 6. पर्णांग पौधा
7. इकसाला पौधा 8. दोसाला पौधा 9. सदाबहार 10. सालाना झड़नेवाला
11. बारह मासी पेड़ / नित हरा पौधा

56 Punctuation

Period / Full stop

☞ *ध्यान दें कि वाक्य के अन्त में लगाए जाने वाले बिन्दु को* American English *में* 'period' *और* British English *में* 'full stop' *कहते हैं।*

☞ Period (full stop) *का प्रयोग निम्नलिखित रचनाओं के बाद करें।*

- Negative or positive statements.
- Polite requests.
- Indirect questions.
- Abbreviations.

Comma

■ जब सहायक क्रिया और मुख्य क्रिया के बीच में, या कर्ता और क्रिया के बीच में 'sentence adverb' आए तो comma से अलग करें।

Example:
(1) My mother, however, did not like it.
(2) My boyfriend has, nevertheless, decided to settle abroad.

■ किसी list या series में वस्तुओं को अलग करने के लिए comma लगाएँ, परन्तु अन्त के दो items के बीच में comma न लगाएँ।

Example:
I visited the Red Fort, Hamayun's Tomb and the Lotus Temple in Delhi.

■ If, when, while, until आदि से आरम्भ होने वाले गौण वाक्य के प्रधान वाक्य से पहले आने पर comma से अलग करें। परन्तु गौण वाक्य के प्रधान वाक्य के बाद में आने पर comma न लगाएँ।

If you invite me, I shall come.

I shall come If you invite me,

- वाक्य में रचना की द ष्टि से अनावश्यक अंश, जो मात्र ब्योरा देने या स्पष्टीकरण के लिए हों, उन्हें comma से अलग करें।
- व्याकरण की द ष्टि से स्वतन्त्र वाक्यों के बीच comma न लगाएँ।

Capitalization .

☞ निम्नलिखित को capital letter से शुरू करें।

- हर वाक्य का पहला शब्द जैसे She is my younger sister.

☞ परन्तु वाक्य के बीच में dash (—) से अलग किए गए वाक्याँश को capital letter सें शुरू न करें। e.g. Having decided to take a day off his work—- he had some fever— he decided to clean his room.

- Inverted commas (quotation mark) के अन्दर वाला वाक्य, e.g. He said, "Get out of this room!"
- नदी, पहाड़, शहर, व्यक्ति के नाम : e.g. Ganges; Himalayas; Kolkata; Anil.
- दिन, महीना, त्योहार, सार्वजनिक छुट्टियाँ : e.g. Monday, Tuesday...; January, February...; Diwali, Dussehra; Independence Day, Thanksgiving.
- Nationality words राष्ट्रीयता सूचक शब्द e.g. Japanese, Indian, Korean.
- कुछ ग्रहों के नाम e.g. Mars, Mercury, Jupiter, Venus, Saturn. परन्तु ध्यान दें : the earth, the sun, the moon छोटे अक्षर से शुरू करें।
- ऐतिहासिक काल और घटनाएँ : e.g. the Mughal Period, the Battle of Plassy, the First World War.
- घर्म अनुयायी, धार्मिक ग्रन्थ : Muslims, Christians, Hindus, Hinduism, Islam, Christianity, God, the Lord, Ramayan,

Bible, Quran.

- Trade names; e.g. National Panasonic, Videocon, Godrej
- Acronyms; e.g. SAIL (Steel Authority of India Ltd.); TISCO (Tata Iron and Steel Company);
- Pronoun 'I', interjection 'O';
  e.g. Finally I decided to come back to India.
  O God please help me!
- Time expression whole hour : O' clock

Colon :

- Business letter में सम्बोधन के बाद colon लगाएँ ।
  e.g. Dear Sir:, Dear Mr. Kapoor:
- किसी title को subtitle से अलग करने के लिए colon का प्रयोग करें । e.g. Nouns: Number and Gender.
- यदि quotation से पूर्व कोई बड़ा सा प्रस्तावनात्मक वाक्यांश (introductory clause) हो तो quotation से पूर्व colon लगाएँ ।
  e.g. Lokmanya Tilak's words will always be remembered: "Self-rule is our birth right".
- कोई list या series के बारे में लिखते समय colon लगाएँ ।
  e.g. Please supply the following at the earliest: (1)... (2)... (3)..
- समय लिखते हुए मिनट को घण्टे से अलग करने के लिए colon का प्रयोग करें ।
  1:10 a.m.
  2:20 p.m.

Parentheses ( )

- वाक्य के ऐसे अंश जिनके बिना वाक्य रचना में दोष नहीं आता, जिनकी भूमिका मात्र कुछ विस्तृत जानकारी देना या दृष्टान्त स्वरूप है, उन्हें

parentheses में रखा जा सकता है।

- कोई सूची लिखते समय संख्या सूचक अंको या अक्षरों को **parentheses** में रखें।
  (1), (2), (3).................
  (a), (b), (c).................

Abbreviations

Examples:

Mrs Bhalla	Mr Kapoor	Ms K.S. Pandey	Dr Jha,
6 a.m.	3 p.m.	729 A.D.	525 B.C.
U.S.S.R.	Hwy	Ph.D.	M.D.

☞ जहाँ **abbreviation** के अन्त में **full stop** लगा हो, वहाँ एक और बिन्दु नहीं लगता। परन्तु यदि प्रश्नवाचक वाक्य है तो **abbreviation** के बिन्दु के बाद भी **question mark** लगता है।
Did he leave at one p.m.?
He left at one p.m.

☞ यदि वाक्य के बीच में **abbreviation** है तो सामान्य **punctuation** का प्रयोग करें।
I meant to be here at one p.m., but I got delayed in a traffic jam.

☞ जब तीन चार शब्दों के **initial letters** (पहले अक्षरों) को साथ रखकर **abbreviation** होता है तो प्रायः बीच में बिन्दु नहीं लगता, जैसे **UNO, NATO, FAO, WHO**

Exclamation mark (!)

- भय, प्रसन्नता, दुःख आदि की पुरज़ोर बलाघातक अभिव्यक्तियों में exclamation mark '!' का प्रयोग होता है।
- विनम्र, मृदु अभिव्यक्तियों में exclamation mark '!' न लगाएँ।

- कितनी ही बलात्मक विस्मयबोधक अभिव्यक्ति क्यों न हो, अंग्रेज़ी में कभी भी एक से अधिक exclamation mark न लगाएँ।
- Exclamation mark को किसी और विराम चिन्ह के साथ न लगाएँ।

1. What a loud noise!	कितना ज़ोर का शोर है!
2. How hot it is!	कितनी गर्मी है!
3. What a fool he is!	कितना मूर्ख है वह!
4. How funny the whole thing sounded!	यह सब मसला इतना मज़किया-सा लगा!
5. If only I knew what they want!	काश मुझे पता होता वे चाहते क्या हैं!
6. Wasn't it an interesting film!	फ़िल्म रोचक थी न!
7. Isn't she clever !	वह सच में होशियार है!

Pronunciation Guidelines

अंग्रेज़ी भाषा में शब्दों के उच्चारण के समय सभी अक्षरों का उच्चारण नहीं होता। यह कठिनाई अभ्यास और कुछ नियमों की जानकारी से साध्य है।

■ जिन शब्दों के अन्त में **'gn'** हो, उनमें **'g'** का उच्चारण नहीं होता।

sign साइन benign बिनाइन foreign फ़ौरेन

■ जिन शब्दों के अन्त में **'mb'** और **'mn'** हो, उनका उच्चारण **'m'** अन्त का होता है।

climb क्लाईम; numb नम; autumn ऑटम; hymn हिम

■ **'kn'** एक साथ होने पर **'k'** का उच्चारण लुप्त हो जाता है।

know ना; knee नी; knife नाइफ़;

■ **'stle'** और **'ten'** अन्तवाले शब्दो पर **'t'** का उच्चारण लुप्त हो जाता है।

hustle bustle हसल-बसल; listen लिसेन;

■ **'ps'** और **'pn', 'pt'** से शुरू होने वाले शब्दों **'p'** का उच्चारण लुप्त हो जाता है।

pseudonym स्यूडोनिम; psychiatry साइक्यिैट्री; pneumonia न्यूमोनिया; ptomaine टोमेन।

■ किसी शब्द के शुरू में **'wh'** का उच्चारण 'ह' की तरह होता है।

who हू; whose हूज़; whole होल।

■ जब **'wh'** के बाद कोई अन्य स्वर हो तो उच्चारण 'व' की तरह होता है।

what व्हाट; which व्हिच; where व्हेयर।

■ शब्द के शुरू में **'wr'** का उच्चारण **'r'** की तरह होता है।

write राइट; writ रिट; wrist रिस्ट।

■ प्राय: **'l + consonant'** होने पर **'l'** का उच्चारण लुप्त हो जाता है।

palm पाम; calm काम; walk वॉक; talk —टॉक।

■ निम्नलिखित शब्द समूहों में कोष्ठक में दिए गए अक्षरों का उच्चारण नहीं होता ।

handkerchief(d)	हैन्करचीफ़	honesty (h)	ऑनेस्टी
hour (h)	आवर	sandwich (d)	सैनविच
Cristmas (t)	क्रिसमस	aisle (s)	आइल
muscle (c)	मसल	depot (t)	डिपो
cupboard (p)	कबर्ड	Wednesday(d)	वैन्सडे

Vocabulary — British : American

British	American	British	American
a.m./p.m.	A.M./P.M.	nappy	diaper
autumn	fall	petrol	gasoline

barrister	attorney	post	mail
bonnet	hood (car)	postman	mailman
biscuit	cookie	post box	mail box
boot	trunk (car)	post code	zip code
car	auto	pub	bar
caretaker	janitor	public toilet	restroom
chemist's	drug store	reel of cotton	spool of cotton
child	kid	rubber	eraser
the cinema	the movies	shop	store
city centre	down town	taxi	cab
public toilet } lavatory }	restroom	tap	{ faucet (indoor) { spigot (outdoor)
crossroads	intersection	tin	can
vest	undershirt	lift	elevator
maths	math	ill	sick
holiday	vacation	maize	corn
wallet	billfold	trousers	pants
flat	apartment	dustbin	garbage can

Spellings — British : American

Given below are some words spelt differently in British and American English. When in doubt, consult a good dictionary.

British	American	British	American
analogue	analog	labour	labor
analyse	analyze	offence	offense
catalogue	catalog	practise	practice*
centre	center	pretence	pretense
cheque	check	programme	program

colour	color	realise	realize
defence	defense	speciality	specialty
honour	honor	theatre	theater
jewellery	jewelry	traveller	traveler

*** In British English, practice is used as a noun.**

Some commonly confused words

accept	except	descent	dissent
accessary	accessory	desert	dessert
affect	effect	die	dye
already	all ready	discuss	discus
allude	elude	elicit	illicit
alter	alter	ensure	insure
amoral	immoral	fair	fare
anecdote	antedote	forth	fourth
anyone	any one	hear	here
ascent	assent	heard	herd
bare	bear	hole	whole
board	bored	hoard	horde
born	borne	knee	nee
brake	break	plain	plane
buy	by	principal	principle
cannon	canon	quiet	quite
capital	capitol	rain	rein
cite	sight, site	raise	raze
clothes	cloths	road	rode
coarse	course	soar	sore
conscience	conscious	their	there
corporal	corporeal	through	thorough, throw
corps	corpse	to	too, two
council	counsel	waist	waste
deprecate	depreciate	weather	whether

★★★★★

57 Vocabulary Practice

Ex.1: Say these verbs in English:

1. दाँत से काटना.........................

2. चबाना ....

3. निगलना.................................

4. चाटना ....

5. चूसना ....

6. घूँट भरना ....

7. डकार लेना ....

8. डकार दिलवाना ....

9. साँस लेना ....

10. अंदर साँस लेना.........................

11. बाहर साँस निकालना.......................

12. आह भरना.........................

13. जंभाई लेना ....

14. ऊँघना ....

15. खर्राटे लेना ....

16. छींकना ....

17. खाँसना ....

18. हिचकी लेना ....

19. पसीना आना ....

20. काँपना ....

21. हँसते-हँसते शरीर का हिलना. ....

22. ठंड या डर से शरीर का हिलना ....

Ex. 2 : Say in English: Adjectives

1. नाराज़ ....

2. व्यस्त ....

3. निराश ....

4. उदास ....

5. खिन्न ....

6. उबाउ ....

7. शर्मिन्दा ....

8. आशावादी ....

9. निराशावादी ....

10. उत्तेजित ....

11. झगड़ालू ....

12. प्रतिभाशाली ....

13. लड़ाकू ....

14. चिन्तित ....

15. आश्चर्यचकित ....

16. प्रसन्न ....

17. सन्तुष्ट ....

18. हाज़िर जवाब ....

Ex.3: Say in English:

1. व्यक्ति जो कैमरे के सामने आने से घबराता है। ....
2. नृत्य रचनाकार/ नृत्य लेखनकार ....
3. 70 -79 साल की उम्र का व्यक्ति
4. 80 - 89 साल की उम्र का व्यक्ति
5. कैमरा प्रचालक ....
6. संगीतकार ....
7. लेखक ....
8. कवि ....
9. धर्मप्रचारक ....
10. कथावाचक ....

Ex.4: Animals

1. चिड़िया ....
2. घोड़ा ....
3. बिल्ली ....
4. सियार ....
5. गाय ....
6. भैंस ....
7. कौवा ....
8. शेर ....
9. कुत्ता ....
10. चूहा ....
11. गधा ....
12. सूअर ....
13. बत्तख़ ....
14. सांप ....
15. हाथी ....
16. मेंढक ....
17. भेड़ ....
18. बकरी ....

Sounds of animals

1. चहचहाना ....
2. हिनहिनाना ....
3. मिंआना ....
4. हुआना ....
5. रंभाना ....
6. कांव-कांव करना ....
7. दहाड़ना ....
8. भौंकना ....
9. किकियाना ....
10. रेंकना ....
11. घुरघुराना ....
12. कां-कां करना ....
13. फुफकारना ....
14. चिंघाड़ना ....
15. टर्र-टराना ....
16. मिमिआना ....

Ex. 5: Baby animals:

1. भालू/शेर/भेड़िया का बच्चा 2. चिड़िया का बच्चा ....
3. इल्ली .... 4. बिल्ली का बच्चा ....
5. बछड़ा .... 6. पिल्ला ....
7. बत्तख़ का बच्चा .... 8. मेंढक का बच्चा ....
9. बकरी/भेड़ का बच्चा ....10. चूज़ा ....
11. घोड़े का बच्चा .... 12 सुअर का बच्चा ....

Ex. 6: Vocabulary – spices

1. नमक .... 2. हल्दि .... 3. लौंग ....
4. लाल मिर्च .... 5. कालीमिर्च .... 6. जीरा ....
7. दारचीनी .... 8. आजवायन 9. सौंफ़ ....
10. जायफल .... 11. जावित्री.............. 12. राई ....
13. हींग .... 14. धनिया .... 15. तेज पत्ता ....
16. कालीमिर्च .... 17. खस खस.............. 18. केसर ....
19. इमली .... 20. लहसुन.............. 21. पोदीना ....
22. तिल .... 23. मेथी दाना.............. 24. सौंफ़ ....

Ex. 7: Vocabulary – Fruits

1. सेब .... 2. संतरा.............. 3. खुमानी ....
4. पपीता .... 5. केला .... 6. आड़ू ....
7. शरीफ़ा .... 8. नाशपाती.............. 9. अंगूर ....
10. अनानास.............. 11. अमरूद .... 12. अनार ....
13. नींबू.............. 14. रसभरी .... 15. लीची ....
16. चीकू.............. 17. लोक़ाट .... 18. आम ....
19. स्ट्राबेरी.............. 20. खरबूजा.............. 21. तरबूज़ ....

Ex 8: Vocabulary – vegetables

1. बैंगन .... 2. चुकन्दर ....
3. करेला .... 4. लौकी ....
5. बन्द/पत्ता गोभी .... 6. शिमला मिर्च ....

7. गाजर ....
8. फूलगोभी ....
9. खीरा ....
10. फलियां ....
11. अदरक ....
12. कटहल ....
13. गांठ गोभी ....
14. कमल ककड़ी ....
15. भिण्डी ....
16. मटर ....
17. आलू ....
18. मूली ....
19. चचिण्डा ....
20. पालक ....
21. शकरकन्दी ....
22. टमाटर ....
23. कचालू / अरबी ....
24. शलजम ....

Ex 9: Vocabulary – grains

1. गेहूँ ....
2. चावल ....
3. बाजरा..............................
4. जौ ....
5. मक्का ....
6. आटा ....
7. बेसन ....
8. मैदा ....
9. सूजी ....
10. दाल मसूर ....
11. राजमाह ....
12. काबुली चना ....
13. काले चने ....

Ex 10: Vocabulary – Fats

1. घी ....
2. मक्खन ....
3. मलाई ....
4. सरसों का तेल ....
5. नारियल का तेल ....
6. तिल का तेल ....

Ex. 11: Cooking verbs:

1. फेंटना..................................
2. छीलना ....
3. उबालना..................................
4. छीलना ....
5. भाप देना ....
6. मसाला मिलाना ....
7. कम आँच पर पकाना................
8. भोजन को सजाना ....
9. काटना ....
10. परोसना ....
11. काटना ....
12. गूँधना ....

13. खुरचना ....
14. आटा गूँधना ....
15. ढकना ....
16. बेलना ....
17 कुचलना ....
18. खुले पानी में धोना ....
19. पीसना ....
20. छानना (चाय आदि) ....
21. छानना (आटा आदि) ....
22. पिघलाना ....
23. कूटना..................
24. भूनना ....
25. धीमा पकाना ....
26. तलना ....
27. भिगोना ....
28. अधिक तेल में तलना ....
29. रेतना ....
30. कम तेल में तलना..................

Ex .12: Vocabulary : Body parts

1. सिर ....
2. माथा ....
3. कनपटी ....
4. आँख ....
5. कान ....
6. दाँत ....
7. जीभ ....
8. गला ....
9. छाती ....
10. पसली ....
11. नाखून ....
12. पैर ....
13. उंगली ....
14. अंगूठा ....
15. बाँह ....
16. हाथ ....
17. घुटना ....
18. टखना ....
19. टाँग ....
20. पेट ....
21. जिगर ....
22. तिल्ली ....
23. फेफड़ा ....
24. दिल ....
25. हड्डी/अस्थि ....
26. उपस्थि ....
27. गुर्दा ....
28. आँतड़ी ....
29. धमनी ....
30. नस ....

31. मांसपेशी .... 32. दिमाग ....

33. भोजन की नली .... 34. श्वास की नली ....

Ex.13 : Vocabulary : Deseases

1. कब्ज़ .... 2. ज़ख़्म ....

3. मरोड़ .... 4. सूजन ....

5. फोड़ा .... 6. सुन्नत ....

7. चर्मरोग .... 8. मिरगी ....

9. लकवा .... 10. गठिया ....

11. बाय .... 12. खट्टी डकार ....

13. चोट .... 14. मुंहासे ....

15. पतली टट्टी .... 16. चक्कर आना ....

17. दाद .... 18. ताउन ....

19. मधुमेह .... 20. बदहज़्मी ....

21. कै होना .... 22. कोढ़ ....

23. आंख की पलक पर फुंसी................ 24. कमज़ोरी ....

25. मानसिक तनाव .... 26. रक्तचाप ....

27. बवासीर .... 28. बेहाशी ....

29. छाला .... 30. खून बहना.....................

31. खरोच .... 32. खुजली ....

33. दमा .... 34. गला ख़राब होना ....

Ex.14: Branches of medicine and their specialists:

1. .... हृदयरोग विज्ञान 2. .... हृदयरोग विशेषज्ञ

2. .... दन्त विज्ञान 4. .... दन्त विशेषज्ञ

5.	चर्म रोग विज्ञान	6.	चर्म रोग विशेषज्ञ
7.	स्त्री रोग विज्ञान	8.	स्त्री रोग विशेषज्ञ
9.	तंत्रिका विज्ञान	10.	तंत्रिका विज्ञानी
11.	नेत्ररोग विज्ञान	12.	नेत्र विज्ञानी
13.	अस्थि विज्ञान	14.	अस्थि विज्ञानी
15.	बाल रोग चिकित्सा	16.	बाल चिकित्सक
17.	विकिरण विज्ञान	18.	विकिरण विज्ञानी
19.	पैथोओलॉजि	20.	पैथोओलॉजिस्ट
21.	शल्य चिकित्सा	22.	शल्य चिकित्सक

Ex. 15: Vocabulary: Astrology---

1. ज्योतिष शास्त्र.......................... 2. ज्योतिषी...............................
3. अंक शास्त्र .... 4. अंकविद.................................
5. हस्तरेखा शास्त्र......................... 6. हस्तरेखा शास्त्र.........................

Planets (ग्रह)

1. सूर्य .... 2. चाँद ....
3. मंगल .... 4. बुध ....
5. बृहस्पति .... 6. शुक्र ....
7. शनि .... 8. राहु ....
9. केतु ....

Zodiac (राशी-चक्र)

Signs of the zodiac (राशियाँ)

1. मेष .... 2. वृषभ ....
3. मिथुन.................... 4. कर्क ....
5. सिंह .... 6. कन्या ....

7. तुला .... 8. वृश्चिक ....

9. धनु .... 10. मकर ... .

11. कुंभ .... 12. मीन ....

Ex.16: Vocabulary---Airport

1. विमान चालक................ 2. जहाज़ श्रमिक ....

3. परिचारक................... 4. परिचारिका ....

5. आगमन .... 6. प्रस्थान ....

7. सीमा शुल्क .... 8. विश्रान्ति कक्ष ....

9. द्वार .... 10. हाथ का सामान ... .

11. सामान ढोने की गाड़ी................ 12. पारगमन यात्री ....

13. सामान नत्थी................ 14. विमान प्रवेश पत्र ....

15. सीट के उपर हाथ का सामान रखने का कक्ष .... 16. सूचना..................

17. अंतर्राष्ट्रीय उड़ान................ 18. राष्ट्रीय सेवाएं...............

19. खाली नहीं .... 20. प्रसाधन कक्ष ....

21. गति................ 22. धूम्रपान निषेध क्षेत्र ....

23. आपकी यात्र सुखद हो। ....

24 कुर्सी की पेटी बांधें। ....

25. रक्षा जाकेट कुर्सी के नीचे है। ....

26. शौचालय में धूम्रपान न करें। ....

27. प्रस्थान स्थान से दूरी। ....

28. गन्तव्य स्थान का स्थानीय समय। ....

29. गन्तव्य स्थान पर पहुंचने का अनूमानित समय।.................................

17: Banks

1. अधिकोश .... 2. यात्री चैक ....
3. आवर्ती जमा .... 4. बचत खाता ....
5. विनिमय दर .... 6. मुद्रा ....
7. चालू खाता .... 8. पैसा जमा करना ....
9. सावधि जमा .... 10. अल्पावधि जमा ....
11. चैक भुनाना .... 12. पैसा निकालना ....
13. नकद भुगतान .... 14. अन्तरण ....
15. खाता पुस्तिका प्रविष्टी .... 16. ब्याज दर ....

Key 1

1. bite	बाइट	2. chew	च्यु
3. swallow	स्वालो	4. lick	लिक
5. suck	सक	6. sip	सिप
7. belch	बैल्च	8. burp	बर्प
9. breathe	ब्रीद	10. inhale	इन्हेल
11. exhale	एक्सेल	12. sigh	साइ
13. yawn	यान	14. snoooze	स्नूज़
15. snore	स्नोर	16. sneeze	स्नीज़
17. cough	कफ़	18. hiccough	हिकप
19. sweat	स्वैट	20. tremble	ट्रैम्बल
21. shake	शेक	22. shiver	शिवर्

Key 2

1. annoyed	अनोएड	2. busy	बिज़ी
3. disappointed	डिस–अपोएण्टिड	4. sad	सैड
5. dejected	डिजैक्टिड	6. boring	बोरिंग
7. embarrassed.	एम्बैरेस्ड	8. optimistic.	आप्टिमिस्टिक
9. pessimistic	पैसिमिस्टिक	10. excited	एक्साइटिड

11.	quarrelsome क्वारलसम	12.	talented	टेलेण्टिड	
13.	belligerant बेलिजरैन्ट	14.	worried	वर्रीड	
13.	wonderstruck वन्डरस्ट्रक	16.	pleased	प्लीज़्ड	
17.	satisfied सैटिसफ़ाइड	18.	witty	विटि	

Key 3

1.	camera-shy	कैमरा शाइ़	2.	choreographer	कोरियोग्राफ़र
3.	septugenarian	सैपच्युअॅजिनेरिअन	4.	octagenarian	ऑक्टाजिनेरिअन
5.	cameraman	कैमरा मैन	6.	composer	कम्पोज़र
7.	writer	राइटर	8.	poet	पोएट
9.	missionary	मिशनरि	10.	narrator	नरेटर

Key 4 Animals

1.	bird	बर्ड	2.	horse	हॉर्स	3.	cat	कैट
4.	jackal	जैकाल	5.	cow	काउ	6.	buffalo	बफ़ेलो
7.	crow	को	8.	lion	लायन	9.	dog	डॉग
10.	mouse	माउस	11.	donkey	डौन्की	12.	pig	पिग
13.	duck	डक	14.	snake	स्नेक	15.	elephant	एलिफ़ैण्ट
16.	frog	फ़्रौग	17.	sheep	शीप	18.	goat	गोट

Sounds of animals

1.	chirp	चर्प	2.	neigh	नी	3.	miao	मिआओ
4.	howl	हाउल	5.	moo	मू	6.	caw	कौ
7.	roar	रोर	8.	bark	बार्क	9.	squeak	सक्वीक
10.	bray	ब्रे	11.	grunt	ग्रन्ट	12.	quack	क्वैक
13.	hiss	हिस्स	14.	trumpet	ट्रम्पेट	15.	croak	कोक
16.	bleat	ब्लीट						

Key 5 Animals babies

1. cub	कब	2. fledgling	फ़्लैजलिंग
3. caterpillar	कैटरपिलर	4. kitten	किटेन
5. calf	काफ़	6. puppy	पपी
7. duckling	डकलिंग	8. tadpole	टेडपोल
9. lamb	लैम्ब	10. chicken	चिकेन
11. foal	फ़ोल	12 piglet	पिगलेट

Key 6 Vocabulary – spices

1. Salt	सॉल्ट	2. turmeric	टर 'मरिक
3. cloves	कलोव्स	4. red pepper	रैड पैपर
5. black pepper	ब्लैक पैपर	6. cumin seed	क्यूमिन सीड
7. cinnamon	सि'नॅ मन	8. carom seed	कैरम सीड
9. fennel	फ़ेनेल	10. nutmeg	नटमैग
11. mace	मेस	12. mustard	मस्टर्ड
13. asafoetida	ऐसॅ फे 'टिड	14 .coriander	कोरिऐण्डर
15. bay leaf	बे-लीफ़	16. black pepper	ब्लैक पैपर
17. poppy seed	पॉपी सीड	18. saffron	सैफ़ॅ रॉन
19. tamarind	टेमेरिण्ड	20. garlic	गार्लिक
21. mint	मिण्ट	22. sesame seed	सेसेमे सीड
23. fenugreek-	फ़ॅनुग्रीक	24.. aniseed	ऐनी सीड

Key 7 Vocabulary – Fruit

1. apple	ऐपल	2. orange	औरेन्ज
3. apricot	एप्रिकौट	4. papaya	पपाया
5. banana	बनानॅ	6. peach	पीच
7. custard apple	कस्टर्ड ऐपल	8. pear	पेऑर
9. grapes	ग्रेप्स	10. pineapple	पाइनैपल
11. guava	गवावॅ	12. pomegranate	पोमेग्रेनेट

13.	lemon	लैमन	14.	raspberry	रैस्पबैरी
15.	litchi	लीची	16.	sapodilla	चीकू
17.	loquat	लोक़ाट	18.	mango	मैन्गो
19.	strawberry	स्ट्राबेरी	20.	musk melon	मस्कमैलन
21.	water melon	वाटर मैलन			

Key 8 Vocabulary – Vegetables

1.	aubergine	ओबर जीन	2.	beet root	बीट रूट
3.	bitter gourd	बिटर गाउर्ड	4.	bottle gourd	बौटल गाउर्ड
5.	cabbage	कैबेज	6.	capsicum	कैप्सीकम
7.	carrot	कैरट	8.	cauliflower	कॉली फ़लावर॑
9.	cucumber	कयुकम्बर	10.	french beans	फ्रैन्च बीन्स
11.	ginger	जिन्जर	12.	jack fruit	जैक फ़्रूट
13.	knol kohl	नोल-खोल	14.	lotus root	लोटस रूट
15.	okra	ओकरा	16.	peas	पीज़
17.	potato	पोटेटो	18.	radish	रेडिश
19.	snake gourd	स्नेक गाउर्ड	20.	spinach	स्पिनेच
21.	sweet potato	स्वीट पोटेटो	22.	tomato	टोमेटो
23.	taro	टारो	24.	turnip	टरनिप

Key 9 Vocabulary – Grains

1.	wheat	व्हीट	2.	rice	राईस
3.	millets	मिलेट्स	4.	barley	बार्ले
5.	maize	मेज़	6.	whole wheat flour	होल व्हीट फ़्लावर
7.	gram flour	ग्रैम फ़्लावर	8.	white flour	व्हाइट फ़्लावर
9.	semolina	सेमोलीना	10.	lentil	लेन्टिल
11.	kidney bean	किडनी बीन	12.	chick peas	चिक पीज़
13.	Bengal grams	बैंगाल ग्रैम्स			

Key 10: Vocabulary – Fats

1.	clarified butter	क्लैरीफ़ईड बटर	2.	butter	बटर
3.	cream of milk	कीम ऑफ़ मिल्क	4.	mustard oil	मस्टर्ड ऑएल
5.	coconut oil	कोकोनट ऑएल	6.	sesame oil	सेसॅमि ऑएल

Key 11 Vocabulary – Cooking

1.	beat	बीट	2.	peel	पील
3.	boil	बौएल	4.	skin	स्किन
5.	steam	स्टीम	6	season	सीज़न
7.	simmer	सिमर	8.	garnish	गार्निश
9.	chop	चौप	10.	serve	सर्व
11.	cut	कट	12.	knead	नीड
13.	scrape	स्क्रेप	14.	make a dough	मेक डो
15.	cover	कवर	16.	roll	रोल
17	crush	क्रश	18.	rinse	खुले पानी में धोना
19.	grind	ग्राइन्ड	20.	strain	स्ट्रेन
21.	sift	सिफ़्ट	22.	melt	मैल्ट
23.	pound	पाउण्ड	24.	roast	रोस्ट
25.	simmer	सिमर	26.	fry	फ्राइ
27.	soak	सोक	28.	deep fry	डीप फ्राइ
29.	grate	ग्रेट	30.	shallow fry	शैलो फ्राइ

Key 12 Parts of the body

1.	head	हैड	2.	forehead	फोरहैड
3.	temple	टैम्पल	4.	eye	आई
5.	ear	ईयर	6.	teeth	टीथ
7.	tongue	टंग	8.	throat	थ्रोट
9.	chest	चैस्ट	10.	rib	रिब
11.	nails	नेल्ज़	12.	feet	फीट

13. finger	फ़िंगर	14. thumb	थम्ब
15. arm	आर्म	16. hand	हैण्ड
17. knee	नी	18. ankle	ऐंकल
19. leg	लैग	20. stomach	स्टॅ मॅक
21. liver	लिवर	22. spleen	स्पलीन
23. lung	लंग	24. heart	हार्ट
25. bone	बोन	26. cartilage	कार्टिलेज
27. kidney	किडनी	28. intestine	इन्टॅ स्टाइन
29. artery	आर्टरी	30. nerve	नर्व
31. muscle	मसल	32. brain	ब्रेन
33. oesophagus	इसॉ फ़ॅगॅस	34. trachea.	ट्रेकिया

Key 13 Common ailments

1. constipation	कान्स्टिपेशन	2. wound	वून्ड
3. cramp	कैम्प	4. swelling	स्वैलिंग
5. boil	बॉएल	6. numbness	नम्बनैस
7. skin disease	स्किन डिज़ीस	8. epilepsy	ऐपिलैप्सी
9. paralysis	पैरेलिसिज़	10. gout	गाउट
11. rheumatism	र्‍युमैटिज़्म	12. acidity	ऐसिडिटी
13. injury	इन्जरी	14. pimples	पिम्पल्स
15. loose motions	लूज़ मोशन	16. giddiness	गिडीनैस
diarrhoea	डायरिया	dizziness	डिज़ीनैस
17. ringworm	रिंग वर्म	18. plague	प्लेग
19. diabetes	डायबटीज़	20. indigestion	इन्डिजैशन
21. vomiting	वोमिटिंग	22. leprosy	लैप्रॅसी

23.	stye	स्टाई	24.	weakness /debility	वीक्नैस डैबिलिटी
25.	hypertension	हाइपॅर टैन्शॅन	26.	blood pressure	ब्लड प्रैशर
27.	piles	पाइल्स	28.	unconscious-ness	अन्कॉन्श्यसनैस
29.	blister	ब्लिस्टर	30.	bleeding	ब्लीडिंग
31.	bruise	ब्रुइज़	32.	eczema	ऐग्ज़ीमा
33.	asthma	आस्थमा	34.	sore throat	सोर थ्रोट

Key 14 Medicine : Branch & specialists

1.	cardiologist	कार्डिओलॅजिस्ट	2.	cardiology	कार्डिओलॅजी
2.	odontologist	ओडोन्टोलॅस्टिज	4.	odontology	ओडोन्टोलॅजी
5.	dermatologist	डर्मा टोलॅजिस्ट	6.	dermatology	डर्मा टोलॅजी
7.	gynaecologist	गाइनिकोलॅजिस्ट	8.	gynaecology	गाइनिकोलॅजी
9.	neurology	न्युरॉलजिस्ट	10.	neurology	न्युरॉलजि
11.	ophthalmologist	ओफ़्थलमालॅजिस्ट	12.	ophthalmology	ओफ़्थलमालॅजि
13.	orthopaedics	ऑर्थोपीडिक्स	14.	orthopaedician	और्थोपीडिशियन
15.	paediatrics	पीडिऐट्रिक्स	16.	paediatrician	पीडिऐट्रिशियन
17.	radiologist	रेडिओलॅजिस्ट	18.	radiology	रेडिओलॅजि
19.	pathologist	पैथोओलॅजिस्ट	20.	pathology	पैथोओलॅजि
21.	surgeon	सर्जन	22.	surgeory	सर्जरी

Key 15 Astrology

1.	astrology	ऐस्टरॉलॅजि	2.	astrologer	ऐस्टरॉलॉजर
3.	numerology	न्युमरॉलॉजि	4.	numerologist	न्युमरॉलॉजिस्ट
5.	palmistry	पामिस्ट्री	6.	palmist	पामिस्ट

Planets (ग्रह)

1. Sun	सन	2. Moon	मून
3. Mars	मार्स	4. Mercury	मर्करी
5. Jupiter	जुपिटर	6. Venus	वीनस
7. Saturn	सैटर्न	8. Rahu	राहू
		(ascending node of moon)	
9. Ketu	केतु	(descending node of moon)	

Signs of the zodiac (राशियाँ)

1. Aries	एरीज़	2. Taurus	टॉरस
3. Gemini	जैमिनी	4. Cancer	कैन्सर
5. Leo	लिओ	6. Virgo	वर्गो
7. Libra	लिब्रा	8. Scorpio	स्कॉर्पिओ
9. Sagittarius	सैजिटेरिअस	10. Capricon	कैप्रिकॉर्न
11. Aquarius	ऐक्वेरिअस	12. Pisces	पाइसीज़

Key 16 Airport

1. pilot	पाइलट	2. crew	क्रियु
3. steward	स्ट्युअर्ड	4. stewardess	स्ट्युअर्डैस
5. arrival	अराइवल	6. departure	डिपार्चर
7. customs	कस्टम्स	8. lounge	लाउन्ज
9. gate	गेट	10. hand luggage	हैण्ड लगेज
11. luggage trolly	लगेज ट्रॉली	12. transit passenger	ट्रांसिट पैसिंजर
13. baggage tag	बैगेज टैग	14. boarding card	बोर्डिन्ग कार्ड
15. overhead bin	ओवरहैड बिन	16. notice	सूचना
17. international flight	इन्टरनैशनल फ़लाइट	18. domestic services	डोमैस्टिक सर्विसिज़

19. occupied	आक्युपाइड	20. lavatory	लैवॅटरी
21. speed	स्पीड	22. no smoking zone	नो समोकिंग ज़ोन

23. Wishing you a pleasant flight. विशिंग यू ए प्लैज़ेन्ट फ़्लाइट

24. Fasten the seat belts. फ़ासेन दी सीट बैल्ट।

25. Life jacket is under the seat. लाइफ़ जैकेट इज़ अन्डर दी सीट।

26. Smoking in lavatories prohibited. स्मोकिंग इन लैवॅटरीज़ प्रौहिबिटिड।

27. Distance from departure. डिस्टैन्स फ्रौम डिपार्चर।

28. Local time at destination. लोकल टाइम ऐट डैस्टिनेशन।

29. Expected time of arrival at the destination. ऐक्सपैक्टिड टाइम आफ़ अर्राइवल ऐट डैस्टिनेशन ।

Key 17: Banks

1. bank	बैंक	2. traveller's cheque	ट्रैवलर्स चैक
8. recurring deposit	रिकरिंग डिपॉज़िट	4. saving account	सेविंग अकाउन्ट
5. rate of exchange	ऐक्सचेंज रेट	6. currency	करेन्सी
7. current account	करेन्ट अकाउन्ट	8. to deposit money	डिपॉज़िट मनी
9. fixed deposit	फ़िक्स्ड डिपॉज़िट	10. short-term deposit	शॉर्ट टर्म डिपॉज़िट
11. encash check	ऐनकैश चैक	12. to withdraw money	विइड्रॉ मनी
13. cash payments	कैश पेमैन्ट्स	14. transfer	ट्रांस्फ़र
15. passbook entry	पासबुक प्रविष्टी	16. interest rate	इन्टरेस्ट रेट

At The Doctor's - 2

Patient: Good evening doctor. I feel feverish.

Doctor : Do you have a headache too?

Patient: Yes, doctor. I have a severe headache.

Doctor : Stomachache?

Patient: No.

Doctor : Any pain in the back or ribs?

Patient: A little.

Doctor : Sore throat?

Patient: Yes, I have difficulty in swallowing.

Doctor : How is your appetite?

Patient: I have absolutely no appetite. My lips are dry and I feel very thirsty all the time.

Doctor : Do you feel nauseous?

Patient: Slightly.

Doctor : How about your stools? Any loose motions or constipation?

Patient: My stools are normal, doctor.

Doctor : Any urinary problems?

Patient: No, doctor, I don't have any such problems.

Doctor : Take this prescription to the chemist's shop next door. He will explain to you when and how to take the medicine. And, yes, drink a lot of water. Eat very light meals. Stay in bed for a couple of days; you will get well soon. If you need my help in any way, see me again.

Patient: Thank you doctor, Goodbye.

Doctor : Goodbye.

INDEX